Frommer's®

Munich & the Bavarian Alps

Here's what the critics say about Frommer's:

"Amazingly easy to use. Very portable, very complete."
—*Booklist*

♦

"The only mainstream guide to list specific prices. The Walter Cronkite of guidebooks—with all that implies."
—*Travel & Leisure*

♦

"Complete, concise, and filled with useful information."
—*New York Daily News*

♦

"Hotel information is close to encyclopedic."
—*Des Moines Sunday Register*

Other Great Guides for Your Trip:

Frommer's Germany

Frommer's Europe

Frommer's Europe on $50 a Day

Frommer's Europe's Greatest Driving Tours

Frommer's Driving Tours: Germany

Frommer's®

2nd
Edition

Munich
& the
Bavarian Alps

**by Darwin Porter
and Danforth Prince**

MACMILLAN • USA

ABOUT THE AUTHORS

Darwin Porter and **Danforth Prince** are coauthors of a number of best-selling Frommer's guides, notably England, France, the Caribbean, Italy, and Spain. Porter, a bureau chief for the *Miami Herald* at 21, was the author of the first-ever Frommer's guide to Germany and has traveled extensively throughout the country ever since. He is joined by Prince, who was formerly of the Paris bureau of the *New York Times*.

MACMILLAN TRAVEL

A Simon & Schuster Macmillan Company
1633 Broadway
New York, NY 10019

Find us online at **www.frommers.com**

ISBN 0-02-862369-X
ISSN 1090-2325

Editor: Alice Fellows
Production Editor: Mark Enochs
Photo Editor: Richard Fox
Design by Michele Laseau
Digital Cartography by Ortelius Design and Roberta Stockwell
Page creation by Carrie Allen and Pete Lippincott

SPECIAL SALES

Bulk purchases (10+ copies) of Frommer's and selected Macmillan travel guides are available to corporations, organizations, mail-order catalogs, institutions, and charities at special discounts, and can be customized to suit individual needs. For more information write to Special Sales, Macmillan General Reference, 1633 Broadway, New York, NY 10019.

Manufactured in the United States of America

Contents

List of Maps

An Invitation to the Reader

In researching this book, we discovered many wonderful places—hotels, restaurants, shops, and more. We're sure you'll find others. Please tell us about them, so we can share the information with your fellow travelers in upcoming editions. If you were disappointed with a recommendation, we'd love to know that, too. Please write to:

Frommer's Munich & the Bavarian Alps, 2nd Edition
Macmillan Travel
1633 Broadway
New York, NY 10019

An Additional Note

Please be advised that travel information is subject to change at any time—and this is especially true of prices. We therefore suggest that you write or call ahead for confirmation when making your travel plans. The authors, editors, and publisher cannot be held responsible for the experiences of readers while traveling. Your safety is important to us, however, so we encourage you to stay alert and be aware of your surroundings. Keep a close eye on cameras, purses, and wallets, all favorite targets of thieves and pickpockets.

What the Symbols Mean

✪ Frommer's Favorites

Our favorite places and experiences—outstanding for quality, value, or both.

The following abbreviations are used for credit cards:

AE	American Express	EC	EuroCard
CB	Carte Blanche	JCB	Japan Credit Bank
DC	Diners Club	MC	MasterCard
DISC	Discover	V	Visa

Find Frommer's Online

Arthur Frommer's Budget Travel Online (www.frommers.com) offers more than 6,000 pages of up-to-the-minute travel information—including the latest bargains and candid, personal articles updated daily by Arthur Frommer himself. No other Web site offers such comprehensive and timely coverage of the world of travel.

Introducing Munich

Sprawling Munich, home of some 1.3 million people, is the capital of Bavaria, and one of Germany's major cultural centers. It's also one of Germany's most festive cities.

Longtime resident of Munich, Thomas Mann, wrote something about the city that might have been coined by an advertising agency: "Munich sparkles." Although the city he described was swept away by two world wars, the quote is still apt. Munich continues to sparkle, drawing temporary visitors and new residents like a magnet from virtually everywhere.

Some of the sparkle comes from its vitality. With its buzzing factories, newspapers and television stations, service and electronics industries, and high-tech laboratories it's one of Europe's busiest and liveliest places. More subtle is Munich's amazing ability to combine Hollywood-type glamour and stylish international allure with its folkloric connections.

Few other large cities have been as successful as Munich in marketing folklore, rusticity, and nostalgia for the golden days of yesteryear, yet this rustic ambience coexists with the hip and the avant-garde, high-tech industries, and a sharp concern for what's going on in Berlin, London, and Washington, D.C.

As Americans migrate to New York or San Francisco to seek opportunity and experience, so Germans migrate to Munich. Munich is full of non-Bavarians. More than two-thirds of the German citizens living in Munich have come from other parts of the country, and tens of thousands are expatriates or immigrants from every conceivable foreign land. Sometimes these diverse elements seem unified only by a shared search for the good life.

Outsiders are found in every aspect of Munich's life. The wildly applauded soccer team, FC Bayern München, is composed almost entirely of outsiders—Danes, Belgians, Swedes, Prussians—and the team was trained by a Rhinelander throughout its spate of recent successes. The city's most frequently quoted newspaper mogul (Dieter Schröder) and many of the city's artistic movers and shakers are expatriates, usually from North Germany.

What's remarkable in Munich is the unspoken collusion of the whole population in promoting Bavarian charm and rusticity, despite the fact that the real dyed-in-the-wool Bavarians risk becoming a distinct minority in their own capital. This is what lends the city such a distinctive flair.

Impressions

In Munich one always has a sense that just over the mountains there is always a way of escape from all German problems, to the lands where the lemons grow.
—Goronwy Rees, "Diary from Berlin to Munich," *Encounter,* April 1964

Virtually everyone has heard the city's many nicknames—"Athens on the Isar," "the German Silicon Valley," and "Little Paris." But none seems to stick. More appropriate is a label that's voiced with more ambivalence both inside and outside Munich—"the secret capital of Germany."

Munich's self-imposed image is that of a fun-loving and festival-addicted city, typified by its Oktoberfest, which began as a minor sideshow to a royal wedding in 1810 and has become a symbol of the city itself. It draws more than 7 million visitors each year. Redolent with nostalgia for old-timey Bavaria, raucous hordes cram themselves into the city during a period of only 16 days.

Oktoberfest is so evocative, and so gleefully and unashamedly pagan, that dozens of places throughout the world capitalize on its success by throwing Oktoberfest ceremonies of their own. These occur even in such unlikely places as Helen, Georgia, where citizens and merchants reap tidy profits by wearing dirndls and lederhosen, playing recordings of the requisite oompah-pah music, and serving ample provisions of beer in oversized beer steins. No one has ever marketed such stuff better than Munich, but then, few other regions of Europe have had such alluring raw material from which to draw.

A somewhat reluctant contender for the role of an international megalopolis, Munich has pursued commerce, industry, and the good life without fanfare. You get the idea that despite its economic muscle and a roaring GNP, Munich wants to see itself as a large agrarian village, peopled by jolly beer drinkers who cling to their folkloric roots despite the presence on all sides of symbols of the computer age.

Underneath expansive, fun-loving Munich is the reality of an unyielding, ongoing conservatism and resistance to change, both religious and political. But as a symbol of a bold, recently reunited Germany forging a new identity for the 21st century, Munich simply has no parallel. As such it continues to exert a powerful appeal.

1 Frommer's Favorite Munich Experiences

- **Socializing at the Biergarten:** If you're in Munich anytime between the first sunny spring day and the last fading light of a Bavarian-style autumn, you might head for one of the city's celebrated beer gardens (*Biergarten*). Our favorite is Biergarten Chinesischer Turm in the Englischer Garten. Traditionally, beer gardens were tables placed under chestnut trees planted above the storage cellars to keep beer cool in summer. Naturally, people started to drink close to the source of their pleasure, and the tradition has remained. Lids on beer steins, incidentally, were meant to keep out the flies. It's estimated that today Munich has at least 400 beer gardens and cellars. Food, drink, and atmosphere are much the same in all of them.

- **Enjoying Munich's World-Class Music:** The city is the home to many outstanding classical music groups, notably the Bavarian State Opera and the Munich Philharmonic. Prices are affordable and the selection is diverse. The season of summer concerts at Nymphenburg Palace alone is worth the trip to Munich.

- **Nude Sunbathing in the Englischer Garten:** A CEO we know in Munich claims that on a summer day he has to go to this park and take off all his clothes and sunbathe naked to regain the strength necessary to work the rest of the day. Whether this is the truth or a far stretch, he is not alone. On any summery sunny day, it seems that half of Munich can be seen letting it all hang out in the Volksgarten (People's Park). The sentimental founding fathers of this park with their Romantic ideas surely had no idea they were creating a public nudist colony. If you're not much of a voyeur, and feel that most people look better with their clothes on, you can still come here to enjoy the park's natural beauty.

- **Snacking on Weisswurst:** Munich's classic "street food" is a "white sausage" made of calf's head, veal, and seasoning, about the size of a hot dog. Weisswurst must be consumed before you hear the chimes of midday, a tradition maintained even in this day of refrigeration. Smooth and light in flavor, it is eaten with pretzels and beer—nothing else. Weisswurst etiquette calls for you to remove the sausage from a bowl of hot water, cut it crosswise in half, dip the cut end in sweet mustard, then suck the sausage out of the casing in a single gesture. When you learn to do this properly, you will have become a true Münchner.

- **Getting Away from It All at the Hirschgarten:** For a glimpse of what Munich used to be like, flee from the tourist hordes and traffic to the Hirschgarten or "Deer Meadow." A "green lung" between Donnersberg Bridge and Nymphenburg Park, the area has been a deer park since 1791. In 1890 the largest beer garden in the world was built here, seating 8,000 drinkers. The Hirschgarten remains Munich's most tranquil retreat, a land of towering oaks, chestnuts, and beeches, attracting those with a love of the great outdoors—and especially those who like to pack a picnic lunch or enjoy an open-air game of chess.

- **Exploring Trendy Haidhausen:** Tourists rarely venture into this district on the right bank of the Isar River. For decades it was known as a blue-collar and low-rent district of Munich. Hippies and artists in the 1970s created a cross-cultural scene that made Haidhausen, not Schwabing, the hip place to hang out. Today it is the place to see and be seen—especially if you're a *Schicki-Micki* (a club-going Bavarian yuppie), a person who dresses only in black, or one of the *Müeslis* (European granolas). The place to go is one of the bars or cafes around Pariser Platz or Weissenburger Platz. Take the S-bahn to Ostbahnhof or Rosenheimerstrasse and get with it!

- **Attending Oktoberfest:** It's called the "biggest keg party" in the world. Münchners had so much fun in 1810 celebrating the wedding of Prince Ludwig to Princess Therese von Sachsen-Hildburghausen that they've been rowdying it up ever since for 16 full days, between September 21 and October 6. The festival's tent city is at the Theresienwiese fairground, and the Middle Ages lives on as oxen are roasted on open spits, brass bands oompah-pah you into oblivion, and some 750,000 kegs of the brew are tapped. There are even tents where *Bierleichen* (beer corpses) can recover from drunkenness, listening to soothing zither music.

- **R&R at Olympiapark:** Site of the 1972 Olympic Games, this 740-acre park is a city unto itself with its own mayor, post office, and elementary school. The stadium is a premier venue for various sporting events and concerts. You can swim in one of the pools that Mark Spitz made famous in his successful pursuit of seven gold medals back in 1972. That's not all: You'll find all the jogging tracks and gyms your heart desires, even an artificial lake. To cap your visit, take the elevator to the top of the Olympiaturm for a panoramic preview of Munich and a look at the Bavarian Alps. In summer, free rock concerts blast from the amphitheater, Theatron, by Olympic Lake.

- **From Vie de Bohème to Schicki-Micki in Schwabing:** In fin-de-siècle Munich, Schwabing was the home of the avant-garde. Artists, writers, poets, and musicians of the era, including Thomas Mann, called it home. *Jugendstil* (art nouveau), the Blue Rider painters, and Richard Wagner made this area the cultural capital of Europe before 1914. A revival came in 1945, as new cultural icons such as Rainer Werner Fassbinder arose. Schwabing lives on, although today it's gentrified and populated by fashion editors and models, along with what have been called "swinging aristocrats." Although you might come here to walk in the footsteps of Wassily Kandinsky or to see where Paul Klee or Rainer Maria Rilke lived and worked, you'll also get exposure to Schicki-Micki (Mickey Mouse chic). Walking, strolling, shopping, and people-watching are the chief activities today. At some point find a chair at **Café Roxy,** 48 Leopoldstrasse, and watch the parade go by.

- **Soaking Up the Wittelsbach Lifestyle:** Just northwest of the city center lies Nymphenburg Palace, begun in 1664, an exquisite baroque extravaganza surrounded by a 495-acre park dotted with lakes, pavilions, and hunting lodges. It was the summer home of the Bavarian rulers. We prefer to visit in either summer, when outdoor concerts are on, or from May through June, when the rhododendrons are in bloom. Go inside the palace for a look at the painted ceiling in the Great Hall. In such works as *Nymphs Paying Homage to the Goddess Flora,* Bavarian rococo reached its apogee.

- **An Afternoon in the Botanischer Garten:** If you're not a plant lover, you'll be converted here. It's one of the finest and most richly stocked botanical wonders in Europe. You can wander among the 40 acres and some 15,000 varieties of plants. Laid out between 1909 and 1914 on the north side of Nymphenburg Park, the park presents one highlight after another, especially an alpine garden with rare alpine specimens—orange hawkweed, the dwarf alpine poppy, or the blue gentian. The flora of steeps, dunes, and moorlands thrive here, as does the heather garden, a delight in late spring.

- **Market Day at Viktualienmarkt:** The most characteristic scene in Munich is a Saturday morning at this food market at the south end of Altstadt. Since 1807, Viktualienmarkt has been the center of Munich life, dispensing fresh vegetables, fruit from the Bavarian countryside, just-caught fish, dairy produce, poultry, rich grainy breads, moist cakes, and farm-fresh eggs. Naturally, there's a beer garden. There's even a maypole, and, as a touch of class, a statue honoring Karl Valentin (1882–1948), the legendary comic actor and filmmaker. Even more interesting than the market produce are the stallholders themselves—a few evocative of Professor Higgins's "squashed cabbage leaf," Eliza Doolittle, in London's Covent Garden of yore.

- **Rafting along the Isar:** Admittedly, it doesn't rival the Seine in Paris, but the Isar is the river of life in Munich. If you can't make it for a country walk in the Bavarian Alps, a walk along the left bank of the Isar is an alternative. Begin at Höllriegelskreuth and follow the scenic path along the Isar's high bank. Your trail will carry you through the Römerschanze into what Münchners call "The Valley of the Mills" (Mühltal). After passing the Bridge Inn (Brückenwirt) you will eventually reach Kloster Schäftlarn, where you'll find—what else?—a beer garden. After a mug you'll be fortified to continue along signposted paths through the Isar River Valley until you reach Wolfrathausen. Instead of walking back, you can often board a raft made of logs and "drift" back to the city, enjoying beer and often the oompah-pah sound of a brass band as you head toward Munich.

- **A Dip at Müller's Public Baths:** Müllersches Volksbad, at Rosendheimer Strasse I (S-Bahn to Isartor), is one of the most magnificent public baths in all of Germany. This is no dull swimming pool but a celebration of grandeur fin-de-siècle style. Karl Hocheder designed this Moorish/Roman spectacle between 1897 and 1901, an era of opulence. When the baths opened they were hailed as the most modern baths in all of Europe, surpassing anything but Budapest. A local engineer, Karl Müller, donated the money to build them. Completely renovated, the baths today have a "gentlemen's pool" with barrel vaulting and a "ladies' pool" with domed vaulting. There are also sweat baths and individual baths for those who like to let it all hang out—but in private. Alas, the *Zamperlbad,* or doggie bath, in the basement is no more.

- **A Night at the Hofbräuhaus:** Established in 1589 by Duke Wilhelm V to satisfy the thirsts of his court, the Hofbräuhaus is not only the city's major tourist attraction but also the world's most famous beer hall, seating more than 4,000 drinkers. In 1828 the citizens of Munich were allowed to drink "the court's brew" for the first time, and it turned out to be habit-forming. A popular song, "In München Steht ein Hofbräuhaus," spread the fame of the brewery. To be really authentic, you drink in the ground-floor *Schwemme* where some 1,000 beer buffs down their brew at wooden tables while listening to the sounds of an oompah-pah band. More rooms, including the *Trinkstube* for 350, are found upstairs, and in summer beer is served in a colonnaded courtyard patio with a Lion Fountain. The waitstaff in Bavarian peasant dress appears carrying 10 steins at once. Pretzels are sold on long sticks, and white *Radis* (radishes) are cut into fancy spirals. Both the radish, which is salted, and the salty pretzel seem designed to make you drink more. The Hofbräuhaus is where the good life of Munich holds forth.

2 History 101

THE BRIDGE OVER THE ISAR
Munich is a very young city compared to some of its neighbors. It had its origins in an unpleasant struggle between two feudal rulers over the right to impose tolls on traffic moving along the salt road that stretched between the then-thriving (and much older) cities of Salzburg, Hallein, Reichenhall, and Augsburg.

The spark that ignited Munich's existence occurred in 1156. Up to that time, Bishop Otto von Freising had controlled a very lucrative toll bridge across the Isar River, directly on the salt route. The ruler of the Bavarian territory, Guelph Heinrich der Löwe (Duke Henry the Lion), was in need of cash. So, with the customary ferocity that had earned him his nickname, he simply burnt down the bishop's bridge and built his own bridge a few miles upstream, preempting the profitable tolls. Emperor Frederick Barbarossa was called upon to settle this dispute between his cousin Henry and his uncle, Bishop Otto, but the bishop's fully justified rage did little to influence the faraway emperor,

Dateline

- **1156** Feudal warlord Henry the Lion demolishes the local bishop's toll-collecting bridge and builds one nearby. The city of Munich is born.

- **1158** Holy Roman Emperor Barbarossa validates Henry's actions. The establishment of Munich is legitimized.

- **1173** Fortified behind walls and watchtowers, Munich's population swells to 2,500.

- **1180** Henry the Lion defies the emperor and is banished. Freising's bishop tries to destroy settlement.

- **1240** The Wittelsbach dukes extend their influence to Munich.

continues

- 1250–1300 Munich's population increases fivefold. New fortifications built.
- 1285 A pogrom burns 150 Jews within their synagogue.
- 1300s Munich's population grows to 10,000, becoming the richest city of the Wittelsbachs.
- 1314 Duke Ludwig IV, Munich's ruler, is elected head of the Holy Roman Empire. Munich is now the most important city in the German-speaking world.
- 1319 A Habsburg, Frederick the Handsome, attacks Munich but is taken captive. Pope's meddling backfires.
- 1322 Munich prospers because of salt trade and becomes center of loose association of German kingdoms.
- 1327 Fire devastates much of Munich's eastern district.
- 1346 Ludwig IV killed in bear hunt. New emperor strips Munich of its honors.
- 1385 Citizens of Munich rebel against Wittelsbach dynasty and execute a representative of the family.
- 1403 Power reverts back to the Wittelsbachs after their armies lay siege to Munich's walls.
- 1492 A mountain pass is carved through the Alps to expedite trade with Italy.
- 1516 Munich passes Europe's first law governing food and beverages.
- 1517 Martin Luther sparks Protestant Reformation. Munich's leaders order their city to remain Catholic.
- 1560 Wittelsbach dynasty makes Munich its official seat and launches massive rebuilding program.
- 1583 Wilhelm IV bans all religion other than Roman Catholicism, making

continues

who was too busy with more important problems to worry about a minor clash between church and state. This particular squabble, however, was to have far-reaching consequences.

Henry's new bridge was adjacent to a tiny settlement of Benedictine monks, whose small community on the banks of the Isar River was referred to as *zu den Münichen*—"at the site of the little monks." The name stuck—it was later shortened to *München*, and the little monk, or *Münichen*, remains today the symbol of the city of Munich.

Henry the Lion had already had experience in the founding of trading centers. Repeating the patterns of his earlier successes, he granted to Munich the right to mint its own coins and to hold markets, basic tools that any city needed for survival. Tolls from his new bridge, which now funneled the lucrative salt trade across the Isar, went directly into Henry's coffers.

Within a few months, Barbarossa validated the crude but effective actions of his duke, legitimizing the establishment of Munich on June 14, 1158, the date that is commemorated as the official debut of the city. Henry, however, had to pay a price: Barbarossa ordered that a third of all tolls generated by the new bridge be paid to the bishop of Freising, whose bridge Henry had destroyed.

MEDIEVAL PROSPERITY   The first of the city's fortifications, a stone wall studded with watchtowers and five gates, was built in 1173 and enclosed 2,500 people. One of the most important survivals from this period (most of the wall was long ago demolished) is the Marienplatz, then and now the centerpiece of the city and the crossing point of the Salzstrasse (Salt Route), a crossroads that is still marked on the city map today. During its early days, the Marienplatz was simply known as "Marketplace" or "Grain Market."

In 1180, Duke Henry quarreled with Emperor Barbarossa and was banished forever from Munich and the rest of Bavaria. Gleefully, Henry's eternal nemesis, the bishop of Freising, attempted to eradicate the upstart young city and reroute the salt trade back through his stronghold of Oberföhring. By this time, however, Munich was simply too well established to succumb.

ENTER THE WITTELSBACHS   By 1240 a new force had arisen in Munich, the Wittelsbach family. They were part of a new generation of merchant princes, and through a shrewd imposition of military and economic power, their family patriarch, Otto von

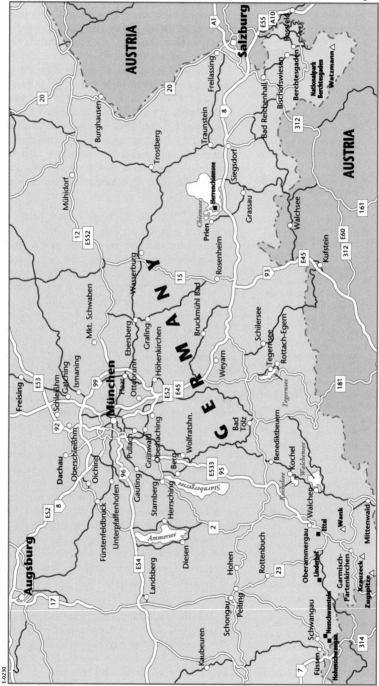

Munich the German-speaking centerpiece of the Counter-Reformation.

- **1608** A policy akin to the Spanish Inquisition persecutes non-Catholics in Munich.
- **1618–1648** The Thirty Years' War leads to siege of Munich by Swedish king who bankrupts city. Plague claims a third of Munich's population.
- **1643** Wittelsbachs secure their power and strip right of Münchners to elect their own mayor.
- **1674** Residenz catches fire but resentful Münchners take their sweet time in putting out the flames.
- **1705** Austria invades and occupies Bavaria. Bavarian peasants marching on Munich in protest are massacred.
- **1758** Porcelain factory at Nymphenburg becomes a resounding success.
- **1759** Academy of Sciences marks the influence of the Enlightenment.
- **1771** King Max III Joseph makes some aspects of public education a legal requirement.
- **1777** Max III Joseph dies, ushering in the much-hated regime of Karl Theodor, who tries to trade Bavaria for the Netherlands.
- **1789** Outbreak of French Revolution causes fear on the throne of Munich's rulers.
- **1799** Armies of Napoléon invade Munich. Napoléon makes Bavaria a kingdom and extends its territory.
- **1807** Maximilian I and Crown Prince Ludwig embark on building program to beautify the city.
- **1818** Liberal administrative reforms are put in place.

continues

Wittelsbach, succeeded in having himself designated as the ruler of Bavaria shortly after the banishment of Henry the Lion. Thus began the longest and most conservative reign of any dynasty in Germany. The Wittelsbachs ruled in Munich and the rest of Bavaria until the forces of socialism swept them away during the final days of World War I. Today they are still viewed by the Bavarians with a kind of nostalgic affection.

Between 1250 and 1300 the population of Munich increased fivefold, the result of migration from the countryside and a period that was relatively free from plagues. Members of at least three religious orders established monasteries, convents, and hospitals within the city walls.

SOCIAL UNREST   As the population (and resultant social tensions) grew, the city's encircling fortifications were enlarged to protect new suburbs. Although predominantly Catholic, the city fostered a small population of much-persecuted Jews as well. The worst pogrom occurred in 1285, when Munich's Jews were accused of the murder of a small child, and 150 of them were burned alive inside their synagogue, which was at the time just behind the present-day location of the Neues Rathaus (New Town Hall). Two years later, other groups of Jews came to Munich, but ironically, the handicaps the city imposed upon them (exclusion from all trades except moneylending) led to a modest if precarious degree of prosperity. Pogroms were repeated throughout the rest of the Middle Ages, and in 1442 the Jews were banished from Munich altogether.

Just before the dawn of the 13th century, the artisans and merchants of Munich staged a revolt against the Wittelsbach family that revolved around the debased coins that were being issued by the dukes' mint. After a mob destroyed the mint and killed its overseer, the dukes exerted a form of punishment that became increasingly standard throughout the tightfisted world of medieval Bavaria—a stiff fine was imposed upon the citizenry as a means of reimbursing the loss.

IMPERIAL MUNICH   During the 1300s, Munich was the richest of the several cities ruled by the Wittelsbachs. Grain, meats, fish, and wine were traded within specifically designated neighborhoods. The collection of tolls from the roads leading in and out of the city helped make whoever controlled them (in this case, the Wittelsbachs) very rich.

In 1314 a Wittelsbach, Duke Ludwig IV, later to be known as Ludwig the Bavarian, was elected as the German kaiser, thanks to his status as the least-threatening choice among a roster of more-powerful contenders. The election suddenly threw Munich into the center of German politics. Ludwig traveled to Rome for his coronation and brought back from his visit one of the treasured religious icons of medieval Munich—the severed arm of St. Anthony, which still can be seen in the church of St. Anna in Lehel.

In 1319 one of the Wittelsbachs's most vindictive enemies, the Habsburg family in the person of Frederick the Handsome, attacked Munich and laid siege to its walls. Against expectations, the Wittelsbachs prevailed, eventually capturing the Habsburg leader and taking him prisoner. However, the pope sided with the Habsburgs and excommunicated Ludwig. Despite this serious handicap, Ludwig retained his throne. Consequences of the excommunication were enormous and widely viewed as an example of a pope overplaying his cards. To reward Munich for its loyalty (and also to line his own pockets), Ludwig created a lucrative monopoly for the city by ordering in 1322 that all the salt mined within Hallein or Reichenhall should pass directly through Munich.

Although Bavaria remained Catholic, and continued to be Catholic even after the Protestant Reformation, Munich had positioned itself as a centerpiece of resistance to papal authority. Along these lines, Ludwig offered shelter to William of Occam, a brilliant scholar trained in the monasteries of both England and France and persecuted as a heretic by the pope. Occam spent the last years of his life in Munich, striving for reform of the Catholic Church. His presence helped to define Munich as a hard-headed Catholic city that catered only reluctantly to the whims of any faraway religious potentate.

Ironically, Ludwig the Bavarian's untimely death (he was killed in 1346 during a bear hunt) came at the perfect time. His unbridled ambition and successful defiance of the pope had alienated many other German princes, who were poised to attack him. However, his death meant that the city's role as headquarters of the German-speaking empire came to an abrupt end.

During Ludwig's tenure, the city experienced explosive growth, and a new wall was built in 1327, designed with so much space that it contained the city throughout the next 400 years. Despite a strong temptation to alter Munich's central core, the Marienplatz was never changed from its original form, which it more or less retains today.

- **1821** Marienkirche is designed as the city's official cathedral (Dom).
- **1826** Munich gets its own university.
- **1846** Revolution leads to voluntary abdication of Ludwig I. Maximilian II ascends Bavarian throne.
- **1855** Maximilian II erects the Bavarian National Museum.
- **1857** Weisswurst makes its debut in the city's beer halls.
- **1860–1890** Munich annexes a half-dozen townships.
- **1864** Maximilian II dies. King Ludwig II ascends to the throne at the age of 18.
- **1864–1865** Wagner resides in Munich, creating some of his major operas before falling out with young Ludwig.
- **1871** Bismarck, ruler of Prussia, unites the quarreling principalities of Germany. Bavarian king becomes a figurehead.
- **1882** Munich electrifies its streets and houses.
- **1886** "Mad" King Ludwig is stripped of power and shortly thereafter drowns mysteriously.
- **1892** Secession movement founded in Munich as a protest against traditional perceptions of Bavarian art.
- **1896** Art nouveau reinforces its grip on Munich thanks to *Jugend* magazine.
- **1902** Lenin spends time in Munich, publishing an incendiary magazine.
- **1911** Klee and Kandinsky found *Der Blau Reiter* school to promote modern and abstract art.
- **1914–1918** World War I throws Munich into bloodshed and disillusionment, climaxed by the bitter Treaty of Versailles.

continues

- **1918** Social unrest prevails as 10,000 workers organize in front of the Residenz. King Ludwig III flees, marking end of Wittelsbach dynasty.
- **1919** Kurt Eisner, leader of short-lived socialist regime, is assassinated. Army sent from Berlin evicts revolutionary government.
- **1923** Hitler instigates Beer Hall Putsch in protest against Weimar government.
- **1933** Munich, along with Germany, is swept by Nazi victories. Swastika flies atop city hall.
- **1934** Hitler consolidates power and crushes archrival Ernst Röhm.
- **1938** *Kristallnacht*—government-sanctioned vandalizing of Jewish-owned homes and businesses—descends on Munich and elsewhere.
- **1939** Assassination attempt against Hitler as he sits with cronies in Munich's Bürgerbräukeller.
- **1942** Most intense Allied bombing of Munich.
- **1945** American troops enter Munich on April 30 to find 45% of the city's buildings in rubble, the population reduced.
- **1945–1947** Mayor Thomas Wimmer directs massive cleanup of World War II debris.
- **1949** Munich redefined as capital of Federal *Land* of Bavaria.
- **1957** Immigrants flood Munich, bringing population to one million.
- **1972** Summer Olympics witness the murder of 11 Israeli athletes by terrorist Palestinians.
- **1985** Gasteig Center for Performing Arts opens.
- **1989** Soviet regime collapses, opening new trade zones.

continues

MORE CIVIC UNREST   Though the Wittelsbachs ruled Munich, often with an iron hand, they were never able to quash their turbulent citizenry, whose resentments broke out periodically in riots and armed conflict. In 1385, Hans Impler, an official Wittelsbach representative, was publicly executed in the Marienplatz. This rebellion was not put down until sympathetic armies had laid siege to the town, quelled the unrest, and granted the citizens a limited influence in the conduct of city affairs.

Ironically, the personal security of the Wittelsbachs was frequently compromised by the rapid growth of the city's boundaries. The site of the Residenz, now near the center of Munich, was originally a rocky, isolated eyrie, built outside the city limits to be safe from rebellion and angry mobs.

BEER, PIGS & PROSPERITY   Throughout the 1400s, Munich became a boom town. More than 28,000 four-wheeled carts bearing marketable goods passed through the city gates every year in addition to the vast number of two-wheeled carts and people on foot. In response to this traffic, some of the town's main avenues, narrow though they were, were paved. Between 1392 and 1492, the city's increasingly prosperous merchant class built or altered into their present form many of the city's centerpieces, including the Ratsturm, the Alte Rathaus (Old City Hall), the Frauenkirche, and St. Peter's Church. Munich had graduated from a dependence on the salt trade, and was now reaping most of its profits from trade with Italy, especially Venice. In the same year Columbus stumbled upon his landfall in the New World, the Münchners opened a mountain pass over the Kesselberg to speed up trade routes to the "Queen of the Adriatic."

By 1500 Munich boasted a population of almost 14,000 persons, 400 of whom were beggars, and 750 of whom were priests, nuns, or monks. It also included about three dozen brewers whose products were quickly becoming associated with the name of the town. Pigs were engaged to eat the garbage strewn in the streets, and about two dozen innkeepers supplied food, drink, and lodgings to the medieval equivalent of the business traveler. The city's core (but not the surrounding fields that kept it fed) was protected from invasion by an ever-expanding ring of fortifications and towers. The most serious dangers were plagues and fires, both of which devastated the city at periodic intervals.

In 1516 the city adopted laws that later helped confirm its role as beer capital of the world. Known as the Bavarian Beer Purity Law, it was the first law in Europe regulating the production of any food or beverage.

THE REFORMATION   Martin Luther's radical message in 1517 fell onto German soil like a torch upon dry tinder. Rome's arrogance, political meddling, and bumbling public relations, coupled with such greedy practices as the sale of indulgences for the forgiveness of sins, had alienated virtually every class of Germany's populace.

- **1991** Munich becomes part of a reunified Germany.
- **1995** The Bavarian Beer Garden Revolution draws 20,000 angry protesters.
- **1998** Munich awaits the euro currency with some apprehension and anticipates capital's final move to Berlin.

If Munich hadn't been so tight in the grip of the Wittelsbach dukes, the Protestant Reformation might possibly have gained a stronger foothold in Bavaria. As it was, although Duke Wilhelm IV was initially attracted to the tenets of the Reformation, he soon drew back. Fearing a dissolution of his own power, he banned the writings of Martin Luther. A series of public banishments or executions of Protestants followed (most took place on everybody's favorite tourist attraction, the Marienplatz).

Fear and suspicion grew as rivalry between Munich (which remained Catholic) and nearby Augsburg (which became Protestant) encouraged Sunday migration by believers, who traveled to and from the two cities to attend their respective houses of worship. As the threat of Protestantism spread, official Munich reacted in ways that were by now predictable—it became more reactionary and more adamantly conservative than ever. In 1583 Wilhelm V banned all religions other than Catholicism from Bavaria, turning Munich overnight into a stronghold of the Catholic Counter-Reformation. Catholic colleges were established, and Protestants were persecuted on sight.

RENAISSANCE EXPANSION   The showy and sometimes pompous building boom associated with the Counter-Reformation marked the debut of the Renaissance in Munich. The lavish building programs as well as the entertainments of the Wittelsbach rulers became legendary, both for their grandeur and extravagance (some feasts lasted for three weeks) and for the burdens they imposed on the citizenry who had to pay for them.

Munich blossomed with the appearance of the Michaelskirche (St. Michael's Church) begun in 1583. The largest Renaissance-style church north of the Alps, it was conceived as a German-speaking response to St. Peter's Basilica in Rome. It took 14 frenetic years to build, and its construction costs almost bankrupted the Bavarian treasury. Despite the grumbling of the taxpayers who financed them, other buildings of equivalent splendor soon followed, including the Wittelsbach family stronghold, the Residenz.

Munich was also becoming a cultural center. By the late 16th century, the city was regarded as an artistic beacon. Credit for this must go to the reigning Wittelsbachs, founders of the art collection that eventually became the Alte Pinakothek, and the book collections that eventually became the Bayerischen Staatsbibliothek (Bavarian State Library).

Despite the prestige all these endeavors conveyed, virtually every tradesman and merchant in town complained of the burden such acquisitions and improvements placed upon the treasury, evidence of a fundamental conservatism that has demarcated Munich ever since.

THE THIRTY YEARS' WAR   Beneath the city's newly acquired glitter, were other, darker tendencies. In the early years of the 17th century, witches were hunted down and burned, flagellants paraded through the town, and foreboding sermons predicted an apocalypse. At least the spirit of those predictions was fulfilled during the Thirty Years' War (1618–1648). This struggle between the Protestant princes and the Catholic League swept across Europe bringing devastation in its wake.

Munich wasn't directly affected until 1632. At that time the Protestant king of Sweden, Karl Gustav Adolf, laid siege to "the German Rome." Munich surrendered almost immediately. The terms of surrender included payment of a huge ransom (450,000 guilders); in exchange, the city was spared being sacked and burned. The war, however, wasn't the only problem faced by the Münchners—at about this time, the Black Plague killed 7,000 people, more than a third of the population. After the disease had run its course, Maximilian I ordered the construction of the Mariensaule on the Marienplatz as a votive offering to God for having spared the city from destruction.

In 1643 the authority of the town's merchants was greatly undermined by the removal of their right to elect the mayor of Munich. The Wittelsbachs were now able to place in power anyone who would cater to their interests.

BAROQUE CASTLES & BAROQUE DREAMS   The legacy of the Thirty Years' War left Munich demoralized and shattered. Although Bavaria was not to play a vital role in European politics during the next century, this period saw a building boom and the development of baroque architecture.

The flamboyant, richly gilded, free-flowing but symmetrical baroque style was used not only by the city's architects to the glory of God but also in secular construction. Notable are Nymphenburg Palace, Munich's answer to the palace at Versailles; the Green Gallery within the Residenz; ornate theaters; and countless villas, pavilions, and garden structures. Funds for the construction of these buildings were derived, as in the past, from sometimes crippling taxes imposed on the citizenry and the forced sale of land to wealthy aristocrats who wanted to build ever-larger palaces for their own use.

Deep resentment was felt by the townspeople. In 1674, when the seat of the Wittelsbach family, the Residenz, accidentally caught fire, the town sullenly and deliberately postponed a response to calls for help for at least an hour, a vital delay that contributed to more enormous rebuilding costs and an increased mistrust among the various levels of society.

Part of the public resentment against Munich's leaders lay in the aristocracy's often disastrous meddling in international affairs. Among these were Bavaria's murky role in the War of the Spanish Succession, which resulted in the occupation of Bavaria between 1705 and 1715 by Austrian soldiers. The first year of this occupation witnessed one of the most cruel massacres in 18th-century history. Led by a local blacksmith, an army of peasants, craftsmen, and burghers armed only with farm implements and scythes marched upon Munich to protest against the Austrian regime. A short march from Munich's city walls, near the hamlet of Sendling, the entire army was betrayed, then obliterated. The *Sendlinger Mordweihnacht* ("Sendling's Night of Murder") has ever since been the source for sculptures, plays, and popular legend.

In 1715 Max Emanuel was able—with the help of the French—to evict the Austrians. Aftereffects of these fruitless conflicts included countless deaths, a profound national disillusionment, and a national debt that historians assess at around 32 million guilders, a burden imposed upon an impoverished population.

REFORM & REFORMERS   The tides of liberalization slowly spread to Bavaria. Newspapers were founded in 1702 and 1750, and in 1751 some vaguely liberal reforms were made in the Bavarian legislature, and an Academy of Sciences, whose discoveries sometimes opposed traditional Catholic teachings, was established in 1759.

To recover from the disasters initiated prior to his reign, Prince Elector Max III Joseph, one of the most enlightened Bavarian rulers, attempted to introduce economic reforms. He inaugurated new industries, including workshops for tapestry making and cloth making. Few of them worked out; the noteworthy exception was the outfit that manufactured Nymphenburg porcelain, founded in 1758, which consistently made a profit, and still does today.

In 1771 he revised the school system, making some aspects of public education a legal requirement. During his regime the city opened its doors to playwrights, composers, and conductors from all over Europe. Munich was the site of the inaugural performance of one of Mozart's early operas (*Idomeneo*) in 1781, but it wasn't particularly well received, and Mozart's request for an ongoing creative stipend from the Wittelsbach family was rejected.

THE REBIRTH OF CONSERVATISM   When Max III Joseph died in 1777, his branch of the Wittelsbach dynasty died with him. The new Wittelsbach, from an obscure family branch in the Palatinate, was Karl Theodor, who was among the least popular of all the Wittelsbachs. Caring little about Bavarian national destiny, he rather amazingly negotiated to cede Munich and all of Bavaria to Austria in exchange for the Habsburg-dominated Netherlands. Relief from this plan came in the form of the French Revolution.

Ironically, although he was despised as a ruler, Karl Theodor as a builder did many things well and skillfully, adding the Karlsplatz and the Englischer Garten to the roster of Munich's attractions. Politically, however, he continued to play his hand badly, outlawing most personal liberties and placing repressive measures on freethinkers. His death in 1799 was the cause of several days of drunken celebration throughout Munich.

THE AGE OF NAPOLÉON   Except for distant rumblings on the western horizon and the hope it gave to Bavaria's liberals, the effects of the French Revolution of 1789 weren't immediately felt in reactionary Munich. All of that changed with the rise of Napoléon. In 1799 French troops laid siege to the capital. The Bavarian court had already fled to the safety of their villas at Amberg. However, the easiest way out for all parties involved the complete and immediate capitulation of the Bavarian court, which decided to side with Napoléon against their brethren in other parts of Germany. On the first night of occupation, in June 1799, French officers enjoyed a performance of Mozart's *Don Giovanni* in the Residenz's royal theater.

To reward his Bavarian vassal, Napoléon more than doubled the territory controlled by Bavaria (at the expense of Franconia and Swabia), thereby tripling the size of its population overnight. Bavaria was made a kingdom, and in 1806 Napoléon personally conducted the coronation of Max IV Joseph as King Maximilian I.

A final irony was the reactivation of the ancient rivalries between Munich and the bishop of Freising (the destruction of whose bridge over the Isar had led to the original founding of Munich). Freising's territory was swallowed up in the new Bavarian nation created by Napoléon, and the bishop's seat moved into the heart of its old "enemy territory"—downtown Munich.

TOWARD A MODERN STATE   The new king's son, Crown Prince Ludwig (later, Ludwig I), gets the credit for establishing what is now the most famous autumn festival in the world, *Oktoberfest*. Originally designated as a *Volksfest*, it was scheduled, along with some horse races, as a sideshow of the crown prince's wedding in 1810.

Beginning around 1820, with the gears of the Industrial Revolution already starting to turn, the first foundations of a modern state were established. A Bavarian constitution was drawn up, and Munich became the seat of a newly founded Bavarian Parliament, designed to afford the citizenry more clearly defined legal rights. Not all Münchners were happy, however—they were attached to their roster of religious holidays, complete with complicated processions and relief from workaday cares, which the new constitution swept away.

"THE ATHENS OF THE NORTH" Crown Prince Ludwig, inspired by an idealized version of ancient Athens, made enormous changes. The old city walls were demolished, with the exception of a small stretch that still runs parallel to the Jungfernturmstrasse. The city moat was filled in and redesignated as the Sonnenstrasse, and new neighborhoods were designed with formal parks and gardens. The prince wanted the Munich equivalent of a triumphal promenade, and commissioned the street that has been known ever since as the Ludwigstrasse. As always, the citizens developed the art of grumbling about the expenses to a high art form.

In 1821 the Frauenkirche became the official cathedral (Dom) of the archbishops of Munich and Freising. In 1826 the university was transferred from the town of Landshut to Munich, bestowing on the Bavarian capital the status of intellectual centerpiece.

BOURGEOIS MUNICH By 1840, with a reported population of around 90,000 residents, the building boom of the early part of the century had made Munich into a neoclassical gem with a distinct identity. Munich's first railway line was laid in 1846, the foundation of a network of railways that soon converged on the city from all parts of southern Germany.

Initially a supporter of liberal reforms, as Ludwig I's reign went on, he gradually grew more and more conservative. In 1832 he began a campaign of censoring the press, repressing student activism, and stressing his role as an absolute monarch, casting himself in a romantic and heroic mold. Münchners considered his affair with actress and dancer Lola Montez even more odious than his rigid politics. All of this came to a head in the revolt of 1848. In a series of events as lurid as anything presently publicized by the Windsor family of England, Ludwig flaunted his affair with Lola so publicly that the fabric of the Wittelsbach dynasty itself was threatened. As the scandal raged out of control, Ludwig was forced to abdicate in favor of his son, Maximilian II.

Maximilian II continued the building programs of his father, established the Bavarian National Museum (1855), and played a role in encouraging writers to emigrate to Munich. One of these, Paul Heyse, was the first German to win the Nobel Prize for literature. Maximilian built an avenue (the Maximilianstrasse) in his own honor and held a series of competitions among architects for the design of such public buildings as the Regierung (Administrative Building) and the Maximilianeum (Bavarian Parliament Building).

The king's role in the promotion of science, industry, and education made him one of the most enlightened despots of the 19th century. When he died in 1864, the administration of many of his programs was continued by what had developed into a massive governmental bureaucracy. The new king, Ludwig II, unfortunately, was not so beneficial to Bavaria.

ROMANTIC BAVARIA & THE DREAM KING Rarely has the king of a nation so despised the citizens of his capital city as Ludwig II did the Münchners.

The Notorious Lola Montez

The sensational career of Lola Montez (1820–1861) was hot copy in the news-papers all over the world during her lifetime. A woman who behaved as she pleased in the Victorian age, she recently surfaced in a song by the Kinks. Her liaison with Bavaria's King Ludwig I led to his forced abdication.

She was born in Limerick, Ireland, as Eliza Gilbert and grew up in India. When she returned there after her first marriage, an outstanding beauty with jet black hair and alabaster skin, an admirer wrote of her, "Mrs. James looked like a star among the others." Her marriage broke up in scandal, and she was forced to leave India. She went to Spain and then to London, where she reinvented herself as the dancer, Lola Montez. Though she was a mediocre performer, her erotic "spider dance" catapulted her to notoriety. During the next years, she went through dozens of lovers, including pianist Franz Liszt and novelist Alexandre Dumas.

When Lola arrived in Munich in 1846, she was refused an engagement at the Hof Theatre. She immediately stormed into the palace and demanded an audi-ence with the king. Whatever happened that evening, she was in—Ludwig was enchanted, and within a week the king was introducing Lola as "my best friend." Ludwig indulged her every whim; in return, the way she indulged him (inclusive of his foot fetish) is renowned. She was called "the Bavarian Pompadour," but Richard Wagner dubbed her a "demonic beast."

Lola was deeply resented in Munich. Ludwig gave her the titles of baroness of Rosenthal and countess of Lansfeld. Her enemies suspected that she meddled in politics and it was said that she virtually ran the Bavarian government. Public sentiment against the king's infatuation and her outlandish behavior was so pow-erful that it contributed to the Revolution of 1848 and ultimately to the king's abdication.

After a brief stint in London, Lola was forced to flee to America to avoid bigamy charges. She fled first to Mexico, then to California, where she ended her days as a cigar-smoking, stage-strutting *artiste* who entertained miners during the California Gold Rush. An amazing life came to an end when she retired, found religion, and devoted the rest of her life to helping wayward women. She died in poverty in Brooklyn. Her life, as she once boasted, was fodder for more biogra-phies than any other woman living in her day.

The trouble began shortly after the new king ascended the Bavarian throne in 1864 at the age of 18. The king had become the patron of Richard Wagner, and four of Wagner's operas—*Tristan und Isolde* (1865), *Die Meistersinger von Nürnberg* (1867), *Das Rheingold* (1869), and *Die Walküre* (1870)—made their debuts in Munich. One of the many visions of the composer and his royal patron was the construction of a glittering opera house. However, this project, and its estimated cost of 6 mil-lion guilders, found little support and led to the collapse of both the hoped-for opera house and the friendship between the king and the composer. A spate of arro-gant public outbursts by the composer (newspapers published his statements that the citizens of Munich had no artistic imagination), led to Wagner and his lofty romantic ideals leaving Munich forever.

Curiously, although viewed as hopelessly eccentric, a bizarre member of a family riddled with other mental aberrations, Ludwig seemed to captivate an age obsessed with romanticism. Although his mania for the building of neo-romantic castles and palaces far from the urban bustle of Munich helped bankrupt the treasury, he rarely meddled in the day-to-day affairs of his subjects and was consequently considered an expensive-to-maintain but relatively unthreatening monarch. If noninvolvement and absenteeism on the part of a king make him more beloved by his subjects, Mad King Ludwig enjoyed a very successful reign.

Actually, the lack of interest in politics on the part of Ludwig II is one of the factors that helped Bismarck, from his base in Prussia, to arrange the unification of Germany in 1871. The unification transformed Berlin into the capital of a united Germany and stripped Bavaria of its status as an independent nation, a designation it had enjoyed since Napoléon's time. Some historians maintain that Bismarck helped induce the mad king to give up his independent status by secretly subsidizing the building costs of his fairy-tale castles. Since the castles, especially Neuschwanstein, have brought billions of tourist dollars to the German nation ever since, he probably made a wise investment.

In 1886 the Bavarian cabinet in Munich stripped the 40-year-old Ludwig of his powers. A few days later, Ludwig's death by drowning in the Starnberg Lake led to endless debate as to whether his death was prearranged because he planned an attempt at a royal comeback. His heir to the tattered remnants of the Bavarian throne was a mentally inept brother, Otto, whose day-to-day duties were assumed by a royal relative, Crown Prince Luitpold, who wore the much-diminished crown until 1912.

The only vestige of Bavaria's imperial past that remained was the designation of the local postal network and railways as "Royal Bavarian" (*Koeniglich-Bayerisch*). The Bavarian monarch was allowed to retain his position as figurehead during a transition period when all eyes, and most real power, slowly flowed toward Berlin.

Munich forged ahead in its role as an economic magnet within a unified Germany. In 1882 Munich began the process of electrifying its street lamps. Three years later public transport was aided by a network of streetcars. And scientist Max von Pettenkofer, who discovered the source of cholera in contaminated water, was instrumental in the installation of a city water supply that was hailed as one of the best in Germany.

ARTISTIC FERMENT   Toward the end of the century, Munich became a center of creativity and artistic ferment. In 1892, the secession movement was founded as a protest against traditional aesthetics. In 1896 the magazine *Jugend* helped define Munich (along with its closest rival, Vienna) as a centerpiece of the German art-nouveau movement, *Jugendstil*. In 1902 a Russian expatriate, Lenin, spent a brief stint in Munich, publishing a revolutionary magazine called *Iskra*. Schwabing, once a farm village, then a summer retreat for the stylishly wealthy, became an icon for the avant-garde, the home base of satirical magazines whose contributors included Thomas Mann (who spent many years of his life in Munich), Rainer Maria Rilke, Hermann Hesse, and Heinrich Mann. In 1911 Franz Marc and Wassily Kandinsky, later joined by Paul Klee, founded the *Der Blaue Reiter* group to promote and define the role of abstract art.

WORLD WAR I & REVOLUTION   World War I (1914–1918) led to more bloodshed and greater disillusionment than Europe had ever known. Hunger was rampant in Munich even in the early years of the war, and by 1918, social unrest was so widespread that a rash of demonstrations, burnings, mob executions, and brawls between advocates of the left and right became increasingly frequent. On the gray day of November 7, 1918, more than 10,000 workers mobilized for a mass demonstration, ending at the gates of the Wittelsbachs's hereditary stronghold, the Residenz. To the rulers' horror, even their guards were persuaded to join the revolutionaries, causing the dynasty's final scion to flee Munich under cover of darkness. The event marked the end of a dynasty that had ruled longer than any other in Europe.

The next day (November 8, 1918) Munich was declared the capital of the Free State of Bavaria (Freistaat Bayern), an independent revolutionary people's republic, led by the Revolutionary Worker's Council. The conservative, so-called "legitimate" Bavarian government went into immediate exile in nearby Bamburg. Kurt Eisner, an articulate political leader who was much less radical than many of those who elected him, ruled briefly and tempestuously. Within a few months, he was assassinated on Munich's Promenadeplatz. Power shifted in a rapid series of events between coalitions of centrists and leftists and ended in a horrendous bloodbath when troops, sent by Berlin in 1919, laid siege to the city as a means of restoring the status quo.

THE RISE OF HITLER   Conservative reaction to the near-takeover of Munich by revolutionaries was swift and powerful, with long-ranging effects. After the events of 1919, and the humiliating terms of surrender imposed upon Germany at Versailles, Munich became one of the most conservative cities in Germany.

In the 1920s sociologists estimated that a full 20% of the city's population of almost three-quarters of a million residents were dependent on welfare, and staggering inflation meant that a wheelbarrowful of Reichsmarks was needed to buy a loaf of bread. The disillusioned city, which retained a deep distrust of Prussian interference from the despised city of Berlin, became a kind of incubator for reactionary, anti-Semitic, and sometimes rabidly conservative political movements.

One of these was the NSDAP (National Socialist Workers Party of Germany) of which Adolf Hitler was a member, and whose meetings were often held in one of Munich's most visited beer halls, the Hofbräuhaus. Hitler's early speeches, as well as the formulation of his ideas as written in *Mein Kampf* (*My Struggle*), were articulated in Munich's beer halls. Ironically, many of the members of Hitler's inner circle (including Heinrich Himmler and Hermann Göring) were from the region around Munich, and thousands of the dictator's rank and file originated from the city's long-suffering, endlessly deprived slums. In 1923 Hitler's "Beer Hall Putsch"—his attempt to lead a popular movement to overthrow the Weimar Republic in Berlin— was quashed, although alert observers of the social scene in Germany could quickly surmise the shape of politics to come.

Under its reactionary civic government, Munich's cultural scene degenerated— anything racy or politically provocative was banned, and many creative persons (including Bruno Walter and Berthold Brecht) opted to change their place of residency to the more sophisticated milieu of Berlin.

After Hitler came to power as chancellor in Berlin, there was little opposition in Bavaria to the National Socialists, whose candidates swept the city's elections of March 5, 1933, and whose swastika flew above city hall by the end of the day. By July of that same year, it was painfully obvious that anyone who opposed the all-Nazi Munich city council would be deported to Germany's first concentration camp, Dachau, on Munich's outskirts.

The headquarters of the Nazi Party was established on the corner of Brienner and Arcis streets, later to be the site of the 1938 signing by Neville Chamberlain, Daladier, Mussolini, and Hitler of the Munich Agreement. Around the same time, a torture chamber was set up in the cellar of what had always been the symbol of power within Munich, the Wittelsbach Palace. Hitler himself even referred to Munich as "the capital of our movement," a statement heard then, as now, with great ambivalence.

Beginning in 1935, vast sums of money were spent on grandiose building projects that followed the Nazi aesthetic. In 1937 a Nazi-sponsored exhibition permeated with anti-Semitic, xenophobic references, *Entartete Kunst* (*Denatured Art*), mocked the tenets of modern art.

Jews began to be persecuted in earnest. The city's largest synagogue was closed in 1938, the same year that *Kristallnacht* (Night of Broken Glass; November 9, 1938) vandalized Jewish-owned homes and businesses across Germany. Only 200 of the city's original population of 10,000 Jews survived the war at all.

In 1939 an attempt to assassinate Hitler as he drank with cronies in a Munich beer hall (the Bürgerbräukeller) failed, and Germany (and Munich) continued the succession of aggressions that eventually led to World War II and the destruction of much of historic Munich.

WORLD WAR II & ITS AFTERMATH   Resistance to Hitler was fatal, and few questioned the mysterious odors emanating from around the once-quiet farm community of Dachau. Nonetheless, a handful of clergymen opposed the Nazi regime. One notable opponent was Father Rupert Mayer, who was imprisoned for many years in Dachau, and who has since been beatified by the Catholic hierarchy. A heroic attempt was made by the Weisse Rose (White Rose) coalition of university students and professors to resist. Their leaders, Hans and Sophie Scholl, Willi Graf, and Hans Huber, were beheaded.

By the war's end, almost half of the city's buildings lay in rubble, many having been blown to pieces as early as 1942. Most of Munich's Renaissance and neoclassical grandeur had been literally bombed off the map, a fact that's easy to overlook by modern visitors who admire the city's many restored monuments.

Munich paid a high price in the blood of its citizens: 22,000 of its sons died in military campaigns, and the civilian population of the city was reduced by almost a quarter million before the end of the war.

THE POSTWAR YEARS & A FOLK HERO   The tone was set after the war by the city's mayor, Thomas Wimmer. He was much beloved by Münchners, and his weekly meet-the-people sessions, when anyone could talk to him personally, made the people in the street feel he was really their representative. His call to clean up the city met with overwhelming response—the rubble was assembled to form decorative hillocks in the city's parks.

Unlike other German cities, Munich was able to unearth the original plans for many of the demolished buildings, which were tastefully restored, even if at astronomical expense, to their original appearance. Today, the city's historic core is surrounded by the same church steeples and towers as in the past.

As capital of the Federal *Land* of Bavaria within the Federal Republic of Germany, Munich took up its new role as focal point for trade between northern and southern Europe. Manufacturers of computers, weapons manufacturers, publishing ventures, fashion houses, movie studios, and companies such as Siemens made Munich their base. The city boomed, with a population that numbered over a million before the end of 1957. As home to BMW (Bayerisches Motoren Werke), Munich is at least partly responsible for Germany's image as home to Europe's fastest drivers.

As the city's population exploded in the 1960s, sprawling masses of concrete suburbs were thrown up hastily, designed for ease of access by cars. Older buildings were demolished to make room for yet another Munich building boom.

Bavarians say the difference between a rich farmer and a poor farmer is that the poor farmer cleans his Mercedes himself.
—J. W. Murray, *Observer,* June 17, 1979

The obsession for rebuilding and modernizing at any price was halted when the then-mayor of Munich paid an official visit to Los Angeles. Munich's press gleefully reported that the automobile-dominated society of L.A. so horrified him that he introduced a new emphasis on historical preservation. Since then, active participation by historic-minded groups has encouraged careful renovations of older buildings.

The 1972 Summer Olympic Games were meant to show all the world the bold new face of a radically rebuilt Munich from the premises of the innovative Olympic City. The terrorist attack on the Israeli athletes, and the collective murder of 11 of them revived recollection of the recent past and left behind ambivalent memories.

MODERN TIMES   Reunification has proved to be something of a mixed blessing to Bavaria. It brought business opportunities in the newly democratized eastern zone, but at the same time, there was an influx of new residents from the east, looking for homes, jobs, and a share in western prosperity, hopes that often aroused resentment and were frequently disappointed.

Social unrest has not disappeared either, although the latest incident, in 1995, had a trivial cause. "The Bavarian Beer Garden Revolution" started when residents in a prosperous neighborhood requested that the local beer garden be closed after 9:30pm because of noise and congestion. Picked up as a *cause célèbre* by thousands of beer drinkers who were afraid that such a rule might become the norm, the event provoked a raucous demonstration by 20,000 angry protesters. Although the owners of the beer garden in question, the Waldwirtshaft, had sown the seeds for the initial protest marches, the number of participants exceeded their wildest imagination. The incident was seen as a visible sign of stress between opposing political and social forces.

As Munich faces the millennium, its citizens are rightly concerned about the impact of Berlin's re-establishment as the official capital of a reunited country in reality as well as in name, and the possible shift of trade and power into the north and east of Germany. Another question is what will happen when the new euro currency makes its debut, replacing the old, reliable Mark—a concern that is shared by the rest of Europe.

3 Famous Bavarians

Albrecht (Albert) V (1528–1579)   This duke of Bavaria did much for regional art and culture during his reign (1550–1579). Although no artist, he established the Kumquat (Cabinet of Art) and the Antiquarium, Germany's first museums, making Munich a cultural center.

Egid Quirin (1692–1750) and **Cosmas Damian Asam** (1686–1739)   These painter-and-architect brothers journeyed to Rome where they were influenced by Bernini. They are known in Munich for their frescoes in such churches as St. Mary's in Thalkirchen and the Church of the Holy Ghost. They brought the flower of Bavarian High Baroque into full bloom.

The Sorrows of Sissi

Elisabeth (1837–1898), "the beautiful girl from Munich," daughter of Munich's Duke Maximilian Joseph, was a kind of 19th-century Princess Di, a revered figure who led a glamorous and tragic life. Despite misgivings, she married Emperor Franz Joseph I of Austria while still a teenager. Her relationship with her husband was not a success, and her mother-in-law, the Grand Duchess Sophie, made her life unbearable.

Willful and independent, she reacted by putting herself through punishing fasts and developing psychosomatic illnesses whenever she was in Vienna. A beautiful and sympathetic woman, she was wildly popular. She spent her time visiting hospitals and old people's homes, and when things got to be too much for her, she fled to Italy or Greece, staying away from Vienna, her beleaguered husband, and the duties of empire as long as possible.

Her public, however, adored her, and knew few of the inner secrets of what might be interpreted as neurotic behavior. She was affectionately known as "Sissi" by the citizens of the Austro-Hungarian Empire, and one of her great successes was her ability to soothe and placate the dour Hungarian faction in her husband's empire.

She devotedly remained at the bedside of the Grand Duchess Sophie during her mother-in-law's last illness, but the death of her old enemy did not really ease her unhappiness. In 1886 her cousin Ludwig, one of her closest friends, drowned, and worse still was to come. Her son, Crown Prince Rudolf, and his mistress were found dead in what appeared to be joint suicide. However, the circumstances were and still are mysterious—Rudolf, libertine and libertarian, was known to hold positions on personal liberties that might have threatened the very fabric of his father's empire.

From this time on, the empress wore black and sank into a deep depression. On September 10, 1898, when she was waiting to board a pleasure craft for a ride on Lake Geneva, she was fatally stabbed by an Italian anarchist who had, in fact, mistaken her for someone else. Her husband, last and longest ruler of the Austro-Hungarian Empire, never remarried.

Today, like her cousin Ludwig, Sissi has a cult following in Bavaria. A recent TV series on her life broke all viewing records there.

François de Cuvilliés the Elder (1695–1768)   Although small in stature, he became the giant of Bavarian rococo architecture and decor. (See the box about him in chapter 6.) His architectural tradition was continued by his son, François, called the Younger.

Rudolf Diesel (1858–1913)   Paris-born Rudolf Christian Carl Diesel studied in Munich, patented the pressure-ignited internal combustion engine (1893), and built the first successful diesel engine (1896). He was also a noted social theorist. He spent the latter part of his life in Munich in elegant Bogenhausen. The name *Diesel* would become famous throughout the world. The inventor was drowned while crossing in a boat from Antwerp to Harwich.

Albert Einstein (1879–1955)   Born in Ulm, one of the greatest modern thinkers spent his formative years in Munich before becoming a Swiss citizen (1901). After the Nazi seizure of Germany he resigned his academic posts and moved to the United States, where he spent his remaining years. His theory of relativity revolutionized modern physics, garnering him the Nobel Peace Prize for physics (1916). A staunch pacifist, he warned the world of the perils of nuclear weaponry after World War II.

Friedrich von Gärtner (1792–1847) After a tour of Italy that familiarized him with forms of classical architecture, this Munich-trained architect was responsible for the development of the Ludwigstrasse in 1827. His synthesis of neoclassical principles of proportional and historical forms manifests itself in such major works as the Munich State Library, the university, the Siegestor, and the Feldherrnhalle.

Hubert Gerhard (1550–1620) This sculptor trained under Giovonni da Bologna in Florence and later worked in bronze in Augsburg, Munich, and Innsbruck. The main exponent of the Bavarian school of bronze around 1660, he led the evolution of sculpture from Mannerism to early Baroque. The figure of St. Michael and the Dragon on the facade of St. Michael's church and the Virgin as Patroness of Bavaria on the Mariensäule are among his most renowned works.

Franz von Lenbach (1836–1904) He was a major artistic figure in the 1870s, a period known in Munich as *Gründerzeit* (a major time of economic progress). He was well known for his copies of Rubens, Titian, and others, commissioned for the Schack Gallery in Munich. His best known original works are *The Arch of Titus, The Shepherd Boy,* and portraits of Emperor William I, Bismarck, Wagner, Liszt, and Gladstone.

Ludwig I, King of Bavaria (1796–1868) Ludwig I became ruler of Bavaria as heir to his father Maximilian I in 1825. He supported the liberal Bavarian constitution of 1818. The reconstruction of the royal capital of Munich owes much to his determination. He envisioned Munich as a grand metropolis, the "Athens of the North." The provincial university was moved from Landshut to Munich by his order in 1826. His retro-tendencies after 1830, combined with his affiliations with dancer Lola Montez, caused a crisis in the Bavarian government, ultimately leading to his abdication amid the confusion of the March revolution in 1848.

Ludwig II, King of Bavaria (1845–1886) Fascinated by German legends since the early years of his upbringing in Schloss Hohenschwangau, King Ludwig II was destined to become a part of romantic lore. When he became king in 1864, he was already an enthusiastic admirer and patron of romantic opera, specifically those composed by Richard Wagner. He earned the title "Mad King" as he constructed his "fairy-tale" castles, and the line between his fantasies and reality became increasingly nebular. He drowned in Starnberg Lake at Schloss Berg amid shrouded circumstances. See the box about him in chapter 11.

Thomas Mann (1875–1955) This famous German author moved to Munich after the death of his father, where he sharpened his skills as editor of the satirical magazine *Simplicissimus* from 1898 to 1899. He remained in Munich until 1933, becoming one of Germany's celebrated writers (*Buddenbrucks,* 1901; *Death in Venice,* 1925; *The Magic Mountain,* 1927). He won the Nobel Prize for literature in 1929. In 1933, wary of the emerging National Socialists, he embarked upon a lecture tour in France and Switzerland, and from abroad he protested the Nazis loudly in essays entitled "Europe, Beware." Naturalized in the United States in 1944, he eventually returned to Europe, but not to Germany, in 1952, settling at Kilchberg on Lake Zurich.

Oskar von Miller (1855–1934) This Munich engineer was a pioneer in the invention and organization of electrical power production. He became acclaimed when in 1882 he scored a major success in transmitting the first electric power in the world from Meisbach to Munich. He was the cofounder and director of

German Edison Company, which developed G.E., and he contributed to the development of high-tension electric power transmission.

Carl Orff (1895–1982)   The composer spent most of his life in his native city of Munich, where he thrived as a conductor and music teacher. In 1924 he and Dorothee Günther founded Güntherschule, to teach children by his widely adopted methods stressing gymnastics and dance. As a composer he became celebrated for lavish theatrical works that combined elements of Greek theater, baroque opera, peasant life, and Christian mystery. *Carmina Burana* (1937) is his most widely recognized work.

Jan Polack (1435–1519)   The Kraków native came to Munich around 1470. His numerous frescoes and altarpieces established him as the most important Munich painter of the late Gothic period. The altarpieces in the chapel of the Blutenburg Castle, the wall paintings in the Pippinger Kirchl, and the high altar of St. Peter's are among his remaining works.

Carl Spitzweg (1808–1885)   The native Münchner and self-taught painter is the most representative of Biedermeyer artists in Germany. His humorously detailed portrayals of small-town misfits, street musicians, postmen, and parting lovers depict their naïvete and simplicity in ironic and mocking tones. In the Neue Pinakothek hangs his best-known work, *The Poor Poet,* who continues to scribble away, despite the leaking roof.

Richard Strauss (1864–1949)   Born in Munich, the composer and conductor was the leader of the New Romantic school. From 1886 to 1898 he was *Kapellmeister* (musical director) of the city, and later with Franz Schalk, headed the State Opera in Vienna, where he worked with all the major European orchestras. He composed both operas and symphonic works. Of his 15 operas, his most famous are *Salome* (1905), *Elektra* (1908), and *Der Rosenkavalier* (1911).

Karl Valentin (1882–1948)   A famous character performer in Munich, Valentin's sketch comedies and extemporaneous commentary are legendary in German-speaking countries. His performances with his partner, Liesl Karlstadt, in small theaters and cabarets bordered on absurd but always remained comical. His twisted logic struck a chord with the common folk, and his films remain popular.

4 Munich & the Flowering of the Baroque

The glory of Bavaria is its baroque and rococo architecture. Even Munich's oldest parish church, St. Peter's, whose foundations date from the early Middle Ages, has an interior overlaid with baroque decoration. The Gothic style never took hold in southern Germany as it did in England and France. The best example of Gothic architecture in the city is, of course, the somber brick profile of the Frauenkirche. Its cornerstone was laid in 1468; the towers were completed in 1525.

THE FLOWERING OF THE BAROQUE   The architecture of the Renaissance, which began in Italy around 1520 and lasted a century, greatly influenced southern German architecture. The most spectacular example appears in the form of the massive St. Michael's Church, the largest baroque building north of the Alps. A symbol of defiance to the growing power of the Protestants farther to the north, it was begun in 1583 and finished in a record-breaking 14 years. When one of its towers collapsed during the seventh year of its construction, its royal patron, Duke Wilhelm V, interpreted the accident as a sign of displeasure from God—the building wasn't impressive enough. Consequently, it was enlarged into the airy and

A Munich for the Millennium

While the dramatic rebuilding of Berlin's no-man's land has captured worldwide attention, Munich is busy with a building spree that will radically transform the city's skyline by the beginning of the millennium.

Presided over by Munich's mayor, Christian Ude, whose passion for high-profile civic monuments seems to rival that of the late French president Mitterand during his *grands travaux,* projects that are underway, nearly completed, or still on paper promise a future cityscape very different from the Munich of today.

Native Münchner architect Stephan Braunfels is in charge of the important expansion of the city's major art museum. His $114 million "Third Pinakothek" is an angular, Bauhaus-inspired glass-and-steel showcase for contemporary art that will supplement the Alte Pinakothek and Neue Pinakothek. The result will be a massive three-part temple to the visual arts, scheduled to be completed sometime in the year 2000—Munich's answer to the showcase Museum Insel of its archrival, Berlin.

Other projects include an all-new rehearsal space for the Kammerspiele theater, with an iconoclastic design by Viennese architect Gustav Peichl. The glass-and-steel structure will straddle both sides of downtown's Falkenbergstrasse, and its most distinctive characteristic will be a rooftop needle-nosed glass pyramid, visible for many blocks around. It's scheduled for completion sometime in 2002. Discussion is ongoing about a possible $230 million overhaul of the aging Olympic Stadium and the neighborhood around it.

Other plans call for the radical transformations of entire neighborhoods into complexes that reflect the city's optimism about its ongoing success in the new millennium. For example, the Thresienhohe district of central Munich around the Deutsches Museum will be transformed into a combination of residential and commercial space and includes an expansion of the museum itself.

High-rises and complexes are growing on at least a dozen other construction sites. A 155-meter tower is going up near the Olympic Stadium, another in central Munich. The Hypobank's icon to postmodernism, the "ultimate high-rise" is currently in design by Christoph Ingenhoven; it has been likened to a graceful-looking stalk of asparagus, and its eventual height will be somewhere between 205 and 263 meters (677 to 868 feet).

Ask any Münchner what he or she thinks about the transformation of the city? The reply will probably be a shrug and a comment about being proud of the city as an architectural powerhouse, so long as the historic core remains untouched. And, of course, amid all this furor, the Altstadt, with its zoning rules that forbid any building to rise higher than the spires of the city's symbol, the Frauenkirche, will remain sacrosanct.

soaring interior you'll see today. It was laboriously reconstructed as a symbol of civic pride after the damages of World War II.

High baroque style, an Italian import whose influence in Germany began around 1660 and continued into the 18th century, brought a different kind of renaissance to Germany. The baroque swept southern Germany, especially Munich and Bavaria. As characterized by art historian Helen Gardner, baroque architecture was "spacious and dynamic, brilliant and colorful, theatrical and passionate, sensual and ecstatic, opulent and extravagant, versatile and virtuoso." This period saw the merging of painting, sculpture, and architecture into an integrated whole. Painting became illusionist, architecture pictorial. Visual impact and sensual delight characterized the movement, as stained glass gave way to floods of natural light. Altarpieces grew monumental, and baroque space provided multiple changing views. Sometimes a baroque building reached out to embrace an entire square and all the buildings surrounding it. The ceilings of baroque churches with their painted scenes, were meant "to lift the viewer to heaven." Illusions like trompe l'oeil, with its whimsical style, often merged with stucco adornment in what one architect called a "form of 3-D trickery."

Outstanding among baroque artists and architects in Bavaria were two sets of brothers. The work of the Asam brothers, painter Cosmas Damian Asam and sculptor Egid Quirin Asam, are the best examples of the southern high baroque style. Their masterpiece is the Asam-Kirche in Munich, whose interior bursts upon the viewer in a riot of gold. Cosmas became particularly celebrated for his vast dome paintings of the heavens. Another pair of brothers, the architect Dominikus Zimmerman (1685–1766) and the fresco master, Johann Baptist Zimmerman (1685–1766), created the towering masterpiece, the Wieskirche near Landsberg. This church is a virtual fantasy, with cherubs and angels peeking out behind garlands of foliage (see the box in chapter 11).

The towering figure of the movement, however, was Balthasar Neumann (1687–1753), whose architecture has been called "music frozen in time." Although he never worked in Munich, his Vierzehnhelligenkirche near Bamberg is Neumann at his most energetic and intricate.

The baroque movement eventually dipped its brushes into the flippant paint of the rococo and brought to the style even greater flamboyance and gaiety. The first rococo church in Bavaria was Johann Michael Fischer's St. Anna im Lehel. The great architect of this movement was François de Cuvilliés whose masterpiece is the Residenztheater (see the box in chapter 6). He is also responsible for the facade of the Theatinerkirche, built by Prince Elector Ferdinand Maria in 1662 in gratitude for the birth of his heir, Max Emanuel. Its construction was among the most complicated in Munich because of its completion date more than a century after its inauguration.

NEOCLASSICAL GRANDEUR By the 19th century, the baroque and rococo styles, with their connections to the *ancien régime,* had been swept away by the French Revolution. In their place neoclassicism made reference to the grandeur of ancient Greece and imperial Rome. Between 1825 and 1848, Munich's transformation into a suitably royal capital of neoclassical splendor owed a great deal to the attempt by the autocratic Crown Prince Ludwig (later Ludwig I) to transform Munich into a second Athens or Rome. The Alte Pinakothek was begun in 1826, and at the time it was the largest art gallery in the world. Ludwig himself is responsible for the collection you see today of early German masters, including Dürer, and such early Italian painters as Giotto, Botticelli, and da Vinci. Other neoclassical examples of Ludwig's efforts are the Königsplatz, the Glyptothek, and, within the Residenz complex, the Königsbau (King's Building).

In the later 1800s, the Romantic movement, which looked back to a rose-colored interpretation of Germany's medieval history, myth, and folklore, introduced an architectural and decorative style sometimes termed *historicism.* This style is exemplified in Fredrich von Gartner's Staatsbibliothek (State Library), the university complex, and such focal points along the Ludwigstrasse as the Feldherrnhalle and the Siegestor. This movement, of course, also inspired Ludwig II, and no other building represents it so well as his palace, Neuschwanstein (see chapter 11).

TOWARD THE MODERN AGE   By the end of the 19th century, the art-nouveau movement—*Jugendstil*—marked the distant beginnings of contemporary architecture, as architects began to use such materials as glass, steel, and concrete. In the aftermath of World War I, the influence of Walter Gropius's Bauhaus movement, whose primary aim was to unify arts and crafts within the context of architecture, began to be felt. Gropius stressed an idea of functional design that reflected the tastes of the postindustrial revolution.

Bauhaus ideas, however, did not suit the tastes of the rising National Socialists, and the Bauhaus was dissolved in 1933. By 1935 the so-called "Third Reich" style of architecture was the law of the land, with Munich (site of most of Hitler's earliest successes) providing the experimental background for many of its ideas. Under Hitler's favorite architect, Albert Speer, art and architecture became propaganda tools; pompous, monumental, and devoid of any real humanity. Postwar Munich did its best to conceal the Nazi roots of some of its buildings by skillfully transforming them into something more human. An example is the Zentralministerium (Central Ministry), a predictably pompous but anonymous building on the Von-der-Tann-Strasse, cutting through the otherwise orderly progression of the Ludwigstrasse. An even better example, recycled after the war into an art gallery, is the Haus der Kunst, which houses the Staatsgalerie Moderner Kunst (State Gallery of Modern Art). Its angular Fascist architecture seems curiously appropriate for the starkly modern paintings it showcases today. Ironically, virtually everything inside would have been anathema to Hitler and outlawed as "degenerate" by its original builders.

RESTORATION & RENEWAL   One of the sad legacies of World War II was the virtual leveling of many of Germany's greatest architectural treasures by Allied bombing raids. On-site witnesses claim that in Munich the first 2 years after the end of the war were devoted almost exclusively to clearing away the rubble. Part of the past had been swept away, but visitors will find that many of the treasured landmarks have been carefully reconstructed in their original style.

New structures for the modern age, ever more innovative, can be seen in such sites as the stadium built for the 1972 Olympics and the performance center at Gasteig, begun in 1979 and opened in 1985.

5 A Taste of Bavaria

THE TRADITIONAL CUISINE

Bavarians like to eat, justifying their appetites with the very reasonable assertion that any type of human interaction operates more smoothly when it's lubricated with ample amounts of food and wine, or even better, food and beer.

Calorie- and cholesterol-conscious North Americans might recoil at the sight of meals made up of dumplings, potatoes, any of a dozen different types of *würste* (sausages), roasted meats flavored with bacon drippings, breads, and pastries. Munich, of course, has many *nouvelle* counterparts to the heavy-handed old-fashioned *kuchen,* as well as restaurants that serve a lighter form of the traditional cuisine.

The Bavarian affair with sausage is of ancient lineage, würst having been a major part of the national diet almost since there were people and livestock in the area. Bavarians tend to view their würst with some superstition, nostalgically adhering to such adages as "Never let the sunshine of noon shine on a Weisswurst," and the reservation of Rotwurst for consumption in the evening.

Every Bavarian professes a love for his or her favorite kind of würst (a choice that's often based on childhood associations). Many visitors' favorite is *Bratwurst,* which came originally from nearby Nürnberg and is concocted from seasoned and spiced pork. *Weisswurst,* Munich's traditional accompaniment to a foaming mug of beer, wasn't "invented" until 1857, a date remembered by Münchners as an important watershed. The ingredients that go into it are less appetizing than the final result—usually including veal, calf's brains, and spleen. Modern versions contain less offal and better quantities of veal, as well as spices and lemon juice to enhance the flavor. Two are usually considered a snack. Five or six are a respectable main course. Most aficionados try not to eat the skin, but some diehards wouldn't think of removing it.

Bauernwurst (farmer's sausage) and *Knockwurst* are variations of the Frankfurter, which, although it originated in the more westerly city of Frankfurt, achieved its greatest fame in the New World. While *Leberwurst* is a specialty of Hesse, and *Riderwurst* (beef sausage) and *Blutwurst* (blood sausage) are specialties of Westphalia, all of them are widely served and enjoyed in Munich. Regardless of which you choose, the perfect accompaniment for würst consists of mustard, a roll (preferably studded with pumpernickel seeds), and beer.

As savory as the würsts of Munich might be, they're considered too simple to grace the table of any truly elaborate Bavarian meal, unless accompanied by a medley of other dishes. These might include dishes from the long-ago repertoire of agrarian Bavarian cuisine, including *Züngerl* (pig's tongue) or *Wammerl* (pig's stomach), most often served with braised or boiled cabbage. Potato dumplings (*Klösse,* or *Kartoffelknödel*) also are served with many dishes, and *Leber* (liver) dumplings are mandatory features several times a month. *Semmelknödel* (bread dumplings) generally accompany the most famous meat dish of Bavaria, *Schweinbraten* (roast pork). Also popular, with many devotees, are *Kalbshaxen* (veal shank) and *Schweinshaxen* (roasted knuckle of pork). Carp is prized by Munich's gastronomes, as is a succulent variety of trout, or *Forelle.*

Feeling hungry during your sightseeing promenades around Munich? Step into the nearest *Metzgerei* (butcher shop) and order such items as a *Warmer Leberkäs,* which has nothing to do either with liver or with cheese, but instead with ground beef and bacon, baked like a meat loaf and sold in slices of about 100 grams each. It's best consumed with mild mustard and a roll. Another worthy choice is *Wurtzsemmel,* sliced sausage meat on a roll, or a *Schinkensemmel,* sliced ham served on a roll. You can carry it away for consumption where there's a view or take it into a *Bierkeller* or Biergarten (it's been legal for centuries to bring in your own food and order a small beer to go with it).

AND WHAT BEER SHOULD YOU DRINK?

No self-respecting Münchener will refuse a sparkling glass of wine, and will even praise highly the light, slightly acidic wines from the Rhineland. But the real glint enters a Münchner's eye when the relative merits of beer are discussed. You won't lack for variety within the beer halls of Munich—there are even beers available according to season.

Both because it's the law, and as a matter of pride, breweries make their beer with yeast, barley, hops, and water. Preservatives aren't usually added—in a city where a 200-liter cask of beer can be drained by a thirsty crowd in fewer than 12 minutes, the beer never lasts long enough to really need them. Legally required adherence to certain standards dates back to 1516—prior to the establishment of standards anywhere else in Europe.

Here's a rundown on what you're likely to need in your dialogues with a Münchner bartender.

"Normal" Bavarian beer, also referred to as light beer (ask for *ein Helles*), is slightly less potent than the brew consumed in North Germany, France, or England. Its relative weakness is the main reason why many visitors can consume several liters before beginning to feel the least bit giddy.

Don't think, however, that "normal" beer is the same as *Weiss* or (in Münchner dialect) *Weizenbier,* which is brewed with a high concentration of fermented wheat. In springtime, along with spring lamb and fresh fruits and vegetables, Munich offers *Bock* and *Doppelbock* (Double Bock), *Märzenbier,* and *Pils.*

Beck's dark is an example of dark beer (*ein Dunkles*) known to many North Americans. There's even a dark Weiss beer, which happens to be wheat beer brewed in such a way as to make it smoky-looking rather than pale. And in case you've forgotten a particularly ugly episode of Munich's civic history, there's even a beer named after the doomed socialists (the Red Guards) who forcibly took over the city's government for a few months in 1918, a *Russe,* which consists of Weiss (wheat) beer and lemonade.

What is the polite thing to ask for if you think you're too drunk to handle another liter of "normal"? Ask for a *Radlermass* (literally, "a mug for the bike"), composed of half "normal" beer, half lemonade.

The ideal place to go for consuming this amazing variety of fermented grains is any of the city's dozens of Bierkellers or Biergartens, which serve simple snacklike food items—sausages, white radishes, cheese, and the kind of salted pretzels that are guaranteed to make you thirstier. Munich's most historic drinking sites include the Hofbräuhaus and the Bürgerbräukeller, both of which carry local associations of everyone from Adolf Hitler to the boy or girl next door.

2

Planning a Trip to Munich & the Bavarian Alps

This chapter is devoted to all the practical information for a visit to Munich and the Alps. Browse through it to be sure you've covered everything you need to get your trip together and take it on the road.

1 Information & Entry Requirements

VISITOR INFORMATION

Nearly all larger towns and all cities in the Federal Republic have tourist offices. The headquarters of the **German National Tourist Board** is at Beethovenstrasse 69, D-60325 Frankfurt am Main (☎ **069/75720**).

Before you go, you'll find a German National Tourist Office in **New York** at 122 E. 42nd St., 52nd Floor, New York, NY 10168 (☎ **212/661-7200**); in **Los Angeles** at 11766 Wilshire Blvd., Suite 750, Los Angeles, CA 90025 (☎ **310/575-9799**); in **Toronto** at 175 Bloor St. E., North Tower, 6th Floor, Toronto, ON M4W 3R8 (☎ **416/968-1570**); and in **London** at Nightingale House, 65 Curzon St., London W1Y 8NE (☎ **0171/495-0081**).

A good travel agent can also be a source of information. Make sure that the agent is a member of the **American Society of Travel Agents** (ASTA). If you get poor service, write to ASTA Consumer Affairs Department, 1101 King St., Alexandria, VA 22314-3200, or you can call their direct line at ☎ **703/739-2782.**

ENTRY REQUIREMENTS

PASSPORTS & VISAS Every U.S. traveler entering Germany must hold a valid passport. It is not necessary to obtain a visa unless you're staying longer than three continuous months. Once you've entered Germany, you won't need to show your passport again at the borders of the European Union countries of Belgium, France, Italy, Luxembourg, the Netherlands, Portugal, or Spain.

In the **United States,** you can apply for a passport in person at one of 13 regional offices or by mail. You'll need a passport application form (available at U.S. post offices), proof of citizenship, and two identical passport-sized photographs. First-time applicants must submit a birth certificate or naturalization papers and are charged a fee of $60 ($40 if under 18 years of age). Applications for renewal must include the old passport and a pink renewal form

(DSP-82); the renewal fee is $40. For an additional $35 passports can be renewed within 3 business days. Call ☎ **202/647-0518** at any time for information or write to Passport Service, Office of Correspondence, Department of State, 1111 19th St. NW, Suite 510, Washington, DC 20522-1075. Information can be obtained on the Internet at **www.travel.state.gov** or by calling the **National Passport Information Center (NPIC)** at ☎ **900/225-5674** (35¢ per minute for 24-hour automated service, or $1.05 per minute for 9am to 3pm live operator service).

In **Canada,** citizens can go to one of 28 regional offices, or mail an application to the Passport Office, External Affairs and International Trade Canada, Ottawa, ON K1A 0GE (☎ **613/996-8885**). Applications are available at passport offices, post offices, and most travel agencies. The fee is $60 Canadian. Passports are valid for 5 years and are not renewable. For more information, call ☎ **800/567-6868** or 800/267-8376**.**

Citizens of the **United Kingdom** and the **Republic of Ireland,** as well as subjects of any other European Union country, need only an identity card to travel to Germany. For more information call ☎ **0990/210410** in London. In Ireland, write to the Passport Office, Setna Centre, Molesworth Street, Dublin 2, Ireland (☎ **01/671-1633**). Irish citizens living in North America can contact the Irish Embassy, 2234 Massachusetts Ave. NW, Washington, DC 20008 (☎ **202/ 462-3939**).

Citizens of Australia, New Zealand, and South Africa need passports to enter Germany. In **Australia,** apply at your nearest post office. Call ☎ **02/131232** for the latest information. Citizens of **New Zealand** should contact the New Zealand Passport Office, Documents of National Identity Division, Department of Internal Affairs, P.O. Box 10-526, Wellington, NZ (☎ **0800/225050**). The fee is NZ 80. **South African** citizens can apply for a passport at any Department of Home Affairs Office.

GERMAN CUSTOMS   Items required for personal and professional use may be brought in duty-free, including a private car, provided it is reported. Gifts are duty-free up to a total value of 780 DM ($444.60).

The following items are permitted into Germany duty-free (imports from European Union countries in parentheses): 200 (300) cigarettes; 1 (1.5) liter(s) of liquor above 44 proof, or 2 (3) liters of liquor less than 44 proof, or 2 (4) liters of wine; 50 (75) grams of perfume and 0.25 (0.375) liters of eau de cologne; 500 (750) grams of coffee; 100 (150) grams of tea. All duty-free allowances are authorized only when the items are carried in the traveler's personal baggage.

2 Money

CURRENCY   The unit of German currency is the **Deutschmark (DM),** which is subdivided into **pfennig.** Bills are issued in denominations of 5, 10, 20, 50, 100, 200, 500, and 1,000 marks; coins come in 1, 2, 5, 10, and 50 pfennig.

CREDIT CARDS   Most major credit cards are accepted throughout Germany. Note, however, that Discover cards are accepted only in the United States.

EURO CURRENCY   The euro, the new single European currency, will become the official currency of Germany and 10 other participating countries on January 1, 1999, but not in the form of cash. The traveler will see prices displayed in euros as well as Marks, and the euro can be used in noncash transactions such as credit cards. Cash will not be introduced, and the Deutschmark and other national currencies will not be replaced, until 2002.

ATMS   PLUS, Cirrus, and other networks connecting automated-teller machines operate in Munich and throughout Germany. Check to be sure that your PIN will work at German ATMs or whether it needs to be reprogrammed for usage in Germany. For Cirrus locations abroad, call ☎ **800/424-7787.** For PLUS usage abroad, dial ☎ **800/843-7587.**

TRAVELER'S CHECKS   Most large banks sell traveler's checks, charging fees that average between 1% and 2% of the value of the checks; if your bank wants more than a 2% commission, it sometimes pays to call the traveler's check issuers directly for the address of outlets where this commission will be less. All the agencies below sell traveler's checks denominated in U.S. dollars, German marks, and other currencies.

American Express (☎ **800/221-7282** in the U.S. and Canada), one of the largest issuers of traveler's checks, has many regional representatives in Germany. No commission is charged to members of the American Automobile Association (AAA) and to holders of certain types of American Express credit cards.

Citicorp (☎ **800/645-6556** in the U.S. and Canada, or **813/623-1709,** collect, from anywhere else in the world) also issues traveler's checks.

Thomas Cook (☎ **800/223-7373** in the U.S. and Canada, or **609/987-7300,** collect, from other parts of the world) issues MasterCard traveler's checks. Depending on individual banking laws in the various states, some currencies might not be available at every outlet.

Interpayment Services (☎ **800/221-2426** in the U.S. and Canada, or **212/858-8500** collect, from other parts of the world) sells VISA traveler's checks.

CHECKS/CASH   If you need a check in German marks before your trip, for example, to pay a deposit on a hotel room, you can contact **Ruesch International,** 700 11th St., NW, 4th Floor, Washington, DC 20001-4507 (☎ **800/424-2923** or 202/408-1200). Ruesch also issues traveler's checks in German marks. If you want to take along an amount in cash, contact your bank or the nearest **Thomas Cook** office (☎ **800/223-7373** in the U.S. and Canada).

MONEYGRAM   If you find yourself out of money, a new wire service provided by American Express can help you tap willing friends and family for emergency funds. Through MoneyGram, 7501 W. Mansfield, Lakewood, CO 80235 (☎ **800/ 926-9400**), money can be sent around the world in less than 10 minutes. Senders should call Amex to learn the address of the closest outlet that handles MoneyGrams. The service includes a short telex message and a 3-minute phone call from sender to recipient. The beneficiary must present a photo ID at the outlet where money is received.

WHAT WILL IT COST?

Munich as well as the rest of Germany is one of the world's more expensive destinations.

Although there are many variations in **accommodations** price structure, based on size and type of room, hotels ranked "Very Expensive" generally charge 350 DM ($199.50) and up for a double room. "Expensive" means that doubles cost about 270 to 350 DM ($153.90 to $199.50); "Moderate" rooms run about 180 to 270 DM ($102.60 to $153.90). A double priced under about 180 DM ($102.60) is considered "Inexpensive." Prices are for two people occupying one room and include tax and service. All rooms are with bath unless stated otherwise. If parking is not specifically mentioned in a listing, the hotel has no garage or other parking facility. You'll need to find a place on the street or at a nearby garage. Parking rates are per day.

The U.S. Dollar & the German Mark

For American Readers   At this writing, $1 = 1.75 DM (or 1 DM = 57¢), and this is the rate of exchange used to calculate the dollar values in this book.

For British Readers   At this writing, £1 = approximately 2.94 DM, and this is the rate of exchange used to calculate the pound sterling values in this table.

Note: The relative value of the Deutschmark to other world currencies fluctuates from time to time and may not be the same when you travel to Germany. This table should be used only as an indication of approximate values.

DM	US$	UK £	DM	US$	UK £
0.25	0.14	0.09	30.00	17.10	10.20
0.50	0.29	.17	35.00	19.95	11.90
0.75	0.43	0.26	40.00	22.80	13.60
1.00	0.57	0.34	45.00	25.65	15.30
2.00	1.14	0.68	50.00	28.50	17.00
3.00	1.71	1.02	60.00	34.20	20.40
4.00	2.28	1.36	70.00	39.90	23.80
5.00	2.85	1.70	80.00	45.60	27.20
6.00	3.42	2.04	90.00	51.30	30.60
7.00	3.99	2.38	100.00	57.00	34.00
8.00	4.56	2.72	125.00	71.25	42.50
9.00	5.13	3.06	150.00	85.50	51.00
10.00	5.70	3.40	175.00	99.75	59.50
15.00	8.55	5.10	200.00	114.00	68.00
20.00	11.40	6.80	250.00	142.50	85.00
25.00	14.25	8.50	500.00	285.00	170.00

Munich offers a wide range of **dining,** in both cuisine and price. In the listings in this guide, a restaurant is considered "Very Expensive" if a meal for one costs more than about 100 DM ($57), without wine. "Expensive" dining runs about 65 to 100 DM ($37.05 to $57); "Moderate," about 35 to 65 DM ($19.95 to $37.05); and "Inexpensive" less than 35 DM ($19.95).

In the small towns and villages of Bavaria, prices will be anywhere from 20% to 40% less than prices in Munich. A moderately priced rail pass will allow you to see a lot of Bavaria in a short time.

Although prices are high, you generally get good value for your money. The inflation rate, unlike that of most of the world, has remained low. Hotels are usually clean and comfortable, and restaurants offer a good cuisine and ample portions made with quality ingredients. The trains run on time, and they're fast, and most service personnel treat you with respect.

For winter sports, the most expensive resorts are in such places as Garmisch-Partenkirchen. You can still enjoy winter fun at a moderate cost if it's not important to you to be seen in chic places. You can stay in the village next to a chic resort where prices are 30% lower.

What Things Cost in Munich	U.S. $
Taxi from the airport to Hauptbahnhof	65.00
Underground from the Hauptbahnhof to Schwabing	2.10
Local telephone call	.20
Double room at the Kempinski Hotel Vier Jahreszeiten (very expensive)	279.30
Double room at the Eden-Hotel-Wolff (expensive)	153.90
Double room at the Adria (moderate)	108.30
Double room at the Pension Westfalia (inexpensive)	65.55
Lunch for one, without wine, at Ratskeller (moderate)	17.10
Lunch for one, without wine, at Nürnberger Bratwurst Glöckl Am Dom (inexpensive)	12.55
Dinner for one, without wine, at Tantris (very expensive)	111.15
Dinner for one, without wine, at Zum Alten Markt (moderate)	25.10
Dinner for one, without wine, at Donisl (inexpensive)	12.40
Glass of wine	2.50
Liter of beer	7.00
Cup of coffee	2.50
Coca-Cola in a restaurant	1.90
Roll of ASA 200 color film, 36 exposures	6.00
Admission to Deutsches Museum	5.70
Movie ticket	7.50
Ticket to Nationaltheater	from 19.95

In Bavaria many prices for children (generally defined as ages 6 to 17) are considerably lower than for adults. Children under 6 often are charged no admission or other fee.

3 When to Go

CLIMATE
In Bavaria and in the Alps, it can sometimes be very cold in winter, especially in January, and very warm in summer, but with cool, rainy days even in July and August. Spring and fall are often "stretched out." In fact, we've enjoyed many a Bavarian-style "Indian summer" until late in October. The most popular tourist months are May through October, although winter travel to the alpine ski areas is becoming increasingly popular.

Munich's Average Daytime Temperature & Days of Rain

	Jan	Feb	Mar	Apr	May	June	July	Aug	Sept	Oct	Nov	Dec
Temp. (°F)	33	35	40	50	60	65	70	73	65	50	39	33
Days rain	19	16	19	19	21	24	18	17	18	15	17	18

HOLIDAYS
The following public holidays are celebrated in Bavaria: January 1 (New Year's Day), January 6 (Epiphany), Easter (Good Friday and Easter Monday), May 1

(Labor Day), Ascension Day (10 days before Pentecost, the seventh Sunday after Easter), Whitmonday (day after Whitsunday/Pentecost), Corpus Christi (10 days after Pentecost), August 15 (Feast of the Assumption), October 3 (Day of German Unity), November 1 (All Saints Day), November 17 (Day of Prayer and National Repentance), and December 25 and 26 (Christmas).

MUNICH CALENDAR OF EVENTS

For details on the following observances, consult the Munich Tourist Bureau at the Hauptbahnof (☎ **089/233-0300**).

January

✪ **Fasching (Carnival).** Pre-Lenten revelry characterizes this bash, with a whirl of colorful parades and masked balls. Special events are staged at the Viktualienmarkt. The celebration culminates on Fasching Sunday and Shrove Tuesday. January 7 to Shrove Tuesday, usually 4 to 6 weeks later depending on the Lenten season. For specifics, contact the Munich Tourist Bureau.

February

• **Munich Fashion Week.** The latest and often most elegant parades of fashion are staged throughout the week at various venues strewn across the city. February 12 to 14.

March

• **Starkbierzeit.** The "strong beer season" provides serious beer drinkers with a fresh crop to tide them over until Oktoberfest. Just one pint of one of the dense brews churned out specifically for the season (beginning the third Friday of Lent and lasting 2 weeks) ought to satiate most buzz seekers. A Lenten loophole from the days of strict fasting, the -ator suffix denotes the brews (e.g., Salvator).

April/May

✪ **Auer Dult.** An old Munich tradition, Auer Dult is a colorful 8-day flea market fair that occurs three times a year. Prize antiques and vintage junk await the keenest eyes and most disciplined bargain hunters. Merchants set up shop on the Mariahilfplatz on the last Saturday in April (Maidult), the end of July (Jakobidult), and the end of October (Herbst Dult).

Corpus Christi street processions are seen all around the region on the Thursday following the eighth Sunday after Easter; the exact date changes annually.

June

• **Munich Film Festival.** This festival isn't as popular as the February International Film Festival in Berlin, but it draws a serious audience. Late June.

• **Tollwood.** This summer music festival, originated by environmentalists, honors the free spirit of jazz, blues, and rock from June 21 to July 9 in Olympiapark. Ask at the Tourist Information Bureau.

July

• **Auer Dult** (see April).

✪ **Opera Festival and Munich Summer of Music.** The Munich Philharmonic Orchestra's Summer of Music and the Bavarian State Opera Festival highlight the work of Munich's prodigal son, Wagner, and other masters including Mozart, Orff, Mahler, and Strauss. Contact the Munich Tourist Board for details.

• **Tollwood** (see June).

September

✪ **Oktoberfest.** Germany's most famous beer festival takes place mostly in September, despite the name. Hotels are packed, and the beer and revelry flow on the Theresienwiese, where gigantic tents that can hold as many as 6,000 beer drinkers are sponsored by local breweries. It lasts from the middle of September to the first Sunday in October.

October

• **Auer Dult** (see April).
• **Oktoberfest** (see September).

November

• **Christkindlmarkt.** Every evening at 5:30pm, classic Christmas music bellows throughout the Christmas market on seasonally lit Marienplatz. You may even catch a glimpse of the *real* St. Nick. Traditionally runs from the end of November to Christmas Eve.

December

• **Christkindlmarkt** (see November).

4 Health & Insurance

HEALTH   German medical facilities are among the best in the world. If a medical emergency arises, your hotel staff can usually put you in touch with a reliable doctor. If not, contact the American embassy or a consulate, as each one maintains a list of English-speaking doctors.

Before you leave home, you can obtain a list of English-speaking doctors from the **International Association of Medical Assistance to Travelers** (IAMAT), in the United States at 417 Center St., Lewiston, NY 14092 (☎ **716/754-4883**); in Canada, at 40 Regal Rd., Guelph, ON N1K 1B5 (☎ **519/836-0102**).

It's a good idea to take with you whatever medication or drugs you'll need to avoid the time and trouble of getting a prescription filled; German, not American or British, pharmaceutical brands prevail. For some chronic conditions, a Medic Alert Identification Tag will tell a doctor about your condition and provide the telephone number of Medic Alert's 24-hour hotline so your medical records can be obtained. For a lifetime membership, the cost is a well-spent $35 for a stainless-steel bracelet. In addition, there is a $15 annual fee. Contact the **Medic Alert Foundation,** 2323 Colorado, Turlock, CA 95382 (☎ **800/825-3785**).

INSURANCE   Credit- and charge-card companies often insure users in case of a travel accident, provided the travel was paid for with their card. Many homeowners' insurance policies cover luggage theft and loss of documents. Coverage is usually limited to about $500. To submit a claim, remember that you'll need police reports or a statement from a local medical authority.

Some insurance policies provide advances in cash or arrange funds transfers so you won't have to dip into your travel money to settle medical bills. Seniors should be aware that Medicare does not cover the cost of illness in Europe.

You may want insurance against trip cancellation. Some travel agencies provide coverage. Often such insurance is written into tickets paid for by credit card. Insurance agents can also provide coverage.

Access America, 6600 W. Broad St., Richmond, VA 23230 (☎ **800/284-8300**), offers travel insurance and 24-hour emergency travel, medical, and legal assistance for the traveler. One call to their hotline center (staffed by multilingual coordinators), connects you to a worldwide network of professionals able to offer specialized help in reaching the nearest physician, hospital, or legal advisor, and in obtaining emergency cash or the replacement of lost travel documents. Varying coverage levels are available.

Travelex Insurance Services, P.O. Box 9408, Garden City, NY 11530, offers tour insurance packages priced at $67 per person for a tour valued at $1,000. Included are travel-assistance services and financial protection against trip cancellation, trip interruption, bankruptcy, flight and baggage delays, accident and sickness, medical evacuation, accidental death and dismemberment, and missed connections and delays, all with the ability to waive preexisting condition limitations. Applications can be made over the phone by credit card (☎ **800/228-9792**).

Travel Guard International, 1145 Clark St., Stevens Point, WI 54481 (☎ **800/ 826-1300** outside Wisconsin, 715/345-0505 in Wisconsin), offers a comprehensive 7-day policy that covers lost luggage, emergency assistance, accidental death, trip cancellation, and medical coverage abroad. The cost of the package is $62, but there are restrictions that you should understand before you accept the coverage.

In **Britain** most big travel agents offer their own insurance and will try to sell you their package when you book a holiday. Think before you sign. Britain's Consumers' Association recommends that you insist on seeing the policy and reading the fine print before buying travel insurance.

You should also shop around for better deals. You might contact **Columbus Travel Insurance Ltd.** (☎ **0171/375-0011** in London), or, for students, **Campus Travel** (☎ **0171/730-3402** in London). Columbus Travel will sell travel insurance only to people who have been official residents of Britain for at least a year.

TRAVEL ASSISTANCE   Several companies offer policies to cover travelers stranded abroad in some emergency; each maintains a toll-free 800 number for out-of-state callers.

Healthcare Abroad (MEDEX), % Wallach & Co., 107 W. Federal St. (P.O. Box 480), Middleburg, VA 22117-0480 (☎ **800/237-6615** or 540/687-3166), offers coverage for between 10 and 120 days at $3 per day; this policy includes accident and sickness coverage to the tune of $100,000. Medical evacuation is included, along with a $25,000 accidental death and dismemberment compensation.

5 Tips for Travelers with Special Needs

FOR TRAVELERS WITH DISABILITIES   Many agencies provide advance data to help you plan your trip. For instance, **Travel Information Service,** Industrial Rehab Program, 1200 W. Tabor Rd., Philadelphia, PA 19141 (☎ **215/ 456-9603** or 215/456-9602 for TTY), offers caller information.

You can obtain a free copy of *Air Transportation of Handicapped Persons,* published by the U.S. Department of Transportation. Write for Free Advisory Circular No. AC12032, Distribution Unit, U.S. Department of Transportation, Publications Division, M-4332, Washington, DC 20590.

For names and addresses of operators of tours specifically for visitors with disabilities, and other relevant information, contact the **Society for the Advancement of Travel for the Handicapped** (SATH), 347 Fifth Ave., Suite 610, New York, NY 10016 (☎ **212/447-7284;** fax 212/725-8253). Yearly membership dues in the society are $45, $30 for senior citizens and students.

For the blind or visually impaired, the best source is the **American Foundation for the Blind,** 11 Penn Plaza, Suite 300, New York, NY 10001 (☎ **212/502-7600,** or 800/232-5463 for ordering of information kits and supplies). It offers information on travel and various requirements for the transport and border formalities for seeing-eye dogs.

One of the best organizations serving the needs of persons with disabilities (wheelchairs and walkers) is **Flying Wheels Travel,** 143 West Bridge St., P.O. Box 382, Owatoona, MN 55060 (☎ **800/535-6790** or 507/451-5005), offering various escorted tours and cruises internationally.

For a $20 annual fee, consider joining **Mobility International USA,** P.O. Box 10767, Eugene, OR 97440 (☎ **503/343-1284;** fax 541/343-6182). It answers questions on various destinations and also offers discounts on videos, publications, and programs it sponsors.

British travelers with disabilities can contact **RADAR** (Royal Association for Disability and Rehabilitation), Unit 12, City Forum, 250 City Rd., London EC1V 8AF (☎ **0171/250-3222**), for useful annual holiday guides. *Holidays and Travel Abroad* costs £5, *Holidays in the British Isles* goes for £7, and *Long Haul Holidays and Travel* is £5. RADAR also provides holiday information packets on such subjects as sports and outdoor holidays, insurance, and financial arrangements for people with disabilities. Each of these fact sheets is available for £2. All publications can be mailed outside the United Kingdom for a nominal fee.

Another good British service is the **Holiday Care Service,** 2nd Floor Imperial Buildings, Victoria Road, Horley, Surrey RH6 7PZ (☎ **01293/774535;** fax 01293/784647), which advises on accessible accommodations. Annual membership costs £15 (U.K. residents) and £30 (abroad) and includes a newsletter and access to a free reservations network for hotels throughout Britain and—to a lesser degree—Europe and the rest of the world.

FOR GAY & LESBIAN TRAVELERS   Gay nightlife in Munich is busy and friendly. Homosexuality in Germany is generally widely accepted, especially among young people. However, in Catholic Bavaria's rural countryside, attitudes can be intolerant. The legal minimum age for consensual sex is 18. For information about the gay and lesbian scene in Bavaria, contact **SUB Info. Laden** in Munich at Mullerstrasse 43 (☎ **089/260-3056**).

Spartacus, the international gay guide for men can be ordered ($32.95), as can *Odysseus 1999, The International Gay Travel Planner,* a guide to international gay accommodations ($27). *Spartacus* is also widely available in Germany. A leading publication for gay men is the glossy German magazine *Männer,* available at street kiosks and often in gay clubs.

Before you go, both lesbians and gay men might want to pick up a copy of *Gay Travel A to Z* ($16), which specializes in general information, as well as listings of bars, hotels, restaurants, and places of interest for gay travelers throughout the world. Books and publications are available from **Giovanni's Room,** 1145 Pine St., Philadelphia, PA 19107 (☎ **215/923-2960;** fax 215/923-0813).

Our World, 1104 North Nova Rd., Suite 251, Daytona Beach, FL 32117 (☎ **904/441-5367**), is a magazine devoted to options and bargains for gay and lesbian travel worldwide. It costs $35 for 10 issues. *Out and About,* 8 West 19th St., Suite 401, New York, NY 10011 (☎ **800/929-2268**), has been hailed for its "straight" reporting about gay travel. It profiles the best gay or gay-friendly hotels, gyms, clubs, and other places, with coverage of destinations throughout the world. Its cost is $49 a year for 10 information-packed issues. It aims for the more upscale gay male traveler and has been praised by everybody from *Travel & Leisure* to the *New York Times.*

The **International Gay Travel Association (IGTA),** 4331 N. Federal, Suite 304, Ft. Lauderdale, FL 33308 (☎ **800/448-8550** for voice mailbox, or 954/ 776-2626), encourages gay and lesbian travel worldwide. With around 1,200 member agencies, it specializes in networking travelers with the appropriate gay-friendly service organization or tour specialist. It offers quarterly newsletters, marketing mailings, and a membership directory that is updated four times a year. Travel agents who are IGTA members will be tied into this organization's vast information resources.

FOR SENIORS   Many discounts are available for seniors, but be advised that you have to be a member of an association to obtain some of them.

Write for a free booklet called *101 Tips for the Mature Traveler,* available from Grand Circle Travel, 347 Congress St., Boston, MA 02210 (☎ **800/221-2610** or 617/350-7500). This tour operator offers extended vacations, escorted programs, and cruises that feature unique learning experiences for seniors at competitive prices.

Saga International Holidays is well known for its affordable all-inclusive tours for seniors, preferably those 50 years old or older. Both medical and trip cancellation insurance are included in the net price of any of their tours except for cruises. Contact SAGA International Holidays, 222 Berkeley St., Boston, MA 02116 (☎ **800/343-0273**).

AARP (American Association of Retired Persons) is the best organization in the United States for seniors. It offers discounts on car rentals and hotels. For more information, contact AARP at 601 E St. NW, Washington, DC 20049 (☎ **202/434-AARP**).

Information is also available from the **National Council of Senior Citizens,** 8403 Colesville Rd., Suite 1200, Silver Spring, MD 20910 (☎ **301/578-8800**). A nonprofit organization, the council charges $13 per person or couple, for which you receive 11 issues annually of a newsletter that is devoted partly to travel tips. Benefits of membership include discounts on hotels, motels, and auto rentals, as well as prescription drug service, long-term-care options, and insurance programs for members.

Mature Outlook, P.O. Box 9390, Des Moines, IA 50306 (☎ **800/336-6330** or 847/286-5024), is a membership program for people 50 years old and up. Members are offered discounts at ITC-member hotels and will receive a bimonthly magazine. The annual membership fee of $14.95 to $19.95 entitles members to free coupons for discounts at Sears & Roebuck Co. Savings are also offered on selected auto rentals and restaurants.

British travelers can contact **Wasteels,** Victoria Station, opposite Platform 2, London SW1V 1JY (☎ **0171/834-6744**), for a Rail Europe Senior pass, sold to British residents 60 years of age and older for £5. The pass entitles seniors to discounted rail tickets on many of the rail lines of Europe. To qualify, British residents must present a valid British Senior Citizen rail card, available for £16 at any BritRail office if proof of age and British residency is presented. Wasteel's main office is just around the corner from Victoria Station, at 120 Wilton Rd., London SW1 V1J (☎ **0171/834-6744**).

FOR SINGLES   Even though millions of adult Americans are single, the travel industry is far better geared for double occupancy of hotel rooms. One company, **Travel Companion Exchange,** has been successful in matching single travelers with like-minded companions. Jens Jurgen, the German-born founder, charges about $99 for a 6-month listing. New applicants fill out a form stating their preferences and needs; then they receive a list of potential partners and travel companions. The same or opposite sex can be requested. A bimonthly newsletter gives numerous money-saving tips of particular interest to solo travelers. A sample copy is available for $5. For an application and more information, contact Jens Jurgen, Travel Companion Exchange, P.O. Box P-833, Amityville, NY 11701 (☎ 516/454-0880).

Since single supplements on tours carry a hefty price tag, some tour companies will arrange for you to share a room with another single traveler of the same gender. One such company that offers a "guaranteed-share plan" is **Globus/Cosmos,** featuring budget touring worldwide offices at 5304 South Federal Circle, Littleton, CO 80123 (☎ 800/851-0728).

FOR FAMILIES Arrange ahead of time for such necessities as a crib and a bottle warmer, and if you're driving, a car seat. Remember that in Germany small children aren't allowed to ride in the front seat. Sitters can be arranged for you at most hotels—finding a sitter with a knowledge of English should not be a problem in Munich.

Special children's menus on airlines must be requested at least 24 hours in advance. If baby food is required, however, bring your own and ask a flight attendant to warm it to the right temperature.

Publications that may help are *Family Travel Times,* published quarterly by **Travel with Your Children** (TWYCH), that includes a weekly call-in service for subscribers. Subscriptions cost $40 a year and can be ordered by writing to TWYCH, 40 Fifth Ave., New York, NY 10011 (☎ 212/477-5524; fax 212/477-5173). The **Family Travel Forum,** 891 Amsterdam Ave., New York NY 10025 (☎ 212/655-6124; www.familytravelforum.com) offers information and travel discounts. Membership costs $48 a year.

FOR STUDENTS Students can secure a number of travel discounts. The most wide-ranging service for students is **Council Travel,** a subsidiary of the **Council on International Educational Exchange (CIEE),** 205 E. 42nd St., New York, NY 10017 (☎ 212/822-2700), which provides details about budget travel, study abroad, working permits, and insurance. It also publishes a number of helpful publications and issues International Student Identity Cards (ISIC) for $19 to bonafide students. Its free copy of *Student Travels* magazine provides information on all of Council Travel's services and CIEE's programs and publications.

The **IYHF (International Youth Hostel Federation)** was designed to provide bare-bones accommodations for serious budget travelers. Regular membership costs $25 annually, only $10 for those under 18 and $15 for those 55 and up. For information, contact Hostelling Information/American Youth Hostels (HI-AYH), 733 15th St. NW, Suite 840, Washington, DC 20005 (☎ 202/783-6161).

Britain's leading specialist in student and youth travel is **Campus Travel,** 52 Grosvenor Gardens, London SW1W 0AG (☎ 0171/730-3402), opposite Victoria Station and open daily. It provides a comprehensive travel service specializing in low-cost rail-, sea-, and airfares, holiday breaks, and travel insurance, plus student discount cards. It issues the International Student Identity Card (ISIC), which sells for £5 and is well worth the cost. Always show your ISIC when booking a trip—you may not get a discount without it.

To stay in youth hostels, you'll need an **International Youth Hostels Association** card, which you can purchase from either of London's youth hostel retail outlets: near Covent Garden at 14 Southampton St., London WC2E 7HY (☎ 0171/836-8541), or 52 Grosvenor Gardens, London SW1W 0AG (☎ 0171/823-4739), in the same building as Campus Travel. To apply for a membership card, take both your passport and some passport-size photo of yourself, plus a membership fee of £9. More information on membership is available from **Youth Hostels Association of England and Wales (YHA),** 8 St. Stephen's Hill, St. Albans, Hertfordshire AL1 2DY (☎ **01727/855215**). The Youth Hostel Association puts together a *YHA Budget Accommodations Guide* (Volumes 1 and 2, £7 each), which lists the addresses, phone numbers, and admissions policies for every youth hostel in the world. The guides can be purchased at the retail outlets listed above or ordered by mail (add 61p for postage to any point within the U.K.). Many youth hostels fill up in the summer, so it's best to book ahead.

6 Getting There

BY PLANE

Most airlines price fares seasonally. During peak season, the summer months, flights to Munich are most expensive. Excluding the Christmas holidays, winter months offer the lowest fares. This fits in fine with those who wish to go skiing in the Bavarian Alps. Shoulder season is in between. Most airlines also offer an assortment of fares from first class, the most expensive, through business class to economy class, the lowest "no frills" regular airfare. Promotional fares are often offered but usually with stringent requirements; the most common such fare is the APEX (advance purchase excursion).

For more about airfares, see "Finding the Best Airfare," below.

THE MAJOR AIRLINES

On most airlines flying to Germany, connections to Munich must be made through Frankfurt, Düsseldorf, or another gateway city. Delta is the only airline that offers direct nonstop flights to Munich.

Lufthansa (☎ **800/645-3880;** www.lufthansa-usa.com), the German national carrier, operates the most frequent service. Convenient connections with flights to Munich can be made through a number of European gateway cities. From North America, Lufthansa serves 14 gateway cities. The largest of these is the New York City area, where flights depart from both JFK and Newark International airports. From JFK daily flights depart nonstop for Frankfurt and Düsseldorf, where easy connections can be made to Munich. From Newark, Lufthansa has daily flights to Frankfurt. Lufthansa's other North American gateways include Atlanta, Boston, Chicago, Dallas/Fort Worth, Houston, Los Angeles, Miami, San Francisco, and Washington, D.C. From Canada and Mexico, Lufthansa flies to Germany from Toronto, Vancouver, Calgary, and Mexico City.

Lufthansa recently entered into the "Star Alliance" with United Airlines, Air Canada, the Scandinavian Airlines System (SAS), Thai Airways International, and Varig. This arrangement allows cross-airline benefits that include travel on one or all the participating airlines on one ticket. Frequent-flyer credit goes to the participating airline of your choice.

American Airlines (☎ **800/443-7300;** www.americanair.com) flies nonstop to Frankfurt every day from Chicago, Miami, and Dallas/Fort Worth, and several times a week from Chicago to Düsseldorf. From Frankfurt and Düsseldorf, American's flights connect easily with ongoing flights to Munich on Lufthansa or British Airways.

Continental Airlines (☎ **800/231-0856;** www.flycontinental.com) offers daily nonstop service between Newark and Frankfurt. Continental maintains excellent connections between Newark and its hubs in Cleveland and Houston. Continental also offers discounts and other benefits to seniors 62 and over and to their traveling companions, regardless of age.

Delta Air Lines (☎ **800/241-4141;** www.delta-air.com) offers daily nonstop service to Munich from JFK airport in New York and from its home base in Atlanta. Delta also offers frequent nonstops to Frankfurt from Cincinnati, Dallas, Los Angeles, and Washington, D.C.

United Airlines (☎ **800/538-2929;** www.ual.com) has steadily increased its European market share and is a participant in the Star Alliance program with Air Canada and Lufthansa. United offers daily nonstops from Washington, D.C., and Chicago to Frankfurt. As part of the alliance, United honors all German flights by Lufthansa or Air Canada as a part of a United ticket. If you're interested in taking advantage of the Star Alliance, be sure to notify the United ticket agent when booking.

KLM (☎ **800/374-7747;** www.klm.nl) has frequent nonstop flights to Amsterdam from New York's JFK, Boston, Washington, D.C.'s Dulles, and Atlanta. From Amsterdam, many flights on both KLM and Lufthansa fly into Munich.

British Airways (☎ **800/AIRWAYS;** www.british-airways.com) offers daily nonstop flights between Munich and London.

FINDING THE BEST AIRFARE
APEX & Other Promotional Fares

The best strategy for securing an economical airfare is shopping around. Keep calling the airlines and checking out their Web sites. Sometimes a cheaper ticket becomes available at the very last minute because the flight is not fully booked, so the airline discounts tickets to achieve full capacity.

Airlines compete in offering the most economical fares encumbered with the least number of restrictions. In general, the early bird almost always gets the lower fare, since price structures are specifically geared to reward travelers who reserve tickets in advance.

There are also special discounts and promotions that airlines frequently offer. You can be sure that any promotional fare announced by an airline without advance notice will probably be quickly matched by its competitors. You can save a bundle on these fares, but they often carry stringent restrictions. Fares are nonrefundable, and payment in full is required within 24 hours of booking. You will probably be asked to fly midweek; there may be time limits on return flights, and less flexibility with return flight dates. Flights on Saturday or Sunday often carry a surcharge of $25 in each direction. Watch the newspapers, consult your travel agent, and remain as flexible as possible about travel dates so you can profit from last-minute price changes.

The lowest airline APEX fares are available roughly from November 1 to late March, with a slight increase over Christmas. Fares go up in shoulder season, the period during April, May, and mid-September to November 1. Midsummer (June through mid-September) is the period when APEX tickets are most expensive.

Lufthansa, the German national airline divides the price structure of most of its transatlantic fares into three separate categories. They include, from the least to the most expensive, nonrefundable APEX fares, instant purchase excursion fares, and full-fledged excursion fares.

The nonrefundable APEX fare requires the purchase of a ticket 21 days or more before departure, with payment and ticketing completed within 72 hours of finalizing the reservation. A stay of between 7 and 21 days is required. Lufthansa's recent nonrefundable APEX fares from New York to Munich ranged from 708 to 1,190

DM ($403.55 to $678.30) round-trip on a weekday (Monday to Thursday) in summer; from 363 to 880 DM ($206.90 to $591.60) for the same flight in winter. Flights on weekends (Friday to Sunday) cost around $60 more, round-trip. Connections to Munich will add an additional fare. Lufthansa sometimes offers promotional fares lower than the best APEX fare, and like most airlines, offers seniors over 62 a 10% discount (the reduction applies to a traveling companion as well). Flying midweek, Delta offers a round-trip APEX fare of $780 in summer and $505 in winter.

From the United Kingdom an APEX ticket to Frankfurt or Munich offers a discount without the usual booking restrictions. You might also ask the airlines about a "Eurobudget ticket," which includes restrictions such as length-of-stay requirements. For promotions and other discount fares, check the newspapers. London's *Evening Standard* maintains a daily travel section, and the Sunday editions of virtually any newspaper in Britain run many ads touting slashed fares. Make sure you understand the bottom line on any special deal you purchase; ask if all surcharges, including airport taxes and other hidden costs are included, and make sure you understand what the penalties are if you're forced to cancel at the last minute. **CEEFAX,** a British television information service included on many home and hotel TVs, runs details on package holidays and flights to Europe and beyond.

Business Class & First Class

Business class features larger seats, upgraded food and service, and more room to spread out papers, calculators, or laptops. Since business travel is not seasonal, prices remain the same year-round. Lufthansa charges $2,554 each way for business class from New York to Munich but imposes absolutely no restrictions concerning length of stay, advance reservation, or prepayment.

First class offers extra comfort and service. The first-class Lufthansa fare from New York to Munich is $3,613 each way, and the amenities can be pleasant and refreshing. At Lufthansa (☎ **800/645-3880**), first- and business-class compartments feature seats with individual TV sets, offering a choice of in-house movies and entertainment in either German or English.

The competition for first- and business-class passengers is fierce through the industry. Delta's (☎ **800/221-1212**) first-class fare between Atlanta and Munich is $3,821 each way; its business fare for the same route is about $2,808 each way.

Excursion or Regular Fares

These are, of course, the most expensive of all, to be used only in cases of sudden emergency. Fares are valid all year, have no minimum stay requirements and a maximum stay of 1 year. No advance purchase is required, and one free stopover is allowed, along with one additional stopover at a charge of $50. Luftansa's round-trip economy fare is $1,806 between New York and Munich.

Some Good-Value Choices

BUCKET SHOPS (CONSOLIDATORS)   The name *bucket shop* originated in the 1960s in Great Britain, where mainstream airlines gave the then-pejorative name to resellers of blocks of unsold tickets consigned to them by major transatlantic carriers. The label stuck, but it might be more polite to use the term "consolidators." They exist in many shapes and forms. In its purest sense, a bucket shop acts as a clearinghouse for blocks of tickets that airlines discount and consign during normally slow periods of travel.

Charter operators (see below) and bucket shops once performed separate functions, but their offerings in many cases have blurred; many outfits perform both functions.

Tickets are sometimes, but not always, priced at up to 35% less than full fare. Terms of payment can vary—anywhere from 45 days prior to departure to last-minute sales in an airline's final attempt to fill up a craft. Tickets can be purchased through regular travel agents, who usually mark up the ticket 8% to 10%, maybe more, thereby greatly reducing your discount. Users of consolidator tickets have voiced only one major complaint: Such a ticket doesn't give you a seat assignment in advance, so you are likely to get a "poor seat" on the plane at the last minute.

Savings have been estimated to be around $200 per ticket off the regular price, and nearly a third of passengers report savings of up to $300, but here's the hitch—many people who book consolidator tickets report no savings at all, since the airline will sometimes match the consolidator price by announcing a promotional fare. The situation is a bit tricky and calls for some careful investigation on your part to determine just how much you're saving, if anything.

800-FLY-4-LESS is a nationwide airline reservation and ticketing service that specializes in finding the lowest fares. For information on available consolidator airline tickets for last-minute travel, call ☎ **800/359-4537.** When fares are high and advance planning time is low, such a service is invaluable.

One of the biggest U.S. consolidators is **Travac,** 989 Sixth Ave., 16th Floor, New York, NY 10018 (☎ **800/TRAV-800** or 212/563-3303 in New York; www.travac.com), which offers discounted seats to most cities in Europe on airlines that include United and Delta. Another Travac office is at 2601 E. Jefferson St., Orlando, FL 32803 (☎ **407/896-0014**).

In New York, try **TFI Tours International,** 34 W. 32nd St., 12th Floor, New York, NY 10001 (☎ **800/745-8000** or 212/736-1140 in New York). This tour company offers services to 177 cities worldwide.

In the Midwest, explore the possibilities of **Travel Avenue,** 10 S. Riverside Plaza, Suite 1404, Chicago, IL 60606 (☎ **800/333-3335;** www.tipc.com), a national agency whose headquarters are here. Its tickets are often cheaper than most, and it charges the customer only a $25 fee on international tickets, rather than taking the usual $10 commission from an airline. Travel Avenue rebates most of that back to customers.

UniTravel, 1177 N. Warson Rd., St. Louis, MO 63132 (☎ **800/325-2222;** fax 314/569-2503; www.unitravel.com), is most useful to travelers who need to get to Munich on short notice. Its ticket prices may or may not be less than what you would be charged if you phoned the airlines directly.

One final option for those with flexible travel plans is available through **Airhitch,** 2641 Broadway, 3rd Floor, New York, NY 10025 (☎ **800/326-2009** or 212/864-2000; www.airhitch.org). Inform Airhitch of any five consecutive days in which you're available to fly to Europe. Airhitch agrees to fly its passengers within those five days from the Northeast, Southeast, Midwest, West Coast, or Northwest. An attempt will be made to fly the passenger to and from the European city of choice, but no guarantees are made, and you could find yourself in a city other than Munich.

In London there are many bucket shops around Victoria and Earl's Court that offer cheap fares. Make sure that the company you deal with is a member of the IATA, ABTA, or ATOL. These umbrella organizations will help you out if anything goes wrong.

One well-recommended company is **Trailfinders** (☎ **0171/937-5400** in London). It offers access to tickets on such carriers as SAS, British Airways, and KLM to Europe and beyond.

STANDBY FARES   Another cheap alternative is **Air-Tech Ltd.,** 588 Broadway, Suite 1007, New York, NY 10012 (☎ **212/219-7000**; www.airtech.com); it is a "space-available" travel service, offering standby fares. All travelers need do is register with Air-Tech, specify preferred destination, give a two- to five-day travel window, and call Air-Tech the Wednesday before their travel window begins. Travelers are then informed of what flights and seating are available. Passengers unable to book a flight within their chosen travel window are given the option to reschedule or receive a full refund.

CHARTER FLIGHTS   A charter is an aircraft reserved months in advance for one-time-only transit to some predetermined point. Before paying for a charter, check the restrictions on your ticket or contract. You may be asked to purchase a tour package and pay far in advance. You'll pay a stiff penalty (or forfeit the ticket entirely) if you cancel. In some cases, the charter-ticket seller will offer an insurance policy for cancellation for good cause (like hospital confinement or death in the family).

Not all charter companies have proved reliable in the past. Charters are sometimes canceled when the plane doesn't fill. One recommended operator is **Council Charter,** run by the Council on International Educational Exchange, 205 E. 42nd St., New York, NY 10017 (☎ **800/2-COUNCIL** or 212/882-2900), which arranges charter seats on regularly scheduled aircraft.

REBATORS   Rebators are firms that pass along part of their commission to the passenger, although many charge a fee for their services. They are not the same as travel agents but can sometimes offer similar services. Most rebators offer discounts averaging 10% to 25%, plus a $25 handling charge.

In the Midwest, **Travel Avenue,** 10 S. Riverside Plaza, Suite 1404, Chicago, IL 60606 (☎ **800/333-3335** or 312/876-6866), is one of the oldest agencies of its kind. They offer up-front cash rebates on every airfare over $300. They pride themselves on *not* offering travel counseling and cater to independent travelers who have already worked out their travel plans. Also available are tour and cruise fares, plus hotel reservations, usually at prices less expensive than if you reserve them on your own.

Another major rebator is **The Smart Traveller,** 3111 S.W. 27th Ave. (P.O. Box 330010), Miami, FL 33133 (☎ **800/448-3338** or 305/448-3338). The agency also offers discounts on package tours, which include hotels, car rentals, and Danube cruises, for which easy connections can be made from Munich.

TRAVELING AS A COURIER   Couriers are hired by overnight air-freight firms hoping to skirt Customs hassles and delays on the other end. Don't worry—the courier service is absolutely legal and can lead to a greatly discounted airfare; sometimes you even fly free. You're allowed one piece of carry-on luggage only (your baggage allowance is used by the courier firm to transport its cargo).

You don't actually handle the merchandise you're "transporting" to Europe; you just carry a manifest to present to Customs. Upon your arrival, an employee of the courier service will reclaim the cargo. Incidentally, you fly alone, so don't plan to travel with anybody. Most couriers operate from Los Angeles or New York; a few out of Chicago or Miami. Courier services are often listed in the *Yellow Pages,* or advertise in travel sections of newspapers.

You might contact **Halbart Express,** 147-05 176th St., Jamaica, NY 11434 (☎ **718/656-8189,** 10am to 3pm daily), or **Now Voyager,** 74 Varick St., Suite 307, New York, NY 10013 (☎ **212/431-1616,** 10am to 5pm daily).

The **International Association of Air Travel Couriers,** P.O. Box 1349, Lake Worth, FL 33460 (☎ **561/582-8320**), publishes *Shoestring Traveler,* a newsletter, and *Air Courier Bulletin,* a directory of courier bargains around the world. The annual membership fee of $45 also includes access to a 24-hour fax-on-demand system and computer bulletin board; both are updated daily with last-minute flights and bulletins.

TRAVEL CLUBS   Another source of low-cost air fares for the traveler with a flexible schedule is the travel club, which sells an inventory of unsold tickets at discounts in the range of 20% to 60%.

After you pay an annual fee, you're given a "hotline" number to call to find out what discounts are available. Many of these become available several days in advance of actual departure, sometimes as long as a week or even a month before the departure date.

Moment's Notice, 7301 New Utrecht Ave., New York, NY 11228 (☎ **718/234-6295;** www.moments-notice.com), charges $25 per year for membership, which allows spur-of-the-moment participation in dozens of tours geared for last-minute getaways. Each offers air and land packages that often represent substantial savings over what you'd have paid through more conventional channels. Although membership is required for participation in the tours, anyone can call the company's hotline (☎ **212/750-9111**) to learn what options are available. Most tours depart from New Jersey's Newark airport.

Travelers Advantage, 3033 South Parker Rd., Suite 900, Aurora, CO 80014 (☎ **800/433-9383** in the U.S.), offers a $50 membership that includes a catalog (issued four times a year), maps, discounts at select hotels, and a limited guarantee that equivalent packages will not be undersold by any other travel organization. It also offers a 5% rebate on the value of all airline tickets, tours, hotels, and car rentals purchased through them (paperwork, including receipts and itineraries required).

FLYING WITH FILM, CAMCORDERS & LAPTOPS

X-ray inspection at airport security counters won't hurt most conventional film or videotapes (don't rely on lead-lined bags as insurance against X-ray exposure: Security staffs just up the intensity of the X-rays. While videotape is not usually damaged by X-rays, it *can* be damaged by the magnetic field of a walk-through metal detector.

In either case, you can ask for a hand check. This might involve taking a picture with your camera, or turning on your camcorder to prove that the machine isn't a disguise for something more sinister.

Passing a laptop computer through a security X-ray machine won't harm the laptop's hard disk, but to be safe, ask for a hand check anyway. You'll be asked to switch on your computer—the security force wants to see the DOS prompt and the memory check to prove that nothing is amiss. It's usually easier to operate your laptop from its battery source, so be sure in advance that the batteries are charged.

Most airlines allow use of laptops and cellphones except during takeoff and landings, when their magnetic fields can interfere with navigational equipment.

Make sure you understand what voltage your laptop requires. Some operate on either North American (110-volt) current or German (220-volt) current; others are much more fussy. Camcorders are usually powered by rechargeable batteries that can be replenished with a universal (worldwide) AC adapter, which can be plugged

Surfing the Web

Great deals on vacation packages and airfares can be found on the Internet. Travel agencies and services are increasingly using the Web as a medium to offer everything from complete tours to plane reservations to budget airline tickets on major carriers. To save you time and effort, we have found sites that may be useful to you in making your travel plans for Bavaria or elsewhere. And don't forget that airline sites are one of the best ways to check for day-to-day fares to get the very best deal on the flight of your choice.

www.travelcom.es allows you to search travel destinations to decide on that perfect vacation and offers link sites to travel agencies all over the world and in all 50 states.

www.previewtravel.com is probably the foremost of these sites, featured prominently on America Online. Preview Travel offers incredible vacation, airline, and hotel deals, updating its offerings every day. The most user-friendly of the travel sites, Preview Travel even lets you book your vacation on its site.

www.moments-notice.com promotes itself as a travel service, not an agency, providing a bargain-hunter's dream. Updated each morning, many of the deals are snapped up by the end of the day. A drawback is that many of these offerings require you to drop everything and go almost immediately. It's safe to say that planning is everything here.

www.180096hotel.com offers budget reservations at prestigious hotels all over the world, many accommodations up to 65% off. Booking can be done on-line, cutting out any travel agent.

www.discount-tickets.com lists discounts on airfares, accommodations, car rentals, and tours.

America Online at **www.aol.com** offers many travel sites that can be customized to a particular region of the world.

www/webmaster@munich-online.de is the city's homepage. For a site in English, try www.munich-tourist.de.

---

into either a 110- or 220-volt electrical outlet (you'll need the appropriate plug, usually included in the package when you buy the camcorder).

ARRIVING AT MUNICH'S AIRPORT

Franz Josef Strauss Airport lies 18 miles northeast of central Munich at Erdinger Moos. Facilities include parking garages; car-rental centers; restaurants, bars, and cafes; money-exchange kiosks; lockers; and luggage-storage facilities. For flight information, call the airline of your choice, or ☎ **089/9752-1313.**

S-Bahn (☎ **089/557575**) trains connect the airport with the Hauptbahnhof (main railroad station) in downtown Munich. Departures are every 30 minutes for the 40-minute trip. The fare is 13.60 DM ($7.75); Eurailpass holders ride free. A taxi into the center costs about 120 DM ($68.40). Airport buses, such as those operated by Lufthansa, also run between the airport and the center.

If you're going to rent a car, refer to "Getting Around" in chapter 3 for more information.

BY TRAIN

Munich has train connections with most major European capitals, and all major German cities are connected to Munich, most with a train arriving and departing almost every hour. Some 20 daily trains connect Munich to Frankfurt, and there are about 23 daily rail connections to Berlin.

From London, four daily trains leave from **Victoria Station,** going by way of the Ramsgate-Ostend ferry or jetfoil. Most trains change at Cologne for destinations elsewhere in Germany. By jetfoil, Cologne is just 9½ hours away; by the Dover-Ostend ferry, 12½ hours. Travel from London to Munich, depending on the connection, can mean a trip of 18 to 22 hours. Tickets can be purchased through British Rail travel centers in London (☎ **0990/484950** within the U.K., or 01603/764-176 for a location near you). For reservations on the Eurostar direct train service between London and Paris or Brussels via the Channel Tunnel, call ☎ **0345/303030,** 01-33-31-58-03 in Paris, and 800/677-8585 in the U.S.

From Paris, the **Orient Express** (☎ **01-45-82-50-50** in Paris, or 0171/928-6000 in the U.K.) leaves from Gare de l'Est at 5:49pm daily and arrives in Munich at 3:05am. If you're in Rome, you can take the **Michelangelo Express** daily at 8:15am. It arrives in Munich at 6:30pm. Other Munich-bound trains leave at 6:20pm and travel via Florence and Innsbruck, arriving in Munich at 8:30am. For train information in Rome, call ☎ **06/484972**.

The **Bavaria** (☎ **01/157-222** in Switzerland) leaves Zurich at 7:41am daily, reaching Munich at 11:51am.

London has an especially convenient outlet for buying railway tickets to virtually anywhere—it's opposite Platform 2 in **Victoria Station. Wasteels Ltd.** (☎ **0171/834-6744**) provides railway-related services and has information on fares and rail passes. Depending on circumstances, Wasteels sometimes charges a £5 fee for its services, but if you are planning to set up an itinerary, the money is well spent.

Many different rail passes are available in the United Kingdom for travel in continental Europe. Stop in at the **International Rail Centre,** Victoria Station, London SW1V 1JYY (☎ **0990/848848** inside the U.K., or 0171/834-2345). Some of the most popular passes, including Inter-Rail and Euro Youth, are offered only to travelers under 26 years of age, entitling them to unlimited second-class travel in 26 European countries.

Most trains arrive at Munich's main rail station, the **Hauptbahnhof,** on Bahnhofplatz, one of Europe's largest. Located near the city center and the trade fairgrounds, it contains a hotel, restaurants, shopping, car parking, and banking facilities. The rail station is connected with the U-Bahn, the city's subway service, and with the S-Bahn rapid-transit system that provides service to outlying city districts and suburbs. In addition, city and suburban buses fan out in all directions.

For information about long-distance trains, call ☎ **089/19419;** for S-Bahn trains, call ☎ **089/557575.**

BY BUS

Long-distance buses arrive and depart in the section of the main train station known as **Westwing-Starnberger Bahnhof.** Bus travel to Germany's major cities, including Munich, is available from London, Paris, and many other cities in Europe.

The continent's largest bus operator, **Eurolines,** operates out of Victoria Coach Station in central London, and in Paris at 28 avenue du Général-de-Gaulle, 93541 Bagnolet (a 35-minute subway ride from central Paris to Métro stop Gallieni). For information in Britain, call ☎ **0990/143219** or 0171/730-8235, or contact any National Express bus lines or travel agent. For information in France, call ☎ **01-49-72-51-51.** Buses on long-haul journeys are equipped with toilets and partially reclining seats. They stop for 60-minute breaks every 4 hours.

Buses from London to Munich depart three times a week and cost £61 ($97.60) one-way, or £94 ($150.40) round-trip. Discounts of about 20% are sometimes offered to qualifying passengers under age 26. From Paris to Munich, the cost is 460 F ($82.80) one-way or 610 F ($109.80) round-trip. Discounts are available to passengers who book their itineraries several weeks in advance, and discounts of around 20% are sometimes offered to those under age 26. For information about Eurolines in Germany, contact **Deutsche Touring** (Eurolines Stadtbüro), Am Römerhof 17, D-60326 Frankfurt am Main (☎ **069/79030**). Eurolines does not maintain a U.S.-based sales agent, although any European travel agent can arrange for tickets.

Deutsche Touring GmbH, Arnulf Strasse 3 (☎ **089/5458-7011**), covers many major cities and also runs buses to the Romantic Road. **Bayern Express Reisen,** Arnulf Strasse 16-18 (☎ **089/553074**), offers daily service to Berlin via Nürnberg. Excursions to such popular Bavarian destinations as Berchtesgaden, Schwangau-Neuschwanstein, Garmisch-Partenkirchen, and Chiemsee (see chapter 11) are offered by several local bus companies, including **Panorama Tours,** at a number of locations (call ☎ **089/591504** for more information).

BY CAR

If you're driving to Munich from England, you face a number of ferry choices. **P&O Ferries** (☎ **800/677-8585** for North American reservations or 01301/212-121 in the U.K.) have between 20 and 25 ferryboat crossings a day, depending on the season, between Dover and Calais. Crossings can take as little as 1 hour and 15 minutes, depending on the craft. **Sealink** (☎ **800/677-8585** in North America or 01233/615-455 in the U.K.) operates ferries from Harwich, in the east of England, to the Hook of Holland; the trip takes about 8 hours. Call ☎ **800/677-8585** or 212/575-2667 in the U.S. or Canada for information about other options. You can also travel with your car through the Chunnel on **Le Shuttle** (☎ **800/4-EURAIL** in the U.S. and Canada; 01304/288-617 or 0990/353-535 in England); the trip takes about 1 hour and you can purchase tickets at the entrance toll booth.

Germany's **Autobahn** system (express highway) links up with its neighbors. From Brussels take the E5 into Cologne; from Innsbruck (Austria), the E17, E86, and E11 lead directly to Munich. From Italy most motorists go from Bolzano in the north along the E6 to Innsbruck, where the road continues north to Munich.

It's slower going from France. From Paris you must take the Autoroute du Soleil to Switzerland and then the Swiss expressways to the German frontier. For Munich, you can continue east from Zurich, heading east for Innsbruck, where you can then make Autobahn connections to Munich.

PACKAGE TOURS

Travelers often find that package tours, land/air packages, or fly/drive packages are more economical than booking everything individually. And travelers planning their first European trip may prefer a tour package that sees to all their needs, from arrival at the airport to the departure back home. Below are some of the leading tour operators.

Lufthansa, the major German airline (☎ **800/645-3880** in the U.S. or 0181/750-3500 in London), offers many fly/drive and fly/rail tour packages to Germany.

American Express Vacations, P.O. Box 1525, Fort Lauderdale, FL 33302 (☎ **800/446-6234** in the U.S. and Canada), is the most instantly recognizable tour operator in the world. Its offerings in Europe are comprehensive, and if it doesn't offer what you want, it will arrange an individualized itinerary for you.

DER Tours, 9501 W. Devon Ave., Rosemont, IL 60018 (☎ **800/782-2424** or 847/692-4141), offers discounted airfares, car rentals, hotel packages, short regional tours, and German Rail, Eurail, and other rail passes.

Delta Air Lines (☎ **800/221-6666**) offers both fly/drive and fly/rail packages to Bavaria and the rest of Germany. For tourists with limited time, it features 3-day "city sprees" in metropolises like Munich.

Getting to Know Munich 3

Munich is a lively place all year—fairs and holidays seem to follow one on top of the other. But this is no "oompah" town. Here you'll find an elegant and tasteful city with sophisticated clubs and restaurants, the best theaters, and the finest concert halls.

One of Europe's most visited cities, Munich is full of monuments and fabulous museums. A place with memories of yesterday, both good and bad, it is very much a city living in its present. Today, with some 1.3 million inhabitants, 16% of which are foreigners, Munich is the third largest city in Germany. It is also the German's first choice as a place to live, according to various polls. It is a major economic center for north-south European trade and for high-tech microelectronics and other industries. It also has a huge publishing center and a burgeoning number of film studios.

A city of art and culture, it is Germany's largest university town. Munich is mainly a city for having fun and enjoying the relaxed lifestyle, the friendly ambience, and the wealth of activities, nightlife, sights, and cultural events.

1 Orientation

It's easy to explore the heart of Munich on foot, and the many attractions in the environs can be reached by Munich's excellent public transportation system.

VISITOR INFORMATION

Tourist information is available at the Franz Josef Strauss Airport in the central area (☎ **089/9759-2815**), as soon as you step off the plane. It's open Monday to Saturday from 8:30am to 10pm and on Sunday from 1 to 9pm. The main tourist office, **Fremdenverkehrsamt,** is at the Hauptbahnhof Bahnhofplatz 2 (☎ **089/233-0300**), at the south exit opening onto Bayerstrasse. It's open Monday to Saturday from 9am to 9pm and on Sunday from 11am to 7pm. You can pick up a free map of Munich and Fremdenverkehrsamt will also reserve rooms.

CITY LAYOUT

Munich's **Hauptbahnhof** lies just west of the town center and opens onto Bahnhofplatz. From the square (platz), the Schützenstrasse leads to a major focal point, **Karlsplatz** (nicknamed Stachus). Many

Munich Orientation

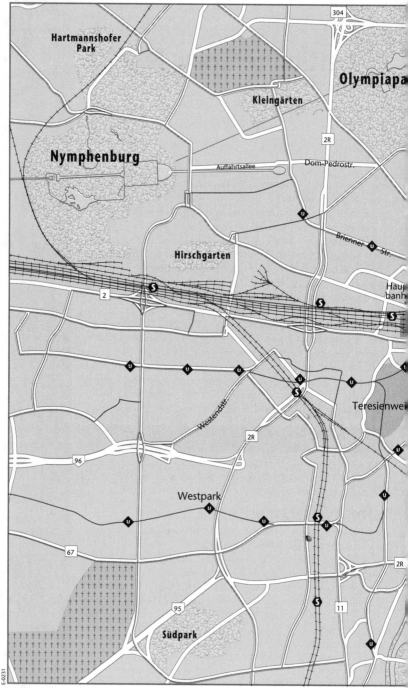

tram lines converge on this square. From Karlsplatz, you can continue east along the pedestrians-only Neuhauserstrasse and Kaufingerstrasse until you reach Marienplatz, where you'll be deep in the **Altstadt** (old town) of Munich.

From **Marienplatz** you can head north on Dienerstrasse, which will take you to Residenzstrasse and finally to **Max-Joseph-Platz,** a landmark square, where the Nationaltheater and the former royal palace, the Residenz, are located. Between Marienplatz and the Nationaltheater is the **Platzl** quarter, the place to head for nighttime fun. Some of Munich's finest (and some of its worst) restaurants are here, along with the Hofbräuhaus, the most famous beer hall in Europe.

North of the old town is **Schwabing,** once an artist/bohemian section whose main street is Leopoldstrasse. The large, sprawling municipal park grounds, the **Englischer Garten,** are due east of Schwabing. Northeast of Schwabing is the Olympic complex (more about that later).

MAIN ARTERIES & STREETS

The best known street in Munich is the **Maximilianstrasse,** the most fashionable shopping avenue, location of the prestigious Hotel Vier Jahreszeiten Kempinski München. It is one of the city's busiest east-west arteries. Other major east-west thoroughfares include **Kaufingerstrasse** and **Neuhauserstrasse.** Both are major shopping avenues in the core of the Altstadt's pedestrian zone. Two of Munich's great 19th-century avenues, **Ludwigstrasse** and **Brienner Strasse,** stretch toward the district of Schwabing. Ludwigstrasse was designed to display the greatness of the kingdom of Ludwig I and is bordered on both sides by impressive neoclassical and neo-Romanesque buildings.

Odeonsplatz, on the southern end of Ludwigstrasse, was established to celebrate the Bavarian kingdom. **Leopoldstrasse** begins on the northern side of Ludwigstrasse and continues through Schwabing. The last of the 19th-century boulevards to be constructed was **Prinzregentstrasse,** lying between Prinz-Carl-Palais and Vogelweide-platz. Along the Prinzregentstrasse at no. 7 is the residence of the prime minister of Bavaria.

FINDING AN ADDRESS/MAPS   Locating an address is relatively easy in Munich, as even numbers run up one side of a street and odd numbers down the other. In the Altstadt "hidden" squares may make it a little difficult; a detailed street map in addition to the more general maps handed out free by the tourist office is a help. The best maps are published by Falk, and they're available at nearly all bookstores and at many newsstands. These pocket-size maps are easy to carry and contain a detailed street index at the end.

NEIGHBORHOODS IN BRIEF

Altstadt   This is historic Munich, the site of the medieval city. Three gates remain to indicate the original town borders: the Sendlinger Tor and Odeonsplatz to the north and south, and the Isar Tor and Karlstor to the east and west. You can walk across the district in about 15 minutes.

The hub is Marienplatz, the town's primary square, with its Rathaus (town hall). In the Middle Ages, Marienplatz was the scene of many jousts and tournaments as well as public entertainments like executions. Today it is brimming with mimes, musicians, and street performers. The square is also the site of many festivals and political rallies and is the traditional stopping and starting place for parades and processions. Included in the Alstadt district is the Fussgänger (pedestrian) Zone, home to many of Munich's elegant shops.

Gasteig   This is the city's primary cultural, educational, and conference center. This modern building in the Haidhausen district houses the city library and the Munich Philharmonic Orchestra. Its various theaters and lecture halls play host to a variety of events, principally musical and theatrical performances.

Lehel   This district, just east of the Altstadt, is part of the original planned expansion of the city that occurred in the latter years of the 19th century. The area is mainly residential and is noted for its fine neo-Renaissance architecture.

Ludwigstrasse   One of Munich's great monumental avenues, it was originally designed for King Ludwig I as a street worthy of his kingdom. The buildings in the southern section of the street adhere to a strict neoclassical style, whereas the architecture in the northern sector is neo-Romanesque. The overall effect is that of uniformity.

Maximilianstrasse   The equivalent of New York's Fifth Avenue, Maximilianstrasse is Munich's Golden Mile. Planned as a showcase for the king's dominion, it has architecture in what is known as Maximilianic style, an eclectic combination of styles with an emphasis on Gothic. Here you find the city's most elegant and expensive boutiques, restaurants, and hotels. Visitors can browse through stores like Armani, Hermès, and Bulgari. Along with numerous chic hotels and restaurants, the street is also home to the Museum of Ethnology and the overpowering monument to the king, the Maxmonument. The street is the primary connector from the Altstadt to the suburbs of Lehel and Haidhausen.

Olympiapark   This residential and recreational area was the site of the 1972 Olympics, which is remembered for the terrorist attack against the Israeli athletes. Located northwest of the city center, this enormous development is practically a city unto itself. It has its own post office, railway station, elementary school, and even its own mayor. On weekends it hosts rock and pop concerts, and its many auditoriums and stadiums are now venues for performances and events of all kinds. The top level of the enormous television tower is the best place to view Munich and its vicinity.

Nymphenburg   Located just northwest of the city center, this district is home to the Nymphenburg Palace and Park, the original home of the Wittelsbach rulers. The baroque palace is home to the Nymphenburg porcelain museum and factory. Adjoining the palace is a vast expanse of lakes and gardens. The original 1664 plan for a small Italian garden has been greatly augmented over the years.

Schwabing   This area in the city's northern sector was once a center of bohemian life, much like New York's Greenwich Village, and like Greenwich Village, it has gentrified into a locale for lawyers, producers, and other professionals, as well as a hangout for university students. At the turn of the century, it was the place where the city's leading artists, actors, poets, musicians, and writers lived or gathered. Many famous literary figures have called Schwabing home, including Thomas Mann. Here you'll find the city's finest examples of art-nouveau architecture.

Arabellapark   The city's ultramodern commercial and industrial quarter, just northeast of the city center, is home to several large international companies. Its glass and concrete buildings have become an outstanding feature of Munich's skyline.

Bogenhausen   Located just northeast of the city center near Arabellapark, the area, like Schwabing, has many excellent examples of art-nouveau architecture.

Once the district where the prosperous had their homes, Bogenhausen is now home to numerous galleries, boutiques, and restaurants.

Brienner Strasse Designed as part of the development of the Maxvostadt during the reign of Maximilian I, this street was home to the aristocratic families and wealthy citizens of Munich. Today it is the location of many galleries and luxury shops.

Maxvorstadt Launched as a planned expansion of the city by Maximilian I, today the area draws its character from the many facilities of the University of Munich. The area is teeming with student bars, book shops, and galleries.

Westpark This 178-acre park, laid out for the fourth International Garden Show, is full of extensive lawns, playgrounds, and ponds. The park is complete with two beer gardens, several cafes, and a lakeside theater that hosts outdoor concerts during the summer months. Also located in the park is the Rudi Sedlmayer Sports Hall, one of Munich's premier venues for large rock concerts.

2 Getting Around

BY PUBLIC TRANSPORTATION

The city's rapid-transit system is preferable to streetcars and certainly to high-priced taxis. The underground network contains many convenient electronic devices, and the rides are relatively noise-free. The same ticket entitles you to ride the **U-Bahn** and the **S-Bahn,** as well as **trams** (streetcars) and **buses.** The U-Bahn, or Untergrundbahn, is the line you will use most frequently; the S-Bahn, or Stadtbahn, services suburban locations.

At the transport hub, Marienplatz, U-Bahn and S-Bahn rails crisscross each other. It's possible to use your Eurailpass on S-Bahn journeys, as it's a state-owned railway. Otherwise, you must purchase a single-trip ticket or a strip ticket for several journeys at one of the blue vending machines positioned at the entryways to the underground stations. These tickets entitle you to ride both the S and U lines, and they're also good for rides on trams and buses. If you're making only one trip, a **single ticket** will average 3.40 DM ($1.95), although it can reach as high as 16 DM ($9.10) to an outlying area.

Costing less per ride is the **strip ticket,** called *Streifenkarte* in German. It's good for several rides and sells for 15 DM ($8.55). A short ride requires only one strip. A **day ticket** for 8 DM ($4.55), called *Tageskarte,* is also a good investment if you plan to stay within the city limits. If you'd like to branch out to Greater Munich (that is, within a 50-mile radius), you can purchase a day card for 16 DM ($9.10). A trip within the metropolitan area costs you two strips, which are valid for 2 hours. In that time, you may interrupt your trip and transfer as you like, traveling in one continuous direction. When you reverse your direction, you must cancel two strips again. Children 4 to 14 use the red *Kinderstreifenkarte,* costing 8.50 DM ($4.85) for eight strips; for a trip within the metropolitan area, they cancel only one strip. Children above the age of 15 pay adult fares. For **public transport information,** dial ☎ **089/210330.**

Where the U-Bahn comes to an end, buses and trams take over; you can transfer as many times as you need to reach your destination, using the same ticket.

ON FOOT & BY BICYCLE

Of course, the best way to explore Munich is on foot, since it has a vast pedestrian zone in the center. Many of its attractions can, in fact, be reached only on foot. Pick up a good map and set out.

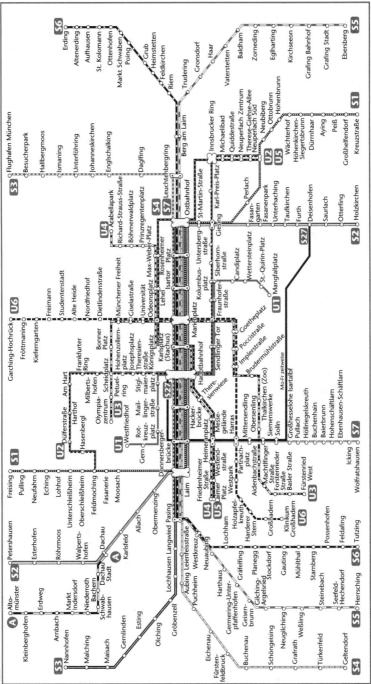

E-0232

55

The tourist office also sells a pamphlet called *Radl-Touren für unsere Gäste,* costing only .50 DM (30¢). It outlines itineraries for touring Munich by bicycle.

One of the most convenient places to rent a bike is **Lenbach & Pöge,** Hans-Sachs-Strasse 7 (☎ **089/266506**), near the U-Bahn station at Frauenhoferstrasse. It's open Monday to Friday from 9:30am to 1pm and 2 to 6pm, and on Saturday from 9:30am to 1pm. Charges are 18 DM ($10.25) for a full day.

BY CAR

Competition in the European car-rental industry is almost as fierce as in the transatlantic airline industry. All the big U.S. car-rental companies, including Avis, Budget, and Hertz, are represented in Germany. You can make reservations and do comparison shopping by calling their toll-free numbers in the United States: **Avis** (☎ **800/331-2112**), **Budget** (☎ **800/472-3325**), and **Hertz** (☎ **800/654-3001**). You can also call **Kemwel Holiday Autos (KHA)** at ☎ **800/678-0678** (www.kemwel.com) and **Auto Europe** at ☎ **800/223-5555** (www.autoeurope.com).

You can rent cars in the city center as well. Companies include **Avis,** Nymphenburger Strasse 61 (☎ **089/1260-0020**), and **Sixt/Budget Autovermietung,** Einsteinstrasse 106 (☎ **089/408-0050**). It's wise to call a number of agencies as prices can vary widely. Rental companies are found under *Autovermietung* in the yellow pages of the Munich phone book. Rental rates may vary by company and type of car. For instance, Avis rents cars ranging from an Opel to a BMW for 104 to 243 DM ($59.30 to $138.50) daily, and Budget rents daily for 139 to 199 DM ($79.25 to $113.45) for a range of cars spanning from an Opel to a Mercedes. Cars at most major rental companies can usually be rented at one Germany city and returned at another for no additional charge.

It's important to understand the many legal and financial implications of auto insurance before you complete your initial paperwork. A collision-damage waiver (CDW) is an optional insurance policy that can be purchased when you sign a rental agreement. For an extra fee, the rental agency agrees to eliminate all but a small percentage of your financial responsibility for liability and collision damage in case of an accident. If you don't have a CDW and do have an accident, you'll usually pay for all damages, up to the cost of actually replacing the vehicle if the accident is serious enough.

Certain credit- and charge-card companies, including American Express and Diners Club, agree to reimburse card users for the deductible in the event of an accident. Because of that, many renters have chosen to waive the cost of the extra CDW. However, although the card issuers will usually reimburse the renter for the cost of damages, this happens several weeks after the accident, when certain documents have been completed. Unless there's a big enough credit line associated with your card, you may be required to pay cash on the spot (sometimes a large sum).

To avoid misunderstandings, the large car-rental companies offer clients the option of either automatically including the CDW as part of the rental price or forgoing it completely in favor of the insurance that sometimes applies automatically through your credit- or charge-card company. Although this confusion has sometimes resulted in "double coverage," it has nonetheless prevented hundreds of renters from having to shell out cash while waiting for reimbursement.

Regardless of the insurance-related options you select, all the major companies maintain competitive rates that tend to be more attractive if you reserve your car from North America between 1 day and 2 weeks in advance of your departure.

Promotional rates offered by car-rental corporations should be researched to ensure the best value.

Cars with automatic transmission cost more in Europe than cars without it. Although all major companies allow dropoffs within Germany at no extra charge, Budget generally offers the most reasonable rates for dropoffs outside Germany.

Some passengers prefer the convenience of prepaying their rental in dollars before leaving the United States. In such circumstances, an easy-to-understand net price (which includes the CDW, all taxes, airport surcharges, and—in some cases—additional personal accident insurance) is quoted and prepaid at least 14 days before departure by credit or charge card. The main benefit to those who opt for this is a somewhat more streamlined rental process, a price structure that is easier to understand, and an ability to avoid unpleasant surprises caused by sudden unfavorable changes in currency exchange rates. Remember, however, that if you opt to prepay, and if your plans change, you'll have to go through some rather complicated paperwork (and in some cases, the payment of a penalty of around $25) for changes or cancellation of any of these prepaid contracts.

Don't overlook the possibility of renting any of Germany's sleekly styled sports cars or luxury sedans. All major companies inventory these cars in abundance, usually at correspondingly elaborate prices.

Because of heavy traffic, don't attempt to see Munich by car. If you're driving into Munich, call your hotel and ask if parking is available on-site. Hotel recommendations (see chapter 4, "Accommodations") indicate if parking is available at the hotel. Otherwise, drive to your hotel, unload your luggage, and ask one of the staff to direct you to the nearest parking garage. Charges tend to be high in most of these garages, often 20 to 30 DM ($11.40 to $17.10) per night.

DRIVING RULES   In Germany, you drive on the right. Easy-to-understand international road signs are posted throughout Germany. Road signs are in kilometers, not miles. In congested areas the speed limit is about 50 kmph, or around 30 mph. On all other roads except the Autobahns the speed limit is 100 kmph, or about 60 mph. In theory, there is no speed limit on the Autobahns (in the left, fast lane), but many drivers reportedly going too fast have written that they have been stopped by the police and fined on the spot. So reasonable precaution is recommended here, for safety if not other reasons. A German driver on the Autobahn can be a ferocious creature, and you may prefer the slow lane. The government nevertheless recommends an Autobahn speed limit of 130 kmph, or 80 mph. Both front-seat and back-seat passengers are required to wear safety belts.

Note: Drinking and driving is a very serious offense in Germany. Therefore, be sure to keep any alcoholic beverages in the trunk or some other storage area. Avoid even the appearance of drinking alcohol while driving.

BREAKDOWNS/ASSISTANCE   The major automobile club in Germany is **Automobilclub von Deutschland (AvD),** Lyoner Strasse 16, D-60329 Frankfurt (☎ **069/66060**). If you don't belong to an auto club and have a breakdown, call from an emergency phone on the Autobahn. These are spaced about a mile apart. On secondary roads, go to the nearest phone and call ☎ **01309/09911.** In English, ask for "road service assistance." Emergency assistance is free, but you pay for parts or materials.

MAPS   The best driving maps, available at all major bookstores throughout Germany, including Munich, are published by Michelin, which offers various regional maps. Other good maps for those who plan to do extensive touring are published by Hallweg.

DRIVER'S LICENSES   If you or your car is from an EU country, all you need is a domestic license and proof of insurance. Otherwise, an international driver's license is required.

For an international driver's license, apply at a branch of the **American Automobile Association (AAA)**. You must be at least 18 years old and have two 2-by-2-inch photographs, a $10 fee, and a photocopy of your U.S. driver's license with an AAA application form. AAA's nearest office will be listed in the local telephone directory, or you can contact AAA's national headquarters at 1000 AAA Dr., Heathrow, FL 32746-5063 (☎ **800/222-4357** or 407/444-7000). Remember that an international driver's license is valid only if physically accompanied by your original driver's license. In Canada you can get the address of the **Canadian Automobile Club** closest to you by calling its national office at ☎ **613/247-0117.**

Both in Germany and throughout the rest of Europe, you must have an international insurance certificate, known as a green card (*carte verte*) to legally drive a car. Any car-rental agency will automatically provide one of these as a standard part of the rental contract, but it's a good idea to double-check the documents the counter attendant gives you at the time of rental just to be sure that you can identify it if asked by a border patrol or the police.

BY TAXI

Cabs are relatively expensive—the average ride costs 8 to 15 DM ($4.55 to $8.55). In an emergency, call ☎ **089/21611,** or 089/19410 for a radio-dispatched taxi.

FAST FACTS: Munich

American Express   Your lifeline back to the States might be American Express, Promenadeplatz 6 (☎ **089/290900**), which is open for mail pickup and check cashing Monday to Friday from 9am to 5:30pm and on Saturday from 9:30am to noon. Unless you have an American Express card or traveler's checks, you'll be charged 2 DM ($1.15) for picking up your mail.

Bookstores   Try Anglia English Bookshop, Schellingstrasse 3 (☎ **089/283642**), in the Schwabing district, which sells English-language titles and travel books. It's open Monday to Friday from 9am to 6:30pm and on Saturday from 10am to 1:30pm.

Business Hours   Most **banks** are open Monday to Friday from 8:30am to 12:30pm and 1:30 to 3:30pm (many banks stay open until 5:30pm on Thursday). Most **businesses** and **stores** are open Monday to Friday from 9am to 6pm and on Saturday from 9am to 2pm. On *langer Samstag* (the first Saturday of the month) stores remain open until 6pm. Many stores in Munich observe a late closing on Thursday, usually 8 or 9pm.

Car Rentals   See "Getting Around," earlier in this chapter.

Climate   See "When to Go," in chapter 2.

Consulates   See "Embassies & Consulates," below.

Currency   See "Money," in chapter 2.

Currency Exchange   You can get a better rate at a bank than at your hotel. American Express traveler's checks are best cashed at the local American Express office (see above). On Saturday and Sunday, or at night, you can exchange money at the Hauptbahnhof exchange, Bahnhofplatz, which is open daily from 6am to 11:30pm.

Dentists   For an English-speaking dentist, go to Klinik und Poliklinik für Kieferchirurgie der Universität München, Lindwurmstrasse 2A (☎ **089/5160-2911**), the dental clinic for the university. It deals with emergency cases and is always open.

Doctors   The American, British, and Canadian consulates keep a list of recommended English-speaking physicians.

Driving Rules   See "Getting Around," earlier in this chapter.

Drug Laws   Penalties for illegal drug possession in Germany are severe. You could go to jail or be deported immediately. Caveat: Drug pushers often turn in their customers to the police.

Drugstores   See "Pharmacies," below.

Electricity   In most places the electricity is 220 volts AC, 50 cycles. Therefore, a transformer will be needed for your U.S. appliances. Many leading hotels will supply one.

Embassies & Consulates   Offices representing various foreign governments are located in Munich. A **United States** Consulate is at Königstrasse 5, D-80539 München (☎ **089/28880**). A Consulate General Office for the **United Kingdom** is located at Burkleinstrasse 10, D-80538 (☎ **089/211090**). **Canada** maintains a consulate at Tal 29, D-80331 (☎ **089/219-9570**). The **Australian** government does not maintain an office in Munich, but if you should need assistance, contact their consulate in Berlin at Uhlandstrasse 181-183 D-10623 (☎ **030/880-0880**). The embassy of **New Zealand** is at Bundeskanzlerplatz 2-10, D-53113 Bonn (☎ **0228/228070**).

Emergencies   For emergency medical aid, phone ☎ **089/557755.** Call the police at ☎ **110.**

Eyeglasses   German optics are among the most precise in the world, and dozens of opticians in central Munich quickly prepare new eyeglasses or contact lenses. Frames and contact lenses are available from **Söhnges Optik,** Kaufingerstrasse 34 (☎ **089/290-0550**) and Brienner Strasse 7 (☎ **089/229-7100**).

Holidays   See "When to Go," in chapter 2.

Hospitals   Munich has many hospitals. Americans, British, and Canadians can contact their consulates for a recommendation of a particular hospital. For emergency medical service, call ☎ **089/557755.**

Language   Many Germans speak English. English is usually spoken at major hotels and restaurants and in the principal tourist areas. A good phrase book to carry with you is the *Berlitz German for Travellers,* available in most big bookstores in the United States.

Liquor Laws   As in many European countries, the application of drinking laws is flexible. Laws are enforced only if a problem develops or if decorum is broken. Officially, someone must be 18 to consume any kind of alcoholic beverage in Germany, although at family gatherings wine or schnapps might be offered to underage imbibers. For a bar or cafe to request proof of age of a prospective client is very rare. Drinking and driving, however, is treated as a very serious offense.

Lost Property   Go to the local lost-and-found office at Ötztalerstrasse 17 (☎ **089/23300**). It's open Monday to Friday 8:30am to noon; on Tuesday it's also open 2 to 5:30pm. If you should lose an item on the German train, then go to the lost-and-found office at Track 24 in the Hauptbahnhof (☎ **089/ 1308-6664**); it's open daily 6:30am to 3:30pm.

Luggage Storage/Lockers   Facilities are available at the Hauptbahnhof on Bahnhofplatz (☎ **089/1308-5047**), which is open daily from 6am to 11pm.

Mail   To post a letter on the street, look for a mailbox painted yellow. The cost to send an airmail letter to the United States or Canada is 3 DM ($1.70) for the first 5 grams (about a fifth of an ounce) and 2 DM ($1.15) for postcards. To mail a package, go to one of the larger post offices in Munich (see below). All letters to the United Kingdom cost 1.10 DM (65¢) or 1 DM (55¢) for postcards.

Newspapers/Magazines   The *International Herald Tribune* is the most widely distributed English-language newspaper in the city. You can also find copies of *USA Today* and the European editions of *Time* and *Newsweek.*

Pharmacies   For an international pharmacy where English is spoken, go to International Ludwig's Apotheke, Neuhauserstrasse 11 (☎ **089/260-3021**), in the pedestrian shopping zone. It's open Monday to Friday from 9am to 6:30pm and on Saturday from 9am to 2pm. There's always a pharmacy open 24 hours in every neighborhood. Every *Apotheke* has a sign in its window indicating where to find the nearest one staying open (it changes from night to night).

Police   Throughout the country, dial ☎ **110** for emergencies.

Post Office   The Postamt München (main post office) is across from the Hauptbahnhof, at Bahnhofplatz 1 (☎ **089/601-0604**). If you want to have your mail sent to you, mark it *Poste Restante* for general delivery (take along your passport to reclaim any mail). Have your mail addressed Poste Restante, Arnulfstrasse 32, D-80074 München. Post office hours are Monday to Saturday 8am to 12:30pm and 2 to 6pm. Closed Sunday and holidays. You can also make long-distance calls here (far cheaper than at your hotel, where you'll be charged for service).

Radio   The BBC World Service broadcasts to Munich, as does the American Forces Network (AFN), which you can hear on 1107 AM. English news broadcasts are presented frequently on the Bavarian Radio Service (Bayerischer Rundfunk).

Rest Rooms   Use the word *Toilette* (pronounced twa-*leht*-tah). Rest rooms may be labeled WC or H (for *Herren,* men) and F (for *Frauen,* women). In the center of Munich are several public facilities that you should not hesitate to use. You can also patronize the facilities at terminals, restaurants, bars, cafes, department stores, hotels, and pubs.

Safety   Munich, like all big cities of the world, has its share of crime. Major crimes are pickpocketing and purse- and camera-snatching. If necessary, store valuables in a hotel safe. Most robberies occur in the much-frequented tourist areas, such as the areas around the Hauptbahnhof, which can be dangerous at night, and the Marienplatz, where tourists gather. Many tourists lose their valuables when they carelessly leave clothing unprotected as they join the nude sunbathers in the Englischer Garten.

Shoe Repairs   Offering the quickest service is **Mister Minit,** at the Hertie department store, Bahnhofplatz 7 (☎ **089/55120**).

Taxes   As a member of the European Union, the Federal Republic of Germany imposes a tax on most goods and services known as a **value-added tax** (VAT), or in German, *Mehrwertsteuer.* Nearly everything is taxed at 15%. That includes vital necessities such as gas and luxury items such as jewelry. Note that the goods for sale, such as German cameras, have the 15% tax already factored into the price; whereas services, such as paying a garage mechanic to fix your car, will have the 15% added to the bill. Stores that display a "Tax Free" sticker work with the **Tax Free Shopping Service.** They will issue you a Tax Free Shopping Check at the time of purchase. When leaving the country before you check your baggage (Customs will want to examine what you purchased), have your check stamped by the German Customs Service as your proof of legal export. You may then be able to obtain a cash refund at one of the Tax Free Shopping Service offices in the major airports and many train stations, even at some of the bigger ferry terminals. Otherwise, you must send the checks to Tax Free Shopping Service, Mengstrasse 19, D-23552 Lübeck, Germany. If you want the payment to be credited to your bank card or your bank account, mention this.

Taxis   See "Getting Around," earlier in this chapter.

Telephone/Telex/Fax   Local and long-distance calls may be placed from all post offices and coin-operated public telephone booths. The unit charge is 0.30 DM or three 10-pfennig coins. More than half the phones in Germany require an advance-payment telephone card from Telekom, the German telephone company. Phone cards are sold at post offices and newsstands, costing 12 DM ($6.85) and 50 DM ($28.50). The 12-DM card offers about 40 minutes and the 50-DM card is useful for long-distance calls. Rates are measured in units rather than minutes. The farther the distance, the more units are consumed. For example, a 4-minute call to the United States costs 41 units. All towns and cities in Germany may be dialed directly by using the prefix listed in the telephone directory above each local heading. Telephone calls made through hotel switchboards can double, triple, or even quadruple the charge. Therefore, try to make your calls outside your hotel at a post office where you can also send telexes and faxes. Credit cards are generally not accepted, but some of the international hotels accept the AT&T calling card. USA Direct can be used with all telephone cards and for collect calls. The number from Germany is ☎ **01-30-00-10.** Canada Direct can be used with the Bell Telephone card and for collect calls. This number from Germany is ☎ **01-30-00-14.** Telephone calls to Germany from the United States and Canada can be made by dialing ☎ **0-11-49.**

Television   There are two national TV channels, ARD (Channel 1) and ZDF (Channel 2). Sometimes these stations show films in the original language (most often English). The more expensive hotels often have cable TV, with programs such as CNN.

Time Zone   Germany operates on central European time (CET), which places it 6 hours ahead of eastern time (ET) in the United States and 1 hour ahead of Greenwich mean time. Summertime in Germany begins in April and ends in September—there's a slight difference in the dates from year to year—so there may be a period in early spring and in the fall when there's a 7-hour difference between U.S. ET and CET. Always check if you're traveling at these periods, especially if you need to catch a plane.

Tipping   If a restaurant bill says *Bedienung,* that means a service charge has already been added, so just round up to the nearest mark. If not, add 10% to 15%. Round up to the nearest mark for taxis. Bellhops get 2 DM ($1.15) per bag, as does the doorman at your hotel, restaurant, or nightclub. Room-cleaning staffs get small tips in Germany, but tip concierges well who perform some special favor such as obtaining hard-to-get theater or opera tickets. Tip hairdressers or barbers 5% to 10%.

Water   Tap water is safe to drink in Munich.

4 Accommodations

Finding a room in Munich is comparatively easy, but tabs tend to be high. Bargains are few and hard to find—but they exist.

If you arrive without a reservation, go to the **Munich Tourist Information Office** on Platform 2 at the Hauptbahnhof (☎ **089/2333-0257**), where general information is also available; it's open daily from 9am to 8pm. Here, the English-speaking personnel, with some 34,000 listings in their files, will come to your rescue. Tell them what you can afford. You must give them a 10% down payment on the room, but this amount will be deducted from your final accommodation bill. Be sure to get a receipt as well as a map with instructions on how to reach the place they've booked for you. Keep your receipt. If you don't like the room, go back to the tourist office and they'll try to find you another lodging at no extra charge. Correspondence, however, should be addressed to Landeshauptstadt München, Fremdenverkehrsamt, D-80313 München. These offices are open Monday to Friday from 9am to 4pm.

Advance Reservations Citi Incoming, Mullerstrasse 11 (Postfach 140163), D-80451 München (☎ **089/260-6914;** fax 089/260-6484), is the best place to go if you want not only to book a hotel room but also to arrange for an Avis rental car and Grey Line sightseeing tour. The service is free and, although this company works with hotels on a commission basis, it guarantees that travelers never pay more than they would if they made the bookings themselves. In some cases, Citi Incoming can even get you a better rate than off-the-street bookings because hotels make special offers to travel agencies. Guaranteed bookings can easily be made by phone or fax. The company provides this service for other areas of Germany as well, even for neighboring countries such as Austria and Switzerland. They'll even provide you with road maps. Both long-term bookings and last-minute requests are handled. There are no fixed open hours; prospective clients can call or fax at any time. If no one is in the office, an answering machine takes requests.

All hotels raise their prices for Oktoberfest and various trade fairs. Some hotels announce their tariffs in advance (see the listings below); others prefer to wait until the last minute to see what the market will bear.

1 Best Bets

- **Best Historic Hotel: Kempinski Vier Jahreszeiten München** (☎ 800/426-3135 in the U.S.) is one of the most famous hotels in the world—the lineage of this hostelry stretches back to 1858. Maximilian II himself took a personal interest in the hotel's establishment, even going so far as to aid its founder financially. The Walterspiel family brought it to worldwide prominence, and over the years it's entertained the greats and near-greats.
- **Best for Business Travelers: München Park Hilton** (☎ 800/445-8687) is a modern 15-story structure, completely geared to welcome the business traveler and provide all needed services. It is close to many corporate headquarters and has the best conference facilities of any hotel in the city. Actually the hotel was an office block until pressed into service as a hotel for the 1972 Olympics. After business is concluded you can unwind at the hotel's health club.
- **Best for a Romantic Getaway: Romantik Hotel Insel Mühle** (☎ 089/81010), constructed around a 16th-century mill, is a romantic choice with its antique decor and its rooms with sloping garretlike ceilings. It also has an old-world restaurant with massive beams and a wine cellar. Though far removed from the hustle and bustle, it's only 6 miles west of Munich's Marienplatz.
- **Best Trendy Hotel: Rafael** (☎ 089/290980), small and deluxe, in a neo-Renaissance building, this hotel dates only from 1990 but has quickly established itself as a choice of visiting celebrities, including fashion models, dress designers, and the media elite. Its discreet style and formal elegance make it the right address for those who don't want to be "too obvious"—that is, by staying at one of the lavish, bigger hotels.
- **Best Lobby for Pretending You're Rich: Bayerischer Hof & Palais Montgelas** (☎ 800/223-6800 in the U.S.) is a real old-fashioned European formal hotel with a deluxe lobby filled with English and French furniture and oriental rugs. It's been called the "living room" of Munich. "Meet you in the lounge of the Bayerischer Hof" is often heard. As hotels go, there's no more impressive place to go for a drink.
- **Best for Families: Arabella Olympiapark Hotel München** (☎ 089/51960) is right at Europe's biggest sports and recreation center and rents many triple rooms that are ideal for families. It's among the most modern and best-kept places in the city, and your kid will enjoy meeting some of the sports heroes who often stay here. At Olympiapark the entire family can use the sports facilities, including a large Olympic-size swimming pool.
- **Best Moderately Priced Hotel: Splendid** (☎ 089/296606), an old-world hotel, is graced with antiques, oriental rugs, and chandeliers, and evokes the aura of a country home. Many rooms are decorated in a style known as "Bavarian baroque." Not all accommodations in this little hotel have private baths, so if you opt for sharing a bathroom, the price becomes budget level.
- **Best Budget Hotel: Pension beim Haus der Kunst** (☎ 089/222127) is one of Munich's better pensions. Ideally located near the Englischer Garten, it has decent and comfortable rooms with shared baths. Its low cost, along with warm hospitality and copious breakfasts, make this little entry a winning choice among those who are watching their Deutsche Marks.
- **Best B&B: Gästehaus Englischer Garten** (☎ 089/392034), close to the Englischer Garten and its summer nudes, is an oasis of charm and tranquillity in

fashionable Schwabing. An ivy-covered former private villa, it offers attractively furnished rooms; those in the annex are really small apartments with tiny kitchenettes. When the weather's right, breakfast is served in the rear garden.

- **Best Service: Eden-Hotel-Wolff** (☎ **089/551150**) employs one of the most thoughtful staffs in Munich. Although hotels like the Bayerischer Hof offer state-of-the-art service, the attentive, efficient, unhurried yet down-to-earth English-speaking staff here gets the job done just as well, anticipating all your needs.
- **Best Location: An der Oper** (☎ **089/290-0270**) is in the virtual heart of Munich. You're just steps away from the central Marienplatz. Moments after leaving the hotel you can be shopping along the Maximilianstrasse or exploring the traffic-free malls just steps from the Bavarian National Theater, and all for a reasonable price.
- **Best Health Club: München Marriott Hotel** (☎ **800/228-9290**) has the best-equipped fitness center of any hotel in Munich—a swimming pool almost 45 feet long, whirlpools, hydrojets, a solarium, and state-of-the-art exercise equipment. There's also a *Kosmetik-Kabine* for beauty treatments and massages, plus separate saunas for men and women. Residents of the Marriott use the club for free; nonresidents pay 30 DM ($17.10) for a day pass.
- **Best Hotel Pool:** The state-of-the-art indoor pool at the **Arabella Hotel Bogenhausen** (☎ **089/51960**) is on the 22nd floor, offering not only views but its own waterfall. Although many hotels in Munich have swimming pools, none competes with this choice. And that's not all—you get five whirlpools, along with saunas and a trio of steam rooms inspired by ancient Rome, each ideal for après-swim. The hotel is in the verdant suburb of Bogenhausen only seven subway stops from the center of town.
- **Best Views: Holiday Inn Crowne Plaza Munich** (☎ **800/465-4329**), near the Olympic Stadium on the northern perimeter of Schwabing, has the best view of Munich along with the added treat of a view of the distant Bavarian Alps. The hotel was constructed with two eight-story towers to house guests for the 1972 Olympics; for the view, ask for a room on an upper floor, facing south.

2　In Central Munich

VERY EXPENSIVE

✪ **Bayerischer Hof & Palais Montgelas.** Promenadeplatz 2-6, D-80333 München. ☎ **800/223-6800** in the U.S., or 089/21200. Fax 089/212-0906. www.lhw.com/munich/ bayerischerhof.html. E-mail: hbhcompuserve.com. 445 units. MINIBAR TV TEL. 446–522 DM ($254–$298) double; 845–1,950 DM ($482–$1,112) suite. Rates include buffet breakfast. AE, DC, MC, V. Parking 33 DM ($18.80). Tram: 19.

A Bavarian version of New York's Waldorf-Astoria, the Bayerischer Hof & Palais Montgelas is in a swank location, opening onto a little tree-filled square. After zillions of marks were spent on it, it is now better than ever, a rival even of the front-ranking Kempinski Hotel Vier Jahreszeiten München. The tastefully decorated central lounge is known as the meeting place of Munich (see "Best Bets" above). Integrating the sumptuously decorated Palais Montgelas into the hotel brought deluxe suites and double rooms, as well as a number of conference and banqueting rooms. Only 80 of the guest rooms are air-conditioned.

Dining/Diversions: The major dining room, the Garden-Restaurant, evokes the grandeur of a small palace with its ornate ceiling and crystal chandeliers. Generous drinks and charcoal specialties from the rôtisserie are served in the clublike bar, where tables are lit by candles and the reflected glow from stained-glass windows. There's also the Kleine Komödie Theater, a Trader Vic's, and the best nightclub in Munich, recommended separately.

Amenities: Room service, laundry service, baby-sitting, rooftop pool and garden with bricked sun terrace, sauna, massage rooms, shopping mall with boutiques and salons.

✪ **Kempinski Hotel Vier Jahreszeiten München.** Maximilianstrasse 17, D-80539 München. ☎ **800/426-3135** in the U.S., or 089/21250. Fax 089/2125-2000. 364 units. A/C MINIBAR TV TEL. 494–797 DM ($281.60–$454.30) double; from 1,291 DM ($735.85) suite. AE, DC, MC, V. Parking 20 DM ($11.40). Tram: 19.

The most elegant place to stay in Munich is this grand hotel with a tradition stretching back to 1858. Rivaled only by the Bayerischer Hof, it is one of Germany's most famous and distinctive hostelries—actually among the finest in the world. For a fine old-world experience, you can do no better. Maximilian II took a personal interest in the establishment of the original hotel and financially helped the founder, restaurateur August Schimon. The hotel gained worldwide fame under the ownership of the Walterspiel family. When it was largely destroyed in a 1944 air raid, they rebuilt the hotel and returned it to its number-one position. Kempinski Hotels took it over in 1970.

The guest rooms and suites, which have hosted royalty, heads of state, and famed personalities from all over the world, combine the charm of days gone by with modern amenities. The windows opening onto Maximilianstrasse are double glazed, and quiet is assured in the units facing the three inner courts. The hotel is not connected to any of the other Vier Jahreszeiten hotel found throughout Germany.

Dining/Diversions: Vier Jahreszeiten Restaurant, its finest dining spot (open daily), is recommended separately. The Four Seasons is under a magnificent glass roof above the lobby. Guests like to linger in the Jahreszeiten Bar, where piano music is played nightly during the cocktail hour, with an international trio performing until 2am. The completely refurnished Bistro Eck surprises guests with its modern yet classical atmosphere.

Amenities: Room service, laundry services, baby-sitting, massages, indoor pool and sauna, solarium, sun terrace.

Königshof. Karlsplatz 25, D-80335 München. ☎ **800/44-UTELL** in the U.S., or 089/551360. Fax 089/5513-6113. 90 units. A/C MINIBAR TV TEL. 395–1,550 DM ($225.15–$883.50) double; 600–11,200 DM ($342–$6,384) suite. AE, DC, MC, V. Parking 24 DM ($13.70) in 180-car underground garage. S-Bahn: S3, S7, or S8 to Karlsplatz. Tram: 19.

In the heart of Munich, the lively, personalized Königshof overlooks the famous Stachus (Karlsplatz) and the old part of the city, where it opened in 1862. The proprietors, the Geisel family, maintain its legend. As a mansion hotel it attracts an extremely upmarket clientele but does not match the Rafael (see below) in this type of premier address. The hotel offers traditional comfort plus up-to-date facilities. All its sleekly styled rooms have soundproofing and picture windows, and there are interesting shopping and sightseeing streets nearby.

Dining/Diversions: On the second floor is the well-known Restaurant Königshof, serving French and international cuisine. A piano bar provides entertainment. The lobby houses an intimate club bar, the Königshof-Bar.

Amenities: Room service, laundry, baby-sitting, concierge, car-rental facilities, shopping boutiques.

Central Munich Accommodations

Adria 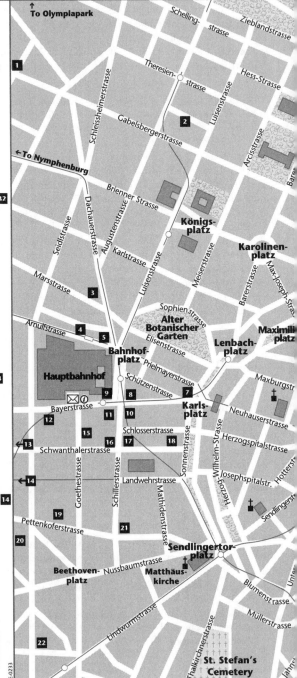37
Advocat Hotel 31
Am Markt 24
An der Opera 26
Arabella-Central 13
Bayerischer Hof & Palais
   Montgelas 6
Carlton 39
City Hotel 10
Concorde 29
Deutscher Kaiser 5
Domus 36
Eden-Hotel-Wolff 4
Europäischer Hof 11
Erzgiesserei Europe 1
Excelsior Hotel 8
Forum Hotel München 37
Gästehaus
   Englischer Garten 40
Germania 16
Hotel Mark 15
InterCity Hotel
   München 9
Jedermann 12
Kempinski Hotel
   Vier Jahreszeiten
   München 27
King's Hotel 3
Königshof 7
Königswache 2
Kraft Hotel 21
München Park Hilton 34
Pension beim Haus der
   Kunst 38
Pension Stadt
   München 23
Pension Westfalia 22
Platzl 25
Preysing 33
Rafael 28
Reinbold 17
SKH-Trustee Park Hotel 14
Splendid 35
Torbräu 30
Uhland Garni 20
Utzelmann 19
Wallis 18

Legend

Church ⸸
Post Office ⊠
Information ⓘ
U-Bahn ──○──
S-Bahn ──▢──

E-0233

66

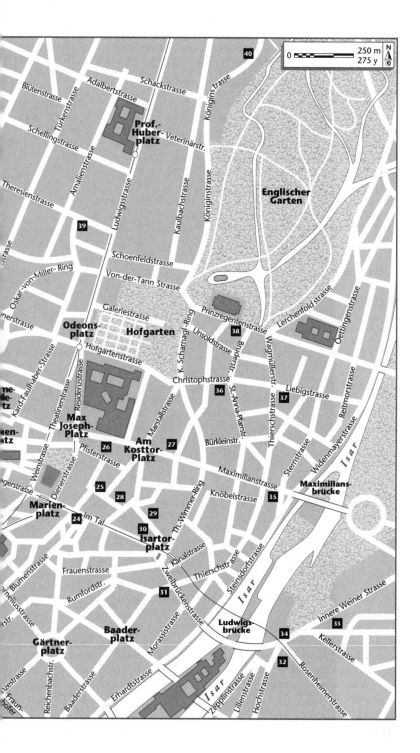

✪ **Rafael.** Neuturmstrasse 1, D-80331 München. ☎ **089/290980.** Fax 089/222539. www. lhw.com/munich/rafael.html. 81 units. A/C MINIBAR TV TEL. 570–730 DM ($324.90–$416.10) double; from 850 DM ($484.50) suite. AE, DC, MC, V. Parking 36 DM ($20.50). U-Bahn or S-Bahn: Marienplatz. Tram: 19.

One of Munich's small hotels is also one of its most posh. Only the Kempinski Hotel Vier Jahreszeiten München and the Bayerischer Hof outclass this sophisticated and luxurious winner. A wedge-shaped neo-Renaissance building within sight of the Frauenkirche, this hotel was inaugurated in 1990 in a format of style and elegance with neoclassical and Biedermeier touches. A marble staircase sweeps upward to the very comfortable guest rooms, each with a richly appointed bathroom and specially crafted furniture or original antiques.

Dining/Diversions: The culinary showplace is Mark's Restaurant, very intimate, with 75 seats and a piano bar.

Amenities: Concierge, 24-hour room service, laundry, baby-sitting, valet parking. The service staff is among the most professional in southern Germany, rooftop pool (May through October) with a view over the historic district, boutiques.

EXPENSIVE

Arabella Westpark-Hotel. Garmischer Strasse 2, D-80339 München. ☎ **089/51960.** Fax 089/519-6100. 258 units. MINIBAR TV TEL. 212–366 DM ($120.85–$208.60) double; 355 DM ($202.35) suite. Rates include breakfast. During Oktoberfest and trade fairs, 361–471 DM ($205.75–$268.45) double; 490 DM ($279.30) suite. AE, DC, MC, V. Parking 24 DM ($13.70). U-bahn: U4 or U5 to Heimeran Platz.

A 10-story, four-star member of the conservative Arabella chain, this hotel is more personalized and more intimate and has a bit less drama and flair than the Arabella Hotel Bogenhausen recommended below. The bedrooms were completely renovated in 1996, with new carpets and draperies and a general upgrade of amenities.

Dining/Diversions: On the premises is a stylish and impeccably maintained restaurant, Ambiente, and a bar.

Amenities: Jacuzzi, concierge, room service, dry cleaning/laundry, solarium, and a swimming pool.

Concorde. Herrnstrasse 38, D-80539 München. ☎ **089/224515.** Fax 089/228-3282. 75 units. MINIBAR TV TEL. 245–295 DM ($139.65–$168.15) double Mon–Thurs, 190 DM ($108.30) Fri–Sun; 220–310 DM ($125.40–$176.70) suite daily. Rates include buffet breakfast. AE, DC, MC, V. Closed Dec 22–Jan 7. Parking 18 DM ($10.25). U-Bahn: U3 or U6 to Isartor platz; then a 3-minute walk to the hotel.

It's set on a quiet side street, a few minutes' walk from some of the most frequently visited attractions in town. This efficiently managed hotel has six floors, an elevator, and was renovated in 1996. Its desirable location and its proximity to both the British and American consulates draw a large number of diplomats. Each bedroom has modern, somewhat bland styling, with a large, comfortable bed and angular contemporary furnishings.

Dining: Although there are no dining or bar facilities on-site, many restaurants are in the neighborhood, and drinks can be served in the lobby on request.

Amenities: Concierge, dry cleaning and laundry service; bicycle rentals are available.

Deutscher Kaiser. Arnulfstrasse 2, D-80335 München. ☎ **089/54530.** Fax 089/ 5453-2255. 174 units. MINIBAR TV TEL. 250 DM ($142.50) double. Rates include breakfast. AE, DC, MC, V. Parking 24 DM ($13.70). U-Bahn or S-Bahn: Hauptbahnhof.

The hotel caters to a high-turnover roster of European business travelers who appreciate its efficiency, its relative anonymity, and its position across the street from the entrance to Munich's main railway station. Rising 15 stories above the congested neighborhood, it contains comfortable, culturally neutral bedrooms that, on the higher floors, offer views of the Alps and the city's distant outskirts. It is similar to the InterCity Hotel München (which we prefer to this one). This is a hotel that, depending on room availability, might be willing to grant a discount if you ask for one.

Dining/Diversions: There is no restaurant on the premises, however there is a casual bar off the main lobby where sandwiches and other snacks are served.

Amenities: There is a separately owned fitness center for women on the premises (discounts available to hotel guests); laundry and dry-cleaning services.

✪ **Eden-Hotel-Wolff.** Arnulfstrasse 4-8, D-80335 München. ☎ **089/551150.** Fax 089/5511-5555. www.ehw.de. E-mail: sales@ehw.de. 211 units. MINIBAR TV TEL. 270–450 DM ($153.90–$256.50) double; 370–500 DM ($210.90–$285) suite. One child up to age 6 stays free in parents' room. Rates include buffet breakfast. AE, DC, MC, V. Parking 20 DM ($11.40). U-Bahn or S-Bahn: Hauptbahnhof.

Opposite the Hauptbahnhof, the stone-clad Eden-Hotel-Wolff misleads with its sedate exterior. The interior is decorated in a richly traditional style, and if you must stay in the railroad station area, this is your best bet. The guest bedrooms are both traditional and modern, with a rather fashionable decor, often with marble-clad baths.

Dining/Diversions: In the main dining room the theme is Bavarian—natural pine ceiling, gleaming brass lantern sconces, thick stone arches, and excellent Bavarian dishes and a savory international cuisine. On a cold night, the fireplace in the bar makes for a snug and cozy retreat.

Amenities: Concierge, baby-sitting, dry cleaning and laundry, secretarial services and conference rooms; bicycle and car rental are at the hotel tour desk.

Excelsior Hotel. Schutzenstrasse 11, D-80335 München. ☎ **089/551370.** Fax 089/5513-7121. 113 units. A/C MINIBAR TV TEL. 295–370 DM ($168.15–$210.90) double; 400–480 DM ($228–$273.60) suite. AE, DC, MC, V. Parking 22 DM ($12.55). U-bahn: Hauptbahnhof.

This solidly comfortable four-star hotel near the city's main railway station prides itself on its restored facade, a pale gray exterior that replicates its original turn-of-the century design, which was destroyed in wartime bombings. Last renovated in 1991, it's under the same management as the Königshof, a few steps away, and is not a member of any chain. Bedrooms are quite spacious, outfitted in a tasteful and conservative style. Overall, this is a low-key, discreet, highly Europeanized hotel with a resolute lack of glitter.

Dining/Diversions: There is a piano bar and a restaurant, Vinothek, on the premises.

Amenities: Concierge, room service, dry cleaning and laundry; clients are welcome to use the sauna, exercise equipment, and whirlpool facilities on the nearby premises of the Königshof.

Forum Hotel München. Hochstrasse 3, D-81669 München. ☎ **089/48030.** Fax 089/448-8277. 593 units. A/C MINIBAR TV TEL. 300–380 DM ($171–$216.60) double; 650 DM ($370.50) suite. During weekend periods of low demand, promotional rates of 195 DM ($111.15) sometimes available Fri-Sun. AE, DC, MC, V. Parking 28 DM ($15.95). S-Bahn: Rosenheimer Platz.

After the Sheraton, this is Munich's largest hotel. It's two subway stops east of the Marienplatz in a congested neighborhood near the Isar River, not far from the Gasteig Center and the Deutsche Museum. An 11-story concrete structure, it offers a handsome, busy, and cosmopolitan environment much favored by airline personnel and business travelers. Rated four stars by the government, it's the kind of place that shows bustling international Munich at its most efficient, but not necessarily at its most charming.

Dining/Diversions: The hotel contains three restaurants, the most formal of which is the Gasteig Taverne. Less formal and less expensive are the Bierstube and Spices which serves EurAsian cuisine and has a likable bar.

Amenities: Room service, baby-sitting, laundry, dry cleaning, indoor pool, sauna, and a network of kiosks and shops.

InterCity Hotel München. Bayerstrasse 10, D-80335 München. ☎ **089/545560.** Fax 089/5455-6610. 200 units. MINIBAR TV TEL. 250–398 DM ($142.50–$226.85) double; 285–460 DM ($162.45–$262.20) suite. AE, DC, MC, V. Parking 17.50 DM ($10). U-Bahn or S-Bahn: Hauptbahnhof.

This four-star hotel was once a late-19th-century *Jugendstil* showplace that rose from the southern precincts of Munich's main railway station. Blasted apart during World War II and rebuilt in a bland angular style, it retains hints of its art-nouveau origins in an otherwise internationally modern interior. Part of its attraction is that you or a porter can carry your luggage from the railway sidings directly to the hotel's lobby without crossing any streets. You'll be disappointed if you're a railway buff, since you won't be able to watch trains arriving or departing, but that's overcome by the fact that bedrooms are soundproofed against urban noise and are comfortable, contemporary, and suited to the needs of international travelers. As a concession to Munich's unending obsession with folklore, a few of the hotel's bedrooms celebrate the Bavarian style with deliberately rustic furnishings.

Dining/Diversions: There's a leather-trimmed bar on the premises, as well as a comfortable restaurant one floor above street level, in a culturally neutral setting, with an otherwise continental menu peppered with a scattering of Bavarian dishes.

Amenities: Services are surprisingly few for a hotel of this classification. Among them are a concierge desk to help guide you around Munich and a dry-cleaning service.

King's Hotel. Dachauer Strasse 13, D-80335 München. ☎ **089/551870.** Fax 089/5518-7300. 120 units. A/C MINIBAR TV TEL. 275–305 DM ($156.75–$173.85) double; 380–420 DM ($216.60–$239.40) suite. Some weekends, depending on bookings (Fri–Sun), 175 DM ($99.75) double. During Oktoberfest and trade fairs, 285 DM ($162.45) double; 445 DM ($253.65) suite. AE, DC, MC, V. U-Bahn: Hauptbahnhof.

The interior of King's Hotel sports the most traditional Bavarian decor of any of the many four-star hotels in Munich. The comfortable, seven-story building looks from the outside like a modern town house, but inside the carved headboards, flowered fabrics, and rich paneling offer a pleasant contrast to the 20th-century anonymity of the area around the city's main railway station. It's a 4-minute walk from the Hauptbahnhof. Built in 1987, the hotel was named after a German family that prides itself on the English spelling of its name.

Dining/Diversions: No meals are served other than breakfast, although the in-house bar offers a limited selection of pizzas, soups, and snack items. Some of the suites have tiny kitchens.

Amenities: Concierge, room service, dry cleaning and laundry services; bicycle rentals upon request.

✪ **München Park Hilton.** Am Tucherpark 7, D-80538 München. ☎ **800/445-8667** in the U.S., or 089/38450. Fax 089/3845-2588. www.hilton.com. 499 units. A/C MINIBAR TV TEL. 355.50 DM ($202.65) double; 817–1,816 DM ($465.70–$1,035.10) suite. 71 DM

($40.45) supplement for room on executive floor, where breakfast and use of a resident's lounge are included. AE, DC, MC, V. Parking 25 DM ($14.25). U-Bahn: U3 or U6 to Giselas-trasse. Bus: E54 from Schwabing.

This sleek, 15-story tower in verdant Trivoli Park was transformed into a hotel from an office complex in time for the 1972 Olympics. Access is sometimes a bit difficult to find for motorists. It lies between the Englischer Garten and the Isar River, in a neighborhood close to the headquarters of many giant corporations. A five-star hotel, it's one of Munich's two Hiltons (the other, the four-star City Hilton, is less plush and has no swimming pool). Bedrooms here have floor-to-ceiling picture windows, balconies affording a distant view of the Alps, and monochromatic color schemes inspired by the earth tones of autumn.

Dining/Diversions: Overlooking the pool is the Isar Terrassen, which combines a rollicking beer garden with a middle-of-the-road restaurant. Fine dining is offered at the Hilton Grill on the ground floor, and at a Chinese restaurant, Tse Yang. The Piano Bar features a pianist and the best martinis in town.

Amenities: 24-hour room service, baby-sitting, laundry, dry cleaning, hair-dresser, health club (renovated in 1996) facing the Englischer Garten, with heated outdoor pool, sauna, Turkish bath, and solarium.

Platzl. Sparkassenstrasse 1, D-80331 München. ☎ **089/237030.** Fax 089/2370-3800. 167 units. TV TEL. 310–430 DM ($176.70–$245.10) double. Rates include buffet breakfast. AE, DC, MC, V. Parking 20 DM ($11.40). U-Bahn: U3 or U6 to Marienplatz.

In the historic Altstadt, this restored hotel stands opposite the world-famous Hof-bräuhaus and close to Marienplatz. It's one of the best choices in Munich for a real taste of *Gemütlichkeit*. Obviously, it's the beer-drinker's favorite—more beer is consumed in and around this hotel than at almost any other place in Europe. The Aying brewery owns the hotel and has decorated the bedrooms—many of which are quite small—in a rustic Bavarian motif. The central location is unbeatable if you'd like to be within walking distance of the major attractions.

Dining/Diversions: The hotel's restaurant, Pfistermühle, serves a Bavarian cuisine. Next door is the folk theater, Platzl's Theaterie.

Amenities: Room service, laundry and dry cleaning service. The hotel has a sauna and a Jacuzzi, in addition to conference rooms for the business traveler, and a boutique.

Torbräu. Tal 41, D-80331 München. ☎ **089/225016.** Fax 089/225019. 67 units. TV TEL. 280–395 DM ($159.60–$225.15) double. Rates include breakfast. AE, MC, V. Closed 1 week at Christmas. Parking 19 DM ($10.85). U-Bahn: Isartor.

The foundations of this four-star hotel in the heart of historic Munich date from the 15th century. Although many vestiges of its folkloric exterior attest to the hotel's distinguished past, the bedrooms are more modern and reasonably comfortable. In all, the place is a lot more charming than many of its bandbox-modern competitors.

Dining/Diversions: The hotel's restaurant, Firenze, is open daily for lunch and dinner, featuring a festive selection of Italian specialties favored by merchants and office workers from the surrounding district. There's also a cafe-conditorei on the premises.

Amenities: Concierge, room service, dry cleaning and laundry services; access to a nearby health club and conference rooms.

MODERATE
Adria. Liebigstrasse 8a, D-80538 München. ☎ **089/293081.** Fax 089/227015. 47 units. MINIBAR TV TEL. 190–280 DM ($108.30–$159.60) double. Rates include buffet breakfast. AE, MC, V. Closed Dec 23–Jan 6. Free parking. U-Bahn: U4 or U5. Tram: 20.

The Adria has an inviting, friendly atmosphere. The lobby sets the stylish contemporary look, and guest rooms are furnished with armchairs or sofas, small desks, and hair dryers. Breakfast, a buffet with waffles, cakes, homemade rolls, health-food selections, and even sparkling wine, is served in the garden room. On Sunday smoked salmon is an added treat. Services include money exchange, laundry, theater tickets, and arrangements for sightseeing tours. For 50 DM ($28.50) the hotel will give you a "license" allowing you to park free in the neighborhood; when you return the license at checkout time, the fee is returned.

Advocat Hotel. Baaderstrasse 1, D-80469 München. ☎ **089/216310.** Fax 089/216-3190. E-mail: advokathot@aol.com. 50 units. MINIBAR TV TEL. Fri–Sun 215 DM ($122.55) double; Mon–Thurs 245 DM ($139.65) double. S-Bahn: Isartor.

This hotel occupies a six-story, oft-rebuilt 1930s apartment house. In 1996 its interior was radically renovated in a stripped-down, streamlined form that borrowed in discreet ways from Bauhaus and minimalist models. One Munich critic remarked that the rooms look as if Philippe Starck had gone on a shopping binge at Ikea. The result is an aggressively simple, clean-lined, and artfully spartan hotel with very few amenities and facilities. Rated three stars by the German government, it's just around the corner from its more upscale neighbor, the Hotel Admiral, with which it shares the same management, but whose rooms cost 50 DM ($28.50) more, double occupancy, per category. There's no restaurant on the premises, and no particular amenities to speak of other than a cozy in-house bar. But the prices are reasonable, and the staff is helpful.

✪ **An der Oper.** Falkenturmstrasse 11, D-80331 München. ☎ **089/290-0270.** Fax 089/2900-2729. 55 units. MINIBAR TV TEL. 250–320 DM ($142.50–$182.40) double. Rates include buffet breakfast. AE, MC, V. Tram: 19.

Located just off Maximilianstrasse, near Marienplatz, this hotel is superb for sightseeing or shopping in the traffic-free malls, just steps from the Bavarian National Theater. In this price category it is better run and more comfortable than the Adria, described above. In spite of its basic, clean-cut modernity, there are elegant touches, such as the crystal chandeliers in the little reception area. The guest rooms offer first-class amenities; each contains a small sitting area with armchairs and tables for breakfast. The rooms have been renovated in a light contemporary style with soft and subdued colors. A restaurant with a French-influenced menu, Bosuirth, occupies space in the same building.

Arabella-Central Hotel. Schwanthalerstrasse 111, D-80339 München. ☎ **089/510830.** Fax 089/5108-3800. 102 units. MINIBAR TV TEL. Sun–Thurs 259–319 DM ($147.65–$181.85) double; Fri–Sat 182–222 DM ($103.75–$126.55) double. AE, DC, MC, V. Closed 2 weeks at Christmastime. Parking 18 DM ($10.25). Tram: 18 or 19.

Managed by a well-respected middle-bracket German hotel chain, this three-star, five-floor hotel was built in the 1960s but has been renovated many times since then. It's about a 5-minute walk from the Messegelände and the Oktoberfest grounds. Everything is modern, often attractively so, and convenient. Some rooms are equipped with balconies; there's a sauna, whirlpool, and solarium on the premises; and the hotel provides both laundry and baby-sitting services. Other than simple bar snacks and a generous morning buffet, there's no food served, but many dining options are nearby.

City Hotel. Schillerstrasse 3a, D-80336 München. ☎ **089/558091.** Fax 089/550-3665. 65 units. A/C MINIBAR TV TEL. 198 DM ($112.85) double during "normal" periods; 248 DM ($141.35) double during Oktoberfest and trade fairs. AE, DC, MC, V. U-Bahn: Hauptbahnhof.

This six-story hotel was built in 1972, not far from Munich's main railway station. Positioned midway between three- and four-star status by the local tourist authorities, it manages to combine coziness with a modern and efficient design and is a pleasant contrast to the congestion that's the norm all around it. Bedrooms are unfussy, uncomplicated, and blandly but comfortably outfitted in a modern international style. No meals are served other than a buffet breakfast, although there's a simple beer-hall-style restaurant on the building's street level that's popular with the crowd from the many offices and businesses nearby.

Erzgiesserei Europe. Erzgiessereistrasse 15, D-80335 München. ☎ **089/126820.** Fax 089/123-6198. 106 units. A/C MINIBAR TV TEL. 200 DM ($114) double; 400 DM ($228) suite. During trade fairs, 295 DM ($168.15) double; 500 DM ($285) suite. Rates include breakfast. AE, DC, MC, V. Parking 20 DM ($11.40). U-bahn: U1 to Steiglmaierplatz.

This clean, comfortable, and well-managed three-star hotel is less expensive than it probably should be. It was designed in a postmodern style in 1984, but its mansard roof and arched, balconied windows suggest turn-of-the-century architecture. It's in a working-class residential neighborhood, a short subway ride from more interesting haunts. Bedrooms are small but comfortable, with modern furniture; some overlook the carefully landscaped inner courtyard that's outfitted with tables, chairs, and potted shrubs and offers cafe service. On the premises is a restaurant decorated in a style of old-timey German nostalgia, Alt Wüttemberg, open daily for lunch and dinner.

✪ Hotel Carlton. Fürstenstrasse 12, D-80333 München. ☎ **089/282061.** Fax 089/284391. 50 units. MINIBAR TV TEL. 180–250 DM ($102.60–$142.50) double. Rates include breakfast. AE, DC, MC, V. Parking 20 DM ($11.40). U-bahn: U3 or U6 to Odeonsplatz.

Employees at this hotel are quick to point out that this Carlton has virtually nothing in common with those grander Carltons in, say, Cannes. But despite that, there's a certain pride in their maintenance of this five-floor arts-conscious hotel whose small but cozy bedrooms are outfitted with copies of Italian faux-baroque furniture and soft pastel colors. The hotel is within a short walk from many of the clubs and restaurants of Schwabing and draws a clientele that appreciates an ambience that's just funky and irreverent enough to be fun. There's an exercise room on the premises, and six of the bedrooms have private balconies.

Hotel Domus. St.-Anna-Strasse 31, D-80538 München. ☎ **089/2217-0408.** Fax 089/228-5359. 47 units. MINIBAR TV TEL. 220–260 DM ($125.40–$148.20) double; 280–300 DM ($159.60–$171) suite. Rates include breakfast. AE, DC, MC, V. Parking 15 DM ($8.55). U-Bahn: U4 or U5 to Lehel.

This sleekly modern, five-story hotel might sound like a university dormitory, but it isn't. Although it's rather large, it has some of the aspects of a private home. It's near the Englischer Garten—not so close to the historic area as the Torbräu (see above)—but parking is easier, a fact that endears it to many of its regular clients. On weekends the clientele might include visitors from other parts of Europe in Munich on a sightseeing binge; on weekdays the place has a high percentage of business travelers. Guest rooms are tastefully furnished in appealing monochromatic earth tones, and to help with an undisturbed night's sleep, the hotel pays special attention to the quality of its carpeting and doors. If you ask for breakfast in your room, you'll miss out on an exceptionally well-presented buffet.

Hotel Germania. Schwanthalerstrasse 28, D-80336 München. ☎ **089/590460.** Fax 089/591171. www.München.DE/Hotel/Germania. E-mail: Hotelgermania@München.DE. 97 units. TV TEL. 180–280 DM ($102.60–$159.60) double. Rates include breakfast. AE, MC, V. U-Bahn or S-Bahn: Hauptbahnhof.

This well-administered three-star contender was built after wartime damage reduced the vicinity of the railway station to rubble. The boxy, sedate building is not a particularly inspired architectural statement, and this is very much a functional hotel geared to busy traffic from business travelers and sightseers. The cost is relatively reasonable and the rooms, although not plush, are superior to those of other three-star hotels in the same neighborhood that charge comparable prices. There's an Italian restaurant, Salioni, on the premises, open Monday to Saturday for lunch and dinner.

Hotel König Ludwig. Hohenzollernstrasse 3, D-80801 München. ☎ **089/335995.** Fax 089/394658. 49 units. TV TEL MINIBAR. Fri–Sun 190 DM ($108.30) double, 250 DM ($142.50) suite; Mon–Thurs 210 DM ($119.70) double, 300 DM ($171) suite. Rates include breakfast. AE, DC, MC, V. Parking 15 DM ($8.55). U-Bahn: Giselastrasse.

Known mostly as a gay-friendly hotel in the 1980s just after it was built, the hotel is now under new management and has assumed a more restrained point of view. Near Munich's university, its six stories rise above a busy landscape. Bedrooms are monochromatic and rather blandly international in style. The staff is invariably tactful, polite, and helpful. The hotel still makes a point of welcoming the dozens of gay clients that continue to show up as a result of trickle-down effect of many years of gay promotion.

Hotel Mark. Senfelderstrasse 12, D-80336 München. ☎ **089/559820.** Fax 089/5598-2333. 90 units. MINIBAR TV TEL. 200–230 DM ($114–$131.10) double. Rates include buffet breakfast. AE, DC, MC, V. Parking 15 DM ($8.55). U-Bahn or S-Bahn: Hauptbahnhof.

This hotel near the Hauptbahnhof's south exit should be considered for its comfort and moderate prices. It offers serviceable amenities and up-to-date plumbing. The guest rooms are modern and functionally furnished, although a bit cramped. Breakfast is the only meal served.

Hotel Reinbold. Adolf-Kolping-Strasse 11, D-80336 München. ☎ **089/597945.** Fax 089/596272. 63 units. A/C MINIBAR TV TEL. 205 DM ($116.85) double; 275 DM ($156.75) suite. Rates include breakfast. Rates about 30% higher at Oktoberfest and during trade fairs. AE, DC, MC, V. Parking 18 DM ($10.25). U-Bahn or S-Bahn: Hauptbahnhof.

A no-nonsense, no-frills hotel, within a 3-minute walk of the railway station, the Reinbold delivers what it promises: a clean, decent room and efficient and polite service. Designed with six concrete and glass stories, it's a boxy-looking structure, most recently renovated in 1996. Bedrooms are compact, monochromatic, and comfortably (but not lavishly) furnished. Laundry services are provided on weekdays, but not on weekends. No meals other than breakfast are served, but there are many restaurants in this busy neighborhood.

Königswache. Steinheilstrasse 7, D-80333 München. ☎ **089/542-7570.** Fax 089/523-2114. 40 units. MINIBAR TV TEL. 290 DM ($165.30) double. Rates include buffet breakfast. AE, MC, V. Parking garage (reservation required) 12 DM ($6.85). U-Bahn: U2 to Königsplatz.

Although not as regal as its name, the Königswache has much to recommend it in spite of its sterile facade. The location, about a 10-minute ride from the Hauptbahnhof and only 2 minutes from the technical university, is between the Stachus and Schwabing. The staff speaks English. The relatively lackluster rooms are modern and comfortable and have writing desks. The hotel bar is decorated in a cozy, rustic style.

Kraft Hotel. Schillerstrasse 49, D-80336 München. ☎ **089/594823.** Fax 089/550-3856. 39 units. TV TEL. 210 DM ($119.70) double; 260 DM ($148.20) double during Oktoberfest and trade fairs. Rates include breakfast. AE, DC, MC, V. U-Bahn: Sendlingertorplatz.

One of the most appealing things about this simple, three-star hotel is its location in the heart of the Altstadt, within a few minutes' walk of the Sendlingertorplatz, and a 5-minute walk from the railway station. Architecturally, it's not very appealing, in the style of boxy architecture so widespread in Munich after World War II. Bedrooms are streamlined and efficiently designed, usually with some built-in furniture. There's no restaurant on the premises, but many dining options are within a short walk of the hotel.

SKH-Trustee Parkhotel. Parkstrasse 31, D-80339 München. ☎ **089/519950.** Fax 089/5199-5420. 35 units. A/C MINIBAR TV TEL. 235 DM ($133.95) double; 395 DM ($225.15) suite. Rates include breakfast. AE, DC, MC, V. Parking 15 DM ($8.55). U-bahn: U1 to Schwanenthalerhöhe.

In a verdant residential neighborhood at the edge of Munich's fairgrounds and Oktoberfest site, this three-story hotel evokes an upscale apartment building. Flowers and plants festoon its balconies, and its blue-and-red bedrooms, with views over a nicely landscaped courtyard, are larger than you might expect. Each well-kept and tastefully furnished unit has floor-to-ceiling windows that flood the interior with sunlight, and an English-speaking staff is able to give advice about diversions within the city. The hotel contains a bistro that's open daily for lunch and dinner, plus a conference room. The hotel is family friendly and provides baby-sitting if requested.

✪ Splendid. Maximilianstrasse 54, D-80538 München. ☎ **089/296606.** Fax 089/291-3176. 40 units (32 with bath). TV TEL. 140–200 DM ($79.80–$114) double without bath, 200–310 DM ($114–$176.70) double with bath; 260–490 DM ($148.20–$279.30) suite. Rates include buffet breakfast. AE, DC, DISC, MC, V. Free parking. U-Bahn: U4 or U5. Tram: 19 or 20.

The Splendid is one of the most attractive old-world hotels in Munich. Public rooms are decorated with antiques, oriental rugs, and chandeliers. Each guestroom reflects the owner's desire to evoke the aura of a country home. Most are in a style known as "Bavarian baroque," although two have recently been remodeled in the Louis XVI style. Room prices are scaled according to time of year, size, furnishings, and plumbing, with the highest prices charged at fair and festival times. On sunny mornings many guests prefer to breakfast on the trellised patio. Baby-sitting can be arranged, and room service is provided.

INEXPENSIVE

✪ Am Markt. Heiliggeiststrasse 6, D-80331 München. ☎ **089/225014.** Fax 089/224017. 32 units (13 with bath). TV TEL. 112 DM ($63.85) double without bath, 160 DM ($91.20) double with bath. Rates include continental breakfast. No credit cards. Parking 12 DM ($6.85). S-Bahn: From the Hauptbahnhof, take any S-Bahn train headed for Marienplatz, a two-stop ride from the station.

This popular Bavarian hotel stands in the heart of the older section. The hotel is not luxurious, but owner Harald Herrler has wisely maintained a nostalgic decor in the lobby and dining room. Behind his reception desk is a wall of photographs of former guests, including the late Viennese chanteuse Greta Keller. As Mr. Herrler points out, at breakfast you're likely to find yourself surrounded by opera and concert artists who stay here because it's close to where they perform. The guest rooms are basic modern—small but trim and neat. All units have hot and cold running water, with free use of the corridor baths and toilets.

Europäischer Hof. Bayerstrasse 31, D-80335 München. ☎ **089/551510.** Fax 089/5515-1222. E-mail: heh_munich@compuserve.com. 153 units (139 with bath or shower and toilet). MINIBAR TV TEL. 109–150 DM ($62.15–$85.50) double without bath or shower and toilet, 179–239 DM ($102.05–$136.25) double with bath or shower and toilet. Rates include breakfast. AE, DC, MC, V. Parking 16 DM ($9.10). U-Bahn or S-Bahn: Hauptbahnhof.

This nine-story hotel opposite the Hauptbahnhof still has the chapel that served its original builders back in 1960, an order of Catholic nuns (order of the Holy Family). Now run by the Sturzer family, the establishment offers simple but clean accommodations, some of which overlook an inner courtyard. Most rooms have some built-in furniture; all have double-glazed windows for soundproofing. All have radios, some contain minibars. Despite its dreary location, the hotel is clean and well managed, with cozy touches. Breakfast is the only meal served, although a likable Italian restaurant, Ca d'Oro, occupies part of the building's street level.

Hotel Jedermann. Bayerstrasse 95, D-80335 München. ☎ **089/533267.** Fax 089/536506. www.hotel-jedermann.de. E-mail: hotel-jedermann@cube.net. 55 units (34 with shower and toilet). TV TEL. 95–140 DM ($54.15–$79.80) double without shower and toilet, 130–220 DM ($74.10–$125.40) double with shower and toilet; 110–185 DM ($62.70–$105.45) triple without shower and toilet, 155–265 DM ($88.35–$151.05) triple with shower and toilet. Rates include buffet breakfast. MC, V. Parking 10 DM ($5.70). Ten-minute walk from Hauptbahnhof (turn right on Bayerstrasse from south exit).

This pleasant, cozy spot has been deftly run by the Jenke family since 1961. Renovated and enlarged in 1990, its central location and good value make it a desirable choice. It has a wood-paneled interior and Bavarian furnishings and is an apt choice for families; cribs or cots are available. A generous breakfast buffet is served in a charming room; Bavarian fare can be arranged for lunch or dinner from one of the restaurants in the vicinity.

Hotel Wallis. Schwanthalerstrasse 8, D-80336 München. ☎ **089/591664.** Fax 089/550-3752. E-mail: Hotel.Wallis@T-online.DE. 54 units. TV TEL. 159 DM ($90.65) double. During trade fairs and Oktoberfest, 289 DM ($164.75) double. AE, DC, MC, V. U-Bahn: Karlsplatz.

Unpretentious, uncomplicated, and comfortable, this three-star hotel's Bavarian-inspired interior is warmer and cozier than you'd imagine after a look at its angular postwar exterior. Bedrooms are relatively small, but they were renovated in 1995 and furnished with a simplified version of alpine-village style. Only breakfast is served, but there's a bar on the premises, and many worthwhile restaurants within a short walk. The staff is polite and helpful to newcomers navigating their way around the city. Don't even think of checking in here during Oktoberfest—its proximity to the Hofbräuhaus virtually guarantees it will be fully booked.

✪ **Pension beim Haus der Kunst.** Bruderstrasse 4, D-80538 München. ☎ **089/222127.** Fax 089/834-8248. www.major.com/bronchen/pension-gb.htm. 9 units (none with bath), 1 apt (with bath). 95 DM ($54.15) double; 220 DM ($125.40) apt for 4. Rates include breakfast. No credit cards. U-Bahn: Lehel.

Noted for an ideal location near the Englischer Garten, copious breakfasts, and warm hospitality, this low-key, inexpensive, and well-run small pension is one of Munich's best. Early reservations are important here. The establishment's apartment contains the only private bath; guests in the other rooms (all doubles) must share the facilities in the hallways. Parking, when available, is free on the street.

Pension Stadt München. Dultstrasse 1, D-80331 München. ☎ **089/263417.** Fax 089/267548. 4 units (all with shower, none with WC). 120 DM ($68.40) double. Rates include breakfast. AE, MC, V. Metro: Marienplatz.

One of the simplest and least expensive hotels in downtown Munich is positioned one floor above street level in an old-fashioned building near the city's most important square. There's a heavy percentage of backpackers and gay men and women at this place, where keys to the front door are distributed as part of the deal. No meals are served other than breakfast. Bedrooms are comfortable, anonymous-looking, and clean, albeit a bit battered and utterly without decorative accessories. Each has a sink and shower, although the WCs are shared facilities accessible via the corridors.

✪ Pension Westfalia. Mozartstrasse 23, D-80336 München. ☎ **089/530377.** Fax 089/543-9120. 19 units (11 with bath). TV TEL. 90 DM ($51.30) double without bath, 115–130 DM ($65.55–$74.10) double with bath. Rates include buffet breakfast. AE, V. U-Bahn: U3 or U6 to Goetheplatz. Bus: 58 from the Hauptbahnhof.

Facing the meadow where the annual Oktoberfest takes place, this four-story town house near Goetheplatz is one of Munich's best pensions, offering immaculately maintained guest rooms, many with TVs. Owner Peter Deiritz speaks English. Parking is free on the street, when available.

Uhland Garni. Uhlandstrasse 1, D-80336 München. ☎ **089/543350.** Fax 089/5433-5250. www.munich_online.de/uhland. E-mail: Hotel_Uhland@compuserve.com. 30 units. MINIBAR TV TEL. 150–280 DM ($85.50–$159.60) double. Rates include buffet breakfast. AE, DC, MC, V. Free parking. Bus: 58.

This family-owned (since 1955) hotel in a residential area offers friendly, personal service and could easily become your home in Munich. The stately art nouveau–style mansion stands in its own small garden. Its bedrooms are soundproof, and all are snug, traditional, and cozy. Only breakfast is served. The hotel is just a 10-minute walk from the Hauptbahnhof.

Utzelmann. Pettenkoferstrasse 6, D-80336 München. ☎ **089/594889.** Fax 089/596228. 11 units (4 with shower and toilet). 95 DM ($54.15) double without bath, 110 DM ($62.70) double with shower only, 145 DM ($82.65) double with shower and toilet. Rates include breakfast. No credit cards. U-Bahn: Sendlingertorplatz.

A 12-minute walk south of Munich's center, this pension is in a stripped-down house originally built about a century ago. The atmosphere inside is familylike. Its owners, Hermann Ernst and his hardworking wife, have freshened everything with furniture, carpeting, and modern toilets.

3 In Schwabing

EXPENSIVE

✪ München Marriott Hotel. Berliner Strasse 93, D-80805 München. ☎ **800/228-9290** or 089/360020. Fax 089/3600-2200. 360 units. A/C MINIBAR TV TEL. 240–285 DM ($136.80–$162.45) double; from 485 DM ($276.45) suite. During selected nonpeak weekends, 200 DM ($114) double. AE, DC, MC, V. Parking 24 DM ($13.70). U-Bahn: U6 to Nord Friedhof.

Marriott's usual postmodern style fits appropriately into this verdant setting along the northern tier of Schwabing. Built in 1990, about 2½ miles north of Munich's historic core, it offers a well-designed, Americanized venue whose German staff welcomes travelers from throughout Europe. Bedrooms are standard and identical, but the lobby is one of the most appealing in Schwabing, with blond wood, marble, potted plants, and sunlight streaming in from all sides. While the hotel caters to conventions and tour groups, individual travelers are not ignored by the highly motivated staff.

Dining/Diversions: A cafe and bar serve simple platters, and the California Grill interprets Pacific coast cuisine into a culinary oddity (at least in Munich) that has enjoyed great success.

Amenities: On the premises is a business center with conference rooms; a hardworking concierge; a health club with sauna, Jacuzzi, and exercise equipment; dry cleaning and laundry services; and baby-sitting.

MODERATE

✪ **Holiday Inn Crowne Plaza Munich.** Leopoldstrasse 194, D-80804 Munich. ☎ **800/ 465-4329** in the U.S., or 089/381790. Fax 089/3817-9888. 367 units. MINIBAR TV TEL. 190–230 DM ($108.30–$131.10) double; 850 DM ($484.50) suite. During Oktoberfest and trade fairs, 550 DM ($313.50) double; 850 DM ($484.50) suite. During selected weekends, 220 DM ($125.40) double, with breakfast included. Breakfast is 29 DM ($16.55). AE, DC, MC, V. Parking 23 DM ($13.10). U-Bahn: U3 or U6 to Münchner Freiheit.

This hotel with its two eight-story towers was built to house visitors to the 1972 Olympics. It's near the Olympic Stadium, about 3 miles north of the historic center. As a member of the deluxe upper tier of the Holiday Inn chain, it offers lots of features to attract guests. The lobby is stylish, and bedrooms are outfitted with big, carefully soundproofed windows and contemporary, uncontroversial furnishings. Rooms on the upper floor, facing south, benefit from views of the city and the faraway Alps; others overlook the suburbs and the urban sprawl surrounding Munich's northern tier.

On the premises are two restaurants, one a folksy Bavarian eatery whose name, *Omas Küche* or "Grandmother's Kitchen," conveys the style of cuisine it serves; another focuses on Italian cuisine. There is a heated indoor pool, a sauna, and a solarium, disco with live entertainment on weekends, and a full roster of business services. Because of the hotel's easy access from the Autobahns funneling into Munich from points north (including Autobahn Nürnberg-Berlin-Frankfurt), it's especially convenient for motorists.

Hotel Leopold. Leopoldstrasse 119, D-80804 München-Schwabing. ☎ **089/367061.** Fax 089/3604-3150. 90 units. TV TEL. 175–225 DM ($99.75–$128.25) double. During trade fairs and Oktoberfest 235 DM ($133.95) double. Rates include breakfast. AE, DC, MC, V. Parking 5 DM ($2.85). U-Bahn: U3 or U4 to Münchner Freiheit.

The core of this unusual hotel is a Jugendstil villa that was built as a private home in 1924. A modern annex is connected to the original house with a glass-sided passageway, and there's a garden area that belonged to the original house. It's close to an exit road of the Autobahn Nürnberg-Würzburg-Berlin, which gives the place the atmosphere of a suburban motel with plentiful parking. Despite the verdant setting, however, the hotel lies only four subway stops from the Marienplatz, and the Englischer Garten is only a few minutes' walk away. Public areas have traditional Bavarian motifs. Rooms in the old section have been modernized to make them equivalent to rooms in the new section, and all have been made as soundproof as possible.

INEXPENSIVE

✪ **Gästehaus Englischer Garten.** Liebergesellstrasse 8, D-80802 München-Schwabing. ☎ **089/383-9410.** Fax 089/3839-4133. 27 units (21 with bath). MINIBAR TV TEL. 130 DM ($74.10) double without bath, 156–192 DM ($88.90–$109.45) double with bath. No credit cards. Parking 10 DM ($5.70). U-Bahn: U3 or U6 to Münchner Freiheit.

This oasis of charm and tranquillity, close to the Englischer Garten, is one of our preferred stopovers in the Bavarian capital. The ivy-covered villa was once a private house, but for some two decades now Frau Irene Schlüter-Hubscher has operated it as a hotel. All the rooms are attractively furnished. Across the street is an annex with 15 small apartment units, all with bath and tiny kitchenettes. Try for rooms 16, 23, 26, or especially 20. In fair weather, breakfast is served in a rear garden.

4 In Olympiapark

✪ **Arabella Olympiapark Hotel München.** Helene-Mayer-Ring 12, D-80809 München. ☎ **089/351-6071.** Fax 089/3575-1800. 105 units. MINIBAR TV TEL. 170–370 DM

($96.90–$210.90) double. AE, DC, MC, V. Free parking. U-Bahn: U2 or U3 to Olympia Centrum.

Near the stadium, right at Europe's biggest sports and recreation center, this hotel will appeal to people who want to be near all the major sports action. Its guest rooms are among the most modern and best kept in the city, and sports heroes, both European and American, often stroll casually through the lobby. There's no need to drive into the city center: The U-Bahn will whisk you there in minutes. If you want to unwind after a tough night in the beer halls, you'll find a refreshing pool, a sauna, and a massage room at the nearby Olympiapark.

5 In Haidhausen

VERY EXPENSIVE

München City Hilton. Rosenheimerstrasse 15, D-81667 München. ☎ **800/455-8687** in the U.S. and Canada, or 089/48040. Fax 089/4804-4804. www.hilton.com. 499 units. A/C MINIBAR TV TEL. 390–550 DM ($222.30–$313.50) double; from 600 DM ($342) suite. AE, DC, MC, V. Parking 25 DM ($14.25). S-Bahn: S1, S2, S3, S4, S5, S6, S7, or S8 to Rosenheimer Platz.

When it opened in 1989, the München City Hilton became the second Hilton to grace the city skyline. Located beside the Deutsches Museum and the Gasteig performing arts center, the low-rise hotel is designed with red brick, shimmering glass, and geometric windows divided by white bands of metal reminiscent of a Mondrian painting. The historic center is an invigorating 25-minute walk across the river. The traditional guest rooms contain modern adaptations of Biedermeier furniture, plush carpeting, and cable TV. The hotel staff is sensitive to visitor needs.

Dining/Diversions: The Hilton offers good drinking and dining facilities, including Zum Gasteig, a Bavarian restaurant decorated in a typical style; Löwen-Schanke, a Bavarian pub; and Café Lenbach, where you can order a leisurely breakfast or afternoon tea.

Amenities: 24-hour room service, laundry, dry cleaning, baby-sitting, flower shop, newsstand.

EXPENSIVE

Preysing. Preysingstrasse 1, D-81667 München. ☎ **089/458450.** Fax 089/4584-5444. 81 units. A/C MINIBAR TV TEL. 328 DM ($186.95) double; 375–540 DM ($213.75–$307.80) suite. Rates include breakfast. AE, DC, MC, V. Closed Dec 23–Jan 6. Parking 18 DM ($10.25). Tram: 18.

If you don't mind a hotel on the outskirts and you want a quiet location, one of the best places to stay is the Preysing, across the Isar near the Deutsches Museum (a short tram ride will take you into the center of the city). When you first view the building, a seven-story modern structure, you may feel we've misled you—but if you've gone this far, venture inside for a pleasant surprise.

The family who runs the hotel has one of the most thoughtful staffs in Munich, and the hotel's style is most agreeable, with dozens of little extras to provide homelike comfort. Fresh flowers are everywhere, and the furnishings, traditional combined with modern, have been carefully selected. Rooms have many amenities.

Dining/Diversions: Preysing's restaurant is one of the finest in Munich (see separate listing chapter 5).

Amenities: Room service, laundry, baby-sitting, indoor pool, sauna, solarium, Jacuzzi.

6 In Bogenhausen

EXPENSIVE

✪ Arabella Hotel Bogenhausen. Arabellastrasse 5, D-81925 München. ☎ **089/92320.** Fax 089/9232-4449. 499 units. A/C MINIBAR TV TEL. 245–305 DM ($139.65–$173.85) double; 385–635 DM ($219.45–$361.95) suite during "normal" times. During Oktoberfest and trade fairs, 285–345 DM ($162.45–$196.65) double; 685–935 DM ($390.45–$532.95) suite. AE, DC, MC, V. Parking 18 DM ($10.25). U-Bahn: U4 to Arabellapark.

In the verdant suburb of Bogenhausen, seven subway stops north of the Odeon-splatz, this is one of Munich's largest hotels and one of the most imaginatively designed in the Arabella chain. It was lavishly renovated in 1995, when all but the cheapest category of rooms were upgraded. Top-category rooms are outfitted in burgundy with lots of paneling in an international style that echoes the feel of the glossy public areas. Other accommodations are in Bavarian *Landhaus* style, with replicas of the kind of solid and dignified furniture you might have found in the home of a prosperous Bavarian burgher early in the century.

Dining/Diversions: Restaurants include The Brasserie and Capriccio (the more formal of the two). Both serve Bavarian, continental, and international cuisine.

Amenities: Room service, concierge, laundry, baby-sitting, indoor pool on the 22nd floor with its own waterfall, five whirlpools, three steam rooms with a decor inspired by ancient Rome, two saunas, solariums, exercise equipment, a poolside bar, and a grove of indoor palm trees.

Hotel Palace. Trogerstrasse 21, D-81675 Bogenhausen. ☎ **089/419710.** Fax 089/4197-1819. 78 units. Sun–Thurs 335–395 DM ($190.95–$225.15) double, Fri–Sat 285–325 DM ($162.45–$185.25) double; 450–1,500 DM ($256.50–$855) suite. AE, DC, MC, V. Parking 25 DM ($14.25). U-bahn: U4 or U5 to Prinzregentenplatz.

A 5-minute walk from Munich's Englischer Garten, this five-star, seven-story hotel was built in a modern internationalist style in 1987. It's located in Bogenhausen, a verdant suburb 3 miles east of Munich's historic core. It has stylish public areas with lots of 19th-century antiques and a well-trained but sometimes overworked staff. Guest rooms are conservatively modern, with big windows, big curtains, and pastel colors.

Dining/Diversions: In addition to the hotel's chic bar, there's a formal restaurant with a reverential hush and an excellent cuisine, both Bavarian specialties and international dishes. In addition, there's a garden terrace where waiters will serve you coffee or a drink.

Amenities: There's an exercise room on the hotel's fourth floor, plus room service, concierge, dry cleaning/laundry, and baby-sitting upon arrangement.

👥 Family-Friendly Hotels

Gästehaus Englischer Garten (*see p. 78*)   An oasis of calm and tranquillity near the Englischer Garten, this ivy-covered villa provides an old-fashioned family atmosphere.

Arabella Olympiapark Hotel München (*see p. 78*)   Right at Europe's biggest sports and recreation center, this hotel rents many triple rooms—ideal for families—and there are lots of activities for kids to enjoy in the area.

Hotel Jedermann (*see p. 76*)   This hotel, which is family run, also caters to families on a budget and has cribs or cots available.

München Sheraton. Arabellastrasse 6, D-81925 München. ☎ **089/92640.** Fax 089/916877. www.Sheraton.com. 653 units. A/C MINIBAR TV TEL. 210–480 DM ($119.70–$273.60) double; 970–2,000 DM ($552.90–$1,140) suite. AE, DC, MC, V. Parking 21 DM ($11.95). U-Bahn: U4 to Arabellapark.

This is the largest hotel in Munich, set in the northern suburb of Bogenhausen, about seven subway stops from downtown Munich. A sprawling giant, and somewhat anonymous, it's well accustomed to welcoming groups of sightseers, salespeople from around the world, and businesspeople from international corporations. This is a hotel that's hard to ignore, towering as it does, 22 stories above the surrounding northern suburbs. Although the hotel has a lot to offer, it's beginning to look just a bit worn, since the last renovations, around 1991, left some parts of the hotel unchanged. But with so many facilities, and a willingness to discount rooms (based on occupancy), it's still a worthy choice.

Dining/Diversions: In addition to its bars, the hotel has two restaurants, the Atrium, with a design of modern, intra-European pizzazz, and the rustic and *gemütlich* Alt Bayern Stube. There's also a nightclub under separate management.

Amenities: Concierge, laundry, health club, 65-foot indoor pool, solarium, fitness room, sauna, massage parlor, shopping arcade, and an in-house branch of Avis Rent-a-Car.

7 At Neu-Perlach

Novotel München. Rudolf-Vogel-Bogen 3, D-18739 München. ☎ **800/221-4542** in the U.S., or 089/638000. Fax 089/635-1309. 253 units. MINIBAR TV TEL. Mon–Thurs 242 DM ($137.95) double, Fri–Sun 158 DM ($90.05) double. During trade fairs and Oktoberfest, weekday rate applies throughout the weekend. Children up to 16 stay free in parents' room. AE, DC, MC, V. U-Bahn: Neuperlach Sud.

Set in a suburb 3 miles southeast of Munich's center, this hotel is a 15-minute (eight-stop) subway ride from the Marienplatz. It's a comfortable, uncharacteristically large member of a worldwide French chain and a favorite with business travelers and families who like the Novotel formula of standardized modern bedrooms, no-nonsense efficiency, pan-European anonymity, and easy access to motorways. There's an indoor pool, a bar that does a brisk business with an international crowd, and a restaurant that serves well-prepared, albeit formulaic, food in generous portions.

8 At Untermenzing

✪ **Romantik Hotel Insel Mühle.** Von-Kahr-Strasse 87, D-80999 München-Untermenzing. ☎ **089/81010.** Fax 089/812-0571. 40 units. TV TEL. 300 DM ($171) double; 410 DM ($233.70) suite. Rates include breakfast. DC, MC, V. Free parking. S-Bahn: Pasing, then bus 76.

Until 1985 this 16th-century stone-sided mill in its isolated position beside the Würm (a tributary of the Isar), 6 miles west of the Marienplatz, was left to ruin and decay. The present-day restoration has retained part of the mill's 1506 construction. Although the hotel's reputation is based mainly on its atmospheric restaurant, it also provides a charming alternative to Munich's many large, modern hotels. The decor and design of each guest room is different—some have sloping garretlike ceilings. Rooms have thick carpets, attractive upholstery, and stylish accessories.

The real beauty of the place can be seen in the massive beams of the dining room and in the mellow brick vaults of the wine cellar. There's a plank-covered wharf where parasols shield diners from the midday sun. The cuisine features well-prepared Bavarian and continental dishes. Down-on-the-farm menu items include medaillons of veal in a mushroom-flavored cream sauce, with fresh vegetables; rack of venison; roasted goose with black-currant dressing; and fish selections that usually include sole and halibut. Meals are served Monday to Saturday from noon to 2pm and 6 to 10pm.

9 Near the Airport

Kempinski Hotel Airport München. Terminalstrasse 20, D-85356 München. ☎ **800/ 426-3135** in the U.S., or 089/97820. Fax 089/9782-2610. www.kempinski-airport.de. E-mail: beatrix.bauer@kempinski.com. 389 units. A/C MINIBAR TV TEL. 350–410 DM ($199.50– $233.70) double; 950–1,400 DM ($541.50–$798) suite. AE, DC, MC, V. Parking 12.50 DM ($7.10). U-Bahn: Airport.

When it was built between the runways of Munich's airports in 1993, it was noted as the most architecturally innovative airport hotel in Europe. Partially owned by Lufthansa, it was designed by a Chicago-based architect of German descent, Helmet Jahn, with a four-story shimmering glass and steel exterior and an interior design whose colorful, postmodern accents ward off the monochromatic landscape of the surrounding airport. Despite its nearness to runways, the hotel's guest rooms are soothing and silent, the result of careful and effective soundproofing. A soaring lobby contains a subtropical garden with palms and has views over one of Europe's busiest airports.

Dining/Diversions: The Charles Lindbergh restaurant, with its bar, serves a well-prepared repertoire of both international and Bavarian dishes.

Amenities: Business center, 24-hour room service, sauna, steam bath, solarium, fitness center.

Dining 5

Munich is one of the few European cities that has more than one "three-star" restaurant, and some of its sophisticated eating places are among the finest anywhere. This is the place to practice *Edelfresswelle* ("high-class gluttony"). There are many local specialties as well as international cuisine. The classic local dish is, of course, Weisswurst, herb-flavored white veal sausages blanched in water and traditionally consumed before noon.

It is said that Münchners consume more beer than people in any other German city. Bernd Boehle once wrote: "If a man really belongs to Munich he drinks beer at all times of the day, at breakfast, at midday, at teatime, and in the evening, of course, he just never stops." The place where every first-time visitor heads for at least one eating and drinking fest is the Hofbräuhaus am Platzl. It's described later in chapter 9.

1 Best Bets

- **Best Spot for a Romantic Dinner: Grünwalder Einkehr** (☎ 089/649-2304) lets you escape from the urban sprawl of Munich to a "green lung" retreat 8 miles south of the center. In a 200-year-old former private home in a rustic setting, you can feast on French-inspired dishes that include many Gallic favorites. It's the best place to get away from it all.
- **Best Spot for a Business Lunch: Mark's Restaurant** (☎ 089/290980), in the deluxe hotel Rafael, is the chic business luncheon spot of Munich. The movers and shakers of the Bavarian capital gather in the informal lobby-level setting of Mark's corner to make the big deal. Menu items change according to the season and the inspiration of the chef, and, as you dine, you can practically feel Deutsche Marks changing hands.
- **Best Spot for a Celebration: Kay's Bistro** (☎ 089/260-3584) is number one on the see-and-be-seen circuit. Sophisticated and chic, it's also lots of fun. It's filled nightly with a glamorous clientele who like not only good food but a festive restaurant in which to celebrate their latest deal, marriage, or divorce (whatever). The decoration is always changing based on the season, but the French and international cuisine remains eternally alluring.
- **Best Decor:** The **Garden Restaurant** (☎ 089/21200), in the Bayerischer Hof Hotel, evokes the interior of a small, pastel-colored

palace with references to gardening and blooming plants. Serving upscale food to a cosmopolitan crowd, it offers completely fresh ingredients—flown in from virtually everywhere—that complement the soothing decor.

- **Best Wine List: Geisel's Vinothek** (☎ **089/5513-7140**), in the Hotel Excelsior, is the best spot in Munich for a taste of the grape. Dedicated to Bacchus, this deliberately unpretentious choice has one of the city's finest collections of Italian, French, Austrian, and German wines—all sold by the glass. You can also order Italian cuisine.
- **Best Value: Palais Keller** (☎ **089/212-0990**) offers great value, although it's housed in the cellar of one of the most elegant hotels in Munich. Its well-prepared cuisine of Bavarian and German dishes is priced about the same as far less desirable beer halls and Weinstuben nearby. Let a smiling waitress in a frilly apron introduce you to *Tafelspitz,* the fabled boiled beef dish of the Teutonic world.
- **Best for Kids: Mövenpick Restaurant** (☎ **089/545-9490**) is right in the heart of Munich and decorated with a whimsical theme; different rooms are devoted to different cuisines, everything from the Longhorn Corner for Texas-style steaks to Grandma's Kitchen for some old-fashioned cookery. Kids like to come here for a full meal of just *Rösti,* those fabled Swiss fried potatoes.
- **Best Continental Cuisine: Tantris** (☎ **089/361-9590**), in Schwabing, serves the city's most refined cuisine, a treat to the eye as well as the palate. Chef Hans Haas is one of the top chefs of Germany and is forever sharpening his culinary skills as he wines and dines the celebrated people of Europe. Nothing in Munich equals the service, flavors, and delight found here.
- **Best French Cuisine: Bistro Terrine's** (☎ **089/281780**) food tastes so authentically French you'll think you're back in Lyon. Menu items are often more inventive than the fin-de-siècle atmosphere of this art-nouveau bistro in Schwabing implies. The menu changes with the seasons—for example, in autumn nuggets of venison might appear with a hazelnut-flavored gnocchi and port wine sauce.
- **Best Italian Cuisine: Buon Gusto** (☎ **089/296383**) is an elegant choice for Italian cuisine, the finest in Munich, where the competition grows increasingly stiff. A rustic-looking bistro with an open kitchen, this restaurant's chefs are masters of Italian cookery, especially the simple but flavorful dishes of Tuscany. Pasta dishes—each homemade and succulent—are meals unto themselves.
- **Best Seafood: Austernkeller** (☎ **089/298787**) prepares not only the freshest oysters in town but also an array of delectable seafood selections that range from mussels to clams and sea snails to the wonderful lobster Thermidor. The kitsch collection of plastic lobsters shouldn't put you off: The food is far more worthy than the decor.
- **Best Bavarian Cuisine: Nürnberger Bratwurst Glöckl Am Dom** (☎ **089/ 295264**) is Munich's coziest restaurant. Here you can enjoy a Bavarian cuisine so authentic that it's hardly changed since the turn of the century (the restaurant opened first in 1893). Bavarians, often looking as stern as one of the Dürer prints on the wall, come here for all their favorite dishes—just like grandmother made a hundred years ago.
- **Best Late-Night Dining: Käfer's Am Hofgarten** (☎ **089/290-7530**) is good and yuppie oriented, and the dining scene goes on weekends until three in the morning. It's a fashionable French bistro with amazingly reasonable prices, and you can enjoy an international array of food, inspired by every place from America to Thailand.

- **Best Outdoor Dining: Locanda Picolit** (☎ **089/396447**), an Italian restaurant in the heart of Schwabing, offers an outdoor terrace in summer with a view over a garden that's one of the most evocative in Munich. The place suggests a Mediterranean world. Menu items change with the season, and you can enjoy the agrarian bounty of Italy while doing some people-watching and soaking up the fresh breezes blowing across Munich at the same time.
- **Best People-Watching: Graffunder** (☎ **089/292427**), is on Marienplatz, the virtual heart of Munich, and here you can take in the passing parade while enjoying a selection of French and Italian wines sold by the glass. Platters of food ranging from simple snacks to more elaborate concoctions are also served. But it's the landmark square of Marienplatz itself, the very center of the city's festive life, that's the real attraction.
- **Best for Pretheater Dinner: Spatenhaus** (☎ **089/290-7060**), across the street from the opera house on Max-Joseph-Platz, is the ideal dining venue if you're going to the opera or one of the theaters nearby. It's Munich's best-known beer restaurant but definitely not a beer hall. It's handsomely appointed and rather conservatively decorated and has excellent Bavarian and international fare. Since the restaurant is open in the afternoon, you can drop in quite early for a meal before a performance.
- **Best Picnic Fare: Alois Dallmayr** (☎ **089/213-5100**) offers not only the best picnic fare in Munich, but the best in Germany. With the food you can gather up here, you could even invite the queen of England for lunch in the Englischer Garten. One of the world's most renowned delis, this supermarket of goodies has elegant selections like foie gras, but it also offers more democratically priced fare.

2 Restaurants by Cuisine

ALPINE

Zum Bürgerhaus (Central Munich, *I*)

AMERICAN

Park Hilton Grill (Central Munich, *VE*)

Planet Hollywood (Central Munich, *I*)

AUSTRIAN

Nymphenburger Hof (Nymphenburg, *M*)

BAVARIAN

Asam Schlössel (South of Center, *I*)

Bamberger Haus (Schwabing, *M*)

Biergärten Chinesischer Turm (Schwabing, *I*)

Chesa Rüegg (Central Munich, *M*)

Donisl (Central Munich, *I*)

Gaststätte zum Flaucher (South of Center, *I*)

Grünwalder Einkehr (Grünwald, *I*)

Halali (Central Munich, *M*)

Hirschgarten (Nymphenburg, *I*)

Hundskugel (Central Munich, *I*)

Nürnberger Bratwurst Glöckl Am Dom (Central Munich, *I*)

Palais Keller (Central Munich, *I*)

Ratskeller München (Central Munich, *M*)

Spatenhaus (Central Munich, *M*)

Straubinger Hof (Central Munich, *I*)

Weinbauer (Schwabing, *I*)

Weinhaus Neuner (Central Munich, *M*)

Weisses Brauhaus (Central Munich, *I*)

Zum Alten Markt (Central Munich, *M*)

Zum Aumeister (Freimann, *I*)

Key to abbreviations: *VE* = Very Expensive, *E* = Expensive, *M* = Moderate, *I* = Inexpensive

BEER GARDENS

Bamberger Haus (Schwabing, *M*))
Biergärten Chinesischer Turm
    (Schwabing, *I*)
Gaststätte zum Flaucher (South of
    Center, *I*)
Hirschgarten (Nymphenburg, *I*)
Zum Aumeister (Freimann, *I*)

CAFES

Café Glockenspiel (Central Munich)
Café Luitpold (Central Munich)
Guglhopf (Central Munich)
Ruffini (Rotkreuzplatz)
Schlosscafé im Palmenhaus
    (Nymphenburg)

CONTINENTAL

Alois Dallmayr (Central Munich, *M*)
Bar-Restaurant Moritzz (Central
    Munich, *M*)
Gastehaus Glockenbach
    (Südbahnhof, *E*)
Lenbach (Central Munich, *M*)
Mark's Restaurant (Central
    Munich, *M*)
Park Hilton Grill (Central
    Munich, *VE*)

FRENCH

Bistro Terrine (Schwabing, *E*)
Graffunder (Central Munich, *I*)
Kay's Bistro (Central Munich, *E*)
Prielhof (Bogenhausen, *E*)
Tantris (Schwabing, *VE*)

GERMAN

Andechser am Dom (Central
    Munich, *I*)
Bogenhauser Hof (Bogenhausen, *E*)
Käfer-Schänke (Bogenhausen, *E*)
Palais Keller (Central Munich, *I*)
Preysing-Keller (Haidhausen, *E*)

HUNGARIAN

Tokajer Weinkeller-und-Pilsstube
    (Schwabing, *M*)

INTERNATIONAL

Asam Schlössel (South of Center, *I*)
Bar-Restaurant Moritzz (Central
    Munich, *M*)

Bogenhauser Hof (Bogenhausen, *E*)
Donisl (Central Munich, *I*)
Garden Restaurant (Central
    Munich, *VE*)
Hunsiger's Pacific (Central
    Munich, *M*)
Kafer's Am Hofgarten (Central
    Munich, *I*)
Käfer-Schänke (Bogenhausen, *E*)
Kay's Bistro (Central Munich, *E*)
Mövenpick Restaurant (Central
    Munich, *M*)
Preysing-Keller (Haidhausen, *E*)
Restaurant Königshof (Central
    Munich, *VE*)
Restaurant Vier Jahreszeiten (Central
    Munich, *VE*)
Spatenhaus (Central Munich, *M*)
Tantris (Schwabing, *VE*)
Zum Alten Markt (Central
    Munich, *M*)

ITALIAN

Al Pino (Solln, *I*)
Buon Gusto (Central Munich, *M*)
Casale (Denning, *M*)
Der Katzlmacher (Schwabing, *M*)
Galleria (Central Munich, *E*)
Geisel's Vinothek (Central Munich, *I*)
Graffunder (Central Munich, *I*)
La Mucca (Schwabing, *M*)
Locanda Picolit (Schwabing, *E*)
Spago (Schwabing, *M*)

MEDITERRANEAN

Garden Restaurant (Central
    Munich, *VE*)
Lenbach (Central Munich, *M*)

SEAFOOD

Austernkeller (Central Munich, *M*)

SWISS

Chesa Rüegg (Central Munich, *M*)
Mövenpick Restaurant (Central
    Munich, *M*)

THAI

Bar-Restaurant Moritzz (Central
    Munich, *M*)

TUSCAN
Buon Gusto (Central Munich, *M*)

VEGETARIAN
Prinz Myshkin (Central Munich, *I*)

3 In Central Munich

VERY EXPENSIVE

✪ **Garden Restaurant.** In the Bayerischer Hof Hotel, Promenadeplatz 2-6. ☎ **089/21200.** Reservations recommended. Main courses 35–56 DM ($20.50–$31.90). Fixed-price lunch 59 DM ($33.65); fixed-price dinners 69–98 DM ($39.30–$56). AE, DC, MC, V. Daily noon–3pm and 6–11:30pm. Tram: 19. MEDITERRANEAN/INTERNATIONAL.

This showcase restaurant within one of the showcase hotels of Munich makes you think of a miniature pastel-colored palace. It's set in a solemnly hushed room filled with blooming plants off the otherwise bustling lobby of the hotel. Upscale food is served to a cosmopolitan crowd. Menu items are about as cultivated and esoteric as you're likely to find in Munich, entirely based on fresh ingredients flown in from virtually everywhere. In some cases there's an emphasis on flavors and textures of the Mediterranean. Examples include salmon carpaccio in lemon-butter sauce, thin noodles with strips of quail and mushroom sauce, a bouquet of salad greens "land and sea" that's accented with lobster meat and calves' liver, a soup of exotic mushrooms in puff pastry, fillet of turbot in puff pastry with champagne sauce served with beans and mashed potatoes, rack of lamb in an herb-flavored crust with a puree of zucchini, and filet of beef stuffed with goose liver and fresh mushrooms. Ironically, despite this restaurant's elaborate menu, one of its most sought after dishes is fillet of Dover sole in lemon-butter sauce, served simply but flavorfully with fresh spinach and boiled potatoes. Desserts are appropriately lavish, and wine choices are among the most varied in Munich.

✪ **Park Hilton Grill.** In the Park Hilton Hotel, Am Tucherpark 7. ☎ **089/38450.** Reservations recommended. Main courses 42–65 DM ($23.95–$37.05). Fixed-price lunch 57 DM ($32.50); fixed-price dinners 92–140 DM ($52.45–$79.80). AE, DC, MC, V. Sun–Fri noon–2:30pm; and daily 7–10:30pm. U-Bahn: U3 or U6 to Giselastrasse, then bus 54. CONTINENTAL/AMERICAN.

In the face of stiff competition from other restaurants on the northern outskirts of Munich, the Hilton's developers used their imagination—they transformed a corner of their modern premises into one of the most sophisticated and well-conceived restaurants in town. The result is a replica of a richly paneled private club that just happens to be open to the public and just happens to be a place with charm, panache, and flair. Tables are elaborately decorated; dishes combine traditional and modern European with North American cuisine. Despite the set luncheon's elegance, management offers a free bottle of champagne if the meal (business lunch) is not completed within an hour of a patron's arrival. A meal might include salmon carpaccio with a white asparagus vinaigrette, spaghettini with morels in an herb sauce, monkfish on lentils with crispy Parma ham, or one of Munich's best Bavarian-style duck dishes on white cabbage with dumplings. Dinners are even more elaborate, including the pièce de résistance, wood pigeon with foie gras and artichokes set in Madeira-flavored aspic, followed by a lavish array of desserts that usually ends in coffee with petits-fours.

✪ **Restaurant Königshof.** In the Hotel Königshof, Karlsplatz 25 (Am Stachus). ☎ **089/ 551360.** Reservations required. Main courses 52–75 DM ($29.65–$42.75); fixed-price menus 148–174 DM ($84.35–$99.20). AE, DC, MC, V. Daily noon–2:30pm and 6:45–10:30pm. S-Bahn: S3, S7, or S8 to Karlsplatz. Tram: 19. INTERNATIONAL.

Munich Dining

Alois Dallmayr 🏮29
Andechser am Dom 🏮28
Austernkeller 🏮22
Bar-Restaurant Moritzz 🏮12
Biergarten Chinesischer
   Turm 🏮18
Bon Gusto (Talamonti) 🏮23
Café Glockenspiel 🏮17
Café Luitpold 🏮34
Chesa Rüegg 🏮31
Donisl 🏮24
Galleria 🏮20
Garden Restaurant 🏮2
Geisel's Vinothek 🏮6
Graffunder 🏮18
Guglhopf 🏮26
Halali 🏮36
Hundskugel 🏮8
Hunsiger's Pacific 🏮1
Käfer's am Hofgarten 🏮35
Kay's Bistro 🏮13
Königshof 🏮5
Lenbach 🏮4
Mark's Restaurant 🏮21
Nürnberger Bratwurst
   Glockl am Dom 🏮27
Nymphenburger Hof 🏮10
Palais Keller 🏮3
Park Hilton Grill 🏮39
Planet Hollywood 🏮30
Prinz Myshkin 🏮16
Ratskeller München 🏮25
Schloss Café im
   Palmenhaus 🏮11
Spatenhaus 🏮33
Straubinger Hof 🏮14
Tantris 🏮37
Vier Jahreszeiten 🏮32
Weinhaus Neuner 🏮7
Weisses Bräuhaus 🏮19
Zum Alten Markt 🏮15
Zum Bürgerhaus 🏮9

Legend
Church ✝
Post Office ✉
Information ⓘ
U-Bahn ──◯──
S-Bahn ──▭──

E-0234

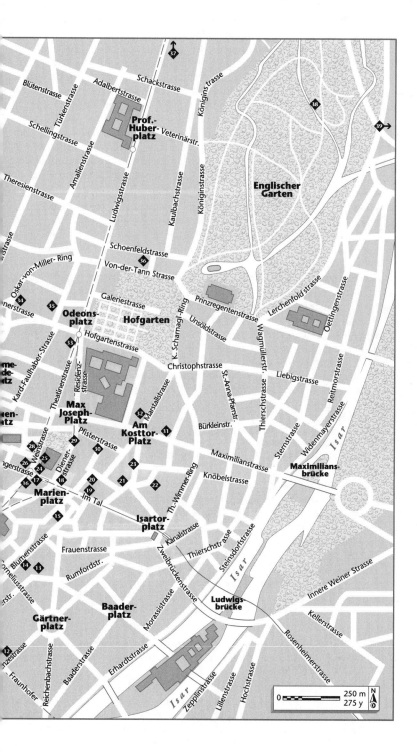

While this hotel dining room is no longer quite Munich's finest— that honor has passed on to the Park Hilton Grill—the Geisel family, who owns this deluxe hotel, wants to keep the Königshof close to the top in culinary delights. Chef Martin Bräuer is both inventive and creative. His "culinary masterpieces" depend on his whim, and, almost as important, on what's available in season. He likes extremely fresh ingredients, and the cuisine here reflects his passion. Perhaps you'll get to try his foie gras with sauterne, lobster soufflé, loin of lamb with fine herbs, lobster with vanilla butter, or sea bass suprême. Renovations have produced a dining room with oyster-white panels of oak, polished bronze chandeliers, and silver candelabra, and the black-jacketed waiters in their long white aprons are both polite and skilled.

Restaurant Vier Jahreszeiten. In the Kempinski Hotel Vier Jahreszeiten München, Maximilianstrasse 17. ☎ **089/21250.** Reservations required. Main courses 39–58 DM ($22.25–$33.05). Five-course fixed-price menu 108 DM ($61.55). AE, DC, MC, V. Daily 6–11pm. Closed Aug. Tram: 19. INTERNATIONAL.

Restaurant Vier Jahreszeiten is in a quiet and elegant location within walking distance of the opera house. The atmosphere is dignified and refined, the service extremely competent, and the cuisine prepared along classic French lines with many imaginative variations. The menu changes every 4 to 6 weeks, but appetizers are likely to include mushroom soufflé served with artichoke cream sauce, freshly made vegetable soup flavored with pesto, or turbot encased in basil-flavored crust. For a main course, you might try breast of Bresse chicken with scampi, flavored with a ginger sauce; or roast medaillons of venison with cherry-pepper sauce. Another main-dish specialty is blanquette of veal and lobster. Desserts include such specialties as strawberries Walterspiel, or, for two, tangerine soufflé served with foamy vanilla sauce.

EXPENSIVE

Galleria. Ledererstrasse 2 at Sparkassenstrasse. ☎ **089/297995.** Reservations recommended. Main courses 15–42 DM ($8.55–$23.95). Fixed-price lunch 50 DM ($28.50); fixed-price dinner 78 DM ($44.45). AE, DC, MC, V. Mon–Sat noon–3pm and 6pm–midnight. Closed Aug 10–30. U-Bahn: Marienplatz. ITALIAN.

This is one of the most appealing of the several Italian restaurants in the historic center and the one that takes the greatest risks with experimental versions of Italian cuisine. It's a few blocks east of the Marienplatz, with a modern and brightly colored setting and modern paintings. Service is gracious, and the menu changes with the availability of ingredients and the inspiration of the chefs. Examples include poached seawolf with fresh vegetables in fennel sauce, an aromatic guinea fowl scented with lavender, fillet of sole with a velvety eggplant mousse and basil, herb-flavored risotto with chunks of lobster and braised radicchio (the best such dish we've ever had in Munich), and roasted soft-shell crabs with a light onion sauce. Dessert might include a smooth zabaglione served with pears marinated in port wine.

✪ **Kay's Bistro.** Utzschneiderstrasse 1. ☎ **089/260-3584.** Reservations required. Main courses 38–45 DM ($21.65–$25.65). AE, MC. Daily 7pm–3am. U-Bahn: U2 or U3 to Marienplatz. INTERNATIONAL/FRENCH.

Munich's most sophisticated dining rendezvous, Kay's is off the historic Viktualienmarkt. It's filled nightly with a glamorous (sometimes media-related) clientele that wants to be seen in the right place. The decoration is changed often—perhaps you'll be there when the walls are covered with Hollywood souvenirs. Not only the interior design but the staff's outfits and even the cuisine reflect the restaurant's current decorative motif. French and international cuisine is light, nouvelle, and avant-garde; many ingredients are bought fresh daily. Kay Wörsching, a magazine columnist, personally greets his guests with a gracious welcome.

MODERATE

✪ **Alois Dallmayr.** Dienerstrasse 14-15. ☎ **089/213-5100.** Reservations required. Main courses 20–37 DM ($11.40–$21.10). AE, DC, MC, V. Mon–Wed 9:30am–7pm, Thurs–Fri 9:30am–8pm, Sat 9am–4pm. Tram: 19. CONTINENTAL.

The Fauchon's of Munich is Alois Dallmayr, whose history goes back to 1700. Near the Rathaus, it is Germany's most famous delicatessen. After looking at its tempting array of delicacies from around the globe, you'll think you're lost in a millionaire's supermarket. Dallmayr has been a purveyor to many royal courts. Here you'll find Munich's most elegant consumers, looking for that "tinned treasure," perhaps Scottish salmon, foie gras, English biscuits, wines and spirits, as well as out-of-season fresh produce.

The upstairs dining room serves a subtle German version of continental cuisine, owing a heavy debt to France. The food array is dazzling, ranging from the best herring and sausages we've ever tasted to such rare treats as perfectly vine-ripened tomatoes flown in from Morocco and papayas from Brazil. The famous French poulet de Bresse, believed by many gourmets to be the world's finest, is also shipped in. The smoked fish is a taste sensation and the soups are superbly flavored, especially one made with shrimp. If you're dining alone, you might prefer to sit at the counter instead of a table. The bustling restaurant is crowded at lunchtime.

✪ **Austernkeller.** Stollbergstrasse 11. ☎ **089/298787.** Reservations required. Main courses 33–49 DM ($18.80–$27.95). AE, DC, MC, V. Daily 5pm–1am. Closed Dec 23–26. U-Bahn: Isartorplatz. SEAFOOD.

The "oyster cellar" is a delight to both visitors and the local trade. You get the largest selection of oysters in town; many gourmands make an entire meal of raw oysters. Others prefer them elaborately prepared—for example, oysters Rockefeller. A delectable dish with which to start is the shellfish platter with fresh oysters, mussels, clams, scampi, and sea snails. Or you might begin with a rich fish soup or cold hors d'oeuvre. French meat specialties are offered, but most guests prefer the fish dishes—no other chef in Munich can make a lobster Thermidor as good as the one served here. The decor, under a vaulted ceiling, is a kitsch collection of everything from plastic lobsters to old porcelain.

Bar-Restaurant Moritzz. Klenzestrasse 43. ☎ **089/201-6776.** Reservations recommended on weekends. Main courses 16–29 DM ($9.10–$16.55). MC. Sun–Thurs 7pm–12:30am, Fri–Sat 7pm–1:30am. U-Bahn: Fraunhoferstrasse. CONTINENTAL/THAI/INTERNATIONAL.

This is the hip gay restaurant of Munich. As estimated by the staff, it has a 70% gay male clientele; lesbian women and gay-friendly straights make up the rest of the clients. Part of the space is devoted to a sprawling, attractive bar with a private club-like atmosphere where red leather chairs, mirrors, and an impeccably trained staff emulate a Paris hotel bar of the 1920s. You can enjoy at least 40 single malt whiskies, a dozen single-barrel bourbons, and a wide array of unusual wines. No one will mind if you decide to eat at the bar, or never move from its premises, but the adjacent dining room offers an appealing combination of international and continental food, prepared by a central-European staff whose interpretation of Thai cuisine is especially enjoyable. Examples include a *vorspeisen-teller* of mixed Thai specialties, and some fans find the lemon-grass soup almost addictive. Continental cuisine includes veal preparations, fresh fish, pastas, and salads (a platter-size version is garnished with strips of confit of duckling).

✪ **Buon Gusto (Talamonti).** Hochbruckenstrasse 3. ☎ **089/296383.** Reservations recommended. Main courses 20–42 DM ($11.40–$23.95). AE, MC, V. Mon–Sat noon–11pm. U-Bahn or S-Bahn: Marienplatz. TUSCAN/ITALIAN.

Devotees—and they may be right—claim this is the finest Italian restaurant in Munich. Its interior features two dining areas: a simple, rustic-looking bistro with an open kitchen and a more formal dining room. Menu items and prices are identical in both areas. It's owned and managed by the Talamontis, an extended family (whose members are likely to speak only Italian and German). Fresh ingredients, strong and savory flavors, and the cooking styles of the Italian Marches and Tuscany are emphasized. Delectable examples include ravioli stuffed with mushrooms and herbs, roasted lamb with potatoes, lots of different forms of scallopini, and fresh fish that seems to taste best when served simply, with oil or butter and lemon. Especially flavorful are the array of risottos whose ingredients change with the seasons and with availability. During Oktoberfest and trade fairs, the place is mobbed.

Chesa Rüegg. Wurzerstrasse 18. ☎ **089/297114.** Reservations recommended. Main courses 25–45 DM ($14.25–$25.65). Fixed-price lunch 25.50 DM ($14.55). AE, DC, V. U-Bahn: Odeonsplatz or Marienplatz. BAVARIAN/SWISS.

The warm coziness of a *gemütlich* inn high in the Bavarian or Swiss Alps is re-created here with roughly textured plaster, wood paneling, oversize cow bells, and kerosene lamps. You can pretend you're far away from the urban setting of Munich's Altstadt. Menu items include Zurich-style strips of veal in cream sauce with *Rösti*, braised fillet of pork with Ticino-style polenta, and filet of beef with truffles and red wine sauce. Bavarian dishes are appearing more frequently on the menu, but they often reflect the chef's inspiration and are lighter than the typical regional fare.

Halali. Schönfeldstrasse 22. ☎ **089/285909.** Reservations recommended. Main courses 26–40 DM ($14.80–$22.80). Fixed-price lunch 35 DM ($19.95); fixed-price dinner 85 DM ($48.45). AE, MC, V. Mon–Sat noon–3pm, Mon–Fri 4pm–1am. U-Bahn: Odeonsplatz. BAVARIAN.

Little has changed here since the place was first decorated around 1900, and very few of the staff or its clients would ever want it to change. The setting is baronial, devoted to a Teutonic version of the Hunt, as its name (which translates into something akin to "Tally-Ho") suggests. Amid high ceilings, solid archways, and a collection of stag's horns, you can order a flavorful array of traditional dishes that include terrine of venison and Blutwurst (blood sausage), both of which are specialties of the house. These might be followed with fillet of venison in wine sauce and succulent versions of grilled Bavarian duck, guinea fowl, or pheasant served in either Beaujolais or cranberry sauce, depending on the whim of the chef. Also recommended are ravioli stuffed with goose meat and mushrooms or with a mixture of ricotta and fontina cheese, fried salmon with champagne sauce, and a gratin of turbot served with mushrooms and white asparagus. A traditional, oft-praised dessert is a warm apple tart with vanilla sauce. Everything here is prepared with a definite style and flair. You get very good value here.

✪ **Hunsiger's Pacific.** Maximiliansplatz 5 (entrance is on the Max-Joseph-Strasse). ☎ **089/5502-9741.** Main courses 24–38 DM ($13.70–$21.65). AE, DC, MC, V. Mon–Fri noon–3pm, daily 6–10:30pm. Closed Sun May–Sept. U-Bahn: Stachus/Odeonsplatz. INTERNATIONAL.

This restaurant is the creative statement of one of the city's most innovative young chefs, Werner Hunsiger. Despite the name, don't expect the menu to be devoted exclusively to Pacific Rim cuisine. Fish is the premier item here—often flown in from Pacific waters just hours after it's caught. Preparation is based on classic French-inspired methods, but the innovative flavors come from Malaysia (coconut milk), Japan (wasabi), Thailand (lemongrass), and India (curry). You could begin with a tuna carpaccio with sliced plum, fresh ginger, and lime. Main courses include a succulent version of bouillabaisse with aïoli, which you might follow with cold melon soup garnished with a dollop of tarragon-flavored granita. Fried monkfish in the Malaysian style and turbot in chili and ginger sauce are evocative of Hawaii. One of the best things about the place is its relatively low prices for food that's superior to what's served at some of its more expensive competitors.

Lenbach. Ottostrasse 6. ☎ **089/549-1300.** Reservations recommended for dinner. In restaurant, main courses 22–120 DM ($12.55–$68.40). In cafe-bistro, main courses 16–27 DM ($9.10–$15.40). Two-course set lunch 18 DM ($10.25). AE, DC, MC, V. Restaurant daily 6pm–midnight; cafe-bistro daily 11am–midnight; bar daily 11am–1am (till 3am Thurs–Sat). S-Bahn: Karlsplatz. CONTINENTAL/MEDITERRANEAN.

An interesting newcomer occupies the grandiose premises of a 19th-century palace (the Bernheimerpalais am Lenbachplatz) whose monumental public rooms became in 1997 a stylish emporium of food, wine, sensuality, and conviviality in an atmosphere more evocative of Berlin.

The decoration revolves around the traditional moralist theme of the Seven Deadly Sins, with a decidedly stylish and highly permissive twist. Adultery is represented by a provocative large-scale pre-Raphaelite–style painting behind the bar. The theme in the drinking lounge is Sloth, and in a stridently red toilet (accessorized with jailhouse bars and manacles) it's Wrath. The view into the kitchen is, of course, Gluttony, and Vanity is represented by a catwalk, illuminated by tri-colored strobe lights, where you can promenade, fashion-model style, high above other diners. More "sins" await your own discovery.

Food sometimes seems less important here than visual stimuli, but the menu is likely to include a "seven sins" platter that contains foie gras, lobster, carpaccio of beef, and mozzarella tarts; a Lenbach salad with prawns, chicory, and olive-enriched bruschetta; goose liver terrine; lamb loin "Lenbach style," served with a gratin of potatoes and zucchini; salmon-trout *en papillote;* lamb cutlets with tarragon and a cassoulet of morels; and heaping platters of fresh shellfish.

✪ **Mark's Restaurant.** In the Hotel Rafael, Neuturmstrasse 1. ☎ **089/290980.** Reservations recommended. Dinner main courses 35–60 DM ($19.95–$34.20). Fixed-price lunch in Mark's Corner 48 DM ($27.35). AE, DC, MC, V. Daily 11am–2pm and 7–10:30pm. U-Bahn: Marienplatz. CONTINENTAL.

The restaurant, in the prestigious Hotel Rafael, is appropriately elegant with impeccably trained staff. If you come here, don't ask to meet a chef named Mark (the place was named after the owner's son) and expect different venues at lunch and dinner. Lunch is served in a small, cozy enclave off the lobby, Mark's Corner, and is usually limited to a set-price menu favored by businesspeople. Dinners are swankier and more elaborate, served one floor above street level in a formal dining room that overlooks a monumental staircase and the lobby below. On Monday night only, the formal dining room is closed, and dinner is in the relatively informal lobby level setting of Mark's Corner.

Menu items change according to the season and the inspiration of the chef and might include dishes that succeed beautifully despite their sometimes experimental nature. Examples include kohlrabi soup with strips of ham, guinea fowl in mustard sauce with herbs, wild salmon with red and green lentils, halibut with fennel sauce, a ragout of fish in puff pastry with balsamic vinegar and herbs, and breast of free-range chicken with curried vinaigrette, sometimes served as a salad.

✪ **Mövenpick Restaurant.** Im Künstlerhaus, Lenbachplatz 8. ☎ **089/545-9490.** Main courses in upstairs dining room 20–40 DM ($11.40–$22.80); main courses in street-level dining room 12–32 DM ($6.85–$18.25). AE, DC, MC, V. Daily 8:30am–midnight. U-Bahn: U4 or U5 to Stachus. SWISS/INTERNATIONAL.

The *Jugendstil* building (Künstlerhaus) was originally constructed in 1898 as a publicly subsidized community of artists. When Munich's Olympic Games came up, the site was transformed into a network of atmospheric dining rooms, each with a different theme. In the Venezia on the ground floor, turn-of-the-century murals have been refurbished. Other rooms have names like Rosenzimmer, the Pub, the garden-style Pastorale (upstairs), and Longhorn Corner, inspired by the plains of Texas. Service and cuisine are more formal and prices more expensive upstairs than on the ground floor, where no one will mind if you ask just for coffee, beer, or a dish of ice cream. Regardless of where you sit, one especially fine choice is Zurich-style veal strips in cream sauce, served with *Rösti* potatoes. Vegetarians might opt for a savory platter of Steinpilz mushrooms served in cream sauce and accompanied by Bavarian dumplings.

Ratskeller München. Im Rathaus, Marienplatz 8. ☎ **089/219-9890.** Reservations required. Main courses 16–35 DM ($9.10–$19.95). Fixed-price menus 30–35 DM ($17.10–$19.95). AE, MC, V. Daily 10am–midnight. Closed Dec 24–Jan 1. U-Bahn: U2 or U3 to Marienplatz. BAVARIAN.

Throughout Germany you'll find Ratskellers, traditional restaurants located in Rathaus (city hall) basements (note that *Rat* means "counsel" in German) serving good, inexpensive food and wine. Munich's Ratskeller, one of the best, is typical: lots of dark wood and carved chairs. The most interesting tables, often staked out by in-the-know locals, are the semiprivate dining nooks in the rear, under the vaulted painted ceilings. Bavarian music adds to the ambience. The menu, a showcase of regional fare, includes some international dishes, many of them vegetarian, which is unusual for a Ratskeller. A freshly made soup of the day is featured, and you can help yourself from the salad bar. Some of the dishes are a little heavy and too porky—best left for your overweight Bavarian uncle—but you can find lighter fare if you search the menu carefully.

✪ **Spatenhaus.** Residenzstrasse 12. ☎ **089/290-7060.** Reservations recommended. Main courses 24.50–42.50 DM ($13.95–$24.20). AE, DC, MC, V. Daily 9:30am–12:30am. U-Bahn: U3, U4, or U6 to Odeonsplatz or Marienplatz. BAVARIAN/INTERNATIONAL.

The wide windows of this well-known beer restaurant overlook the opera house on Max-Joseph-Platz. Of course, to be loyal, you should accompany your meal with the restaurant's own beer, Spaten-Franziskaner-Bier. You can sit in an intimate, semiprivate dining nook or at a big table. The Spatenhaus has old traditions, offers typical Bavarian food, and is known for generous portions and reasonable prices. If you want to know what the fabled Bavarian gluttony is all about, order the "Bavarian plate," which is loaded with pork, sausages, and other meats. After eating it, you'll have to go to a spa.

Weinhaus Neuner. Herzogspitalstrasse 8. ☎ **089/260-3954.** Reservations recommended. Main courses 24–33 DM ($13.70–$18.80). Fixed-price menus 34–58 DM ($19.40–$33.05). AE, MC, V. Mon–Sat 11:30am–3pm and 6:30pm–midnight. U-Bahn: U4 to Stachus. S-Bahn: All trains to Stachus. BAVARIAN.

👥 Family-Friendly Restaurants

Nürnberger Bratwurst Glöckl Am Dom *(see p. 97)*   Hot dogs will never taste the same after your child has tried one of those delectable little sausages from Nürnberg.

Mövenpick Restaurant *(see p. 94)*   The food at this Swiss-run restaurant is so varied, and the dining options so different, that your kids will surely find something they like. Dining rooms range from a garden-style Pastorale to Grandma's Kitchen, with even a corner inspired by the plains of Texas. You can order a light meal or a big spread—whatever you want. It's all very informal and moderately priced.

Ratskeller München *(see p. 94)*   All parents eventually take their kids to the centrally located Marienplatz in Munich. Once here, there is no better place for dining than the architecturally interesting Ratskeller, one of the finest in Germany. It's got everything needed to fill up your kid, ranging from vegetarian dishes to a freshly prepared salad bar. The hearty soups served here make a complete lunch unto themselves.

This is an *Ältestes Weinhaus Münchens,* one of the city's landmark taverns. It dates to the late 15th century and is the only building in Munich that has its original Tyrolean vaults. The place brims over with warmth and charm. Once young priests were educated here, but after secularization by Napoléon the place became a wine tavern and a meeting place for artists, writers, and composers, including Richard Wagner. Its rooms have been renovated and its paintings restored.

It's divided into two parts. The less expensive place to dine is the casual Weinstube, with lots of local atmosphere, where you can order typical Bavarian dishes such as home-smoked beef. The restaurant, on the other hand, is elegant, with candles and flowers. The chef happily marries cuisine moderne and regional specialties.

✪ **Zum Alten Markt.** Am Viktualienmarkt, Dreifaltigkeitsplatz 3. ☎ **089/299995.** Reservations recommended. Main courses 20–38 DM ($11.40–$21.65). No credit cards. Mon–Sat noon–10pm. U-Bahn: U2 or U3 to Marienplatz. Bus: 52. BAVARIAN/INTERNATIONAL.

Snug and cozy, Zum Alten Markt serves beautifully presented fresh cuisine at a good price. Located on a tiny square just off Munich's large outdoor food market, the restaurant offers a mellow charm and a warm welcome from its owner, Josef Lehner. The interior decor with its intricately coffered wooden ceiling was taken from a 400-year-old Tyrolean castle. In summer there are outside tables. Fish and fresh vegetables come from the nearby market. You might begin with a tasty home-made soup, such as cream of carrot, or perhaps black-truffle tortellini in cream sauce with young onions and tomatoes. The chef makes some of Munich's best Tafelspitz (the elegant boiled-beef dish so beloved by Emperor Franz Josef of Austria). You can also order classic dishes such as Bavarian goose and savory roast suckling pig.

INEXPENSIVE

Andechser am Dom. Weinstrasse 7a. ☎ **089/298481.** Reservations recommended. Main courses 17.50–28 DM ($10–$15.95). AE, DC, MC, V. Daily 10am–midnight. U-Bahn and S-Bahn: Marienplatz. GERMAN.

Located just behind the Frauenkirche, this restaurant and beer hall serves Andechser, a beer brewed in a monastery near Munich, along with generous portions of German food. No one will mind if you order a snack, a full meal, or just a beer. The menu features such dishes as veal schnitzel, steak, turkey croquettes, roasted lamb, fish, and several kinds of sausages that taste best with tangy mustard. They are often accompanied with German-style potato salad and green salad. In good weather, tables are set up both on the building's roof and on the sidewalk in front.

✪ **Donisl.** Weinstrasse 1. ☎ **089/220184.** Reservations recommended. Main courses all 12 DM ($6.85). AE, DC, MC, V. Daily 9am–midnight. U-Bahn: U3 or U6 to Marienplatz. S-Bahn: All trains. BAVARIAN/INTERNATIONAL.

Donisl is Munich's oldest beer hall, dating from 1715, with a relaxed and comfortable atmosphere. The seating capacity is about 550, and in summer you can enjoy the hum and bustle of Marienplatz while dining in the garden area out front. The restaurant has two levels, the second of which is a gallery. English is spoken. The standard menu offers traditional Bavarian food as well as a weekly changing specials menu. Specialties include the little white sausages, Weisswürste, a decades-long tradition of this place. The chef also prepares a succulent duck. Select beers from Munich's own Hacker-Pschorr Brewery top the evening. A zither player at noon and an accordion player in the evening entertain guests.

✪ **Geisel's Vinothek.** In the Hotel Excelsior, Schützenstrasse 11. ☎ **089/5513-7140.** Reservations recommended for dining, not necessary for wine tasting. Main courses 26–30 DM ($14.80–$17.10). Fixed-price meals 38–40 DM ($21.65–$22.80). Glasses of wine 4.50–9.50 DM ($2.55–$5.40). AE, DC, MC, V. Warm food daily noon–12:30am; wine daily noon–1am. U-Bahn: Hauptbahnhof. ITALIAN.

The Excelsior made a deliberate choice when it decided not to compete with the *grand chic* restaurants of hotels like the Bayerischer Hof, with its super-upscale Garden Restaurant. Instead, this four-star hotel opted for a cozy, gemütlich enclave of rustic charm that evokes an unpretentious trattoria high in the Italian Alps. It's known for its assortment of Italian, French, Austrian, and German wines, dispensed by the glass. Clients can sit at the bar or at one of about a dozen tables for those who want a full-fledged meal. The menu is conceived mostly as a savory foil for the wine. Examples include carpaccio, mozzarella with fresh basil and tomatoes, *vitello tonnato,* platters of assorted grilled fish, veal and chicken dishes, and pastas whose composition changes with the season and mood of the chef. The fare is routine Italian, but with the wine as a backup, almost everything tastes good.

✪ **Graffunder.** Tal 1. ☎ **089/292427.** Snack items and platters 10–19 DM ($5.70–$10.85); glasses of wine 6–7.80 DM ($3.40–$4.45). No credit cards. Mon–Fri 4pm–midnight, Sun 5pm–midnight. U-Bahn: Marienplatz. ITALIAN/FRENCH.

Don't expect the grace notes and service rituals of a full-fledged restaurant at this informal place. It specializes in French and Italian wines, usually sold by the glass. It's the kind of breezy, easygoing spot that's been the rage in London for almost a decade now. Food, while not actually an afterthought to the wine, is nonetheless considered an accompaniment. Platters range from the very simple (tomato, basil, and mozzarella salads or a platter of carpaccio) to the somewhat more elaborate (pastas, escalopes of veal, chicken with morels or chanterelles, or Mediterranean ratatouille). In all, it's an excellent French/Italian alternative to the predictable regime of beer-hall–style suds and würsts served in so many restaurants in Munich's Altstadt.

Hundskugel. Hotterstrasse 18. ☎ **089/264272.** Reservations required. Main courses 16–38 DM ($9.10–$21.65). No credit cards. Daily 10am–midnight. U-Bahn: U2 or U3 to Marienplatz. BAVARIAN.

The city's oldest tavern, Hundskugel dates back to 1440 and apparently serves the same food now as it did back then—if it was good a long time ago, why mess with the menu? Built in an alpine style, it's within easy walking distance of the Marienplatz. Perhaps half the residents of Munich at one time or another have made their way here to be wined and dined in style. The cookery is honest Bavarian with no pretensions. Although the chef makes a specialty of Spanferkel (roast suckling pig with potato noodles), you might prefer Tafelspitz (boiled beef) in dill sauce or roast veal stuffed with goose liver. To begin, try one of the hearty soups, made fresh daily.

✪ **Käfer's Am Hofgarten.** Odeonsplatz 6. ☎ **089/290-7530**. Reservations recommended for dinner. Main courses 24–35 DM ($13.70–$19.95). AE, V. Mon–Thurs 10:30am–1am, Fri 10:30am–3am, Sat 9:30am–3am, Sun 9:30am–1am. U-Bahn: U3, U4, U5, or U6 to Odeonsplatz. Bus: 54. INTERNATIONAL.

Even its staff (most are under 30) make jokes about the affluent and youthful clientele that hangs out at this French bistro at the foot of the Ludwigstrasse. Almost everyone who comes here is between 27 and 35. The 200-year-old historic building, with a decor that could have been lifted directly from gaslight-era Paris is part of its allure, an ambience eminently suited for relaxing, gossiping, and convivial chitchat. The other powerful allure is the food—it's the most self-consciously eclectic in Munich, combining Thai curries with dim sum and spring rolls with Bavarian duckling, American rib-eye steaks, English lamb chops, and Italian tagliatelle. There's additional seating upstairs, and a staff that thinks nothing is strange at all about serving breakfast to recovering night-owls at 3pm.

✪ **Nürnberger Bratwurst Glöckl Am Dom.** Frauenplatz 9. ☎ **089/295264.** Reservations recommended. Main courses 29–35 DM ($16.55–$19.95). No credit cards. Daily 9am–1am. U-Bahn: U2 or U3 to Marienplatz. S-Bahn: All trains. BAVARIAN.

The homesick Nürnberger comes here just for one dish: those delectable little sausages, Nürnberger Schweinwurst mit Kraut. This old restaurant first opened in 1893. It was rebuilt after World War II and is the coziest and warmest of all the local restaurants. Chairs look as if they were made by a Nuremberg carver, and upstairs, reached through a hidden stairway, is a dining room hung with reproductions of Dürer prints. Tables are shared, and food is served on tin plates. Last food orders go in at midnight. A short walk from Marienplatz, the restaurant faces the Frauenkirche.

✪ **Palais Keller.** In the Hotel Bayerischer Hof (Palais Montgelas), Promenadeplatz 2. ☎ **089/212-0990.** Reservations recommended. Main courses 15–30 DM ($8.55–$17.10); platter of the day 19–25 DM ($10.85–$14.25). AE, DC, MC, V. Daily 11am–midnight. Tram 19. BAVARIAN/GERMAN.

Massive, with a high turnover and a sense of bustling energy, this richly folkloric restaurant lies down a flight of stone steps, deep in the cellar of one of Munich's finest hotels. Despite its elegant associations, its prices are competitive with those of Munich's many beer halls and Weinstuben. Waitresses speak English and wear frilly aprons and genuine smiles. There is a tempting array of such German dishes as veal in sour cream sauce with glazed turnips, cabbage, and carrots; pike balls on buttery leaf spinach with shrimp sauce; and Tafelspitz (boiled beef) with horseradish and vinaigrette sauce. Some diners, especially those who make the place a regular stopover, order whatever Tageseller (platter of the day) is being served, along with a foaming mug of beer or one of the restaurant's broad selection of German wines. Wines are sold by the bottle or glass.

Planet Hollywood. Platzl 1. ☎ **089/2903-0500.** Reservations accepted only Mon–Wed and Sun. Main courses 20–25 DM ($11.40–$14.25). AE, DC, MC, V. Daily noon–1am. S-Bahn: Marienplatz or Isartor. AMERICAN.

This is the Munich branch of Hollywood, USA's, embassy of good will to the world at large. It's across the street from the Hofbräuhaus, an establishment that's light-years away from everything that Planet Hollywood tries desperately to promote. In the commodious bar area of this bastion of Americanism, cocktails commemorate the success of recent films in alcoholic form. Surrounded by memorabilia associated with *Titanic* and every film ever made by Bruce Willis or Sly Stallone, you can eventually gravitate into either the main dining room or a satellite room that immortalizes the achievements of Hollywood's favorite Teuton, Arnold Schwarzenegger—the staff is quick to tell you he was once a resident of Munich. Menu items are firmly grounded in American pop culture and include burgers (several vegetarian versions), T-bone steaks, chili, club sandwiches, tacos, and ice cream sundaes. Want a little taste of an Arnold-inspired dessert before you exit this place? Then order a slice of the "famous" apfelstrudel, which is reputedly made according to his mother's recipe. You can have a good time here, even if you find the venue very similar to everything you left America to forget. Unless you find the cultural schizophrenia unbearable, check out the souvenir stand on the way out.

Prinz Myshkin. Hackenstrasse 2. ☎ **089/265596.** Reservations recommended. Main courses 16–30 DM ($9.10–$17.10). Fixed-price meals 13.80–28.50 DM ($7.85–$16.25). AE, MC, V. Daily 11am–1am. U-Bahn: U2 or U3 to Marienplatz. VEGETARIAN.

One of the best known and most popular vegetarian restaurants in Munich, it's set near Marienplatz, with hanging plants and a window view. Freshly made salads with names like "Aphrodite" and "Barbados," vegetarian involtini and casseroles, soups, and nine zesty pizzas are some of the choices, many of which are excellent. This is not a buffet—rather, it's a full-fledged restaurant with table service from a helpful staff. Wine and beer are available. Smaller portions of many items are available for 8.50 DM ($4.85).

Straubinger Hof. Blumenstrasse 5. ☎ **089/260-8444.** Reservations necessary only for 4 or more. Main courses 18–28 DM ($10.25–$15.95). AE, V. Mon–Sat 9am–9:30pm (last order). U-Bahn: Marienplatz. BAVARIAN.

This is one of the most recommendable and popular restaurants in the Altstadt, a well-managed, unpretentious, folkloric place sponsored by the brewers of Paulaner beer. Stop in just for a brew during the morning and afternoon, but during peak lunch and dinner hours, it's good form to order at least a small platter of cheese, Blutwurst, Weisswurst, or Rotwurst, if not a steaming platter of Tafelspitz (boiled beef with horseradish), Sauerbraten, or roasted knuckle of pork. In something approaching an orgy of Teutonic nostalgia for the kind of food old-time Bavarians were served as children, you're likely to see in the menu the term *Grossmutter Art,* or "in the style of grandmother." A large stein of beer costs from 5.20 to 5.50 DM ($3.65 to $3.85), depending on the type you order. This restaurant's position close to the Viktualienmarkt guarantees—at least in theory—the use of ultrafresh produce. Portions are ample, prices are reasonable, and in summer, seating spills out onto the pavement. Looking for a traditional Bavarian dessert? The specialty of the house is old-fashioned *Apfelschmarrn,* an apple-laced pastry. The restaurant also has all-vegetarian options.

Weisses Bräuhaus. Tal 7. ☎ **089/299875.** Reservations recommended, especially for the back room. Main courses 20–32 DM ($11.40–$18.25). No credit cards. Daily 8am–midnight. U-Bahn: U2 or U3 to Marienplatz. BAVARIAN.

In the heart of the city, Weisses Bräuhaus is big, bustling, and Bavarian with a vengeance. Not for the pretentious, this informal place does what it has done for centuries: It serves home-brewed beer. At one time the famous salt-trade route between Salzburg and Augsburg passed by its door, and salt traders were very thirsty back then.

In a world of smoke-blackened dark-wood paneling and stained glass, the front room is for drinking and informal eating; the back room has white tablecloths and black-outfitted waiters. You can begin with smoked fillet of trout or rich-tasting potato soup, then try roast pork with homemade potato dumplings and cabbage salad or Viennese veal goulash with mushrooms and cream sauce. You'll invariably share your table, but that's part of the fun here.

Zum Bürgerhaus. Pettenkoferstrasse 1. ☎ **089/557909.** Reservations recommended. Main courses 20–35 DM ($11.40–$19.95). Lunch platter 17 DM ($9.70). Fixed-price menu 23 DM ($13.10). AE, MC, V. Mon–Fri 11:30am–2:30pm and Mon–Sat 7:30pm–midnight. U-Bahn: Sendlinger Tor. ALPINE.

Originally built in 1827, this is one of the few restaurants in the Altstadt that escaped relatively unscathed from the devastation of World War II. It's still outfitted with the traditional dark-stained wood paneling and all the gemütlich accessories you'd expect. Appropriate to its nostalgic charm, it places culinary emphasis on alpine food. Menu choices change with the seasons, but at one time or another might include a Bürgerhaus salad (garnished with herbed croutons and bacon); lamb with rosemary sauce; fillet of venison with red wine sauce; Zurich-style veal with Rösti and cream sauce; Viennese-style pork schnitzels; Bavarian duck with orange sauce; Angus steak bordelaise, and a cold-weather favorite, a *Bürgerhaus Pfanne* that combines cutlets of turkey, veal, and pork in one well-seasoned pan. The homemade version of noodles with cream sauce, herbs, and mushrooms may sound a little bland, but it is actually one of the more savory dishes.

4 Near the Südbahnhof

✪ **Gastehaus Glockenbach.** Kapuzinerstrasse 29, corner of Maistrasse. ☎ **089/534043.** Reservations recommended. Main courses 25–43 DM ($14.25–$24.50). Fixed-price menus 40–95 DM ($22.80–$54.15). AE, MC, V. Tues–Fri noon–1:30pm (last order), Tues–Sat 7–9:30pm (last order). Closed 1 week at Christmas. U-Bahn: U3 or U6 to Goetheplatz. CONTINENTAL.

Despite a deliberately low-key approach, this unpretentious restaurant holds its own against the more expensive *grand bourgeois* icons. The setting is a 200-year-old building close to a tributary (the Glockenbach) of the nearby Isar. Originally a brewery, it was transformed into its present incarnation in 1983. The dignified country-baroque interior is accented with vivid modern paintings, and the most elegant table settings in town, including a lavish array of porcelain by a company not well known in the New World, Hutchenreuther.

Cuisine changes with the season and according to the inspiration of the chef, Karl Ederer. Examples include imaginative preparations of venison and pheasant in autumn, lamb and veal dishes in springtime, seasonal shellfish, and a medley of ultrafresh vegetables from local farms. Exotica is imported from sophisticated purveyors throughout the world. Wines are mostly European, with goodly representatives from Italy, France, and Austria.

5 Near the Isar, South of Center

Asam Schlössel. 45 Maria-Einsiedel-Strasse. ☎ **089/723-6373.** Main courses 20–30 DM ($11.40–$17.10). AE, MC, V. Daily 11am–1am. U-Bahn: Talkirchen (zoo). BAVARIAN/ INTERNATIONAL.

A relaxed, relatively informal hideaway from the congestion of Munich, this restaurant is housed in a building dating from 1724 that was once the private villa of a pair of artists. Many of the original castlelike architectural features were retained during the conversion into an Augustiner brewery restaurant. Several brews, all products of Augustiner, are offered, including both pale and dark versions fermented from wheat (*Weissebier*). Menu items include roasted shoulder of pork (*Schweinsschulterbraten*) basted with (what else?) beer and served with braised red cabbage, and potato dumplings; beef braised in red wine (*Böfflamott*) with bread dumplings (*Semmelknödel*); and a dish beloved by the last of Austria's Habsburg emperors, a savory form of boiled beef with horseradish (*gesottener Tafelspitz mit frischen Kren*).

6 In Schwabing

This district of Munich, which used to be called "bohemian" in the 1940s, overflows with restaurants, many of which are awful, although there are also notable places and some that attract a youthful clientele. Evening is the best time for a visit.

VERY EXPENSIVE

✪ **Tantris.** Johann-Fichte-Strasse 7, Schwabing. ☎ **089/361-9590.** Reservations required. Fixed-price 5-course lunch 148 DM ($84.35); fixed-price dinner 192 DM ($109.45) for 5 courses, 218 DM ($124.25) for 8 courses; special 5-course dinner Tues–Thurs (including red and white wine) 225 DM ($128.25). AE, DC, MC, V. Tues–Sat noon–3pm and 6:30pm–1am. Closed public holidays; annual holidays in Jan and May. U-Bahn: U6 to Dietlindenstrasse. FRENCH/INTERNATIONAL.

Tantris serves Munich's finest cuisine—it's simply the best. Chef Hans Haas was voted the top chef in Germany in 1994 and, if anything, he has refined and sharpened his technique since winning that honor. His penchant for exotic nouvelle carries him into ever greater achievements. No restaurant in Munich comes close to equaling this place, not even Preysing-Keller, Boettner, or Gastehaus Glockenbach. The setting is unlikely, but once you're inside, you're transported into an ultramodern atmosphere with fine service. Leading Munich businesspeople like to entertain here.

The food is a treat to the eye as well as to the palate, and the beautiful interior adds to your enjoyment. The cooking is both subtle and original. Choice of dishes is wisely limited: There's an eight-course menu that changes daily, plus a five-course table d'hôte, served at noon. You might begin with one of the interesting soups, or a terrine of smoked fish served with green cucumber sauce, then follow with classic roast duck on mustard-seed sauce, or a delightful concoction of lobster medaillons on black noodles. These dishes show a refinement and attention to detail, plus a quest for technical perfection, that is truly rare anywhere.

EXPENSIVE

✪ **Bistro Terrine.** Amalienstrasse 89. ☎ **089/281780.** Reservations recommended. Main courses 28–45 DM ($15.95–$25.65). Fixed-price lunch 45 DM ($25.65); fixed-price dinner 85 DM ($48.45). AE, MC, V. Mon–Sat noon–1:45pm and 6:30–10:30pm. U-Bahn: U3 or U6 to Universität. FRENCH.

The restaurant looks like an art-nouveau French bistro, and its nouvelle cuisine is based on traditional recipes as authentic and savory as anything you'd find in Lyon or Paris. There's room for up to about 50 diners at a time, but because of the way the dining room is arranged, with banquettes and wood and glass dividers, it seems bigger than it actually is. During clement weather, there's additional seating on an outdoor terrace.

Menu items are often more innovative than the restaurant's turn-of-the-century setting would imply and might include tartar of herring with freshly made potato chips and salad, watercress salad with sweetbreads, cream of paprika soup, an autumn fantasy that includes nuggets of venison served with hazelnut-flavored gnocchi and port wine sauce, zander fish baked in an herb-and-potato crust, or an alluring specialty salmon with a chanterelle-studded risotto. After all this novelty, the most satisfying desserts might include a traditional tarte tatin or even an old-fashioned crème brûlée that's jazzed up with Tahitian-style vanilla sauce.

✪ **Locanda Picolit.** Siegfriedstrasse 11. ☎ **089/396447.** Reservations recommended. Main courses 38–60 DM ($21.65–$34.20). Fixed-price menu 95 DM ($54.15). AE, DC, MC, V. Mon–Tues and Thurs–Fri noon–2:30pm and Thurs–Tues 4–11pm. Closed in June. U-Bahn: U3 or U6 to Münchner Freiheit. ITALIAN.

If you come here in the summer and sit on the outdoor terrace with a view over a garden, it's easy to believe that you've suddenly been transported to the Mediterranean world. Set in the heart of Schwabing, the restaurant is the result of the imagination and hard work of Danillo Munisso and his Munich-born wife, Ingrid. In the heart of Schwabing in a 1960s building, the restaurant has a decor of streamlined furnishings and dramatic oversize modern paintings. Menu items come from all over Italy, but you might suspect that Sr. Munisso's favorites are those from his native Friuli district, near Venice. Even the locanda's name, Picolit, comes from one of that region's well-known wines.

The menu is influenced by whatever is in season. There's a lavish use of asparagus, arugula, shellfish, rabbit, wild mushrooms, and venison in such alluring preparations as ravioli stuffed with lobster, tagliatelle, rotini, or linguini with braised radicchio and shellfish, and, when available, saltimbocca (veal with ham).

MODERATE

Der Katzlmacher. Kaulbacherstrasse 48. ☎ **089/348129.** Reservations recommended. Main courses 28–39 DM ($15.95–$22.25). Fixed-price lunches 40–50 DM ($22.80–$28.50); fixed-price dinners 60–90 DM ($34.20–$51.30). AE, MC, V. Tues–Sat noon–3pm and 6:30pm–1am. U-Bahn: Universität. ITALIAN.

Few Italian restaurants would have had the nerve to adopt as their name a pejorative German term referring to Italians. This one did, however, as whimsical proof of a sense of humor that's made them beloved by loyal local fans. The setting is a postwar building whose two dining rooms are evocative of a mountain lodge high in the Italian Alps. Starched white napery contrasts pleasantly with the rustic setting. The cooking is based on the culinary traditions of the Italian Marches, Friulia, and Emilia-Romagna, all known for their fine cuisines and agrarian bounty. Menu specialties might include calzone stuffed with spinach and pine nuts, ravioli with ricotta and herbs, a commendable grilled swordfish with red wine vinaigrette, eel with champagne sauce, John Dory in saffron sauce, and a succulent version of *fritto misto del pesce* based on whatever is seasonal.

La Mucca. Georgenstrasse 105. ☎ **089/271-6742.** Reservations recommended. Main courses 25–34 DM ($14.25–$19.40). AE, DC, MC, V. Tues–Sun noon–2:15pm and 6–11:30pm. U-Bahn: U2 to Josephsplatz. ITALIAN.

This is an unpretentious and charming Italian restaurant in the heart of Schwabing, run by Italian expatriates who manage to infuse the ambience here with Mediterranean charm, Mediterranean humor, and—when things get too busy—Mediterranean hysteria. It's small and convivial, with only 55 seats in two dining rooms. Arguably, the most delectable item on the menu is *lotte* (sea bass) baked in a salt crust. The chef shows flair with his carpaccio of lamb with olive oil and white beans and also prepares that famous dish of Rome, *saltimbocca* (literally "jump-in-your-mouth," with ham and veal). However, you have to be born and bred in Italy, or else a true devotee of Italian cuisine as we are, to opt for a platter of grilled sardines in arugula. Both the antipasti and pasta selections are excellent, especially rigatoni with zucchini strips.

Spago. Neureutherstrasse 15 at Arcisstrasse. ☎ **089/271-2406.** Reservations recommended. Main courses 25–39 DM ($14.25–$22.25). Fixed-price lunch 39 DM ($22.25); fixed-price dinner 59 DM ($33.65). AE, DC, V. Mon–Fri noon–4:30pm and daily 6–11:30pm. U-Bahn: U2 to Josephsplatz or U3 to Universität. ITALIAN.

Less self-conscious and self-promotional as its Los Angeles namesake, this amiable multilingual Italian restaurant in Schwabing nevertheless offers lots of Italian pizzazz as well as good, upscale Italian food. Some of the dishes are tagliatelle with porcini mushrooms, braised breast of chicken stuffed with herbs and spinach, ravioli with artichoke hearts or with potatoes and chanterelles, an especially delectable fish baked with herbs in a salt crust and wild mushrooms sautéed with herbs and arugula, a perfectly prepared suckling lamb with mint and balsamic vinegar, and an array of desserts as beautiful as they are tasty.

Tokajer Weinkeller-und-Pilsstube. Belgradestrasse 61. ☎ **089/308-6825.** Reservations recommended. Main courses 20–26 DM ($11.40–$14.80). Daily platter 9.90 DM ($5.65). No credit cards. Daily 5pm–2am. U-Bahn: U3 to Bonnerplatz. HUNGARIAN.

This north Schwabing dining room is filled with wood carvings, paintings, Hungarian needlecraft, and the wild and poignant strains of gypsy violins and xylophones. As Munich's only Hungarian restaurant, it's something of a focal point for the expatriate Hungarian community. Cuisine is as paprika-laden and pungent as you might hope, and it tastes wonderful when washed down with Bavarian beer or with the strong, ruby-red wines from the Danube in western Hungary, especially the celebrated "bull's blood" and the Tokay reds. Dishes include a peppery and creamy hors d'oeuvre, *palatschinken Hortobágy,* beloved by Hungarians from childhood; at least five different kinds of goulash; stuffed peppers; and a "Toikayer platter," three kinds of meat bound together by a peppery paprika seasoning.

INEXPENSIVE

Weinbauer. Fendstrasse 5. ☎ **089/398155.** Reservations recommended. Main courses 10.50–26.50 DM ($6–$15.10). No credit cards. Mon–Fri 11am–midnight, Sat 3pm–midnight. U-Bahn: U3 or U5 to Münchner Freiheit. BAVARIAN.

Just off Leopoldstrasse is this small, relatively untrammeled budget restaurant. Despite a complete renovation in 1993, it retains many traditional Bavarian accessories, evoking an unglossy dining room in a small town somewhere in the Alps. Menu items include Wiener schnitzel, Nürnberger wurst'l with sauerkraut, sirloin steak with an herb-butter sauce, goulash soup, and Blutwurst and Leberwurst platters. The food is reliable but hardly spectacular. Any of these might be washed down with a half liter of tap beer.

7 In Haidhausen

✪ Preysing-Keller. Preysingstrasse 1. ☎ **089/4584-5260.** Reservations recommended. Main courses 32–46 DM ($18.25–$26.20). Fixed-price menus 89–125 DM ($50.75–$71.25). AE, DC, MC, V. Mon–Sat 6pm–1am. Tram: 18. GERMAN/INTERNATIONAL.

Preysing-Keller is a "find," but you have to cross the Isar to discover its superb cookery and wines. It's connected to the Hotel Preysing (see chapter 4). You'll dine in a 300-year-old cellar with massive beams and high masonry arches; the decor is simple, with wooden tables and chairs. Daily market excursions are made by the staff, who select only the freshest ingredients. Fresh fish and seafood are kept in aquariums on the premises. Everything on the menu appears seductively fresh. The cuisine is derived from classic Bavarian dishes made new by the innovative chef. Goose-liver pâté is a specialty, as is lobster in butter sauce and venison steak tartar.

8 In Bogenhausen

Bogenhauser Hof. Ismaninger Strasse 85, Bogenhausen. ☎ **089/985586.** Reservations recommended. Main courses 40–55 DM ($22.80–$31.35). AE, DC, V. Mon–Sat 11:30am–3pm and 6–10pm. U-Bahn: U5 to Max-Weber-Platz, then tram no. 18 to Essnerplatz. GERMAN/INTERNATIONAL.

In the verdant residential suburb of Bogenhausen, 3 miles east of the Marienplatz, this stylish and sought-after restaurant occupies a stately looking villa that was originally built as a hunting lodge in 1825. With its reputation for well-conceived food and intelligent, sensitive service, the restaurant has flourished here since it was established in the mid-1980s. You'll dine within a high-ceilinged dining room decorated in the Jugendstil style, or in good weather, outside in a manicured garden beneath the spreading limbs of massive chestnut trees. (Four additional rooms cater to private parties.) The cuisine is as elegantly prepared as the decor; only market-fresh ingredients are used and deftly handled by the skilled chefs. Menu items change with the season but are likely to include a salad of fresh wild greens garnished with grilled scampi and rock lobster; carpaccio of venison with fresh herbs and olive oil; an excellent saddle of lamb served with thyme sauce, green beans, and gratin of potatoes; fillets of veal with morel sauce; glazed sweetbreads with truffle sauce; and a medley of sophisticated desserts that are rolled from table to table on a trolley.

✪ Käfer-Schänke. Prinzregentenstrasse 73. ☎ **089/41680.** Reservations required. Main courses 25–45 DM ($14.25–$25.65). Fixed-price lunch 43 DM ($24.50). AE, DC, MC, V. Mon–Sat 11:30am–midnight. Closed holidays. U-Bahn: U4 to Prinzregentenplatz. Bus: 55. GERMAN/INTERNATIONAL.

For casual dining prepared with elegant style, this spot on the second floor of a famous gourmet shop, Käfer, is one of the best in Munich. The setting resembles a chalet, and the cuisine roams the world for inspiration—everywhere from Lombardy to Asia. You select your hors d'oeuvres from a dazzling display and are billed according to how many pâtés or croûtes you choose. Waiters serve the main dishes. Often Käfer-Schänke devotes a week to a particular country's cuisine. On one visit, we enjoyed the classic *loup* (sea bass) with fennel as presented on the French Riviera. The salads have what one reviewer called "rococo splendor." From a cold table, you can choose smoked salmon or smoked eel. Venison, quail, and guinea hen are regularly featured. There's a deluxe gourmet shop on the main floor.

Prielhof. Oberföhringer Strasse 44. ☎ **089/985353.** Reservations required. Main courses 25–45 DM ($14.25–$25.65). Fixed-price lunch 50 DM ($28.50); fixed-price dinner 78 DM ($44.45). No credit cards. Wed–Mon noon–2:30pm and 6–11pm. U-Bahn: U4 to Arabella-park. FRENCH.

It's one of the most glamorous French restaurants in town. The decor is Austrian and urbane. A green ceramic *Kachelofen* (porcelain stove) dominates one side of the main dining room. Menu items are influenced by modern French cuisine and are written in a very French scrawl on the frequently changing menu. They include cream of potato soup with chanterelles; sautéed sweetbreads with asparagus and fresh tomatoes; a heavenly braised guinea fowl with wild greens and shiitake mushrooms; vegetable risotto with braised goose liver; gratin of saltwater fish with leafy salad and chive sauce; braised hen with rosemary, tomatoes, and parslied potatoes; and our favorite, rack of lamb in an herb crust with creamed potatoes, ratatouille, and green beans. Dessert might be an amaretto parfait with marinated berries. The restaurant is named, incidentally, after the upscale neighborhood where it's located.

9 In Denning

Casale. Ostpreussenstrasse 42. ☎ **089/936268.** Reservations recommended. Main courses 36–63 DM ($20.50–$35.90). Fixed-price menus 65–98 DM ($37.05–$55.85). AE, DC, MC, V. Daily noon–3pm and 6–11pm. U-Bahn: U4 to Arabellapark. ITALIAN.

It's one of the more restrained, discreet, upscale, and formal of Munich's many Italian restaurants, with a decor more self-consciously "expensive" than many of its competitors. It's north of the city center, near the mega-hotels of the Bogenhausen district. It works hard on such tours de force as a nine-course *menu dégustazione* that requires several hours to consume gracefully. Menu items are savory and stylish and usually served with flair. They include sea bass prepared with rosemary in a salt crust, filet of beef with Barolo sauce, and an array of pastas that include ravioli stuffed with pulverized veal and spices and an excellent linguine with fresh asparagus or exotic seasonal mushrooms.

10 In Solln

Al Pino. Frans-Hals-Strasse 3, Solln. ☎ **089/799885.** Reservations recommended for dinner. Main courses 29–39 DM ($16.55–$22.25). AE, MC. Sun–Fri noon–2:30pm and daily 6–8:30pm (last order). S-Bahn: S7 to Solln. ITALIAN.

Set in the southern suburb of Solln, seven subway stops from Munich's main railway station, this is a likable and unpretentious restaurant with well-prepared food. It's busier in the evening than at lunch, and although diners are welcome to linger at the table as long as they want, management prefers that they be seated before 8:30pm, a fact that might cramp your style if you're a night owl. The venue evokes the ambience of a comfortable, upscale trattoria in a bustling northern Italian city like Milan (though some Sicilian items appear on the menu). Especially delectable are freshly made pasta with fresh chanterelles or salmon, baked lamb with red wine sauce and onions, ravioli stuffed with herbs and mozzarella, platters of perfectly grilled fresh fish, and desserts that might include mascarpone. These can be accompanied by a bottle of Italian wine from the establishment's well-stocked cellar.

11 In Grünwald

✪ **Grünwalder Einkehr.** Nördlicher Münchner Strasse 2, in Grünwald. ☎ **089/
649-2304.** Reservations recommended. Main courses 14–35 DM ($8–$19.95). AE, DC, MC, V.
Tues–Sun noon–3pm and 6pm–10:30pm. U-Bahn: U2 to Silberhornstrasse, then tram 25.
BAVARIAN.

This restaurant, 8 miles south of the city, was the home of a prosperous landowner
around 200 years ago. Its trio of dining rooms are outfitted in an elegantly rustic
Bavarian style that a temporary refugee from city streets might find very appealing.
The cuisine, however, reflects a different tradition—menu items are conservative
and French, featuring such dishes as a succulent roast rack of lamb with rosemary
sauce, fried trout with almond-butter sauce, filet of beef with green peppercorn
sauce, pistou, and a satisfying, old-fashioned version of *tarte tatin.*

12 In Nymphenburg

Nymphenburger Hof. Nymphenburger Strasse 24. ☎ **089/123-3830.** Reservations recommended in summer. Main courses 28–38 DM ($15.95–$21.65). Fixed-price lunch 33.50
DM ($19.10); fixed-price dinner 65–85 DM ($37.05–$48.45). AE, DC, MC. Mon–Sat
noon–3pm and 6–11pm. U-Bahn: U1 to Steiglmaierplatz. AUSTRIAN.

Many Münchners consider an outing to its verdant outdoor terrace, 6 miles west of
the Marienplatz and 3 miles from Schloss Nymphenburg, the next best thing to a
week in the country. Although the modern blue-and-white interior is attractive in
any season, the place is especially appealing in summer when the outdoor terrace,
separated from the busy avenue by a screen of trees, is open.

Don't expect even a hint of tradition, as everything is streamlined and modern.
The only nostalgic thing about the place is the courtly but amused service and the
cuisine, inspired by what used to be known as the Austro-Hungarian Empire.
Examples include Wiener schnitzel, Tafelspitz (the favorite of Austrian Emperor
Franz Josef), *Kaiserschmarr* (a sweet dessert made with apples), a variety of Czech
pastries made with honey and plums, and the gooey sticky dessert beloved across
the border, *Salzburger knockerl.*

13 Cafes

Many Münchners take a break during the day to relax over coffee or a beer, read the
newspaper, or meet friends. For afternoon coffee and pastry, also see the cafes listed
in chapter 9.

Café Glockenspiel. Marienplatz 28. ☎ **089/264256.** Daily 10am–1am. U-Bahn or S-Bahn:
Marienplatz.

This is the most frequented cafe in Munich. It's across from the Rathaus, and a
crowd gathers here every day at 10:30am to watch the miniature tournament staged
by the clock on the Rathaus facade. In addition to the view, the cafe has good coffee
costing from 4.30 to 5.90 DM ($2.45 to $3.35), with pastries beginning at 4.80
DM ($2.75). It also makes a fine place to end your day tour of Munich and fortify
yourself for Munich after dark. Arrive around 5pm for a drink and watch the square
change its stripes as it goes from daytime to night. It's an ideal place for people-
watching.

Café Luitpold. Briennerstrasse 11. ☎ **089/292865.** Mon–Fri 9am–8pm, Sat 8am–7pm.
U-Bahn: Königsplatz or Odeonsplatz.

Opened in 1888 and rebuilt in a blandly modern style after the ravages of World War II, this cafe once attracted such notables as Ibsen, Kandinsky, Johann Strauss the Younger, and other musicians, artists, and authors, as well as members of the royal court of Bavaria. What you'll find today, however, is mainstream workaday Munich stopping in for a pastry, a platter of food, coffee, or a mug of beer. There's a more formal restaurant associated with the place, but we tend to prefer the cafe section. A large beer costs 5.75 DM ($3.30); coffee costs from 4.35 DM ($2.50).

Guglhopf. Kaufingerstrasse 5. ☎ **089/260-8868.** Mon–Fri 7am–8pm, Sat 8am–8pm, Sun 10am–7pm. U-Bahn: Marienplatz.

Though it opened in the 1970s, this cafe's ambience of old-fashioned nostalgia and Bavarian rusticity will make you think it's older than it really is. It's named for the closest thing to a Bavarian "national pastry," the *Guglhopf.* Made with flour, eggs, and sugar, the pastry comes in at least four different variations, including chocolate and/or nuts. Equally nationalistic is the apfelstrudel served with vanilla sauce. If you're craving more than just dessert try the pan-fried mushrooms with cream and herb sauce, served over a bed of homemade noodles. You can borrow any of a half-dozen newspapers while you eat your pastry and drink your coffee or beer. A slice of the namesake pastry costs 3.90 DM ($2.20), beer or Weissbeer is 5.20 DM ($2.95), and platters are 8.50 to 18 DM ($4.85 to $10.25).

Ruffini. Orffstrasse 22–24. ☎ **089/161160.** Tues–Sat 10am–midnight, Sun 10am–6pm. U-Bahn: U1 to Rotkreuzplatz.

Münchners head for this turn-of-the-century former residence at the end of U-bahn Line 1 for a respite from the pressures of the inner city. It offers everything you'd expect from a traditional cafe. You can relax over your coffee or beer with the most recent edition of several different newspapers, or view the cafe's current painting exhibition (most are for sale). The cafe maintains its own bakery in the cellar, and a wine shop and delicatessen on a corner nearby. Coffee costs 3.60 to 5.30 DM ($2.05 to $3); snacks such as cheese platters go for 12 DM ($6.85). Warm platters are 15 to 25 DM ($8.55 to $14.25). The cafe offers natural food, free from artificial fertilizers, flavors, or coloring.

Schlosscafé im Palmenhaus. In the gardens of Schloss Nymphenburg, near entrance 43 and the rose gardens. ☎ **089/175309.** Daily 9:30am–6:30pm. Closed on Mon Nov–Mar. Tram: 17.

This cafe is in a historical reconstruction of a 17th-century building that once functioned as a conservatory for palm trees. The original building, older than the Schloss itself, was destroyed in World War II. Here you can have your coffee capped with whipped cream or drink your beer in the garden, weather permitting. Coffee costs from 3.80 DM ($2.15), and beer goes for 5.40 DM ($3.10). Luncheon platters of unpretentious food include rice curries, schnitzels with french fries, and salads, and cost from 6.50 to 38 DM ($3.70 to $21.65).

14 Beer Gardens

If you're in Munich anytime between the first sunny spring day and the last fading light of a Bavarian-style autumn, you might head for one of the city's celebrated beer gardens. Traditionally, beer gardens were simple tables placed under the chestnut trees that were planted above the storage cellars to keep the beer cool in summer. People, naturally, started to drink close to the source of their pleasure, and the tradition has remained. Lids on beer steins, incidentally, were meant to keep out flies. It's estimated that today Munich has at least 400 beer gardens and cellars. Food, drink, and atmosphere are much the same in all of them.

Bamberger Haus. Brunnerstrasse 2. ☎ **089/308-8966.** Main courses 15.50–32 DM ($8.85–$18.25); large beer 4.60 DM ($2.60). Restaurant, daily 11am–10pm; beer hall, daily 11am–1am. AE, MC, V. U-Bahn: U3 or U6 to Scheidplatz.

In a century-old house northwest of Schwabing at the edge of Luitpold Park, Bamberger Haus is named after the city of Bamberg, most noted for the quantity of its beer drinking. Most visitors head for the street-level restaurant. Bavarian and international specialties include well-seasoned soups, grilled steak, veal, pork, and sausages. If you want only to drink, you might visit the rowdier and less expensive beer hall in the cellar.

✪ Biergärten Chinesischer Turm. Englischer Garten 3. ☎ **089/383-8730.** Meals from 15 DM ($8.55); large beer 10 DM ($5.70). Daily 11am–9pm. AE, MC, V. U-Bahn: U3 or U6 to Giselastrasse.

Our favorite is in the Englischer Garten, the park lying between the Isar River and Schwabing. The biggest city-owned park in Europe, it has several beer gardens, of which the Biergärten Chinesischer Turm is the best. The largest and most popular of its kind in Europe, it takes its name from its location at the foot of a pagodalike tower, a landmark that's easy to find. Beer and Bavarian food, and plenty of it, are what you get here. For a large glass or mug of beer, ask for *ein mass Bier*, which is enough to bathe in. It will likely be slammed down, still foaming, by a server carrying 12 other tall steins. The food is very cheap. Homemade dumplings are a specialty, as are all kinds of tasty sausage. You can get a first-rate *Schweinbraten* (braised loin of pork served with potato dumpling and rich brown gravy), which is Bavaria's answer to the better-known Sauerbraten of the north. Huge baskets of pretzels are passed around, and they're eaten with *radi*, the large, tasty white radishes famous from these parts. Oompah bands often play, and it's most festive. It's open May through October until midnight, but from November through April, its closing depends on the weather and the number of guests.

Gaststätte zum Flaucher. Isarauen 8. ☎ **089/723-2677.** Meals 9.50–24.50 DM ($5.40–$13.95); large beer 9.50 DM ($5.40). May–Oct, daily 10am–10pm; Nov–Apr, Fri–Sun 10am–8pm. Bus: 52 from Marienplatz.

If you're going to the zoo, which we'll recommend later, you might want to stop close by for fun and food. The word *Gaststätte* tells you that it's a typical Bavarian inn. This one is mellow and traditional, with tables set in a tree-shaded garden overlooking the river. Here you can order the local specialty, *Leberkäse*, a large sausage loaf eaten with freshly baked pretzels and plenty of mustard, a deli delight. The most expensive food platter goes for 16.50 DM ($9.40).

Hirschgarten. Hirschgartenstrasse 1. ☎ **089/172591.** Meals 9–30 DM ($5.15–$17.10); large beer 9.50 DM ($5.40). MC. Daily 10am–midnight. S-Bahn: Laim. Tram: Romanplatz.

In the Nymphenburg Park sector (near one of Munich's leading sightseeing attractions, Schloss Nymphenburg), west of the heart of town, this beer garden is part of a 500-acre park with hunting lodges and lakes. The largest open-air restaurant in Munich, it seats some 8,000 beer drinkers and Bavarian merrymakers. A 1-liter stein of Augustiner tap beer goes for 9.50 DM ($5.40).

Zum Aumeister. Sondermeierstrasse 1. ☎ **089/325224.** Main courses 15–40 DM ($8.55–$22.80); large beer 4.80 DM ($2.75). Tues–Sun 10am–10pm. No credit cards.

If you have a car, and have a nostalgic streak, you'll enjoy dining and drinking beer in the historic and evocative atmosphere of Zum Aumeister. Few places so authentically recapture the life gone by—surely the Bavarian royals, if they could miraculously return, would be delighted to see that their old hunting lodge is still around, and not much changed. It lies off the Frankfurter Ring at München-Freimann, a 20-minute drive north of the center. It offers a daily list of seasonal Bavarian specialties. Especially enjoyable is the cream of cauliflower soup and the rich oxtail soup.

Exploring Munich 6

Munich is a city of art and culture, one of Europe's most visited. It has innumerable monuments, and more museums than any other city in Germany. In quality, its collections even surpass those of Berlin. The Wittelsbachs were great collectors—some might say pillagers—and have left behind a city full of treasures.

Go to Munich to have fun and to enjoy the relaxed lifestyle, the friendly ambience, and the wealth of activities, sightseeing, and cultural events. You'll never be at a loss for something to do or see here, and on a short trip, you'll only be able to sample a few of the city's wealth of offerings.

SUGGESTED ITINERARIES

If You Have 1 Day

Local tourist tradition calls for a morning breakfast of Weisswurst (little white sausages). Head for Donisl (see chapter 5), which opens at 9am. A true Münchner downs them with a mug of beer. Then walk to Marienplatz (see "Exploring the City Center," below), with its Glockenspiel and Altes Rathaus (town hall). Later stroll along Maximilianstrasse, one of Europe's great shopping streets.

In the afternoon, visit the Alte Pinakothek and catch at least some exhibits at the Deutsches Museum. Cap the evening with a night of Bavarian food, beer, and music at the Hofbräuhaus am Platzl (see chapter 9).

If You Have 2 Days

Spend the first day as detailed above. In the morning of day 2, visit the Staatsgalerie Moderner Kunst and, if the weather's right, plan a lunch in one of the beer gardens of the Englischer Garten. In the afternoon, explore Nymphenburg Palace, summer residence of the Wittelsbachs.

If You Have 3 Days

Spend days 1 and 2 as outlined above. Occupy your third day exploring the sights you've missed so far: the Residenz, the Städtische Galerie im Lenbachhaus, and the Bavarian National Museum. If you have any more time, return to the Deutsches

Munich Attractions

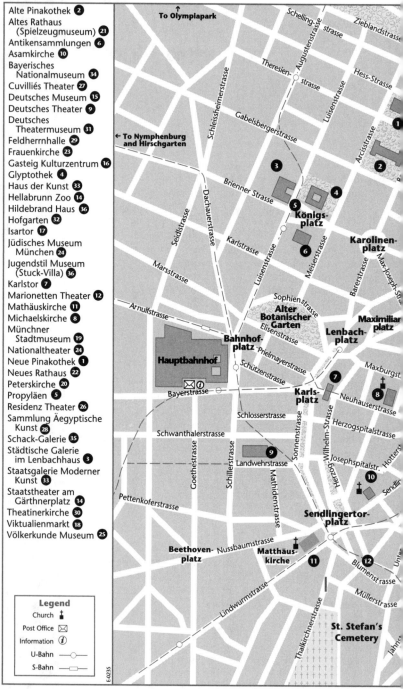

Legend

Church ✝
Post Office ✉
Information ⓘ
U-Bahn ─○─
S-Bahn ─▭─

E-0235

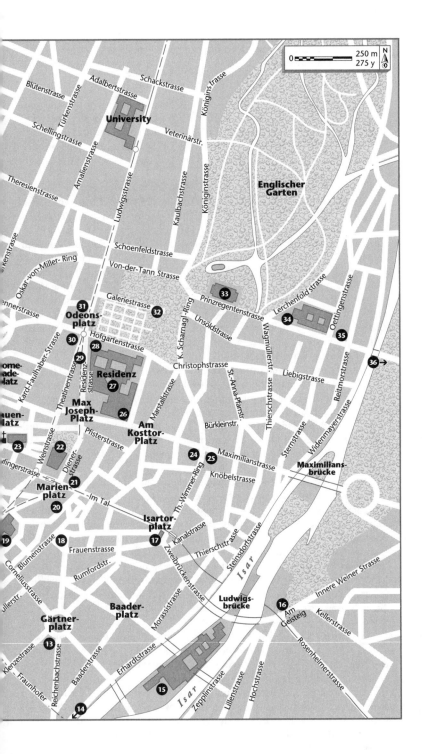

Museum. Have dinner, or at least a drink, at the Olympiapark Tower, enjoying a panoramic view of the Alps.

If You Have 4 or 5 Days

Spend the first three days as outlined above. As fascinating as Munich is, tear yourself away for a side trip on day 4 to one of the Royal Castles built by the "mad king," Ludwig II (see chapters 10 and 11). On day 5, visit Dachau, the notorious World War II concentration camp (see chapter 10), or go farther afield to Garmisch-Partenkirchen for a taste of the Bavarian Alps (see chapter 11).

1 Exploring the City Center

Marienplatz, dedicated to the patron of the city, whose golden statue atop a huge column (the Mariensaüle) stands in the center of the square, is the heart of the Altstadt. On its north side is the **Neues Rathaus** (New City Hall) built in 19th-century Gothic style. Each day at 10:30am, and also at noon and 5pm in the summer, the Glockenspiel on the facade stages an elaborate performance, including a miniature tournament, with enameled copper figures moving in and out of the archways. Since you're already at the Rathaus, you may wish to climb the 55 steps to the top of its tower (an elevator is available if you're conserving energy) for a good overall view of the city center. **Altes Rathaus** (Old City Hall), with its plain Gothic tower, is to the right. It was reconstructed in the 15th century, after being destroyed by fire.

South of the square you can see the oldest church in Munich, **St. Peter's.** The outdoor **Viktualienmarkt,** just off Marienplatz and around the corner from St. Peter's church, has been a gathering place since 1807. Here people buy fresh country produce, wines, meats, and cheese as well as gossip, browse, and snack.

To the north lies **Odeonsplatz,** Munich's most beautiful square, near the **Residenz** (Royal Palace) and the **Theatinerkirche.** Adjoining the Residenz is the restored **Nationaltheater,** home of the acclaimed Bavarian State Opera and the Bavarian National Ballet.

Running west from Odeonsplatz is the wide shopping avenue, Briennerstrasse, leading to **Königsplatz.** Flanking this large Grecian square are three classical buildings constructed by Ludwig I—the **Propyläen,** the **Glyptothek,** and the **Antikensammlungen.** Returning to Odeonsplatz, note the **Feldherrnhalle,** a loggia designed after a Florentine model, at the south end of the busy Ludwigstrasse. The Ludwigstrasse leads north to the section of Munich known as **Schwabing.** This is the Greenwich Village or Latin Quarter of Munich, proud of its artistic and literary heritage, numbering among its own such writers as Ibsen and Rilke. The Blue Rider group, which influenced abstract art in the early 20th century, originated here. Today Schwabing's sidewalk tables are filled with young people from all over the world.

The **Isartor** (Isar Gate) is one of the most photographed Munich landmarks. Take the S-Bahn to Isartor. This is the only tower left from the wall that once encircled Munich, forming part of the city's fortifications against invaders.

The other major gate of Munich is the **Karlstor,** once known as Neuhauser Tor, lying northeast of Karlsplatz (nicknamed Stachus). Take Tram 18 to Karlsplatz. Karlstor lies at the end of Neuhauser Strasse, which formed part of the town's second circuit of walls, dating from the 1500s. It takes its present name from Elector Charles Theodore in 1791. Unlike the Isartor, the Karlstor lost its main tower (1302) in an 1857 explosion.

2 Museums & Palaces

⭐ **Alte Pinakothek.** Barerstrasse 27. ☎ **089/2380-5216.** Admission 7 DM ($4) adults, 4 DM ($2.30) students, free for children 14 and under. Daily 10am–5pm (until 8pm Thurs). U-Bahn: U2 to Königsplatz. Tram: 27. Bus: 53.

This is not only Munich's most important art museum, but also one of the most significant collections in Europe. The nearly 900 paintings on display (many thousands more are in storage) in this huge neoclassical building represent the greatest European artists from the 14th through the 18th centuries. Begun as a small court collection by the royal Wittelsbach family in the early 1500s, the collection grew and grew. There are only two floors with exhibits, but the museum is immense, and we do not recommend that you try to cover all the galleries in one day. Try to see some of the more important works, described below.

The landscape painter *par excellence* of the Danube school, Albrecht Altdorfer, is represented by no fewer than six monumental works. The works of Albrecht Dürer include his greatest—and final—*Self-Portrait* (1500). Here the artist has portrayed himself with almost Christlike solemnity. Also displayed is the last great painting by the artist, his two-paneled work called *The Four Apostles* (1526).

Several galleries are given over to works by Dutch and Flemish masters. The *St. Columbia Altarpiece* (1460–62), by Roger van der Weyden, is the most important of these, in size as well as significance. Measuring nearly 10 feet across, it is a triumph of van der Weyden's subtle linear style and one of his last works (he died in 1464).

A number of works by Rembrandt, Rubens, and Van Dyck include a series of religious panels painted by Rembrandt for Prince Frederick Hendrick of the Netherlands. A variety of French, Spanish, and Italian artists are found in both the larger galleries and the small rooms lining the outer wall. The Italian masters are well represented by Fra Filippo Lippi, Giotto, Botticelli, Raphael (*Holy Family*), and Titian.

You'll also see a *Madonna* by da Vinci, a famous self-portrait by the young Rembrandt (1629), and a number of works by Lucas Cranach, including his *Venus*. In the *Land of Cockaigne,* Pieter Brueghel has satirized a popular subject of European folk literature: The place where no work has to be done and where food simply falls into one's mouth. Note the little egg on legs running up to be eaten and the plucked and cooked chicken laying its neck on a plate. In the background you'll see a knight lying under a roof with his mouth open, waiting for the pies to slip off the eaves over his head.

Important works are always on display, but exhibits also change. You'd be wise to buy a map of the gallery to guide you through the dozens of rooms.

⭐ **Residenz.** Max-Joseph-Platz 3. ☎ **089/290671.** Museum and Treasury, 6 DM ($3.40) adults, 4 DM ($2.30) students and seniors; Old Residenz Theater, 3 DM ($1.70) adults, 2 DM ($1.15) students, free for children under 15. Combined ticket 10 DM ($5.70) adults, 6 DM ($3.40) students and children. Museum and Treasury, Tues–Sun 10am–4:30pm (last tickets sold at 4pm); Theatre, Mon–Sat 2–5pm, Sun 10am–5pm. U-Bahn: U3, U5, or U6 to Odeonsplatz.

When a member of the royal Bavarian family said that he was going to the castle, he could have meant any number of places, especially if he was Ludwig II. But if he said that he was going home, he could only be referring to the Residenz. This enormous palace, with a history almost as long as that of the Wittelsbach family, was the official residence of the rulers of Bavaria from 1385 to 1918. Added to and rebuilt over the centuries, the complex is a conglomerate of various styles of architecture.

Depending on how you approach the Residenz, you might first see a German Renaissance hall (the western facade), a Palladian palace (on the north), or a Florentine Renaissance palace (on the south facing Max-Joseph-Platz).

The Residenz has been completely restored since its almost total destruction in World War II and now houses the Residenz Museum, a concert hall, the Cuvilliés Theater, and the Residenz Treasure House.

Residenz Museum, Max-Joseph-Platz 3, comprises the southwestern section of the palace, some 120 rooms of art and furnishings collected by centuries of Wittelsbachs. To see the entire collection, you'll have to take two tours, one in the morning and the other in the afternoon. You may also visit the rooms on your own.

The **Ancestors' Gallery** is designed like a hall of mirrors, with one important difference: Where the mirrors would normally be, there are portraits of the members of the Wittelsbach family, set into gilded, carved paneling. The largest room in the museum section is the **Hall of Antiquities,** possibly the finest example of interior Renaissance secular styling in Germany. Frescoes, painted by dozens of 16th- and 17th-century artists, neatly adorn every inch of space on the walls and ceilings. The room is broken into sections by pilasters and niches, each with its own bust of a Roman emperor or a Greek hero. The central attraction is the two-story chimney-piece of red stucco and marble. Completed in 1600, it's adorned with Tuscan pillars and the coat-of-arms of the dukes of Bavaria.

On the second floor of the palace, directly over the Hall of Antiquities, the museum has gathered its enormous collection of Far Eastern porcelain. Note also the fine assemblage of oriental rugs in the long, narrow **Porcelain Gallery.**

If you have time to view only one item in the **Schatzkammer** (Treasure House), make it the 16th-century Renaissance statue of *St. George Slaying the Dragon.* The equestrian statue is made of gold, but you can barely see the precious metal through the thousands of diamonds, rubies, emeralds, sapphires, and semiprecious stones embedded in it.

Both the Residenz Museum and the Schatzkammer are entered from Max-Joseph-Platz on the south side of the palace. From the Brunnenhof, you can visit the Alte Residenztheater, better known as the **Cuvilliés Theater,** whose rococo tiers of boxes are supported by seven bacchants. Directly over the huge center box, where the royal family sat, is a crest in white and gold topped by a jewel-bedecked crown of Bavaria held in place by cherubs in flight. In summer this theater is the scene of frequent concert and opera performances. Mozart's *Idomeneo* was first performed here in 1781.

The Italianate **Hofgarten,** or Court Garden, is one of the special "green lungs" of Munich. To the north of the Residenz, it's enclosed on two sides by arcades; the garden dates from the time of Duke Maximilian I and was laid out between 1613 and 1617. In the center is the Hofgarten temple, a 12-sided pavilion dating from 1615.

✪ **Bayerisches Nationalmuseum (Bavarian National Museum).** Prinzregentenstrasse 3.
☎ **089/211241.** Admission 3 DM ($1.70) adults, 2 DM ($1.15) students and seniors, free for children under 15. Tues–Sun 9:30am–5pm. U-Bahn: U4 or U5 to Lehel. Tram: 17. Bus: 53.

King Maximilian II in 1855 began an institution to preserve Bavaria's artistic and historical riches. So rapidly did the collection grow in the next 100 years that the museum moved to larger quarters several times. Its current building, near the Haus der Kunst, contains three vast floors of sculpture, painting, folk art, ceramics, furniture, and textiles, as well as clocks and scientific instruments.

Residenz

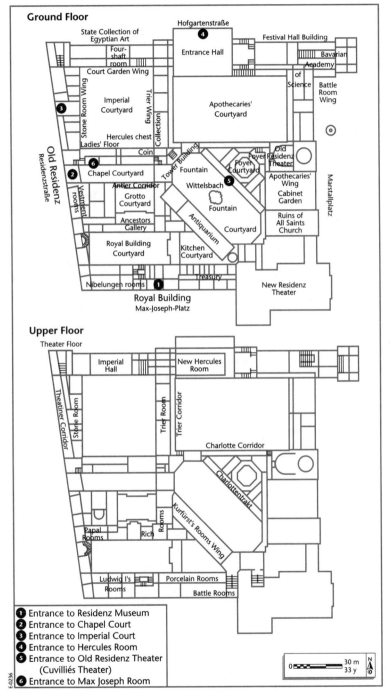

Ground Floor

State Collection of Egyptian Art

Hofgartenstraße

④

Festival Hall Building

Four-shaft room

Entrance Hall

Bavarian Academy

Court Garden Wing

of Science

Battle Room Wing

Trier Wing

Imperial Courtyard

Apothecaries' Courtyard

Stone Room Wing

③

Hercules chest

Ladies' Floor

Coin Collection

Old Residenz Theater

Old Residenz

Residenzstraße

②

⑥ Chapel Courtyard

Tower Building

Fountain

Foyer

Foyer Courtyard

Apothecaries' Wing

Cabinet Garden

Antler Corridor

Wittelsbach

⑤

Grotto Courtyard

Fountain

Ruins of All Saints Church

Vestment rooms

Ancestors Gallery

Antiquarium

Courtyard

Marstallplatz

Royal Building Courtyard

Kitchen Courtyard

Nibelungen rooms **①**

Treasury

New Residenz Theater

Royal Building
Max-Joseph-Platz

Upper Floor

Theater Floor

Imperial Hall

New Hercules Room

Theatiner Corridor

Stone Room

Trier Room

Trier Corridor

Charlotte Corridor

Charlottentrakt

Kurfürst's Rooms Wing

Rooms

Papal Rooms

Rich

Ludwig I's Rooms

Porcelain Rooms

Battle Rooms

① Entrance to Residenz Museum
② Entrance to Chapel Court
③ Entrance to Imperial Court
④ Entrance to Hercules Room
⑤ Entrance to Old Residenz Theater (Cuvilliés Theater)
⑥ Entrance to Max Joseph Room

0 ▄▄▄▄ 30 m / 33 y

N

E-0236

An Unlikely Genius: François Cuvilliés

In the 17th and 18th centuries, Bavaria's rulers were determined to rival Rome itself by adorning their city with churches and abbeys and monuments. In the cut-throat competition for commissions that followed, an unexpected candidate emerged to become Munich's most brilliant master of rococo style.

François Cuvilliés (1695–1768) was born in Belgium, a dwarf. Few roles were open to those like himself, who were regarded as freaks and collected by the rich as if they were curious objects. Like many of his peers, he became a page boy and later court jester to Max Emanuele, elector of Bavaria. Ambitious and witty, with a charm that transcended his stature, he won his patron's friendship and support.

When the elector was exiled, François went with him. It was during this exile, at St-Cloud near Paris, that he first encountered the French baroque style and began to absorb his patron's interest in French aesthetics. When the elector was later recalled to Bavaria and reinstated as ruler with pomp and ceremony, François was allowed to become a draftsman for the court's chief architect.

Cuvilliés proved himself so talented that in 1720 the elector sent him for a 4-year apprenticeship to one of the leading architects of Paris, Jacques-François Blondel. When he returned to Munich, his work soon eclipsed that of his master, and by 1745, the former jester had been elevated to the title of chief architect to the Bavarian court.

Commissions he received between 1726 and his death in 1768 include some of southern Germany's most important rococo monuments. Noted for a flam-boyant sinuousness, his work includes the interior of the Amalienburg Pavilion in the park at Nymphenburg Palace and the facade of the Theatinerkirche. His most famous masterpiece is, of course, the remarkable Altes Residenztheater, familiarly called by his name.

Cuvilliés's son, François Cuvilliés the Younger (1731–1777), also became an architect, although he never achieved the greatness of his father. Most notably, he put the final touches on the facade of the Theatinerkirche that his father had left unfinished at his death.

Entering the museum, turn right and go into the first large gallery (the Wesso-brunn Room). Devoted to early church art from the 5th through the 13th cen-turies, this room holds some of the oldest and most valuable works. The desk case contains medieval ivories, including the so-called Munich ivory, from about A.D. 400. The carving shows the women weeping at the tomb of Christ while the resur-rected Lord is gingerly stepping up the clouds and into heaven. At the crossing to the adjoining room is the stone figure of the *Virgin with the Rose Bush,* from Straubing (ca. 1300), one of the few pieces of old Bavarian church art to be influ-enced by the spirit of mysticism.

The Riemenschneider Room is devoted to the works of the great sculptor and carver Tilman Riemenschneider (ca. 1460–1531) and his contemporaries. Charac-teristic of the sculptor's works is the use of natural, unpainted wood. Note especially the 12 apostles from the Marienkapelle in Würzburg (1510), St. Mary Magdalene, the central group from the high altar in the parish church of Münnerstadt (1490–1492), and the figure of St. Sebastian (1490). Also on display are famous collections of arms and armor from the 16th to 18th centuries.

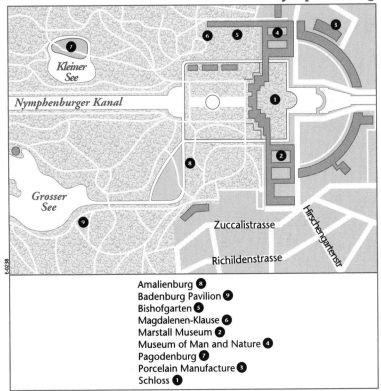

Amalienburg **8**
Badenburg Pavilion **9**
Bishofgarten **5**
Magdalenen-Klause **6**
Marstall Museum **2**
Museum of Man and Nature **4**
Pagodenburg **7**
Porcelain Manufacture **3**
Schloss **1**

On the second floor is a fine collection of stained and painted glass—an art in which medieval Germany excelled. Other rooms on this floor include baroque ivory carvings, Meissen porcelain, and ceramics. One novelty addition to the museum is the collection of antique clocks, some dating from the 16th century.

In the east wing of the basement level are many Christmas cribs from Germany, Austria, Italy, and Moravia. The variety of materials competes with the variety of styles—wood, amber, gold, terra-cotta, and even wax were used in making these nativity scenes. Also on this level is a display of Bavarian folk art, including many examples of wood carving.

✪ **Schloss Nymphenburg.** Schloss Nymphenburg 1. ☎ **089/1790-8668.** The 8 DM ($4.55) ticket includes the palace, Marstallmuseum (carriages), museum of porcelain, and the pavilions in the park; free for children 13 and under. For Nymphenburg palace, Amalienburg, Marstallmuseum, and museum of porcelain only, 6 DM ($3.40) for adults, free for children 13 and under. Apr–Sept, Tues–Sun 10am–noon and 1:30–5pm; Oct–Mar, Tues–Sun 10am–noon and 1:30–4pm. Parking beside the Marstallmuseum. U-Bahn: U1 to Rotkreuzplatz, then tram 12 toward Amalienburgstrasse. Bus: 41.

In summer, the Wittelsbachs would pack their bags and head for their country house, Schloss Nymphenburg. A more complete, more sophisticated palace than the Residenz in Munich, it was begun in 1664 by Elector Ferdinand Maria in Italian villa style and took more than 150 years and several architectural changes to complete. The final palace plan was the work of Elector Max Emanuel, who in 1702 decided to enlarge the villa by adding four large pavilions connected by arcaded passageways. Gradually the French style took over, and today the facade is in a subdued baroque style.

The palace interior is less subtle, however. Upon entering the main building, you're in the great hall, decorated in rococo colors and stuccos. The frescoes by Johann Baptist Zimmermann (1756) depict incidents from mythology, especially those dealing with Flora, goddess of the spring, and her nymphs, for whom the palace was named. This hall was used for both banquets and concerts during the reign of Max Joseph III, elector during the mid–18th century. Concerts are still presented here in summer.

From the main building, turn left and head for the arcaded gallery connecting the northern pavilions. The first room in the arcade is the Great Gallery of Beauties, painted for Elector Max Emanuel in 1710. More provocative, however, is Ludwig I's Gallery of Beauties in the south pavilion (the apartments of Queen Caroline). Ludwig commissioned no fewer than 36 portraits of the most beautiful women of his day. The paintings by J. Stieler (created from 1827 to 1850) include the *Schöne Münchenerin* (lovely Munich girl) and a portrait of Lola Montez, the dancer whose "friendship" with Ludwig I caused a scandal that factored into the Revolution of 1848.

To the south of the palace buildings, in the rectangular block of low structures that once housed the court stables, is the **Marstallmuseum.** In the first hall, look for the glass coronation coach of Elector Karl Albrecht, built in Paris in 1740. From the same period comes the elaborate hunting sleigh of Electress Amalia, adorned with a statue of Diana, goddess of the hunt; even the sleigh's runners are decorated with shellwork and hunting trophies.

The coaches and sleighs of Ludwig II are displayed in the third hall. His constant longing for the grandeur of the past is reflected in the ornately designed state coach, meant for his marriage to Duchess Sophie of Bavaria, a royal wedding that never came off. The fairy-tale coach wasn't wasted, however, since Ludwig often used it to ride through the countryside at night, and from castle to castle, creating quite a picture. The coach is completely gilded, inside and out; rococo carvings cover every inch of space except for the panels, faced with paintings on copper. In winter the king would ride in his state sleigh, nearly as elaborate as the Cinderella coach.

Nymphenburg's greatest attraction is the **park.** Stretching for 500 acres in front of the palace, it's divided into two sections by the canal that runs from the pool at the foot of the staircase to the cascade at the far end of the English-style gardens.

Within the park are a number of pavilions. The guided tour begins with the **Amalienburg,** whose plain exterior belies the rococo decoration inside. Built as a hunting lodge for Electress Amalia (in 1734), the pavilion carries the hunting theme through the first few rooms and then bursts into salons of flamboyant colors, rich carvings, and wall paintings. The most impressive room is the Hall of Mirrors, a symphony of silver ornaments on a faint blue background.

The **Badenburg Pavilion** sits at the edge of the large lake of the same name. As its name implies, it was built as a bathing pavilion, although it's difficult to visualize Ludwig dashing in from the water in a dripping swimsuit and across those elegant floors. A trip to the basement, however, will help you appreciate the pavilion's practical side. Here you'll see the unique bath, surrounded by blue-and-white Dutch tiles. The ceiling is painted with frescoes of mythological bathing scenes.

The octagonal **Pagodenburg,** on the smaller lake on the other side of the canal, looks like a Chinese pagoda from the outside. The interior, however, is decorated with pseudo-Chinese motifs, often using Dutch tiles in place of Chinese ones.

Magdalenenklause may look like a ruin, but that was the intention when it was built in 1725. Also called the Hermitage, it was planned as a retreat for prayer and solitude. The four main rooms of the one-story structure are paneled with uncarved stained oak, with simple furnishings and a few religious paintings—a really drastic change from the other buildings.

Neue Pinakothek. Barer Strasse 29. ☎ **089/2380-5195.** Admission 8 DM ($4.55) adults, 4 DM ($2.30) students, children, and seniors. Tues and Thurs 10am–8pm, Wed and Fri–Sun 10am–5pm. U-Bahn: U2 to Königsplatz. Tram: 27. Bus: 53.

Neue Pinakothek offers a survey of 18th- and 19th-century art. Across Theresienstrasse from the Alte Pinakothek, the museum was reconstructed after its destruction in World War II; it reopened in 1981. The museum has paintings by Gainsborough, Goya, David, Manet, van Gogh, and Monet, and many other works. Among the more popular German artists represented are Wilhelm Leibl and Gustav Klimt; you'll encounter a host of others whose art is less well known. Note particularly the genre paintings by Carl Spitzweg.

⭐ **Staatsgalerie Moderner Kunst (State Gallery of Modern Art).** Haus der Kunst, Prinzregentenstrasse 1. ☎ **089/2112-7137.** Staatsgalerie, 6 DM ($3.40) adults, 3.50 DM ($2) students, children, and seniors. No admission fee on Sun. Tues–Wed and Fri–Sun 10am–5pm, Thurs 10am–8pm. Closed some holidays. U-Bahn: Odeonsplatz. Bus: 53.

Munich's State Gallery of Modern Art is housed in the west wing of the massive Haus der Kunst, which was constructed in 1937. Some art critics claim that it has one of the 10 finest modern art collections in the world. It shows about 400 paintings, sculptures, and art objects from the 20th century. The largest exhibit is devoted to modern German art. You'll see paintings by Klee, Marc, Kirchner, Beckmann, and Lovis Corinth as well as Italian art, with stars such as Marino Marini and Renato Guttoso; American abstract expressionism; minimalist art; and a host of younger modern artists such as Anselm Kiefer. There are 14 works by Picasso, the earliest dating from 1903.

The east wing of the **Haus der Kunst**, Prinzregentenstrasse 1 (☎ **089/ 2112-7113**), is entered separately and requires a separate ticket. It's devoted to changing exhibitions, which are often cutting-edge and feature exciting new artists whose canvases are for sale when on display. Traveling exhibitions of worldwide importance stop here. Admission ranges from 8 to 12 DM ($4.55 to $6.85) for adults, depending on the exhibition, and 4 DM ($2.30) for children 6 to 18; children 5 and under free. Open Tuesday to Thursday from 10am to 10pm and Friday to Monday from 10am to 6pm.

⭐ **Deutsches Museum (German Museum of Masterpieces of Science and Technology).** Museuminsel 1. ☎ **089/21791.** Admission 10 DM ($5.70) adults, 7 DM ($4) seniors, 4 DM ($2.30) students, 3 DM ($1.70) children 6–12, free for children 5 and under. Daily 9am–5pm (closes at 2pm the second Wed in Dec). Closed major holidays. S-Bahn: Isartor. Tram: 18.

On an island in the Isar River, in the heart of Munich, this is the largest technological museum of its kind in the world. Its huge collection of priceless artifacts and historic originals includes the first electric dynamo (Siemens, 1866), the first automobile (Benz, 1886), the first diesel engine (1897), and the laboratory bench at which the atom was first split (Hahn, Strassmann, 1938). There are hundreds of buttons to push, levers to crank, and gears to turn, as well as a knowledgeable English-speaking staff to answer questions and demonstrate how steam engines, pumps, or historic musical instruments work.

Deutsches Museum

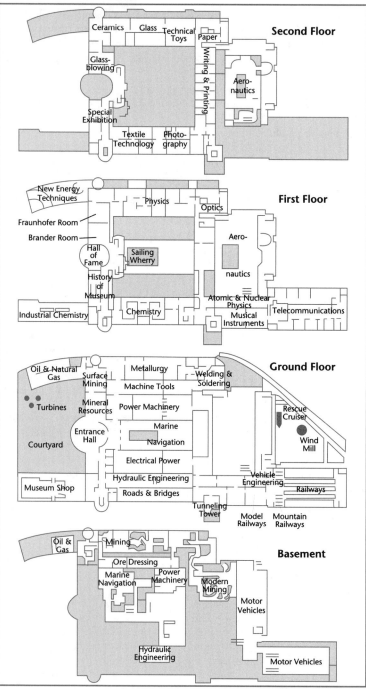

Second Floor

Ceramics · Glass · Technical Toys · Paper

Glass-blowing

Writing & Printing

Aero-nautics

Special Exhibition

Textile Technology · Photo-graphy

First Floor

New Energy Techniques

Physics

Optics

Fraunhofer Room

Brander Room

Hall of Fame

Sailing Wherry

Aero-nautics

History of Museum

Atomic & Nuclear Physics

Telecommunications

Industrial Chemistry

Chemistry

Musical Instruments

Ground Floor

Oil & Natural Gas

Surface Mining

Metallurgy

Welding & Soldering

Turbines

Mineral Resources

Machine Tools

Power Machinery

Rescue Cruiser

Entrance Hall

Marine Navigation

Wind Mill

Courtyard

Electrical Power

Museum Shop

Hydraulic Engineering

Vehicle Engineering

Roads & Bridges

Railways

Tunneling Tower

Model Railways

Mountain Railways

Basement

Oil & Gas

Mining

Ore Dressing

Marine Navigation

Power Machinery

Modern Mining

Motor Vehicles

Hydraulic Engineering

Motor Vehicles

E-0237

Among the most popular displays are those on mining, with a series of model coal, salt, and iron mines, as well as the electric power hall, with high-voltage displays that actually produce lightning. There are also exhibits on transportation, printing, photography, textiles, and many other activities, including glass-blowing and paper-making demonstrations. The air-and-space hall is the largest in the museum. A hall for high-tech exhibits, computer science, automation, microelectronics, and telecommunications is also very intriguing. The museum's astronomy exhibition shows how this science developed from its earliest beginnings to its current status and is the largest permanent astronomy exhibition in Europe. A good restaurant and a museum shop are on the premises.

3 The Great Churches

In addition to the historic churches described below, visitors might also want to visit the **Matthäuskirche,** Nussbaumstrasse 1 (U-Bahn: Sendlinger-Tor-Platz), an Evangelical cathedral built between 1953 and 1955.

✪ **Frauenkirche (Cathedral of Our Lady).** Frauenplatz 12. Free admission. Daily 7am–7pm. U-Bahn and S-Bahn: Marienplatz.

When the smoke cleared from the 1945 bombings, only a fragile shell remained of Munich's cathedral, which is affectionately known as Liebfrauenkirche. Workmen and architects who restored the 15th-century Gothic cathedral used whatever remains they could find in the rubble. The overall effect of the rebuilt Frauenkirche is strikingly simple, yet dignified.

The twin towers, or Liebfrauendom, which remained intact with their strange early Gothic onion domes, have been the city's landmark since they were added to the church in 1525. Instead of the typical flying buttresses, huge props on the inside support the edifice and separate the side chapels. The Gothic vaulting over the nave and chancel is borne by 22 octagonal pillars.

Entering the main doors at the cathedral's west end, you first notice no windows (actually, except for the tall chancel window, they're hidden by the enormous pillars). According to legend, the devil was delighted at the notion of hidden windows and stamped in glee at the stupidity of the architect—you can still see the strange footlike mark called "the devil's step" in the entrance hall.

In the chapel directly behind the high altar is the cathedral's most interesting painting: *The Protecting Cloak,* a 1510 work by Jan Polack, showing the Virgin holding out her majestic robes to shelter all humankind. The collection of tiny figures beneath the cloak includes everyone from the pope to peasants.

Peterskirche (St. Peter's Church). Rindermarkt 1. ☎ **089/260-4828.** Church, free; tower, 2.50 DM ($1.40) adults, 1.50 DM (85¢) students, .50 DM (30¢) children. Apr–Oct, daily 9am–7pm (or later); Nov–Mar, daily 9am–6pm. U-Bahn: Marienplatz.

Munich's oldest church (1180), known locally as Old Peter, has turned over a new leaf, and it's a gold one at that. The white and gray interior has been decorated with painted medallions of puce and gilded baroque. It contains a series of murals by Johann Baptist Zimmermann, but nothing tops the attraction of the bizarre relic in the second chapel on the left: the gilt-covered and gem-studded skeleton of St. Mundita. It stares at you with two false eyes in its skull, which rests on a cushion. Jewels cover the mouth of rotten teeth, quite a contrast to the fresh roses usually kept in front of the black and silver coffin.

St. Peter's also has a tall steeple, although you may be discouraged from going up since it lacks an elevator. Colored circles on the lower platform tell you whether the climb is worthwhile: If the circle is white, you can see as far as the Alps.

Theatinerkirche. Theatinerstrasse 22. Free admission. Church, daily 6am–7:30pm; crypt, daily 10:30am–5pm. U-Bahn: Odeonsplatz.

Named for a small group of Roman Catholic clergy (the Theatines), this church, dedicated to the scholar-saint Kajetan, is Munich's finest example of Italian baroque. Two Italian architects, Barelli and Zucalli, began building it in the mid-17th century. It was completed in 1768 by the son of the court architect, François de Cuvilliés.

The arched ceiling of the nave is supported by fluted columns that line the center aisle. Above the transept, dividing the nave from the choir, the ceiling breaks into an open dome with an ornate gallery decorated with large but graceful statues. Nothing detracts from the whiteness of the interior, except the dark wooden pews and the canopied pulpit. Since 1954 the church has been under the care of the Dominican Friars.

Michaelskirche. Neuhauserstrasse 6. ☎ **089/231-7060.** Free admission. Guided tour, 5 DM ($2.85) Wed at 2pm. Church, daily 9am–7pm. Crypt, Mon–Fri 10am–1pm and 3–4:45pm, Sat 10am–3pm. U-Bahn or S-Bahn: Karlsplatz, Stachus, or Marienplatz.

The largest Renaissance church north of the Alps, it was constructed by Duke Wilhelm the Pious in 1583. Seven years into construction, the tower collapsed. The duke took this as divine portent that the church was not large enough. During the second phase of construction, the size of the church was dramatically increased, making it not only the largest north of the Alps, but the possessor of the world's second largest barrel-vaulted roof. Among those who have been laid to rest in the crypt are Duke Wilhelm himself, more than 40 Wittelsbachs, and, perhaps the family's most notorious member, Mad King Ludwig II.

Asamkirche. Sendlingerstrasse 62. Free admission. Daily 9am–8pm. U-Bahn: Sendlinger Tor.

St.-Johann-Nepomuk-Kirche, commonly referred to as the Asamkirche after its builders, was constructed by the Asam brothers, Cosmas Damian and Egid Quirin. Although modest on the outside, the interior of this small 18th-century church is a baroque fantasy. Above the entrance stands the statue of St. Nepomuk (the church's patron), a 14th-century monk who drowned in the Danube. Upon entering the chapel, visitors are greeted with a burst of frescoes surrounded by rich red stucco and lavishly gilded woodwork, a superb illustration of the Bavarian passion for ornamentation.

4 More Attractions

MUSEUMS

Antikensammlungen (Museum of Antiquities). Königsplatz 1. ☎ **089/598359.**
Admission 6 DM ($3.40) adults. Joint ticket to the Museum of Antiquities and the Glyptothek, 10 DM ($5.70) adults, free for children under 14, free for everyone on Sun. Tues and Thurs–Sun 10am–5pm, Wed 10am–8pm. U-Bahn: U2 to Königsplatz.

After 100 years of floating from one museum to another, the Museum of Antiquities finally found a home in the 19th-century neoclassical hall on the south side of Königsplatz. The collection grew around the vase collection of Ludwig I and the Royal Antiquarium, both of which were incorporated after World War I into a loosely defined group called the Museum Antiker Kleinkunst (Museum of Small Works of Ancient Art). Many pieces may be small in size but not in value or artistic significance.

Entering the museum, you're in the large central hall. The five main-floor halls house more than 650 Greek vases, collected from all parts of the Mediterranean. The pottery has been restored to near-perfect condition, although most of it dates as far back as 500 B.C. The oldest piece is "the goddess from Aegina" from 3000 B.C. Technically not pottery, this pre-Mycenaean figure, carved from a mussel shell, is on display with the Mycenaean pottery exhibits in Room I. The upper level of the Central Hall is devoted to large Greek vases discovered in Sicily and to Etruscan art.

Returning to the Central Hall, take the stairs down to the lower level to see the collection of Greek, Roman, and Etruscan jewelry. Note the similarities to today's design fashions. Included on this level, as well, are rooms devoted to ancient colored glass, Etruscan bronzes, and Greek terra-cottas.

Bavarian Film Studio. Bavariafilmplatz 7, Geiselgasteig. ☎ **089/6499-2304.** Admission 15 DM ($8.55) adults, 13 DM ($7.40) students and senior citizens, 10 DM ($5.70) children 4–14; Action Show 9 DM ($5.15). Tours, Mar–Oct daily 9am–4pm, Nov–Feb daily 10am–3pm; show, Mar–Oct daily 11:30am and 1:30pm, additional shows Sat–Sun 2:30pm. Tram: 25.

This is Europe's largest filmmaking center. Production was begun here as early as 1920. In the 1970s, Fassbinder, Wim Wenders, and Herzog worked here; Stanley Kubrick shot his interiors for *Paths of Glory,* and Bob Fosse produced *Cabaret.* Tours take you through the sets of famous films like *Das Boot* and *The Neverending Story,* and you can watch films on the Showscan, a superwide movie screen. Children enjoy the Action Show, a demonstration of movie stunts.

Deutsches Theatermuseum. Galeriestrasse 4a. ☎ **089/210-6910.** Free admission. Tues–Fri 10am–4pm; library, Tues 10am–4pm and Thurs 2–4pm. U-Bahn: Odeonsplatz.

Founded in 1910, the German Theatermuseum is a haven for theater fans from all over the world. Its collection includes theater plans and stage sets, as well as various props, costumes, and masks used in productions around the world. The archive contains thousands of manuscripts, programs, and revues. The museum's library houses additional manuscripts, scores, and journals. Available at the museum is the *Münchner Spielplan,* a service providing information on all current theatrical performances in the Munich area.

Glyptothek. Königsplatz 3. ☎ **089/286100.** Admission 6 DM ($3.40) adults. Joint ticket to the Museum of Antiquities and the Glyptothek, 10 DM ($5.70) adults, free for children under 14, free for everyone on Sun. Tues–Sun 10am–4:30pm. U-Bahn: U2 to Königsplatz.

The ideal neighbor for the Museum of Antiquities, the Glyptothek supplements the pottery and smaller pieces of the main museum with an excellent collection of ancient Greek and Roman sculpture. Included are the famous pediments from the temple of Aegina, two marvelous statues of *kouroi* (youths) from the 6th century B.C., the colossal figure of a *Sleeping Satyr* from the Hellenistic period, classical masterpieces of sculpture from ancient Athens, and a splendid collection of Roman portraits. In all, the collection is the country's largest assemblage of classical art. King Ludwig I, who had fantasies of transforming Munich into another Athens, ordered it built.

Hildebrand Haus. Maria-Theresia Strasse 23. ☎ **089/419-4720.** Free admission. Mon–Wed 9am–5pm, Thurs 10am–7pm, Fri 9am–3pm. U-Bahn: Prinzregentenplatz. Tram: 18.

Hildebrand Haus, former home and studio of sculptor Adolf von Hildebrand, now houses the Monacensia Library. Hildebrand, who is best known for designing the Wittelsbach Fountain, created and built the house in 1897. The library's collection is comprised of numerous manuscripts and unpublished works by various Bavarian writers and artists such as Frank Wedekind, Klaus Mann, and Ludwig Ganghofer.

Jüdisches Museum München. Maximilianstrasse 36. ☎ **089/297453.** Free admission. Tues–Wed 2–6pm and Thurs 2–8pm. U-Bahn: Isartor. Tram: 18.

This small, private museum portrays the history of Jews in Nazi Germany through photographs, letters, and exhibits. The horrors suffered during Nazi occupation are startlingly illuminated through powerful portraits of daily life. The yellow stars that Jews were forced to wear continuously are on display, as well as an exhibit that chronicles the hunt for Raoul Wallenberg, the Swedish diplomat who spirited hundreds of Jews to safety during World War II.

Münchner Stadtmuseum (Municipal Museum). St. Jakobsplatz 1. ☎ **089/2332-2370.** Admission 5 DM ($2.85) adults, 2.50 DM ($1.40) children. Tues and Thurs–Sun 10am–5pm, Wed 10am–8:30pm. U-Bahn or S-Bahn: Marienplatz.

Munich's Municipal Museum is to the city what the Bavarian National Museum is to the whole state. Housed in the former armory building, the museum offers insight into the city's history and the daily lives of its people. Special exhibitions about popular arts and traditions are frequently presented. A wooden model shows Munich in 1572. The extensive furniture collection is changed annually so that visitors have a chance to see various periods from the vast storehouse.

The museum's most important exhibit is its Moorish Dancers (*Moriskentanzer*) on the ground floor. These 10 figures, each two feet high, carved in wood and painted in bright colors by Erasmus Grasser in 1480, are among the best examples of secular Gothic art in medieval Germany. In the large Gothic hall on the ground floor you can admire an important collection of armor and weapons from the 14th to 18th centuries.

The second-floor photo museum traces the early history of the camera back to 1839. Every day, at 6 and 9pm, the film museum shows two films from its extensive archives. The historical collection of musical instruments on the fourth floor is one of the greatest of its kind in the world. It includes an ethnological collection.

Enter the Municipal Museum through the main courtyard, where there's a cafeteria.

Stadtische Galerie im Lenbachhaus. Luisenstrasse 33. ☎ **089/2333-2000.** Admission 8 DM ($4.55) adults, 4 DM ($2.30) children 6–12, free for children 5 and under. Tues–Sun 10am–6pm. U-Bahn: U2 to Königsplatz.

This gallery, in the ancient villa of painter Franz von Lenbach (1836–1904), exhibits works by von Lenbach and others. Entering the gold-colored mansion through the gardens, you'll be greeted by a large collection of early works by Paul Klee (1879–1940)—mainly those predating World War I. There's an outstanding group of works by Kandinsky, leader of the Blue Rider movement, and many 19th- and 20th-century paintings throughout the villa. The enclosed patio is pleasant for a coffee break.

Staatliche Sammlung Ägyptischer Kunst (State Collection of Egyptian Art). Hofgartenstrasse 1. ☎ **089/298546.** Admission 5 DM ($2.85) adults, 3 DM ($1.70) children. Tues 9am–4pm and 7–9pm, Wed–Fri 9am–4pm. U-Bahn: Odeonsplatz. S-Bahn: Marienplatz.

The Egyptian Collection is located in the Residenz. The museum evolved from the collections made by Duke Albrecht V and King Ludwig I and contains pieces from every period of Egyptian history, from the predynastic period (4500–3000 B.C.) to the Coptic period (A.D. 4th–9th centuries). On exhibit are sculptures, reliefs, jewelry, tools, weapons, as well as sarcophagi.

Stuck-Villa (Jugendstil Museum). Prinzregentenstrasse 60. ☎ **089/4555-5125.** Free admission. Daily 10am–5pm, Thurs until 9pm. U-Bahn: U4 to Prinzregentenplatz.

This splendid house was designed by painter Franz von Stuck (1863–1928) for himself and mingles art-nouveau style with elements of the late neoclassical. The ground-floor living rooms contain frescoes by the artist himself, and many of his paintings are on display. On the first floor is a permanent collection of *Jugendstil.*

Staatliches Museum für Völkerkunde (Ethnology Museum). Maximilianstrasse 42. ☎ **089/210-1360.** Admission 2 DM ($1.15). Tues–Sun 9:30am–4:30pm. Tram: 17 or 19.

The museum, housed in an imposing building completed in 1865, has an extensive collection of art and artifacts from all over the world and is one of the principal museums of its kind in Europe. Particularly interesting is the Peruvian collection; the museum also has exhibitions from other parts of South America, East Asia, and West and Central Africa.

5 Parks, Gardens & the Zoo

Bordering Schwabing on the east and extending almost to the Isar River is Munich's city park, the 18th-century **Englischer Garten,** one of the largest and most beautiful city parks in Germany. It was the idea of Sir Benjamin Thompson, the English scientist who spent most of his life in the service of the Bavarian government. The Englischer Garten was laid out in 1785. You can wander for hours along the walks and among the trees, flowers, and summer nudes, stopping for tea on the plaza near the Chinese pagoda or having a beer at the nearby beer garden. You might also take along a picnic put together at the elegant shop of Alois Dallmayr, or less expensive fare from **Hertie,** across from the Hauptbahnhof, from Kaufhof at Marienplatz, or from Munich's famous open-air market, the Viktualienmarkt.

Bordering Nymphenburg Park to the north is the **Botanischer Garten.** The garden is composed of 49 acres of land, teeming with more than 15,000 varieties of flora. Each subdivision is devoted to a particular variety of plant. The highlight of the Botanischer Garten is the alpine garden, laid out according to geographic region and altitude. It's at its peak during the summer months. Another favored attraction is the heather garden. Visitors to the garden during the late summer months are treated to an explosion of vibrant violets and purples. Other attractions include the rose garden, fern gorge, and the series of hothouses that are home to numerous exotic tropical plants. To reach the Botanischer Garten (☎ **089/ 1786-1310**), take the U-Bahn to Rotkreuzplatz, then tram 12. The garden is open November through January daily from 9am to 4:30pm; February and March daily from 9am to 5pm; April, September, and October daily from 9am to 6pm; and May through August daily from 9am to 7pm. The hothouses close half an hour before the garden does. During the day, the garden closes from 11:45am to 1pm. Admission is 4 DM ($2.30) for adults and 2 DM ($1.15) for children.

In west Munich, between Schloss Nymphenburg and the main railway line, stands the **Hirschgarten.** Designated by elector Karl Theodor as a deer park in 1791, this 67-acre tract of land is home to one of Munich's most tranquil stretches of greenery. In the 19th century, Münchners would visit the meadow to view the protected game as they grazed. The head huntsman secured the right to sell beer, which prompted the Hirschgarten to soar in popularity. Eventually a beer garden was established, now the largest in the world, with a capacity for 8,000 thirsty patrons. To reach the park, you can take the S-Bahn to Laim; or you can catch bus no. 32 or 83 from Steubenplatz. Although no longer a wildlife preserve, the Hirschgarten still draws the citizens of Munich for picnics, barbecues, or afternoon chess games.

About 4 miles south of the city center, the **Hellabrunn Zoo** stands in the Tierpark Hellabrunn, Tierparkstrasse 30 (☎ **089/625080**). It's one of the largest zoos in the world and may be visited daily from 8am to 6pm (in winter, daily from 9am to 5pm) for an admission of 10 DM ($5.70) for adults, 7 DM ($4) for students and seniors, and 5 DM ($2.85) for children. To reach the park, you can take bus no. 52, leaving the Marienplatz, or U-Bahn U3 to Thalkirchen. Hundreds of animals roam in a natural habitat. A walk through the park is so attractive that it's recommended even if you're not a zoo buff. There's also a big children's zoo as well as a large aviary.

6 The Olympic Grounds

Olympiapark (☎ **089/3067-2414**), site of the 1972 Olympic Games, is 740 acres at the city's northern edge. More than 15,000 workers from 18 countries transformed the site into a park of nearly 5,000 trees, 27 miles of roads, 32 bridges, and a lake. Here you'll find Germany's greatest sports complex, also one of the greatest in Europe.

Olympiapark is a city in itself: It has its own railway station, U-Bahn line, mayor, post office, churches, and elementary school. It broke the city skyline by adding a 960-foot television tower in the center of the park.

The showpiece is a huge stadium, which hosts major sporting events. The stadium is capable of seating 69,200 spectators and is topped by the largest tent-style roof in the world—nearly 90,000 square yards of tinted acrylic glass. The supports for the stadium are anchored by two huge blocks, each capable of resisting 4,000 tons under stress. The roof serves the additional purpose of collecting rainwater and draining it into the nearby Olympic lake.

Olympia Tower, Olympiapark (☎ **089/3067-2750**), is open daily from 9am to midnight. A ticket for a ride up the tower in the speediest elevator on the continent costs 5 DM ($2.85) for adults and 2.50 DM ($1.40) for children under 15. Four observation platforms look out over the Olympiapark, and the extraordinary view reaches to the Alps.

The most expensive dining spot in the tower is the **Tower Restaurant** (☎ **089/ 308-1039**), featuring a selection of French and German dishes. Food is served daily from 11am to 5:30pm and 6:30pm to midnight. A complete dinner costs 65 to 78 DM ($37.05 to $44.45). The Tower Restaurant revolves around its axis in 36, 53, or 70 minutes, giving the guests who linger a changing vista of the entire Olympic ground. American Express, Diners Club, MasterCard, and Visa are accepted.

At the base of the tower is the **Restaurant Olympiasee,** Spiridon-Louis-Ring 7 (☎ **089/3067-2808**), serving genuine Bavarian specialties, with meals costing 12.50 DM ($7.10) and up. Favored items include half a roast chicken and various hearty soups, and food is served daily from 9:30am to 7pm (until 9pm in summer). The restaurant is popular in summer because of its terrace. No credit cards are accepted. Take U-Bahn U3 or U8 to Olympiazenturm.

Near Olympiapark, you can visit the **BMW Museum,** Petuelring 130 (☎ **089/ 3822-3307**), where the history of the automobile is stunningly displayed in an atmosphere created by Oscar winner Rolf Zehetbauer, a "film architect." The exhibition "Horizons in Time," housed in a demisphere of modern architecture, takes you into the future and back to the past. You can view 24 video films and 10 slide shows (an especially interesting one shows how people of yesterday imagined the future). The museum is open daily from 9am to 5pm, charging 5.50 DM ($3.15) for adults and 4 DM ($2.30) for children. While here, you might also ask about BMW factory tours. Take U-Bahn U3 or U8 to Olympiazentrum.

Munich's Soccer Craze

Like Italy, England, and Brazil, Germany is crazed on soccer. Munich's equivalent of the Chicago Bulls or the New York Yankees is its famous soccer team, **Bayern München.** One of Europe's most outstanding teams, Bayern München has won the German National Championship 13 times since 1932. Most recently, they won the European Football Federation championship in 1995, and in 1996 the *Welttokalsieger* championship, an event that designated the team as the best non-national team in the world (national teams play in the World Cup).

However, it's a matter of civic pride to many Münchners, especially when they're soaked with beer, to root enthusiastically for a less-well-rated local team, **T.S.V. 1860 München.** This team was around about 40 years before Bayern München was founded, and it still arouses local loyalty—something like the Chicago White Sox as opposed to the much beloved and beleaguered Chicago Cubs. Both teams call the Olympic Stadium in Olympiapark their home.

7 Especially for Kids

From the Deutches Museum to the Marionetten Theater to the Bavarian Film Studio, kids love Munich.

Take your children to the **Münchner Stadtmuseum,** St. Jakobsplatz 1 (☎ 089/2332-2370). On the third floor is an array of puppets from around the world, with star billing going to the puppeteer's art. The comical and grotesque figures include both marionettes and hand puppets. The collection also includes detailed puppet theaters and miniature scenery, a Lilliputian version of the world of the stage. A special department is devoted to fairground art, including carousel animals, shooting galleries, roller-coaster models, and wax and museum figures. The main exhibit contains the oldest-known carousel horses, dating from 1820. For hours and admission fees, see "More Attractions," above.

If children have a favorite museum in Munich, it's the **Deutsches Museum,** Museumsinsel 1 (☎ 089/21791), which has many interactive exhibits. For details, see "Museums & Palaces," above.

The **Spielzeugmuseum,** in the Altes Rathaus, Marienplatz 15 (☎ 089/294001), is a historical toy collection. It is open daily from 10am to 5:30pm. Admission is 5 DM ($2.85) for adults, 1 DM (55¢) for children, and 10 DM ($5.70) for a family.

At the **Münchner Marionetten Theater,** Blumenstrasse 32A (☎ 089/265712), you can attend puppet shows and the *théâtre de marionnettes*. Adults as well as children are delighted with the productions; many are of Mozart operas. Performances are on Wednesday, Thursday, Saturday, and Sunday at 3pm. Performances Saturday at 8pm cost 15 DM ($8.55). Admission is 8 DM ($4.55) for adults and 6 DM ($4.20) for children. Matinees tend to be more animated and crowded than evening performances and are particularly well-suited to younger children age 4 and up. To reach the theater, take the U-Bahn to Sendlinger Tor.

At the **Bavarian Film Studio,** Bavariafilmplatz 7, Geiselgasteig (☎ 089/6499-2304), children enjoy the film presentations and the Bavaria Action Show, where stunt teams demonstrate fistfights, escape from burning buildings, fall down staircases, and even plunge off a 92-foot-high building. The show lasts about 30 minutes. For more information, see "More Attractions" above.

The **Hellabrunn Zoo** has a large children's zoo where children can pet the animals. For details, see "Parks, Gardens & the Zoo," above.

Not to be ignored is the **Circus Krone,** Marstrasse 43 (☎ **089/558166**). It might be compared to London's Albert Hall, since its productions are so varied. From December 25 to March 31 a circus show is presented. There are matinee performances on Wednesday, Friday, Saturday, and Sunday.

8 Sightseeing Tours

CITY TOURS   Blue buses, with sightseeing tours conducted in both German and English, leave from the square in front of the Hauptbahnhof, at Hertie's, all year round. Tickets are sold on the bus and no advance booking is necessary.

A 1-hour tour, costing 17 DM ($9.70) for adults and 9 DM ($5.15) for children 6 to 12, leaves at 10am, 11:30am, and 2:30pm daily from May through October. Winter departures are from November through April, daily at 10am and 2:30pm.

A 2½-hour tour, including the Olympic Tower, costs 30 DM ($17.10) for adults and 15 DM ($8.55) for children. Departures are at 10am and 2:30pm from May through October and at 10am and 2:30pm from November through April.

A second 2½-hour tour, costing 30 DM ($17.10) for adults and 15 DM ($8.55) for children, visits the famous Neue Pinakothek, the cathedral, and the performing clock at Marienplatz. It departs Tuesday to Sunday at 10am.

A third 2½-hour tour, costing 30 DM ($17.10) for adults and 15 DM ($8.55) for children, visits Nymphenburg Palace and the Schatzkammer, departing Tuesday to Sunday at 2:30pm.

DAY TRIPS NEARBY   If you'd like to visit some of the Bavarian attractions outside of Munich, you can sign up with **Panorama Tours,** an affiliate of Gray Line. Their office is at Arnulfstrasse 8 (☎ **089/5490-7560**), to the north of the Hauptbahnhof. Hours are 7:30am to 6pm Monday to Friday, 7:30am to noon on Saturday, and 7:30am to 10am on Sunday and holidays. The firm offers about a half-dozen tours of the region around Munich, usually priced at 78 DM ($44.45) per adult and 40 DM ($22.80) per child.

If you want to visit Ludwig's famous castles, there's a 10½-hour tour to Neuschwanstein and Linderhof costing 78 DM ($44.45). A 10½-hour tour for 78 DM ($44.45) takes you to Ludwig's castle at Herremchiemsee. You can also book a tour to Salzburg in Austria that includes a boat ride on the Wolfgangsee and takes about 11½ hours, costing 78 DM ($44.45). A tour to the Alpine town of Berchtesgaden and to the site of Hitler's once luxurious retreat at Obersalzburg takes 10½-hours and costs 78 DM ($44.45)

On a darker note is a 4½-hour excursion to Dachau, departing every Saturday at 1:30pm. The tour incorporates a visit to the notorious concentration camp and also a tour through the historic town of Dachau itself and the medieval Schloss Dachau. During the visit to the death camp, participants are requested to respect the dignity of the site by wearing appropriate attire. It is priced at 40 DM ($22.80).

TOURING BY BIKE   Pedal pushers will want to try Mike Lasher's **Mike's Bike Tour,** St. Bonifatiusstrasse 2, (☎ **089/651-4275**). His bike-rental service for 27 DM ($15.40) includes maps, locks, helmets, and child and infant seats at no extra charge. Bike tours in English and bilingual tours of central Munich run from March through November at a cost of 28 DM ($15.95). Tours leave at 11:30am and 4pm daily (call to confirm). This unique enterprise has been praised widely by its clients, thanks in part to the charm of its American owner. Participants meet under the tower of the old town hall, a gray building at the east end of Marienplatz. Mike, the consummate guide, will be there—whistle in mouth—letting everyone know who he is. The tour veers from the bike paths only long enough for a lunch stop at a *Biergarten.* Fear not faint-hearted, the rides are nonstrenuous with plenty of photo opportunities, historical explanations, and question and answer sessions.

9 Activities & Outdoor Pursuits

The best place to enjoy the great outdoors is not in Munich itself, but just outside the city limits. Munich is surrounded by mountains and alpine lakes that afford some of the finest skiing and hiking in the world. Avid skiers will want to make an excursion to the Zugspitze, the highest mountain peak in Germany. Ski slopes begin at an elevation of 8,700 feet. For information on ski resorts and other snow-related activities in the Munich area, contact **Bayerischer Segler-Verband,** Georg-Brauchle-Ring 93 (☎ **089/1570-2366**). The mountains are a haven for hikers and nature lovers during the summer months. Trails abound for all levels of experience. See chapter 11 for details. The alpine lakes around Munich are excellent for swimming and water sports. The Ammersee and Starnbergersee, both a short drive from the city, are favorites for sailing, windsurfing, and other water sports. See chapter 10 for more information. Visitors can also go for a dip in the frigid, snow-fed waters of the Isar River.

BIKING   The city is full of bike paths, and most major streets maintain bike lanes. The many parks and gardens scattered throughout Munich offer hours of riding. The tourist office provides suggested tours in its *Radi Touren.* Although printed in German, the maps are excellent and easily followed. You can rent bikes at **City Hopper Tours,** Hohenzollern Strasse 95 (☎ **089/272-1131**); **Mike's Bike Tour,** St. Bonifatiusstrasse 2 (☎ **089/651-4275;** see above); and **Radius Touristik,** Arnulfstrasse 9 (☎ **089/4366-0383**). Many S-Bahn stations also rent bikes and allow them to be returned at other S-Bahn stations.

BOATING   Rowboats add to the charm of the lakes in the **Englischer Garten.** (There's also a kiosk located at the edge of the Kleinhesselcher See for rentals during clement weather.) There are rowboat rentals on the southern bank of the **Olympiasee,** in the Olympiapark.

Raft trips on the Isar River between the town of Wolfrathausen and Munich begin in early May and last until late September. A raft may contain up to 60 other passengers, but if the idea appeals to you, contact **Franz and Sebastian Seitner,** Heideweg 9, D-82515 Wolfrathausen (☎ **08171/18320**).

GOLF   You might want to take a break from sightseeing for a round or two of golf. One of the best courses is **Golf Club Feldafing,** Tutzingerstrasse 15, D-82340 Feldafing (☎ **08157/93340**). Situated beside a clear Bavarian lake, the Starnbergersee, it's open from April through mid-November every day from 8am to 7pm (closed in winter.) Depending on the day of the week you arrive, greens fees range from 100 to 120 DM ($57 to $68.40) for 18 holes. Be warned in advance that although you can play without a reservation every Monday to Friday, if you have a handicap of 34 or less, on Saturday and Sunday you'll need to be accompanied by a club member.

You can also play at the **Golfclub Strasslach** (also known as the Munich Golf Club), Grünwald (☎ **08170/450**). The course is open daily from 8am to 8pm, charging greens fees of 100 DM ($57). Visitors must reserve their tee-times in advance. Both of the above-mentioned clubs lie within a 45-minute drive south of Munich's center.

HIKING & HILLCLIMBING   Bavaria is packed with well-marked hiking trails. For information about nearby terrains and itineraries, contact the **Deutscher Alpenverein,** Van-Kahr-Strasse 2–4 (☎ **089/140030**). Also see chapter 11.

ICE-SKATING   During the winter's coldest months, a lake in the Englischer Garten freezes over and is opened to ice skaters. A section of the Nymphenburger Canal is also blocked off for skaters. Be alert to the GEFAHR (Danger) signs that are posted whenever temperatures rise and the ice becomes too thin. The **Olympic Icestadium,** Spiridon-Louis-Ring 3 (☎ **089/3067-2150**), in the Olympiapark, is the indoor rink. Information on hockey matches and other ice-skating events is available from **Bayerischer Eissportverband,** Georg-Brauchle-Ring 93 (☎ **089/81820**).

JOGGING   Regardless of the season, the most lushly landscaped place in Munich is the **Englischer Garten** (U-Bahn: Münchener Frieheit), which has a 7-mile circumference and an array of dirt and asphalt tracks. Other possibilities for jogging are the grounds of the **Olympiapark** (U-Bahn: Olympiazentrum) or the park surrounding **Schloss Nymphenburg.** Convenient to the city center's commercial district is a jogging track along the embankments of the Isar River.

SWIMMING   Although most Münchners head to the lakes to swim, there are several excellent facilities within the city. The largest public swimming pool is the giant competition-size pool in the Olympiapark, the **Olympia-Schwimmhalle** (☎ **089/3067-2015**). Admission is 13 DM ($7.40). The graceful turn-of-the-century **Müllersches Volksbad (Müller's Public Baths),** Rosendheimer Strasse I (☎ **089/2361-343**) evokes the baths of Budapest, and offers an unusual experience. See "Frommer's Favorite Munich Experiences" in chapter 1.

TENNIS   At least 200 indoor and outdoor tennis courts are scattered around greater Munich. Many can be booked in advance through **Sport Scheck** (☎ **089/9928-7460**). For information on Munich's many tennis tournaments and competitions, contact the **Bayerischer Tennis Verband,** Georg-Brauchle-Ring 93, D-80992 München (☎ **089/1570-2640**).

SPECTATOR SPORTS

If you want to attend a soccer match between opposing teams from different ends of Europe, chances are good that there'll be one in Munich's enormous **Olympiastadium** (☎ **089/3067-2424**). Originally built for the 1972 Olympics, Olympiapark is the largest recreational and sports venue in Europe and has facilities for competitions of virtually every kind. To get tickets for any sports event, call ☎ **089/5418-1818,** Monday to Friday from 9am to 6pm and on Saturday from 10am to 3pm.

Munich Strolls

A walk through the city is the only true way to get to know it. The Altstadt (old town) is the traditional walking tour for most visitors, but travelers with more time may enjoy visiting some of the lesser known but equally interesting sights near the city center. And a walk through Schwabing is a must for those who want to have a more offbeat experience.

WALKING TOUR 1
The Historic Center

Start: Frauenkirche.
Finish: Königsplatz.
Time: 2½ hours, not counting visits to interiors or shopping.
Best Times: Daylight hours during clement weather.
Worst Times: Monday to Friday from 7:30 to 9am and 4:30 to 6pm, because of heavy traffic.

With a history spanning centuries of building and rebuilding, Munich is one of Europe's most interesting cities architecturally.

Begin your tour at the dignified cathedral with its impressive brickwork, the:

1. **Frauenkirche.** It was begun in 1468 on the site of a much older church and was completed in 20 years. The majestically somber building is capped with twin towers that survived World War II bombings—the symbol of Munich.

After admiring the towers' design, walk for about a block southeast along any of the pedestrian alleyways radiating away from the rear of the church. In a couple of minutes you'll find yourself in the most famous medieval square of Munich:

2. ✪ **Marienplatz,** in whose center a golden statue of the Virgin Mary (the **Mariensäule**) rises above pavement that was first laid in the 1300s when the rest of the city's streets were a morass of mud and sewage. On the square's northern boundary sits the richly ornamented neo-Gothic Neues Rathaus (New City Hall), built between 1867 and 1908 as a symbol of Munich's power. On its facade is the famous the mechanical clock with its Glockenspiel that performs a miniature tournament several times a day.

At the square's eastern border, beyond a stream of traffic, is the simpler and smaller Altes Rathaus (Old City Hall), which was rebuilt in its present form in 1470 after fire destroyed an even earlier version.

From the square, walk south along Rindermarkt, encircling the masonry bulk of the:

3. Peterskirche. Its foundations date from A.D. 1000, and the interior is a sun-flooded fantasy of baroque stucco and gilt. Walk around the church to the back, where you'll find the sprawling premises of one of the best-stocked food emporiums in Europe, the:

4. Viktualienmarkt. Known as "Munich's stomach," it's where you can snack, have a beer, pick up the makings of a picnic, or just observe the ritual of European grocery shopping. At the northern end, at the corner where the streets Rosen Tal and Im Tal meet, rises the richly ornate baroque walls of the:

5. Heiliggeist (Holy Ghost) Church. Its foundations were laid in the 1100s, but the form in which you see it today was completed in 1730.

From here, cross the busy boulevard identified as Im Tal and walk north along Maderbraustrasse (within a block it will change its name to Orlandostrasse and then to Am Platz). Here, look for the entrance to the most famous beer hall in Europe, the state-owned:

6. Hofbräuhaus. For a description, see chapter 9. For the moment, note its location for an eventual return. Now, walk east along Pfisterstrasse. To your left are the walls of the:

7. Alter Hof, originally built in 1255, and once the palace of the Wittelsbachs, although eclipsed later by grander palaces. Since 1816 it has housed the rather colorless offices of Munich's financial bureaucracies. On the opposite (northern) edge of Pfisterstrasse rise the walls of the:

8. Münzhof (built 1563–1567). During its lifetime it has housed in turn, the imperial stables, the first museum north of the Alps, and (between 1809 and 1986) a branch of the government mint. Today it's headquarters for Munich's Landmark Preservation office (Landesamt für Denkmalschutz). If it's open, the double tiers and massive stone columns of the building's Bavarian Renaissance courtyard are worth a visit.

Pfisterstrasse funnels into a broader street, Hofgraben. Walk west for 1 block, then turn right (north) along Residenzstrasse. The first building on your right will be the city's main post office (Hauptpost) and a few paces farther on you'll reach:

9. Max-Joseph-Platz. Designed as a focal point for the monumental avenue (Maximilianstrasse) that radiates eastward, the plaza was built during the 19th century on the site of a Franciscan convent in honor of Bavaria's first king. At the north edge of the plaza lie the vast exhibition space and labyrinthine corridors of one of Munich's finest museums, the:

10. ✪ **Residenz.** Constructed in different stages and styles from 1500 to 1850, it served as the official home of the rulers of Bavaria until 1918. Restored and rebuilt in its original form after the bombings of World War II, its complicated plan contains seven semiconcealed courtyards, lavish apartments that have housed foreign visitors like Elizabeth II and Charles de Gaulle, and museums that include the Residenz Museum, the Treasure House of the Residenz, the richly gilded rococo Cuvilliés Theater (1753), and the Herkulessaal, a concert hall noted for its baroque decorations.

Walking Tour 1—The Historic Center

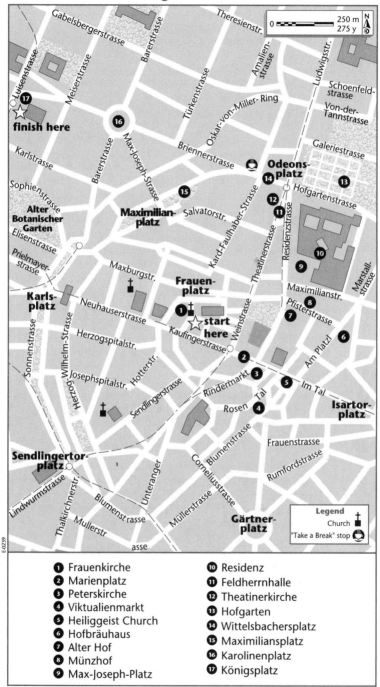

0   250 m
275 y   N

① Frauenkirche
② Marienplatz
③ Peterskirche
④ Viktualienmarkt
⑤ Heiliggeist Church
⑥ Hofbräuhaus
⑦ Alter Hof
⑧ Münzhof
⑨ Max-Joseph-Platz
⑩ Residenz
⑪ Feldherrnhalle
⑫ Theatinerkirche
⑬ Hofgarten
⑭ Wittelsbachersplatz
⑮ Maximiliansplatz
⑯ Karolinenplatz
⑰ Königsplatz

Legend

✝ Church
🕬 "Take a Break" stop

133

Walk from Max-Joseph-Platz north along Residenzstrasse. Make the first left and walk west along Salvatorstrasse; then, within another block, turn right (north) along Theatinerstrasse. On your right you'll immediately notice an important Munich landmark, the:

11. Feldherrnhalle. This open-air loggia was designed and constructed by Friedrich von Gärtner between 1841 and 1844. Von Gärtner chose as his model the famous Loggia dei Lanzi in Florence. King Ludwig I commissioned the construction of the loggia as a tribute to the Bavarian army. The bronze figures honoring Bavarian generals Tilly (1559–1632) and Wrede (1767–1838) were based on drawings by Ludwig Schwanthaler. The two lions on the steps were the work of a sculptor, Ruemann, in 1906. Although Hitler's attempted putsch in Munich failed, along with the subsequent march to the Feldherrnhalle, the loggia later became a Nazi rallying point. Today the brown shirts are gone, replaced by street singers and musicians who hold out their hats, hoping for coins.

On the western (opposite) side of the same street (Theatinerstrasse) is the:

12. Theatinerkirche (Church of St. Kajetan). Completed in 1690, its triple-domed Italian baroque facade was added about a century later by the Cuvilliés father and son. Its crypt contains the tombs of many of the Wittelsbachs.

Now, continue walking north passing through Odeonsplatz, below which several subway lines converge. On the northeastern side of this square lie the flowers, fountains, and cafes of one of Munich's most pleasant small parks, the:

13. Hofgarten. Originally laid out for members of the royal court in 1613, it was opened to the public in 1780. Along the edges of the Hofgarten, as well as along the avenues radiating away from it, lie many opportunities for you to:

TAKE A BREAK   Do as the Münchners do and enjoy the panorama of Odeonsplatz and the nearby Hofgarten. One particularly attractive choice is **Café Luitpold,** Briennerstrasse 11 (☎ **089/292865**). Rebuilt in a streamlined design after the bombings of World War II, it has in the past welcomed such cafe-loving habitués as Ibsen, Johann Strauss the Younger, and Kandinsky.

Now, walk westward along Briennerstrasse, through a neighborhood lined with impressive buildings. On your right, notice the heroic statue of Maximilian I, the Great Elector (1597–1651), rising from the center of:

14. Wittelsbachersplatz. In a short time, the gentle fork to your left leads into the verdant and stylish perimeter of:

15. Maximiliansplatz. Shop at your leisure or plan to return later for a more in-depth sampling of this prestigious neighborhood. For the moment, return to Briennerstrasse, turn left (west), and head toward the 85-foot obelisk (erected in 1833) that soars above:

16. Karolinenplatz. Its design commemorates Bavarians killed in the Napoleonic invasion of Russia. Continuing west, you'll come upon:

17. Königsplatz. In the early 19th century, Crown Prince Ludwig (later Ludwig I) selected its formal neoclassical design from an architectural competition. Its perimeter is ringed with some of Germany's most impressive museum buildings, the Doric-inspired Propyläen monument (west side), the Antikensammlungen (south side), and the Ionic-fronted Glyptothek (north side).

WALKING TOUR 2
Exploring West of Marienplatz

Start: Marienplatz.
Finish: Viktualienmarkt.
Time: 2 hours.
Best Times: Daylight hours during clement weather.
Worst Times: Monday to Friday from 7:30 to 9am and 4:30 to 6pm, because of heavy traffic.

This tour takes you on a second discovery of the Altstadt. To reach the starting point from the Marienplatz, walk down the shop-lined Koffingerstrasse to Liebfrauenstrasse and past the Frauenkirche (visited on the previous tour) and continue west to:

1. ✪ **St. Michael's,** Hubert Gerhard's larger-than-life creation. The figure of St. Michael slaying the dragon adorns the church's rich Renaissance facade. The church, constructed in 1597, possesses an interior that merits a glance as well. Its barrel vault is second in size only to St. Peter's in Rome. King Ludwig II's final resting place, it also houses other Wittelsbach rulers. Continue west on Neuhauserstrasse to the:

2. **Richard Strauss Fountain.** The fountain's central column has scenes from Strauss's *Salome* (1905), interpreted with flair in bas-relief.

   Then continue to the:

3. **Bürgersaal.** The two-story church completed in 1710 has an appealing facade with the Virgin and Child in a crescent moon over the doorway. The lower floor was once the worship hall of a Jesuit community called the Marian Congregation.

   At the end of the pedestrian mall, you'll see the fountain of the little boy at the medieval Karlstor. You've come to the:

4. **Stachus (Karlsplatz),** a busy intersection that was engineered when the old town walls were demolished in 1791. The unpopular Elector Karl Theodor lent his name to the square only to suffer the indignity of having the nickname, *Stachus,* become the common usage of the local citizenry. The name *Stachus* dates back either to an 18th-century local eatery, or to a marksman who practiced nearby, depending on which story you find most plausible.

   Diagonally and to the right is the 19th-century Palace of Justice. Directly in front of you, at a distance, is the main train station. Now turn 180° and walk back to the Strauss fountain. You will enjoy one of the finest views in town as the Cathedral ascends before the walker. Turn right at Eisenmannstrasse and head for:

5. **St.-Anna-Damenstift** (1735), a large church on the corner. Rebuilt in the 1950s, it replicates the old church that was collapsed by bombs during World War II. The attached building (now a secondary school for girls) was once a convent. The church, built by Johann Baptist **Gunetzrhainer** in 1732–1735, features stucco work and frescoes by the brothers Egid Quirin and Cosmas Damian Asam.

   The street name changes to Damenstiftstrasse for the duration of the block as we pass a pretty, old house numbered 4 and the 18th-century Palais Lerchenfeld. Although we've not made a turn, the street is now named Kreuzstrasse, home of the:

6. **Allerheiligenkirche am Kreuz.** Built around 1478 by Ganghofer, it now houses Ukranian Catholics. The Gothic building features baroque touches, such as the

Walking Tour 2—West of Marienplatz

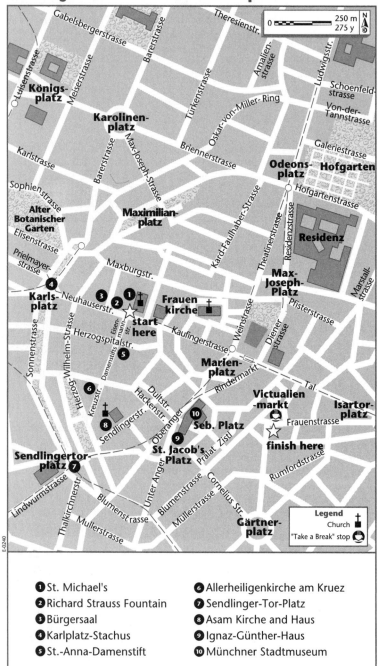

1 St. Michael's
2 Richard Strauss Fountain
3 Bürgersaal
4 Karlplatz-Stachus
5 St.-Anna-Damenstift
6 Allerheiligenkirche am Kruez
7 Sendlinger-Tor-Platz
8 Asam Kirche and Haus
9 Ignaz-Günther-Haus
10 Münchner Stadtmuseum

apse from a remodeling in 1620 and Renaissance altarwork in the pattern of J. B. Strauss (1770).

The street merges into Herzog-Wilhelm-Strasse, which veers left and ends at:

7. Sendlinger-Tor-Platz. The Sendlinger Tor, once a medieval fortification, was built in 1318, about the same time as the Karlstor. The two side towers of the gates are the only original survivors. Sendlinger Strasse, a lengthy, brightly colored avenue of small commercial outlets, leads us back into the center. Stay on the right side of the street as you walk back until you come to:

8. Asamkirche and Haus. The Asam brothers created the building in 1746 as a sort of monument to themselves. Be sure to step inside to see the extravagant Bavarian rococo interior, courtesy of Egid Quirin, along with frescoes and paintings by brother Cosmas Damian. A wax figure of St. John of Nepomuk, to whom the building is dedicated, graces the altar.

Turn left, heading northeast along the Sendlinger Strasse; take the second right southeast onto Dultstrasse, cross the Oberanger Rinder, and head into the St.-Jakobs-Platz. You'll see the:

9. Ignaz-Günther-Haus. This memorial house is a tribute to the 18th-century Bavarian rococo artist who lived and worked out of the edifice during his lifetime. Restoration was completed in 1977, and it is now maintained by the Munich Stadtmuseum (see below). The Madonna out front is a Günther replica, and an exhibit inside displays some of his other works.

In the same block is the:

10. Münchner Stadtmuseum. Housed in the old, 15th-century city Arsenal, the building is turreted in front. Exhibits vary seasonally, often featuring one of the countless local artists in Munich's cultural history. Several displays, however, are permanent and are reviewed in chapter 6.

Continue down the street veering left into Sebastiansplatz and admire the old houses lining the street. Exit the Sebastiansplatz from its eastern edge and walk for 3 blocks along the meandering length of the Prälat-Zistl-Strasse until you reach the Viktualienmarkt.

TAKE A BREAK   The **Münch'ner Suppenkücke** (no phone) is a Munich legend, a true "soup kitchen" at what is called "the stomach of the city." Münchners can be seen here on the coldest days devouring hearty soups such as Goulashsuppe, sausage and sauerkraut, and Krustis (sandwiches). Or, buy some bread and fruit at one of the many stands, sit back, and enjoy the fountains and statues that surround you.

WALKING TOUR 3
Schwabing

Start: Wedekindplatz.
Finish: Englischer Garten.
Time: 2½ hours with minimal stopovers.
Best Times: Morning to mid-afternoon while students bustle to and from class.
Worst Times: Monday to Friday from 7:30 to 9am and 4:30 to 6pm.

Schwabing was incorporated into the city in 1890. Its golden era as an artists' center was from 1890 to 1914. Novelists Thomas Mann and Herman Hesse, the poet

Rainer Maria Rilke, satirist Karl Kraus, and playwright Franz Wedekind were some of the better-known authors who lived in the area. For a short period after World War II, it became legendary as Germany's hip center.

The tour begins in the section of Schwabing behind the Münchener Freiheit station known as Old Schwabing. Movie theaters, music clubs, and even a handful of cabarets give it the markings of cosmopolitanism.

1. **Wedekindplatz,** once the community market, is named for Franz Wedekind, whose "Lulu" plays provided the basis for the 1929 Louise Brooks film, *Pandora's Box,* and for Alban Berg's opera, *Lulu.* The platz is the focal point of the neighborhood.

Head west down Fellitzschstrasse, pass the Freiheit rail station and cross the:

2. **Leopoldstrasse,** the most famous street in Schwabing, the best known *Jugendstil* district in Munich. *Jugend* ("Youth"), an avant-garde magazine published in Schwabing, lent its name to the German art-nouveau movement at the turn of the century, urging artists to turn away from old-world nostalgia in favor of a newer, fresher perspective.

A block farther on, take a left on Wilhelmstrasse, travel south for 2 blocks, then take a right on:

3. **Hohenzollernstrasse.** Here you can further study Jugendstil. The facades that adorn the buildings lining this street are fine examples of the bright and geometric decoration that typify the style. Look also for the little, quirky fashion boutiques that give the street its fame. Turn left on Römerstrasse, travel south a block, then head back east on:

4. **Ainmillerstrasse.** The artistic unshackling of the Jugendstil movement laid the foundation for a further development of artistic consciousness that was the basis for many of the eager manifestos set forth by the Blaue Reiter (Blue Rider) school. Appropriately, Wassily Kandinsky, the premiere artist associated with the movement, lived down the street. You will find many of the finest examples of Jugendstil on the east end of the street—including the facade at no. 22 that sports Adam and Eve lying at the base of the tree of knowledge.

🖎 **TAKE A BREAK**   The cafe-bar, **Café Roxy,** Leopoldstrasse 48 (☎ **089/ 349393**), is owned by Iris Berben, star of German TV. She presides over the neo-deco interior, the Italian cuisine, and an affectedly urbane crowd. It's chic, it's hip, and it's the best place to relax in the neighborhood.

Head south down Leopoldstrasse until you approach the:

5. **Akademie der Shönen (Academy of Fine Arts).** The building, erected at the end of the 19th century, enthusiastically recalls the Italian Renaissance. The academy is best known for the "secession" movement, spearheaded by its students in the 1890s. This protest against "traditional aesthetics" and a call for a new creativity in the arts led quickly to the growth of Jugendstil and helped define Munich as a centerpiece of the art nouveau movement. Continue south on Leopoldstrasse and you will enter the:

6. **Ludwig-Maximilian Universität (University of Munich)** campus. Frederich von Gärtner engineered the construction of the edifice, one of the aesthetically finest in all of Munich. Gärtner relieved Leo von Klenze (Alte Pinakothek) as Bavaria's court architect, and the relative flamboyance of this structure is compared favorably to Klenze's more staid approach. It was here that the student

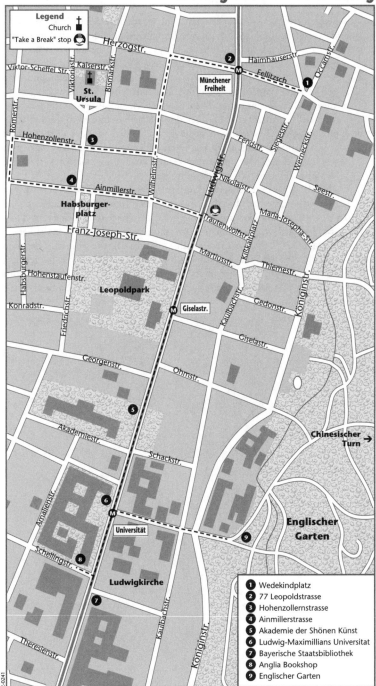

Legend

✝ Church

"Take a Break" stop

① Wedekindplatz
② 77 Leopoldstrasse
③ Hohenzollernstrasse
④ Ainmillerstrasse
⑤ Akademie der Shönen Künst
⑥ Ludwig-Maximillians Universitat
⑦ Bayerische Staatsbibliothek
⑧ Anglia Bookshop
⑨ Englischer Garten

139

society, the White Rose, made a last effort to resist Hitler in 1942 to 1943. Its leaders, Sophie and Hans Scholl, were brutally executed for "civil disobedience."

Across the street, three smaller buildings complete the university complex: a conference building, the twin-spired St. Ludwig's Church, and the:

7. **Bayerische Staatsbibliothek (Bavarian State Library).** This mammoth library is one of the largest in all of Europe. It stands where the Schwabing Gate of medieval Munich once cast its shadow. Check out its proportional staircase within. Before leaving campus, duck down Schellingstrasse and drop in at:

8. **Anglia English Bookshop,** Schellingstrasse 3. The student district's liveliest street is south of the university in a suburb of Schwabing known as Maxvorstadt. Munich is Germany's publishing center, and the bookstores throughout Schwabing will satisfy the most avid reader.

Head back north up Leopoldstrasse, returning to the university's center. Take a left on Veterinärstrasse, directly across the street from Gärtner's famed building. Those without inhibition may want to begin disrobing. You're being routed to the:

9. ✪ **Englischer Garten,** Munich's most famous park, full of nude sunbathers. The Chinese Tower is the most recognizable landmark of the gardens. The wooden tower, trimmed with gold leaf, was destroyed during World War II but reemerged in the 1950s to the delight of its beer-garden devotees—a Munich tradition revered even by upstart Schwabingers, and a good place to take a break and end your walk.

Shopping 8

Visitors to Munich usually come for the fun, the beer gardens, the cultural scene, or the nightlife, not for the shopping. However, Munich is full of beautiful and elegant (and expensive) shops and has a number of really intriguing retailers.

1 The Shopping Scene

Here you'll find some of the foremost shops and boutiques in Europe. There's an extensive pedestrian shopping area in the city center. **Kaufingerstrasse** and **Neihauserstrasse,** the principal shopping streets, extend from the Haubtbahnhof to Marienplatz, then north to Odeonsplatz. For even more upscale shopping, head to **Maximilianstrasse.** The street houses numerous chic boutiques and fashion houses that rival any on Fifth Avenue.

For funkier wares, head to Schwabing, the former bohemian quarter. **Schellingstrasse** and **Hohenzollernstrasse** are home to many unusual galleries and hip boutiques. Shops in the downtown area are generally open from 9am to 6pm during the week. Stores may stay open until 8:30pm on Thursday. On Saturday the shops generally close around 2pm. The smaller neighborhood stores usually open their doors from 8:30am to 12:30pm and reopen from 3 to 6pm. On the first Saturday of the month, *Langer Samstag,* the downtown stores are open until 4pm from April through September and until 6pm from October through March.

2 Shopping A to Z

ANTIQUES

Munich is not a center for antique buyers, since not a lot remained after the World War II bombings, and anything really valuable is snapped up instantaneously by the prosperous bourgeoisie. There is some estate-sale stuff "from Grandmother's cupboard" but little of major consequence. In fact, many older pieces come from England or France.

If you enjoy random wanderings, window-shopping for collectibles, the streets that are particularly rich in antique shops radiate outward from the Viktualienmarkt. One of the most important of these is the Westenriederstrasse.

Antike Uhren Eder. Prannerstrasse 4. ☎ **089/220305.** U-Bahn: Marienplatz.

Here you'll find antique clocks from the 19th and early 20th centuries. Along with a roughly equivalent nearby competitor, Antike Uhren Eder can supply you with timepieces that have told many, many other people exactly what time it is for a very long time. Both stores are adjacent to the Hotel Bayerischer Hof, and attract a glamorous clientele from virtually everywhere. They're open Monday to Friday from 10am to 6pm and Saturday from 10am to 2pm.

Carl Jagemann. Residenzstrasse 3. ☎ **089/225493.** U-Bahn: Marienplatz.

Ancestors of the present owner established this store more than a century ago, and today, you're likely to see the grandchildren of former clients coming in for appraisals of objects their forebears might have received as long-ago wedding presents. The specialty here is estate and antique jewelry, plus reproductions of baroque clocks. It's open Monday to Friday from 10am to 6pm and Saturday from 10am to 2pm.

Philographikon Galerie Rauhut. Pfisterstrasse 11. ☎ **089/225082.** U-Bahn or S-Bahn: Marienplatz.

This important gallery is one of the great successes of Munich's art world—it was established in 1978 by a television producer, Rainer Rauhut, who transformed his hobby of collecting rare engravings, prints, and manuscripts into a career. It's on two floors of a century-old building near the Marienplatz. Merchandise ranges from 19th-century steel engravings priced from 30 DM ($17.10), to pre-Gutenberg illuminated manuscripts (sold, depending on circumstances, as individual sheets or as entire folios) worth hundreds of thousands. Other curiosities include antique maps; botanical prints from English, French, and German sources; and a series of rare prints by a Swiss-born engraver, Karl Bodmer, whose depictions in the 1820s of Native Americans are increasingly valuable on both sides of the Atlantic. It's open Monday to Friday from 10am to 6pm and Saturday from 10am to 2pm.

Squirrel. Schellingstrasse 54. ☎ **089/272-0929.** U-Bahn: U3 or U6 to Universität.

This unusual shop was established 21 years ago by its charming owner, Urban Geissel and his wife Gisela. A delightful alternative for dedicated antique buyers, it carries a collection of luggage made by English and French purveyors to the aristocrats and millionaires of the Jazz Age. There are suitcases and steamer trunks from Louis Vuitton, whose *LV* logo was inaugurated about 20 years after the company's establishment in 1878; some antique pieces by Hérmès; and examples from English makers such as Finnegan's and Harrods. Although they tend to be heavy, they're still serviceable and richly imbued with the nostalgia of the great days of oceangoing travel. An expenditure of 500 DM ($285) buys a worthy suitcase from circa 1910 to 1925; 22,000 DM ($12,540) buys one of tailored crocodile with silver clasps. The place is open Monday to Friday from 11am to 6pm and Saturday from 11am to 2pm.

ARTS

Galerie für Angewandte Künst München. Pacellistrasse 8. ☎ **089/290-1470.** U-Bahn: Karlsplatz.

This is the largest, most visible, and most historic art gallery of its type in Germany, established by the Bavarian government in the 1840s as a showcase for local artists. One of its two interconnected buildings is a *Jugendstil* monument, the other "of no artistic importance." Works by more than 400 artists are displayed and sold in the art gallery, where merchandise begins at 2,000 DM ($1,140). In a sales outlet, the Ladengeschäft, crafts in all kinds of media, textiles, and woven objects are sold at prices that begin at 45 DM ($25.65). It's open Monday to Friday from 9:30am to 6pm and Saturday from 9:30am to 2pm.

Romi Senn. Frauenstrasse 12. ☎ **089/292798.** S-Bahn: Isartor.

This gallery is across from the Viktualienmarkt. It sells original art-nouveau stained-glass windows extracted from old houses and public buildings in Belgium, Germany, France, England, and Austria; it has a scattering from 19th-century America as well. Hours are Monday to Friday from 11am to 6pm and Saturday from 11am to 2pm.

BOOKS

Anglia English Bookshop. Schellingstrasse 3. ☎ **089/283642.**

Words'Worth. Schellingstrasse 21. ☎ **089/280-9141.** U-Bahn: U3 or U6 to Universität.

Few competitors in Munich cooperate with each other as gracefully as these two independent stores that deal exclusively in English-language periodicals and books. Their stock runs the gamut from 19th-century English and American classics to the most recent releases, with art books and offbeat modern literature thrown in as well. Words'Worth is a bit larger than Anglia. One corner is devoted to a display of English tea caddies and marmalades, profits from which go directly to Britain's National Trust. Both stores are open Monday to Friday from 9am to 6:30pm and Saturday from 10am to 2pm, and both will cheerfully refer you to the other if they don't have what you're looking for.

Hugendubel. Marienplatz 22. ☎ **089/23891.** U-Bahn or S-Bahn: Marienplatz.

Not only is this Munich's biggest bookstore, but it also enjoys the most central location. It sells a number of English-language titles, both fiction and nonfiction, and also offers travel books and helpful maps. Open Monday to Friday from 9am to 6:30pm and Saturday from 9am to 2pm.

CHINA, SILVER & GLASS

Georg Jensen. Amiraplatz 1. ☎ **089/2916-1084.** U-Bahn: Odeonsplatz.

This is the only outlet in Munich for the products of the most famous silversmith in Denmark. Many of the designs were first produced shortly after World War I—they helped to alter forever the way the Scandinavians interpreted modern design. Inventory includes hollowware, jewelry, cutlery, clocks, and wristwatches. It's open Monday to Friday from 9:30am to 6pm and Saturday from 9:30am to 2pm.

✪ **Kunstring Meissen.** Briennerstrasse 4. ☎ **089/281532.** U-Bahn: Odeonsplatz.

This establishment's close links to the porcelain factories of Meissen and Dresden in what was then East Germany stretch back to the coldest days of the Cold War. It was then Munich's exclusive distributor of Meissen and Dresden. Though exclusive access is now a thing of the past, Kunstring's still carries one of Munich's largest inventories of elegant porcelain. *Note:* With two of the most impeccable pedigrees in Europe, neither Meissen nor Dresden have adopted the assembly-line methods used by many of their more industrialized modern-day competitors. Anything you buy can be shipped, although if you're looking for the more esoteric objects, there might be a delay if Kunstring doesn't have the object in stock. Kunstring is open Monday to Friday from 9:30am to 5pm and Saturday from 9:30am to 2pm.

✪ **Nymphenburger Porzellanmanufaktur.** Nordliches Schlossrondell 8. ☎ **089/ 179-1970.** Bus: 41.

At Nymphenburg, about 5 miles northwest of the heart of Munich, you'll find one of Germany's most famous porcelain factories on the grounds of Schloss Nymphenburg. You can visit its exhibition and sales rooms Monday to Friday from 8:30am to noon and 12:30 to 5pm. Shipments can be arranged if you make purchases. (This is a bit of a trek, but you'll probably be taking a sightseeing trip to Schloss Nymphenburg anyway). There's also a more central branch in Munich's center at Odeonsplatz 1 (☎ **089/282428**; U-Bahn: U1 to Rotkreuzplatz, then tram no. 12 toward Amalienburgstrasse).

✪ **Rosenthal.** Dienerstrasse 17. ☎ **089/222617.** U-Bahn or S-Bahn: Marienplatz.

Established in 1879 in the Bavarian town of Selb near the Czech border, Rosenthal is one of the three or four most prestigious names in German porcelain. Although traditional patterns are still made, most of the line now focuses on contemporary design. Prices for Rosenthal designs are preestablished by the manufacturer, and there are no price breaks at this factory outlet. The outlet is owned and operated by Rosenthal itself, so you will find here the widest selection of Rosenthal patterns available in Germany. In addition to porcelain, the line includes furniture, glass, and cutlery, all scattered over two floors of spotlessly maintained showrooms. It's open Monday to Friday from 9:30am to 8:30pm and Saturday from 9:30am to 2pm.

CHOCOLATE & CONFISERIE

Confiserie Kreutzkann. Maffeistrasse 4. ☎ **089/993-5570.** Tram: 19.

This is one of Munich's most famous purveyors of elaborate chocolates, pastry, and the artistically shaped and colored almond paste, marzipan. It dates back to 1861. If you want to consume your high-calorie treats on the spot, there's a cafe on the premises where you can order coffee or tea to go with whatever appeals to you. It's open Monday to Saturday from 8am to 6:30pm.

Kaffe Hause Reber. Herzogspitalstrasse 9. ☎ **089/265231.** U-Bahn: Stachl.

Pralines, chocolates, and marzipan are the products of this famous and nostalgia-laden store. It has been here since 1876, and many locals remember coming here on childhood outings with their grandparents. About eight bite-size morsels (100 grams) cost 7.20 DM ($4.10). There's a cafe on its street-level premises that has a reputation for chocolate-slathered cakes filled with Cointreau-flavored whipped cream. Slices of this sell for 4.80 DM ($2.75) and can be consumed with coffee, or for chocoholics, with hot chocolate.

CRAFTS & FOLKLORE

Bayerischer Kunstgewerbeverein (Bavarian Association of Artisans). Pacellistrasse 6-8. ☎ **089/290-1470.** U-Bahn: Karlsplatz.

At this showcase for Bavarian artisans, you'll find excellent handcrafts: ceramics, glass, jewelry, wood carvings, pewter, and Christmas decorations. It's open Monday to Friday from 9:30am to 6pm and on Saturday from 9:30am to 2pm.

Haertle. Neuhauserstrasse 15. ☎ **089/231-1790.** U-Bahn: Marienplatz or Stachus.

Although much of what it sells is crafted from wood, don't look for carvings of the saints or depictions of woodcutters and alpine farmers here. Instead you'll find racks of nostalgic, and in some cases, kitschy wooden implements for the home and kitchen. Much is rustic, charming, and crafted in Bavaria, though the regional merchandise is offset with racks of porcelain, glassware, and gift items. The shop has thrived at its central location for at least a century. The store is open Monday to Friday from 9:30am to 6:30pm (Thursday until 8:30pm) and Saturday from 9:30am to 2pm.

Horst Fuchs. Westenriederstrasse 17. ☎ **089/223791.** U-Bahn: Marienplatz.

The venue is Bavarian beer-drinking in all its well-accessorized splendor. Even if, after you return home, you fill a genuine beer stein from this store with a mass-market beer from an aluminum can, it will somehow taste better because of its association with Bavaria. It's open Monday to Friday from 10am to 6pm and Saturday from 10am to 2pm.

✪ Ludwig Mory. Marienplatz 8. ☎ **089/224542.** U-Bahn or S-Bahn: Marienplatz.

This is the most famous purveyor of Bavarian beer steins in Munich. It's near the cathedral, its one-room setting is folkloric, and it basks in a reputation that has been building since the 1830s. After seeing this place, you'll never want to drink Budweiser from a can again. Fashioned from pewter, and to a lesser degree, ceramic, sometimes lidded, sometimes without, the steins range from the honest but unpretentious to richly decorative works of art that might round off a private collection. For your souvenir of Munich you can pay anywhere from 45 DM ($25.65) to 1,200 DM ($684). It's open Monday to Friday from 9am to 6pm and Saturday from 9am to 1pm.

Otto Kellnberger Holzhandlung. Heiliggeistrasse 8. ☎ **089/226479.** U-Bahn or S-Bahn: Marienplatz.

Established just after World War II, this is a small but choice emporium of traditional wood carvings. In the Altstadt near the Marienplatz, it evokes the bucolic charms of remote alpine Bavaria. Inventory includes all the folkloric charm and some of the folkloric kitsch you might have found if you had made the trek to remote Oberammergau, but with a lot less time, trouble, and expense. It's open Monday to Friday from 9:30am to 6:30pm and Saturday from 10am to noon.

Prinoth. Guido Schneblestrasse 9A. ☎ **089/560378.** U-Bahn: U4 or U5 to Laimerplatz.

Most of the wood carvings sold here are produced in small workshops in South Tyrol, that folklore-rich part of Austria that was annexed to Italy after World War I. The selection is wide-ranging and broad, and since the setting lies 3½ miles west of Munich's tourist zones, prices are substantially reasonable compared to shops closer to the Marienplatz. It's open Monday to Friday from 9am to 6pm.

✪ Wallach. Residenzstrasse 3. ☎ **089/220871.** U-Bahn or S-Bahn: Marienplatz.

Established more than a century ago, Wallach is the largest emporium in Munich for Bavarian handcrafts, both new and antique, as well as the evocative, sometimes kitschy folk art. You'll find antique butter churns, hand-painted wooden boxes and trays, painted porcelain clocks, wooden wall or mantelpiece clocks, and doilies whose use faded along with antimacassars, but which are charming nonetheless. Most of the store's street level is devoted to hand-crafted folklore. One floor above street level, you'll find dirndls, lederhosen, loden coats, and other traditional Bavarian garments for men, women, and children. Look also for fabrics (sold by the meter), and housewares like sheets and towels, many patterned in Bavarian themes. The store is open Monday to Friday from 10:30am to 6pm (Thursday until 8:30pm) and Saturday from 10:30am to 4pm.

DEPARTMENT STORES

Hertie. Bahnhofplatz 7. ☎ 089/55120. U-Bahn: Hauptbahnhof.

This is our favorite Munich department store, a sprawling four-story-plus-basement emporium of all aspects of the good life as interpreted by Teutonic tastes. A fixture near the main railway station since the turn of the century, it has survived wars and revolutions with predictable mercantile style. It's open Monday to Friday from 9am to 6:30pm (Thursday until 8:30pm) and Saturday from 9am to 2pm.

Karstadt. Neuhauserstrasse 18. ☎ 089/290230. U-Bahn: Karlsplatz-Stachus.

One of Munich's most well-respected department stores can sell you just about everything you'd need to maintain a well-accessorized home, to dress yourself for virtually any occasion, or to pursue almost any activity. Temporary visitors to Munich especially value the collection of Bavarian handcrafts on the third floor, many of which would look fetching as a souvenir of your trip to Munich. It's open Monday to Friday from 9am to 8pm and Saturday from 9am to 4pm.

Kaufhof. Marienplatz. ☎ 089/231851. U-Bahn or S-Bahn: Marienplatz.

This is the Munich branch of the upscale department store chain that was originally established in Cologne during the late 19th century. It came to Munich in 1972 and is one of the largest stores in town, on five floors in a building on the city's historic square. Wander freely among displays that are art forms in their own right. You'll find men's, women's, and children's clothing, housewares, groceries, and virtually everything else you might think of. It's open Monday to Friday from 9am to 6:30pm (Thursday until 8:30pm) and Saturday from 8:30am to 2pm. There's a smaller branch of this emporium at Karlsplatz 2 (☎ 089/51250; U-Bahn: Karlsplatz) that maintains the same hours and accepts the same credit cards.

Ludwig Beck am Rathauseck. Am Marienplatz 11. ☎ 089/236910. U-Bahn or S-Bahn: Marienplatz.

This is Munich's major department store. Most merchandise is intended for local residents; however, visitors will also be interested in this four-floor shopping bazaar, which sells handmade crafts from all over Germany, both old and new. Items include decorative pottery and dishes, etched glass beer steins and vases, painted wall plaques depicting rural scenes, and decorative flower arrangements. There's unusual kitchenware, colored flatware, calico hot pads and towels, and a collection of casually chic leather-trimmed canvas purses. The shop also offers fashions, textiles, and even jazz recordings. Within the same block the store has opened two more outlets: Wäsche-Beck, selling lingerie, linens, and curtains, and Strumpf-Beck, featuring the town's largest selection of stockings and hosiery. All three locations are open Monday to Friday from 9:30am to 6:30pm and on Saturday from 9am to 2pm.

ELECTRONICS

Media Markt. Drygalski-Allee 31. ☎ 089/780280.

Saturn Electro Technocenter. Schwanenthaler Strasse 115. ☎ 089/510850.

Anyone interested in electronics will enjoy comparing what's available at home to what's widespread and selling like gangbusters in Germany. For insight into design, speed, capabilities, and accessories, head for Munich's two superstores that deal exclusively in computers, cameras, VCRs, sound systems, and all kinds of electronics. If it's sold anywhere in Europe, you'll almost certainly find it here.

FASHION
MEN & WOMEN

Bogner Haus. Residenzstrasse 15. ☎ **089/290-7040.** U-Bahn or S-Bahn: Marienplatz.

Founded by Willy Bogner, former Olympic champion downhill racer, this store stocks well-made women's clothing upstairs, men's clothing on the street level, and clothing suited for whatever sport happens to be seasonal at the time of your visit in the cellar. Somewhere in the store, you'll find whatever you need to be appropriately clad for any occasion. One of its best is the Fire & Ice Department, in the cellar, where garments for young men and women have the kind of flair that might please some of the most demanding people in your life—your teenage children. The store is open Monday to Wednesday and Friday from 9:30am to 6:30pm, Thursday from 9:30am to 7:30pm, and Saturday from 9:30am to 2pm.

✪ **Dirndl-Ecke.** Am Platzl 1/Sparkassenstrasse 10. ☎ **089/220163.** U-Bahn or S-Bahn: Marienplatz or Isartor.

One block up from the famed Hofbräuhaus, this shop gets our unreserved recommendation as a stylish place specializing in high-grade dirndls, feathered alpine hats, and all clothing associated with the alpine regions. Everything sold is of fine quality—there's no tourist junk. Other merchandise includes needlework hats, beaded belts, and pleated shirts for men. You may want to buy the stylish capes, the silver jewelry in old Bavarian style, the leather shoes, or the linen and cotton combinations, such as skirts with blouses and jackets. Bavarian clothing for children is also available. The store is open Monday to Friday from 9am to 6pm and Saturday from 9am to 1pm.

Exatmo. Franz-Josef-Strasse 35. ☎ **089/335761.** U-Bahn: Giselastrasse.

Only a district like Schwabing could sustain a business like this one. One of the most unusual clothiers in Munich, it operates from a showroom complete with mock-medieval murals. The store purchases old pieces of antique fabric (such as linen bedsheets from army surplus inventories) and makes them into jackets, vests, and ruffled shirts that hang beautifully, styles that would have been appreciated by the Elizabethans. Among the racks of clothing are garments inspired by the puffy sleeves and dramatic flair of 17th-century fashions that might have been worn by the Three Musketeers—you can dress yourself here as a fencing champion even if you don't know a thrust from an *en garde*. Virtually everything in stock is manufactured from linen or leather. It's open Monday to Friday from 9am to 6:30pm, and Saturday from 10am to 2pm.

Frankonia. Maximiliansplatz 10. ☎ **089/290-0020.** U-Bahn: Karlsplatz or Odeonsplatz.

This store carries Munich's most prestigious collection of traditional Bavarian dress (called *Tracht*). If you see yourself dressed hunter style, this place can outfit you well. There's a fine collection of wool cardigan jackets with silvery buttons. It's open Monday to Friday from 9am to 6:30pm and Saturday from 9am to 2pm.

Loden-Frey. Maffeistrasse 7-9. ☎ **089/210390.** U-Bahn or S-Bahn: Marienplatz.

The twin domes of the Frauenkirche are visible above the soaring glass-enclosed atrium of this shop's showroom. Go here for the world's largest selection of Loden clothing and traditional costumes, as well as for international fashions from top European designers such as Armani, Valentino, and Ungaro. It's open Monday to Friday from 9am to 6pm, except on Thursday when hours extend to 8:30pm, and on Saturday from 9am to 2pm.

Red/Green of Scandinavia. Kauflingerstrasse 9. ☎ **089/260-6489.** U-Bahn or S-Bahn: Marienplatz.

This shop near the Marienplatz will sell you everything you need for appearing relaxed, casual, and at home on someone's private yacht or on the local golf links. Most of the inventory comes from Denmark, and since it was all designed to withstand the blustery winds or the clear sunlight of the Baltic, everything is ready to outfit you appropriately for whatever outdoor activity (or *après-sport* fireside chitchat) you're planning. Garments for men, women, and children are all available. It's open Monday to Friday from 10am to 6pm and Saturday from 10am to 2pm.

MEN

Moshammer's. Maximilianstrasse 14. ☎ **089/226924.** U-Bahn: Isartor.

This store could be your first resource in a search for appropriate menswear. Merchandise is continental, and the staff seems aware of their own prestige and the glamour of their address. In other words, although a visit won't necessarily leave you with a warm and fuzzy feeling of *Gemütlichkeit,* you might at least learn how high some of the prices can be in an upscale Münchner menswear store. It's open Monday to Friday from 10:30am to 8:30pm and Saturday from 11am to 4pm.

Uli Knecht. Residenzstrasse 19-20. ☎ **089/2916-0406.** U-Bahn: Odeonsplatz.

This is the men's division of the same retailer recommended below, the kind of place where a business executive could clothe himself for the office, the golf course, a hunting lodge, or an amorous weekend getaway. Designers represented on the two floors of the showroom include Ralph Lauren, Armani, an Italian designer named Antonio Fusco, and such German outfitters as Closed and Strenesse. It's open Monday to Friday from 10:30am to 6pm and Saturday from 9am to 2pm; it's closed Sunday.

WOMEN

Furore. Franz-Joseph Strasse 41. ☎ **089/343971.** U-Bahn: U3 or U6 to Giselastrasse.

This elegant store offers fashionable lingerie (brassieres, bustiers, slips, etc.) with tasteful designs, in some cases filmy, feminine, and subtly erotic, in silk, cotton, and a few synthetics by Spain-born André Sard. It also has a homewear collection: nightgowns, pajamas, sheets, towels, and decorative accessories from New York design superstar Donna Karan. Furore was the first store in Germany to distribute her designs. The store is open Monday to Friday from 10am to 6:30pm and Saturday from 10am to 2pm.

Maendler. Theatinerstrasse 7. ☎ **089/291-3322.** U-Bahn: Odeonsplatz.

This store caters to the well-dressed woman with a series of boutiques scattered over two floors. You may prefer to just wander around the store, appreciating the creative vision of Joop, Claude Montana, New York New York, and Jil Sander, but a quick consultation with any of the staff poised near the store's entrance can point you in the right direction. Looking for that special something for your dinner with the city's mayor or the president of Germany? Ask to see the formal evening wear of English designer David Fielden. Looking for something more daring and avantgarde? Head for this outfit's other branch, **Rosy Maendler,** Maximiliansplatz 12 (same phone). Here you'll find a youthful version of the same store and garments by Madonna's favorite designer, Jean-Paul Gaultier, whose exhibitionistic and/or erotic leather and rubber clothing will cause a stir on either side of the Atlantic.

Both shops are open Monday to Friday from 9:30am to 6:30pm and Saturday from 9:30am to 2pm.

Uli Knecht. Residenzstrasse 15. ☎ **089/221510.** U-Bahn: Odeonsplatz.

Its employees are quick to tell you that Uli Knecht is not a designer, but rather, a clever and successful retailer with a gift for distributing the creations of some of the best-known clothiers in the world. This branch for women, two doors down from the Uli Knecht store for men, covers two floors. It's laden with garments that include sportswear and some formalwear, but the emphasis is on upscale, elegant, and highly wearable clothing—everything from business suits to cocktail dresses. It is open Monday to Wednesday 10am to 7pm, Thursday and Friday 10am to 8pm, and Saturday 10am to 4pm.

FOOD

British Stop. Schellingstrasse 100. ☎ **089/542-0270.** U-Bahn: Theresienstrasse.

Popular with expatriates, this store specializes in British and Irish food and drink. Featured are British cheeses, breads, bacon, sausages, and pies, along with a goodly selection of sweets and gift chocolates. Also sold are sandwiches composed of English bread and "fillings." The store also sells British greeting cards, secondhand and new books, and British magazines. It is open Monday to Wednesday 9:30am to 7pm, Thursday and Friday 9:30am to 8pm, and Saturday 9:30am to 4pm.

✪ **Dallmayr.** Dienerstrasse 14-15. ☎ **089/21350.** Tram: 19.

What Fauchon is to Paris, and Fortnum & Mason is to London, the venerable firm of Dallmayr is to Munich. Gastronomes as far away as Hamburg and Berlin sometimes telephone orders for exotica not readily available anywhere else, and its list of prestigious clients reads like a Who's Who of German industry and letters. Wander freely among racks of foodstuffs, some of which are too delicate to survive shipment abroad, others that can be shipped anywhere. The shop is open Monday to Friday from 9am to 6:30pm and Saturday from 9am to 1pm. The restaurant associated with this store is separately recommended in chapter 5.

Zerwirk Gewölbe. Ledererstrasse 3. ☎ **089/226824.** U-Bahn or S-Bahn: Marienplatz.

The amazing thing about this place is that it has survived in a form more or less evocative of medieval times, which is when it was originally established, in 1206. It's the oldest purveyor of venison and game in Bavaria, with so much history associated with it that it's easy to forget its modern, workaday function as a supplier of würsts, pâtés, terrines, roasts, and cutlets (most of which are made from venison, wild boar, pheasant, or game birds) to private homes and restaurants around the city. Most temporary visitors stop in for a simple platter of food, priced from 8 DM ($4.55), perhaps preceded by a steaming bowl of one of the *Tagessuppes* (soups of the day) that are dispensed from an *Imbiss* (snack bar) set up in one corner. Look for this venerable upscale delicatessen and butcher shop near the landmark restaurant Haxnbauer, on a small street near the Marienplatz. It's open Monday to Friday from 9:30am to 6pm and Saturday from 9:30am to 3pm.

JEWELRY & WATCHES

Andreas Huber. Weinstrasse 8. ☎ **089/298295.** U-Bahn or S-Bahn: Marienplatz.

This store sells all the big names in Swiss and other European wristwatches, as well as clocks. It offers some jewelry, but the specialty is timepieces. It's open Monday to Friday 10am to 7pm and on Saturday 10am to 4pm.

Carl Jagemann's. Residenzstrasse 3. ☎ **089/225493.** U-Bahn: Marienplatz.

Its reputation for quality and honesty goes back to 1864, as does some (but not all) of the merchandise it sells. It's one of the Altstadt's largest purveyors of new and antique timepieces of all types, ranging from wristwatches to grandfather clocks, from the severely rectilinear to rococo kitsch. There's also a collection of new and antique jewelry. It's open Monday to Friday from 10am to 6pm and Saturday from 10am to 2pm.

✪ **Gebruder Hemmere.** Maximilianstrasse 14. ☎ **089/220189.** U-Bahn: Odeonsplatz or Max-Weber Platz.

This is *the* place for jewelry. The original founders of this stylish shop made their fortune creating bejeweled fantasies for the Royal Bavarian Court of Ludwig II. Today, in a setting of southern baroque-style pastel-painted paneling, you can buy some of the most exciting jewelry in the area. All pieces are limited editions, designed and made in-house by Bavarian craftspeople. The company also designs its own wristwatch, the Hemmerle, and distributes what is said to be one of the world's finest watches, the Breguet. The story is open Monday to Friday from 9:30am to 6pm and Saturday from 9:30am to 1pm.

KITCHENWARE

Biebl. Karlsplatz 25. ☎ **089/597936.** U-Bahn: Karlsplatz (for both outlets).

In the central pedestrian zone, this reputable and fairly priced emporium sells razor-sharp German steel. They're quick to debunk the myth that anything that's made in the town of Solingen, in the Ruhr Valley near the French border, is of flawless quality. Instead, they point you to the impeccable quality of the implements made by a select group of Solingen-based companies—Trident Wuesthof or Henckels (for kitchen knives), Dovo (for scissors), and W.M.S. (for table cutlery). Your first impression of the premises may make you think you're in a warehouse for surgical implements, but the choice is so overwhelming and the prices so fair that you'll soon see why it's one of the best-recommended stopovers in this survey. Many excellent knives can be had for 20 DM ($11.40) and up. Even the best rarely exceed 60 DM ($34.20) each. The outlet is open Monday to Friday 9:15am to 6:15pm and Saturday from 9:15am to 2pm.

MARKETS

In addition to those listed below, a traditional market, **Auer Dult,** is held three times a year in the Mariahilfplatz. Dates vary but the months are April, July, and October (see also the "Munich Calendar of Events," in chapter 2). Antiques dealers, food, and Bavarian bands are present; it's a great place to find bargains. Take tram 7, 15, 25, or 27.

Christkindlmarkt. Marienplatz. U-Bahn: Marienplatz.

One of the most visible and traditional in Munich, this December Christmas market attracts visitors from all over Germany and Europe—only the Christmas market in Nürnberg is more famous. Hundreds of stalls offer Christmas ornaments, handmade children's toys, carved figures, and nativity scenes. The square is full of local color; the stallkeepers are picturesque in their woolen coats, hats, and gloves; and the scene is enhanced by frequent snowfalls. Opening hours vary with the enthusiasm of the merchants. In most cases, stalls are open 10am to 8pm on Monday to Saturday, although as Christmas approaches, many open on Sunday as well, until 7pm.

Elisabethmarkt. Elisabethplatz. Tram: 18.

This is Schwabing's smaller and less dramatic version of Munich's premier outdoor market, the Viktualienmarkt. It's held every Monday to Saturday from 7am to about 11am, although some die-hard merchants manage to hold out until 1:30pm. Completely decentralized, each individual vendor operates exclusively on his or her own account. Stalls tend to be more laden with bounty in spring, summer, and fall, but a few hardy souls maintain a presence here even in the depths of winter.

Grossmarkthalle. Thalkirchen. U-Bahn: U3 to Fürstenried West.

This is Munich's equivalent of Paris's Rungis (formerly Les Halles). Buyers from virtually every restaurant in Munich make an early morning pilgrimage to this industrial-looking complex in the city's southern suburbs. Purveyors arrive with lorries from as far away as Italy; buyers congregate from throughout Bavaria and beyond. Be warned, though, that there's an entrance fee of 5 DM ($2.85) that allows you only to browse and admire the way business is conducted; buying is wholesale only—homemakers who do show up usually bring bushel baskets or wheeled carts to haul away impressive quantities of peaches, apples, or whatever. It's open Monday to Saturday from 5am to 10:30am.

Viktualienmarkt. U-Bahn or S-Bahn: Marienplatz.

Unless you happen to be staying in a place where you have access to a kitchen, it's doubtful that you'll want to be hauling groceries back to your hotel room during your stay in Munich. That doesn't detract, however, from the allure of wandering through the open-air stalls of the city's most prominent food market, a few minute's walk south of the Marienplatz. It's composed of hundreds of independently operated merchants who maintain whatever hours they want, often closing up their cramped premises whenever the day's inventory is sold out. Most economy-minded shoppers, however, show up, shopping basket in hand, around 8am, to stock their larders before noon. By 5pm, only the hardiest of merchants remain in place, and by early evening, the kiosks are locked up tight. On the premises are a worthy collection of wine, meats, cheeses, and all the other bounty of the Bavarian agrarian world.

MUSIC

Hieber Musikhaus. In the Rathaus, Landschaftstrasse (without number). ☎ **089/ 2900-8040.** U-Bahn or S-Bahn: Marienplatz.

This is the largest music store in Munich, and with a history going back to 1884, it's also one of the oldest. Its stockpiles of librettos for Wagner, Mozart, Puccini, and Verdi operas are among the most extensive anywhere, and in many cases, they inventory German-language translations even of operas originally written in Italian or French. You'll have to use a bit of ingenuity to determine which building contains whatever it is you're looking for, but in the process of educating yourself, you're likely to run into at least one or two musicians employed by the city's many orchestral groups. Looking for a musical instrument? Check out the company's branch at Liebfrauenstrasse 1 (☎ **089/2900-0840**). Looking for keyboards and an idiosyncratic collection of secondhand sheet music, some of it antique, and some dog-eared and annotated by anonymous musicians of yesteryear? Head for the company's branch on the Mazaristrasse 1 (☎ **089/2900-0800**). All three are within a short walk of each other, and all maintain the same hours: Monday to Friday from 9am to 6:30pm (Thursday until 7:30pm) and Saturday from 9am to 2pm.

PEWTER

Sebastian Wesely. Petersplatz 1. ☎ **089/264519.** U-Bahn: Marienplatz.

This is one of the best sites in Munich for the acquisition of everybody's favorite utilitarian metal, pewter. Favored throughout the 16th and 17th centuries because of the ease with which it can be crafted into baroque forms, it burnishes to a low luster that's still prized today. This shop carries an impressive array of reproductions, any of which would make a valuable addition to your home. It's open Monday to Friday 8:30am to 6:30pm and Saturday 8:30am to 4pm.

TOYS

Münchner Poupenstuben und Zinnfiguren Kabinette. Maxburgstrasse 4. ☎ **089/ 293797.** U-Bahn: Karlsplatz.

This is the kind of store you either thrill to or find impossibly claustrophobic. Here is a miniature world where houses, furniture, birdcages, and people are cunningly crafted from pewter or carved wood. Many of the items look deceptively realistic. Famous throughout Germany, the shop has been managed for 150 years by women of the same family, and some of the figures are still made from the original 150-year-old molds that are collectors' items in their own right. Anything in this place would make a great gift not only for a child but for an adult with a nostalgic bent. Ilse Schweizer is the present owner. It's open Monday to Friday from 10am to 6pm and Saturday from 10am to 1pm.

Obletter's. Karlsplatz 11–12. ☎ **089/231-8601.** U-Bahn: Karlsplatz.

Established in the 1880s, this is one of the largest emporiums of children's toys in Munich, with five floors of inventory containing everything from folkloric dolls to computer games. Some of the most charming are replicas of middle European antique toys, some of which look suspiciously capable of coming alive beneath someone's Christmas tree, à la the *Nutcracker* ballet. It's open Monday to Friday 9am to 7:30pm and Saturday from 9am to 4pm.

WINE

Geisel's Vinothek. Schützenstrasse 11. ☎ **089/5513-7140.** U-Bahn: Hauptbahnhof.

Other than Dallmayr, which does this kind of thing on a much bigger scale, this is the most sophisticated wine shop in Munich. It's next to the Excelsior Hotel, with displays that celebrate grapes and wine making in one way or another. (It doubles as a restaurant, recommended separately in chapter 5.) Its inventory includes wines from Germany, Austria, Italy, and France, with bottles ranging from 15 DM ($8.55) to as much as 1,400 DM ($798) for a vintage *Château Petrus*. Many worthy bottles sell for 30 DM ($17.10). Because the chef here is a passionate advocate of wines from western France, there's an especially strong selection of Bordeaux. Most of the selections offered by the glass at the restaurant's bar are sold by the bottle in the wine shop, allowing you to taste before you buy the whole bottle. The shop is open daily 10am to 1am.

Munich After Dark

9

Munich is a major performing arts center and has a lively nightlife as well. Munich is home to no less than four major orchestras plus a world-class opera company and a ballet company. Many theaters are scattered throughout the city, offering everything from classic to modern German drama.

Munich's nightlife varies with the weather. When the weather is fair, and the night air balmy, the *Biergartens* and *Biersteins* are brimming with cheer. During the winter months, patrons of the beer gardens turn to Munich's beer halls, such as the illustrious Hofbräuhaus, to quaff beer and share in the typical Bavarian singsong. Beer gardens and beer halls usually empty around midnight; then the club scene cranks up. Munich's club scene is quite eclectic. It is possible to find almost any type of club, from country-western bars to ultratechno dance halls. Many clubs rave until the wee hours of the morning. The district of Schwabing, home to the numerous cabarets and funky dance clubs, is the place to go.

To find out what's happening in the Bavarian capital, go to the tourist office at platform 12 in the Hauptbahnhof and request a copy of *Monatsprogramm*, costing 2.50 DM ($1.40). It contains a complete cultural guide, telling you not only what's being presented—from concerts to opera, from special exhibits to museum hours—but how to purchase tickets.

1 The Performing Arts

Nowhere else in Europe, other than London and Paris, will you find so many musical and theatrical performances. And the good news is the low cost of seats—so count on indulging yourself and going to several concerts. You'll get good tickets if you're willing to pay anywhere from 15 to 75 DM ($8.55 to $42.75). Pick up a *Monatsprogramm* for information and schedules.

If you speak German, you'll find at least 20 theaters offering plays of every description: classic, comic, experimental, contemporary—take your pick. The best way to find out what current productions might interest you is to go to a theater-ticket agency: The most convenient one is at Marienplatz at the entrance to the S-Bahn.

For events that sell out and popular events where the number of available tickets is reduced by season tickets and long-term subscriptions (such as soccer games, or the opera, especially the summer festival performances), you'll have to make a trip to the box office—organizers of these events tend not to cooperate with outside ticket agencies. But for virtually everything else in Munich, you'd be well advised to head for **WOM (World of Music)**, Kaufingerstrasse 15 (☎ **089/2185-1920**), whose employees can obtain tickets to virtually every cultural venue, concert, or sporting event in Bavaria. Be warned in advance that use of a credit card for payment, both at WOM and at its competitors, carries a surcharge of at least 20 DM ($11.40) per order. WOM's leading competitors include **München Tickets** (☎ **089/5481-8181**) and **Hieber am Dom** (☎ **089/2900-8014**), both of which deal basically in the same tickets, with access to the same computer database.

OPERA & CLASSICAL MUSIC

Besides the organizations listed below, Munich is home to the **Bavarian State Radio Orchestra** (Bayerischer Rundfunk Münchner Rundfunkorchestra), Roberto Abbado, musical director; the **Bavarian Radio Orchestra** (Bayerischer Rundfunk Symphonieorchester), Loren Mazel, musical director; and the **Graunke Symphony Orchestra,** directed by Kurt Graunke.

✪ **Bayerischen Staatsoper.** Performing in the Nationaltheater, at Max-Joseph-Platz 2. ☎ **089/2185-1920.** Tickets 8–375 DM ($4.55–$213.75), including standing room. U-Bahn or S-Bahn: Marienplatz.

The **Bavarian State Opera** is one of the world's great companies. The Bavarians give their hearts, perhaps even their souls, to opera. Productions are beautifully mounted and presented, and the company's roster includes some of the world's greatest singers. Hard-to-get tickets may be purchased Monday to Friday from 10am to 6pm, plus 1 hour before each performance (during the weekend, only on Saturday from 10am to 1pm). The Nationaltheater is also the home of a younger company, the **Bavarian State Ballet.**

Münchner Philharmoniker (Munich Philharmonic). Performing in the Gasteig Kulturzentrum, at Rosenheimerstrasse 5. Tel. ☎ **089/5481-8181.** Tickets, 18–95 DM ($10.95–$54.15). S-Bahn: Rosenheimerplatz. Tram: 18 to Gasteig. Bus: 51.

This famous orchestra was founded in 1893. James Levine is its newly appointed music director. Its home is the Gasteig Cultural Center, where it performs in Philharmonic Hall. The center, which opened in 1985, also shelters the Richard Strauss Conservatory and the Munich Municipal Library, and has five performance halls. The Gasteig stands on the bluffs of the Isar River in the Haidhausen District. You can purchase tickets to events at the ground-level Glashalle, Monday to Friday from 9am to 6pm and on Saturday from 9am to 2pm. The Philharmonic season begins in mid-September and runs to July.

MAJOR THEATERS & CONCERT HALLS

There are theaters and performance halls all over town. Concerts are given in the **Herkulessaal** (in the Residenz, Hofgarten; ☎ **089/290671**). The **Staatstheater am Gärtnerplatz** (☎ **089/201-6767**) offers a varied program of operetta, ballet, and musicals.

✪ **Altes Residenztheater (Cuvilliés Theater).** Residenzstrasse 1. ☎ **089/2185-1920.** Opera tickets, 30–255 DM ($17.10–$145.35); play tickets, 10–71 DM ($5.70–$40.45). U-Bahn: U3, U4, U5, or U6 to Odeonsplatz.

A part of the Residenz (see "Museums & Palaces" in chapter 6), this theater is a sightseeing attraction in its own right. The Bavarian State Opera and the **Bayerisches Staatsschauspiel (State Theater)** perform small-scale works here in keeping with the tiny theater's intimate character. Box-office hours are the same as those for the Nationaltheater. The theater is celebrated as Germany's most outstanding example of a rococo tier-boxed theater. Seating an audience of 550, it was designed by court architect François de Cuvilliés in the mid–18th century. During World War II the interior was dismantled and stored. After the war it was reassembled in the reconstructed building. For an admission of 3 DM ($1.70), visitors can look at the theater Monday to Saturday from 2 to 5pm and on Sunday from 10am to 5pm.

Deutsches Theater. Schwanthalerstrasse 13. ☎ **089/5523-4444.** Tickets 29–90 DM ($16.55–$51.30); higher for special events. U-Bahn: Karlsplatz/Stachus.

The regular season of the Deutsches Theater lasts throughout the year. Musicals are popular, but operettas, ballets, and international shows are performed as well. It's the only theater in Germany that's both a theater and a ballroom. During Carnival in January and February, the seats are removed and stored, replaced by tables and chairs for more than 2,000 guests. Handmade decorations by artists combined with lighting effects create an enchanting ambience. Waiters serve wine, champagne, and food. The costume balls and official black-tie festivities here are famous throughout Europe.

Münchner Kammerspiele. Maximilianstrasse 26-28. ☎ **089/2372-1328.** Tickets 10.50–47.50 DM ($6–$27.10). U-Bahn: Marienplatz. S-Bahn: Isartorplatz. Tram: 19 to Maximilianstrasse.

Contemporary plays as well as classics from German or international playwrights, ranging from Goethe to Brecht and Shakespeare to Goldoni, are performed here. The season lasts from early October through the end of July. You can reserve tickets by phone Monday to Friday from 10am to 6pm, but you must pick them up at least 2 days before the performance. The box office is open Monday to Friday from 10am to 6pm and on Saturday from 10am to 1pm, plus 1 hour before performances.

The theater also has a second smaller venue called **Werkraum,** where new productions—mainly by younger authors and directors—are presented. The location is at Hildegardstrasse 1 (call the number above for more information).

2 The Club & Music Scene

NIGHTCLUBS

Bayerischer Hof Night Club. In the Hotel Bayerischer Hof, Promenadeplatz 2-6. ☎ **089/ 212-0994.** Cover 18 DM ($10.45) Fri–Sat after 10pm; higher for special events. Admission is free to hotel guests. Tram: 19.

This sophisticated club is in a large room in the extensive cellars of the Bayerischer Hof. Between 7 and 10pm every night, the club is a piano bar. After 10pm a partition opens, revealing the bandstand where a band plays to a dancing crowd until 3 or 4am. Entrance to the piano bar is free, but there's a cover charge to the nightclub on Friday and Saturday nights. Drinks begin at 15.50 DM ($8.85). It's open daily from 6pm to 3 or 4am. Daily happy hour is at 8:30pm with drinks starting at 9.50 DM ($5.40).

Night Flight. Franz-Joseph Strauss Airport, Wartungsallee 9. ☎ **089/9759-7999.** Cover 6 DM ($3.40) Tues–Thurs 10pm–2am, 10 DM ($5.70) Fri–Sat. S-Bahn: S8 to Flughafen.

It's one of only two or three nightclubs in Europe that dramatizes the landings and takeoffs from an airport as part of a visual thrill. To reach it, you'll have to either drive 25 miles north of the city or take a 30-minute ride on the S-Bahn. The site is on the periphery of the Munich Airport, in an industrial-looking building midway between three enormous hangars. You can drink at three different bars, dance, and listen to the loud music that changes according to the night of the week. There's even a restaurant, serving main courses from 16 to 22 DM ($9.10 to $12.55) and drinks that cost from 6.50 DM ($3.70). In summer, there's an outside terrace where virtually everything at the airport can be seen with eerie clarity. Friday nights, with techno-rap as the theme, draw the youngest audience. Other nights, the crowd ranges from 25 to a youthful 40. It's open Tuesday to Saturday from 9pm to at least 3am, and in some cases, until 8am the following morning.

A MEDIEVAL FEAST

Welser Kuche. Residenzstrasse 27. ☎ **089/296565.** U-Bahn: U3 to Odeonsplatz.

Welser Kuche re-creates a hearty medieval feast. Meals begin every night of the week at 8pm, and guests must be prepared to stick around for 3 hours as they are served by *Magde* and *Knechte* (wenches and knaves) in 16th-century costumes. In many ways this is a takeoff on the Tudor banquets that are so popular with tourists in London. Food is served in hand-thrown pottery, and guests eat the medieval delicacies with their fingers, aided only by a stilettolike dagger. Many recipes are authentic—they are based on a 16th-century cookbook discovered in 1970. You can order a 6- or 10-course menu, called a *Welser Feast,* for 69 or 79 DM ($39.35 or $45.05), respectively. On Tuesday only, a *Bürgermahl* of five courses costs 59 DM ($33.65). The place can be good fun if you're in the mood; but it's likely to be overflowing with tourists, so reservations are recommended. It's open daily from 7pm to 1am.

JAZZ

Jazzclub Unterfahrt. Kirchenstrasse 96. ☎ **089/448-2794.** Cover 15–28 DM ($8.55–$15.95) Tues–Sat, 10 DM ($5.70) Sun jam session. U-Bahn or S-Bahn: Ostbahnhof.

This is Munich's leading jazz club, lying near the Ostbahnhof in the Haidhausen district. Within a *gemütlich* ambience of pinewood paneling and flickering candles, the 120-seat club presents live music Tuesday to Sunday from 9pm to 1am. In one corner is an art gallery where a changing collection of paintings and sculptures is sold. Sunday night there's a special jam session for improvisation.

Mister B's. Herzog-Heinrichstrasse 38. ☎ **089/534901.** Cover 8–10 DM ($4.55–$5.70). U-Bahn: Goetheplatz.

Small, dark, and popular with blues and jazz aficionados, this club hosts a slightly older, mellower crowd than the rock and dance clubs. Blues, jazz, and rhythm-and-blues combos take the stage Thursday to Saturday. Hours are Tuesday to Sunday from 8pm to 3am.

Tilt. Helmholtzstrasse 12. ☎ **089/129-7969.** Cover 8–10 DM ($4.55–$5.70). S-Bahn: Donnersbergerbrücke.

Weekends, this is the place for acid jazz; dancers pack the floor during the slamming Disco Orange. It's balanced by world-beat Thursdays and indie Tuesdays. Hours are Tuesday and Thursday to Saturday from 10pm to 4am.

COUNTRY

Oklahoma. Schäftlarnstrasse 156. ☎ **089/723-4327.** Cover 10–20 DM ($5.70–$11.40). U-bahn: U3 or U6 to Implerstrasse, then bus no. 31 or 57.

File under surreal. German and European bands decked out in cowboy hats and boots struggle with a kind of music that makes no sense at all when taken so far out of context. Even when the results are dead-on mimicry, there's something strange about watching German "cowboys" line dance or lean on the bar while guzzling Spaten. The cover charge is usually at the low end of the scale, with higher rates when English and American acts hit the stage. Depending on your mood, this place can be a lot of fun. Pull on your jeans and come on in Tuesday to Saturday from 7pm to 1am.

Rattlesnake Saloon. Schneeglöckchenstrasse 91. ☎ **089/150-4035.** Cover 10–15 DM ($5.70–$8.55). S-Bahn: S1 to Fasanerie.

One of Munich's two country-western saloons, this is a down-home homage to the redneck charms of hound dogs, battered pickup trucks, and cowboy hats and boots. Rib-sticking platters (rib-eye steaks, barbecued pork, chili) can be ordered to wash down with the steins of Spaten beer that go so well with the live country music. Performers come from Munich, England, Canada, and even in some cases, Nashville, Tennessee. Regardless of how authentic the twang in the music might be, you'll have a fun evening here, and someone will invariably rise to the challenge of conducting a rodeo-style line dance lesson for anyone who's interested in learning. Rattlesnake is open Wednesday to Sunday from 7pm to 1am.

DANCE CLUBS & DISCOS

Feierwerk. Hansastrasse 39-41. ☎ **089/769-3600.** Cover 10–20 DM ($5.70–$11.40). U-Bahn or S-Bahn: Heimeranplatz.

Alterna-scene central. If it's independent theater or rock and roll, the multiple stages inside this complex have hosted it. Entertainment ranges from the commercially viable to the truly underground. In the summer, this already-roomy complex expands outside into circus tents. It's open daily from 9pm to 4am.

Kunstpark Ost. Grafingerstrasse 6. ☎ **089/4900-2730.** S-Bahn: Ostbahnhof.

Munich's newest complex of bars, restaurants, and dance clubs is in a sprawling former factory. There are more than 23 places, including K41, Babylon, Colosseum, Incognito, the Bongo Bar, and the Natray Temple. Your best bet is to show up after 8pm, when the bars open; discos begin to roar around 10:30pm. Entrance to the discos usually costs from 5 to 10 DM ($2.85 to $5.70), depending on the night of the week.

Max Emanuel Brauerei. Adalbertstrasse 33. ☎ **089/271-5158.** Cover 10 DM ($5.70) Wed, 13 DM ($7.40) Fri–Sat, including the first drink. U-Bahn: U3 or U6 to Universität.

Beer hasn't been brewed here since the 1920s, when the place was transformed into a showcase for Löwenbräu beer. It serves robust food and steins of beer every day from 11am to 1am. Three nights a week, the cavernous floor above street level reverberates with salsa music (Wednesday and Friday from 9pm) or 1950s-style rock and roll (Sunday beginning at 8pm). During salsa nights, most of Munich's Latino population, from Puerto Rico to southern Chile, make it a point of honor to show up to show off their merengue steps. Sunday nights the site can also be fun in a convertible-Chevy and saddle-shoes kind of way.

Nachtwerk. Landesbergerstrasse 185. ☎ **089/578-3800.** Cover 10 DM ($5.70). S-Bahn: Donnersbergerbrücke.

Both bands and disco are featured in this festive, unpretentious club in an old factory warehouse. The club is open Thursday from 10pm to 4am and Friday and Saturday from 10:30pm to 4am.

Parkcafé. Sophienstrasse 7. ☎ **089/598313.** Cover 10 DM ($5.70). U-Bahn: Königsplatz.

Male dancers in black leather and feather boas gyrate on elevated platforms, and beautiful people trance out to heavy repetition on the dance floor below them. Who'd ever guess this home to chic freaks was a Nazi hangout in the 1930s? Hours are Wednesday and Thursday from 10pm to 4am and Friday and Saturday from 10pm to 5am.

Schwabinger Podium. Wagnerstrasse 1. ☎ **089/399482.** No cover charge. U-Bahn: Münchener Freiheit.

Loud, urban, underground, smoky, crowded, and often raucous—this place's fans wouldn't change it even if they could. There's some kind of live music every night, and a crowd that seems up on the musical scenes in London and Los Angeles. It's open Sunday to Thursday from 8pm to 1am and Friday and Saturday from 8pm to 2am.

Wunderbar. Hochbrückenstrasse 3. ☎ **089/295118.** Cover 7 DM ($4). U-Bahn or S-Bahn: Marienplatz.

In 1995 this once-staid cellar bar reinvented itself, changed its musical direction, and became a dance bar. The result is an animated watering hole with music that includes recent releases of hip-hop, Brit-pop, and house in an industrial-looking environment with lots of chrome. Clients range from ages 18 to 35. It's open nightly from 9pm to 4am.

3 The Bar & Cafe Scene

Alter Simpl. Türkenstrasse 57. ☎ **089/272-3083.** Tram: 18. Bus: 53.

Once a literary cafe, Alter Simpl takes its name from a satirical review of 1903. There's no one around anymore who remembers that revue, but Alter Simpl is still on the scene, made famous by its legendary owner, Kathi Kobus. Lale Andersen, who popularized the song "Lili Marlene," frequented this cafe/bar when she was in Munich. (She always maintained that the correct spelling of the song was "Lili Marleen," as pointed out repeatedly in her autobiography—she died while promoting the book.) Today it attracts locals, including young people, counterculturists, and *Gastarbeiter* (foreign workers). The real fun occurs after 11pm, when the artistic ferment becomes more reminiscent of iconoclastic Berlin than Bavaria. Light meals cost 10 to 20 DM ($5.70 to $11.40). It's open daily 11am to 3am, or even later on weekends.

Café Extrablatt. Leopoldstrasse 7, Schwabing. ☎ **089/333333.** U-Bahn: U3 or U6 to Universität.

Owned by a prominent Munich newspaper columnist, Michael Grater, this cafe epitomizes the nocturnal essence of Schwabing. The sprawling, sometimes smoky room is adorned with photographs of celebrities, a commodious bar extends across one wall, and warm-weather tables spill onto the sidewalk. The cafe attracts many of Munich's writers, artists, and counterculture fans. A simple *Tagesmenu* will fend off starvation for around 15 DM ($8.55), while a large beer costs around 5.50 DM ($3.15). It's open Monday to Thursday from 7am to midnight, Friday and Saturday from 9am to 1am, and Sunday from 9am to midnight.

Cafe Puck. Türkenstrasse 33. ☎ **089/280-2280.** U-Bahn: U3 or U6 to Universität.

This is a convivial, dark-paneled combination of cafe, restaurant, and bar—depending on what time of day or night you happen to drop in. You'll find a hip scene, from locals who come to dine to students who use it as a beer- and wine-drinking hangout. Menu items change daily, and dishes can be German, North American, Mexican, or Chinese. Platters range in price from 15 to 23 DM ($8.55 to $13.10), and full-fledged American breakfasts—which can even include pancakes with maple syrup—are served every day between 9am and 6pm. These are sometimes requested late in the afternoon as a kind of status symbol by those recovering from too many drinks consumed the night before. One particular favorite is a pork steak *teller* that's actually a meal in itself. The atmosphere is convivial and infectious, encouraged by the foam and suds of Spaten and Franziskaner, but if you get bored, you'll find a selection of German and English-language newspapers to read. It's open daily from 9am to 1am.

Cocorico. Schellingstrasse 22. ☎ **089/284372.** U-Bahn: U3 or U6 to Universität.

At first glance, the place might appear like a more-elaborate-than-usual snack bar, where a French-inspired menu lists a selection of crêpes—both salt and sweet—as well as salads, sandwiches, and light platters of food designed to go with wine or beer. Prices range from 5.50 to 17.50 DM ($3.15 to $10). The cafe is a popular meeting place and has an appealing atmosphere of chitchat and banter from table to table. It's open Monday to Friday from noon to midnight and Saturday from noon to 6pm.

Haus der 111 Biere. Franzstrasse 3. ☎ **089/331248.** U-Bahn: Münchener Freiheit.

This unassuming corner bar is the type of small dark place that adds character to any urban neighborhood. Among the beer selections is the strongest brew in the world—EKU Doppelbock Kulminator, a 22-proof treat. It's open Sunday to Thursday from 4pm to 1am and Friday and Saturday from 4pm to 3am.

Havana Club. Herrnstrasse 30. ☎ **089/291884.** S-Bahn: Isartor.

It's a lot less *Cubano* than its name suggests—it's named after a brand of rum. Gloria Estefan once appeared during a sojourn in Munich; most of the rest of the time, however, it functions as a singles bar where rum-based cocktails, ranging in price from 15 to 20 DM ($8.55 to $11.40) each, help lubricate the rolling good times. The only food served is salty, snacklike fare, usually peanuts. It's open Monday to Thursday from 6pm to 1am and Friday and Saturday from 7pm to 2am.

Master's Home. Frauenstrasse 11. ☎ **089/229909.** S-Bahn: Marienplatz or Isator.

One of the historic center's most animated and convivial bars attracts a wide range of clients. The setting is the ground floor of an imposing, 19th-century building close to the Marienplatz, within a large room outfitted with antiques and warm colors in the style of an Edwardian-era club in London; the place suggests a living room in a comfortably battered but upscale private home. There's also a restaurant offering Italian-inspired cuisine, serving fixed-price seven-course meals that cost 68 DM ($38.75). The bar is open nightly from 6:30pm till 3am, with the last order accepted in the kitchen at 1:30am.

Nachtcafé. Maximiliansplatz 5. ☎ **089/595900.** Tram: 19.

It hums, it thrives, and it obviously has captured the nocturnal imagination of the people that count: No other nightspot in Munich attracts so many soccer stars, film celebrities, literary figures, and, as one employee put it, "ordinary people, but only the most sympathetically crazy ones." Waves of patrons appear at different times of the evening—at 11pm when live concerts begin, at 2am when the restaurants close, and at 4am when die-hard revelers seek a final drink in the predawn hours. There are no fewer than four indoor bars (and an additional three on an outdoor terrace in summertime) and lots of tiny tables. The decor is updated 1950s; the music jazz, blues, and soul. Beer costs 7 DM ($4), drinks run 12 DM ($6.85), and meals go for 18 to 40 DM ($10.25 to $22.80). It's open daily from 9pm to 6am.

O'Reilly's Irish Pub. Maximilianstrasse 29. ☎ **089/293311.** U-Bahn or S-Bahn: Marienplatz.

Too constant a diet of Bavarian folklore can tax even the heartiest of beer drinkers, so for a Gaelic alternative head for this pub near the Marienplatz that's awash with Guinness, Irish stew, and—on some evenings—Gaelic music. You'll find it in a historic vaulted cellar close to the Vier Jahreszeiten hotel, where tiled floors and an all-Irish staff help keep the place reverberating until late at night. The best-known brands of beer from England, Ireland, the Czech Republic, and Germany are available. If you're hungry, you can order filet steaks, Irish stew, burgers, and mixed grills. Beer costs from 4 to 7 DM ($2.30 to $4), main courses from 16.50 to 33 DM ($9.40 to $18.80). Hours are Monday to Thursday from 4pm to 1am, Friday and Saturday from 4pm to 3am, and Sunday from noon to 1am.

Pusser's. Falkenturmstrasse 9. ☎ **089/220500.** U-Bahn: Marienplatz.

This themed bar/restaurant is about British navy nostalgia and the grog that helped keep it afloat throughout the 18th and 19th centuries. It's on two levels of a prewar building near the Marienplatz; look for the fishing boat from Tortola (British Virgin Islands) suspended from the ceiling. The most popular drink is a rum-based Painkiller in a special mug that holds a whopping 16 ounces of Caribbean kick. Menu items are international but with a Caribbean flair (black bean soup, grilled fish in Mexican salsa). Main courses range from 18 to 26 DM ($10.25 to $14.80). Everybody's favorite is a half pound of peel-it-yourself shrimp for 30 DM ($17.10). Despite its international outlook, Pusser's is much more of a local hangout than you might expect, with a clientele from around the Altstadt. In the cellar bar a pianist performs every day from 9pm until closing. It's open Monday to Saturday from 5pm to 3am and Sunday from 5pm to 2am.

Schultz. Barerstrasse 47. ☎ **089/271-4711.** U-Bahn: U3 or U6 to Universität.

Schultz is a New York–style bar in Schwabing, popular with theater people who crowd in for smoke-filled chatter. The food is uncomplicated. The decor, as they say here, is "unobvious and understated." Beer starts at 5 DM ($2.85); drinks run from 14 DM ($8) and up. It's open daily from 5pm to 1am.

Schumann's. Maximilianstrasse 36. ☎ **089/229060.** Tram: 19.

Located on Munich's most desirable shopping street, Schumann's is known as a "thinking man's bar." Charles Schumann, author of three bar books, wanted a bar that would be the artistic, literary, and social focus of the metropolis, and his bar is said to have contributed to a remarkable renaissance of bar culture in the city. Schumann's doesn't waste any money on decor: Popular with the film, advertising, and publishing worlds, it doesn't have to—it can depend on its clientele to keep it fashionable. The drinks run 8.50 to 25 DM ($4.85 to $14.25). Beer is 6.50 DM ($3.70). It's open Monday to Friday 5pm to 3am and Sunday 6pm to 3am, but it's closed on Saturday.

Shalom. Leopoldstrasse 130. ☎ **089/366662.** U-Bahn: U3 or U6 to Münchener Freiheit.

You might be reminded here of a 1980s singles bar in a large urban North American city. In a room that can hold 300 persons, there's a surprisingly small bar where bodies are sometimes four and five deep. Most crowded is Thursday to Saturday, when most of the clients are divorced, almost-divorced, or nominally unattached in one way or another. A small dance floor rocks and rolls to Latino merengue, French dance tunes, or North American disco. It's open every night from 9pm to 4am. Beer costs from 8 DM ($4.55).

Shamrock. Trautenwolfstrasse 4. ☎ **089/331081.** U-Bahn: Universität.

Despite differences in language, culture, and the way beer is brewed, the Germans and the Celts seem to get along famously, at least at this rollicking Irish pub near the university. It features the brews of both countries, including Kilkenny and Guinness, which usually sell for between 6.50 DM and 7.50 DM ($3.70 and $4.25) per mug. A modest assortment of food is served (nothing to write home about), such as baguette-style sandwiches and stuffed pita pockets, but most clients come here to drink. Try to schedule your visit between 9pm and midnight, when there's some kind of music (not necessarily Irish). It's open Monday to Thursday from 5pm to 1am, Friday from 5pm to 3am, and Saturday and Sunday from 11am to 3am.

Tomato Sports. Siegesstrasse 19. ☎ **089/348393.** U-Bahn: U3 or U6 to Münchener Freiheit.

Its large-screen TV and emphasis on American-style football might remind you of the sports bars you left behind at home, even though this one speaks with a distinctive Teutonic accent. It has thrived in this site since 1975, partly because it screens U.S. sporting events as well as rugby and soccer. Despite its name, there are almost no references inside to the tomato. Owned and operated by the Paulaner brewery, whose beer is showcased, the place is open Sunday to Thursday from 7:30pm to 1am and from 7:30pm to 3am on Friday and Saturday. Beer costs 6.50 DM ($3.70).

4 Beer Halls

The *Bierhalle* is a traditional Munich institution, offering food, entertainment, and, of course, beer.

Augustinerbrau. Neuhauserstrasse 27. ☎ **089/2318-3257.** U-Bahn or S-Bahn: Karlsplatz. Tram: 19.

On the principal pedestrian-only street of Munich, this beer hall offers generous helpings of food, good beer, and a mellow atmosphere. Dark-wood panels and ceilings in carved plaster make the place look even older than it is. It's been around for less than a century, but beer was first brewed on this spot in 1328, as the literature about the establishment claims. The long menu changes daily, and the cuisine is not for dieters: It's hearty, heavy, and starchy, but that's what customers want. Half a liter of beer begins at 6.50 DM ($3.70); meals cost from 20 to 39 DM ($11.40 to $22.25). It's open Monday to Saturday from 10am to midnight.

✪ **Hofbräuhaus am Platzl.** Am Platzl 9. ☎ **089/221676.** U-Bahn or S-Bahn: Marienplatz.

The Hofbräuhaus is a legend among beer halls. Visitors with only one night in Munich usually target the Hofbräuhaus as their number-one nighttime must-do. The present Hofbräuhaus was built at the end of the 19th century, but the tradition of a beer house on this spot dates from 1589. In the 19th century it attracted artists, students, and civil servants, and it was called the Blue Hall because of its dim lights and smoky atmosphere. When it grew too small to contain everybody, architects designed another, in 1897. This was the 1920 setting for the notorious meeting of Hitler's newly launched German Workers Party, when a brawl erupted between the Nazis and their Bavarian enemies.

The Bavarian Brew

Few cities in the world cling to a beverage the way Munich clings to beer. Münchners—with a little help from their visitors—consume a world's record of the stuff: 280 liters a year, per capita (as opposed to a wimpy 150 liters in other parts of Germany). This kind of heroism usually prompts a cynical comment from the wine drinkers of Berlin and the Rhineland—they say that Bavarians never open their mouths except to pour in more beer. The Münchner response is that to settle questions of politics, art, music, commerce, finance, as well as the affairs of the human heart, requires plenty of beer and lots of good, unfussy food.

Some of Munich's most notable events have floated on the suds of steins of lager. There was Hitler's Beer Hall Putsch (Hofbräuhaus, 1923); a bungled attempt to assassinate Hitler (in the Burgerbräukeller, 1939); and most recently, the Beer Garden Revolution, a 1995 event where a threat to the civil liberties of beer drinkers prompted mass rallies of infuriated Münchners. These, along with dozens of smaller but still very sudsy tempests, have trained Munich's politicians to view the effects of the brew on their constituents with considerable respect.

Statistics regarding Oktoberfest are daunting indeed. Seven million visitors flood into the city in less than 16 days, surging into every beer hall in town and filling the sprawling network of tents set up in the Theresienweise specifically for the event. But while the festival promotes the consumption of millions of liters of beer during the two drink-sodden weeks of its duration, beer drinking continues on year-round. Under the trees of the Biergarten in summer, and in the noisy Bierhalle and cellars, solid citizens in feathered hats, Schicki-Mickies, grandmothers, students, and tourists rub shoulders as they down their hefty liter mugs of beer. Over your stein of beer, it's a tradition to complain about anything and everything—linguists have even coined a word for the local habit of mumbling into a stein of beer—*guanteln*. And why not? It's a therapeutic, relatively inexpensive way to let off steam.

The perfect accompaniment for beer (especially if it happens to be consumed before noon), as everyone knows, is Weisswurst, those little white sausages. And every year the anniversary of their invention, in 1857, is celebrated as something of a national holiday. *Prost!*

Today 4,500 beer drinkers can crowd in here on a given night. Several rooms are spread over three floors, including a top-floor room for dancing. With its brass band (which starts playing at 11am), the ground-floor Schwemme is most typical of what you probably expected—here it's eternal Oktoberfest. In the second-floor restaurant, strolling musicians, including an accordion player and a violinist, entertain. Dirndl-clad servers bring beer to your table between sing-alongs. Every night the Hofbräuhaus am Platzl presents a typical Bavarian show in its Fest-Hall, starting at 8pm and lasting until midnight. The entrance fee is 9 DM ($5.15), and the food is the same as that served in other parts of the beer palace. A liter of beer costs 9.90 DM ($5.65); meals run 10 to 28 DM ($5.70 to $15.95). It's open daily from 9am to midnight.

Türkenhof. Türkenstrasse 78. ☎ **089/280-0235.** U-Bahn: U3 or U6 to Universität.

With its 150-year-old setting, this place looks at first glance like a traditional beer hall. But you'll quickly realize by the animated dialogue and the youthful energy of many of the patrons that it's more than a venue for conventional Bavarian schmaltz. One of the owners is Greek, a fact that accounts for the relatively cosmopolitan food. Within an oversize room where humming conversations reverberate against the walls, you can hoist a stein of five kinds of Augustiner beer, the only brand sold in this brewery-sponsored place. Salads and platters of food are relatively inexpensive, priced from 10.50 to 15.80 DM ($6 to $9).

Waldwirtschaft Grosshesslohe. George-Kalb-Strasse 3. ☎ **089/795088.** Tram: 7.

This popular summertime rendezvous has seats for some 2,000 drinkers. The gardens are open daily from 11am to 11pm (they have to close early because neighborhood residents complain). Music, from Dixieland to English jazz to Polish band music, is played throughout the week. Entrance is free and you bring your own food. It's located above the Isar River in the vicinity of the zoo. A liter of beer costs 10 DM ($5.70).

5 Gay & Lesbian Clubs

Much of Munich's gay and lesbian scene takes place in the blocks between the Viktualienmarkt and Gärtnerplatz, particularly on Hans-Sachs-Strasse. Lesbians may want to check out the bars, **Klemper Kastel,** Mainstrasse 28 (☎ **089/537639**) or **Inges Karotte,** Baaderstrasse 13 (☎ **089/301-0669**) or hit the disco, **Fortuna,** Maximiliansplatz 5 (☎ **089/554070**).

Moritz. Klenzestrasse 43. ☎ **089/201-6776.** No cover. U-Bahn: U2 to Frauenhoferstrasse.

One of Munich's most stylish gay bars, it sprawls over mirror-ringed premises outfitted with red leather armchairs and marble-topped tables. Full meals, including Thai dishes, cost from 50 DM ($28.50) and are served until midnight. Despite a clientele that tends to be 70% gay and male, the place prides itself on a convivial welcome for straight clients. Hours are Sunday to Thursday 7pm to 2am and Friday and Saturday 7pm to 3am.

New York. Sonnenstrasse 25. ☎ **089/591056.** No cover Mon–Thurs, 10 DM ($5.70) Fri–Sun, including first drink. U-Bahn: U1, U2, U3, or U6 to Sendlingertorplatz.

The strident rhythms and electronic sounds might just have been imported from New York, Los Angeles, or Paris. The sound system is accompanied by laser light shows. This is Munich's premier gay (male) disco. Most clients, ranging in age from 20 to 35, wear jeans. It's open daily 11pm to 4am.

Soul City. Maximiliansplatz 5. ☎ **089/595272.** Cover 10 DM ($5.70). U-Bahn: Karlsplatz.

It's the most popular and animated gay disco in Munich. There are enough nooks and crannies for quiet dialogue and a sound system that's among the best in the city. Lesbians make up a respectable proportion of the clients, although gay men comprise the majority. Don't even try to phone this place—whenever staff members are there, they're usually so busy monitoring the crowd that there's barely time to answer the phone. It's open Thursday 10pm to 6am, Friday 10am to 4pm, and Saturday 10pm to 9:30am.

Stadtcafé. St. Jakobsplatz 1. ☎ **089/266949.** No cover. U-Bahn or S-Bahn: Marienplatz.

It considers itself the communications center of gay Munich, an intellectual beacon that attracts creative people. By Munich nightlife standards, it closes relatively early; night owls drift on to other late-night venues. Expect lots of chitchat from table to table, and there's sure to be someone scribbling away at his or her unfinished story (or unfinished novel). It's open Sunday to Thursday 10am to midnight and Friday and Saturday 10am to 2am.

Teddy Bar. Hans-Sachstrasse 1. ☎ **089/260-3359.** No cover. U-Bahn: Sendlingertor. Tram: 18 or 25.

Teddy Bar is a small, cozy, gay bar decorated with teddy bears. It draws a congenial crowd, both foreign and domestic. From October through April, there's Sunday brunch from 11am to 3pm. it's open nightly 6pm to 3am.

Side Trips from Munich

10

Mountains, lakes, spas, and medieval towns lie within an hour of Munich. The landscape is dotted with castles, including the fairy-tale castles of Ludwig II, as well as villas and alpine resorts (see chapter 11).

A short drive from Munich delivers visitors to the heart of Starn-berg's "Five Lakes Region." The **Starnberger See** and **Ammersee** are weekend destinations that afford an enormous assortment of sports: sailing, windsurfing, waterskiing, cycling, golf, hiking, and skiing, to name a few. The **Tegernsee** region is also a popular desti-nation. The spa town of **Bad Tölz** is known for its healing waters and clear mountain air. The environs of Munich are as rich in culture and history as in natural beauty, as is **Dachau,** symbol of Germany's cultural nadir.

1 Starnberger See

17 miles SW of Munich

This large lake southwest of Munich is a favorite with Münchners on holiday. If you take a cruise on the lake, you can observe how the terrain changes from low-lying marshlands on the north to alpine ranges towering above the lake in the south.

ESSENTIALS
GETTING THERE

BY TRAIN   The suburban train (S6) is a 40-minute ride from Marienplatz in the heart of Munich.

BY CAR   From Munich motorists can follow Autobahn 95 toward Garmisch to the Starnberg exit.

VISITOR INFORMATION

For information contact the tourist office (☎ 08151/90600) at Kirchplatz 3, Berg, June through October, Monday to Friday from 8am to 6pm and Saturday from 9am to 1pm; November through May, Monday to Friday from 8am to 6pm.

EXPLORING THE LAKE

Around the 40-mile shoreline you can see no fewer than six castles, including the Schloss Berg, where Ludwig II was sent after he was certified insane in 1886. Across the lake from Berg, the unofficial capital of the lake, stands the castle of Possenhofen, the home of Ludwig's favorite cousin, Sissi. It was in this lake that the king drowned under mysterious circumstances—local legend asserts that he was trying to swim to Possenhofen to ask his cousin's help. Many historians suggest he was murdered. A cross on the water marks the spot where his body was found. A Votivkapelle (memorial chapel) dedicated to Ludwig is on the shore above the cross. It is reached by walking up the hill from the village of Berg, into the Hofgarten and along the wall of the Schloss Berg (no connection with the hotel of the same name recommended below), which lies 3 miles southeast of Starnberg (the Schloss is not open to the public).

CRUISES & OUTDOOR PURSUITS   The main attractions here are sunshine and water sports. Speedboats, paddleboats, and Windsurfers crowd the lake. All of these can be rented from **Surf Tools (☎ 08151/89333).**

Two of the most appealing beaches on the lake include **Possenhofer Strand,** at the lakefront in the village of Possenhofen, and **Perchen Strand** at the village of Perchen. Access to the beaches is free, but parking costs 5 DM ($2.85). Lifeguards are on duty between May and September from 9:30am to 5:30pm.

For information on cruises around the lake, contact the **Staatliche Schiffahrt (☎ 08151/8061)** at Dampfschiffstrasse 5, in Starnberg. Cruises are frequent in the summer months.

WHERE TO STAY & DINE

Dorint Hotel Leoni am Starnberger See. Ortsteil Leoni, Assenbucher Strasse 44. D-82335 Berg. **☎ 08151/5080.** Fax 08151/506140. 73 units. MINIBAR TV TEL. 270–290 DM ($153.90–$165.30) double; 350–395 DM ($199.50–$225.15) suite. AE, DC, MC, V. Parking 15 DM ($8.55).

Comfortable and low-slung, this hotel rises three stories between the edge of the lake and a rolling Bavarian hillside. Built in the early 1970s, it has a cozy country-cousin decor, and the public rooms offer big-windowed views of the lake with its swimmers and sailboats. The bedrooms are outfitted in a dignified 19th-century *Landhaus* style. On the premises are a rustic bar, the Dorfstubl, and two restaurants, the informal Damfersteg and the more formal König Ludwig. A swimming pool has direct access to a swimming pier that juts into the lake. A sauna, solarium, and steam bath round out the facilities. In summer, when the place is most popular, a *Biergarten* serves frothy mugs of beer in a setting a few feet from the edge of the water.

Strandhotel Schloss Berg. Seestrasse 17, D-82335 Berg. **☎ 08151/9630.** Fax 08151/96352. 50 units. MINIBAR TV TEL. 165–250 DM ($94.05–$142.50) double; 250–320 DM ($142.50–$182.40) suite. Rates include breakfast. AE, MC, V. Free parking.

It's within about 500 yards of the town's famous Schloss (privately owned) and is the most luxurious and comfortable hotel in town. It occupies two buildings, one a 1994 remake of an older building, the other an all-new chalet-style structure. They are separated from one another by a parking lot and copses of trees.

Rooms on the upper end of the prices listed above are in the older building, whose windows overlook the lake. Bedrooms are comfortable, conservatively decorated, and eminently appropriate for weekend getaways from Munich. Our favorite hangout here is the bar, an atmospheric prelude to a Bavarian-style restaurant that charges 35 to 65 DM ($19.95 to $37.05) for a full meal.

Side Trips from Munich

2 Tegernsee

30 miles SE of Munich

This alpine lake and the resort town on its eastern shore have the same name. Although small, this is one of the loveliest of the Bavarian lakes, with huge peaks reaching to 6,300 feet, seemingly rising right out of the water.

ESSENTIALS
GETTING THERE

BY TRAIN The station of Tegernsee is a 1-hour-and-20-minute ride from Munich's Hauptbahnhof. To reach the hotels in Rottach-Egern, you must take a taxi from the station.

BY CAR From Munich take the A8/A9 Autobahn toward Salzburg. At exit 97 (Holzkirchen) veer south and follow the signs to Tegernsee.

VISITOR INFORMATION

For information contact the tourist office (☎ **08022/180140**) at Haus de Gastes, Hauptstrasse 2, open April through October, Monday to Friday from 8am to 6pm and Saturday and Sunday from 10am to noon and 3 to 5pm; November through March, Monday to Friday from 8am to noon and 1 to 5pm and Saturday and Sunday from 10am to noon and 3 to 5pm.

EXPLORING THE LAKE

One of the most scenic drives in Bavaria is around the tiny Tegernsee, an easy morning drive. Around the lake is a string of resort towns, including the elegant Rottach-Egern with its ritzy health clinics. Bad Wiessee is a year-round resort with curative springs, used in the treatment of rheumatism and heart and respiratory conditions.

In the town of Tegernsee, the two major sights span some 12 centuries. The oldest of these is the former Benedictine monastery. Built in the 8th century, it was turned into a secular castle and village church in the 19th century by Bavarian king Maximilian I when he bought it for a summer retreat. The other attraction is a contemporary church, a fine example of modern German church architecture, designed by Olaf Gulbransson of Munich.

CRUISES & OUTDOOR PURSUITS   Sailing and windsurfing are the most popular sports here. Both can be arranged (June through September) at **Steck Segel-und-Surf Schule** (no phone) near the town of Gmund, 6 miles north of Rottach-Egern. Windsurfers cost from 35 DM ($25.65) for a half-day rental.

You can take a 1-hour cruise around the lake on one of the ferryboats operated by **Bayerischer Zehnschiffart GambH** (☎ 08022/93311). Boats operate about every 1½ hours from 8am to 8pm, and a circular tour from Tegernsee costs 11 DM ($6.25).

In summer you can walk and hike along the lakeshore. In winter, because of its small size, the lake freezes over, making it an attraction for skaters.

WHERE TO STAY
VERY EXPENSIVE

✪ **Bachmaier Hotel am See.** Seestrasse 47, D-83700 Rottach-Egern. ☎ **08022/2720.** Fax 08022/272790. www.highlights.de/hotels/bachmaier.htm. 266 units. MINIBAR TV TEL. 320–900 DM ($182.40–$513) double; 900–2,000 DM ($513–$1,140) suite. Rates include half board. AE, DC, MC. Free parking.

This posh resort is the most elegant beside the Tegernsee and is set in the heart of town. Today, eight additional buildings supplement the original, generously proportioned *Gartenhaus,* which was constructed in 1827 as a farmhouse. It is almost like a village of minihotels, ringed with terraced gardens. Public rooms include an eclectic blend of Biedermaier, Directoire, and Louis XV styles. Bedrooms are outfitted with lots of varnished pine and country-baroque pieces.

Dining/Diversions: On-site restaurants include two folkloric bistros, a main dining room, and the upscale Gourmet Restaurant. Virtually everyone who has ever checked in here does so on the half-board plan, including former clients Helmut Kohl, Tom Jones, Englebert Humperdinck, and many of Munich's influential movers and shakers.

Amenities: On the premises are all the major resort amenities: a swimming pool, a bathing pier, and a state-of-the-art sports and fitness center in a separate building. There is also a Jacuzzi, a sauna, two tennis courts nearby, a car-rental desk, a beauty salon, boutiques, room service, a concierge, dry cleaning/laundry service, a courtesy minibar, and a solarium.

EXPENSIVE

Bachmaier-Alpina. Valepper Strasse 24, D-83700 Rottach-Egern. ☎ **08022/2041.** Fax 08022/272790. 23 units. MINIBAR TV TEL. 260 DM ($148.20) double; 415 DM ($236.55) suite. AE, DC, MC. Closed late Oct to mid-Dec and Mar–Apr.

This is the inexpensive, two-star sibling of the more glamorous, better located Bachmaier Hotel am See, described above. It's in a pleasant but uninspired modern Swiss chalet style and is inland from the lake, in a quiet residential neighborhood. Bedrooms are simple but comfortable.

Dining: Although the Alpina serves no meals other than breakfast, guests can arrange half board in the main dining room of the Bachmaier for a surprisingly reasonable supplement of 25 DM ($14.25) per person per day.

Amenities: Although there are very few grace notes and extra facilities on-site, guests are welcome to enjoy the sprawling physical plant of the Bachmaier, 2 miles west of the hotel.

Parkhotel Egerner Hof. Aribostrasse 19, D-83700 Rottach-Egern. ☎ **08022/6660.** Fax 08022/666200. 86 units. MINIBAR TV TEL. 310–422 DM ($176.70–$240.55) double; 446–562 DM ($254.20–$320.35) suite. Half board 48 DM ($27.35) supplement per person per day. AE, DC, MC, V. Free parking.

Its detractors suggest that this modern hotel maintains a constant struggle to become a more up-to-date version of the town's five-star aristocrat, the Bachmaier. Despite that, many urbanites from Munich prefer its four-star comfort and alert staff, although there's no lake view—the hotel is surrounded by meadows and trees—and the establishment is a 20-minute walk south of the town center. Bedrooms are traditionally cozy and warm.

Dining/Diversions: There are three charming restaurants. The hotel's main dining room, the Sankt-Florian, accommodates guests on half board. Most nonresidents, however, opt for a meal in the Dichterstube (dinner only), or the Hubertus-Stüberl (lunch and dinner). Both of these latter choices are separately recommended in "Where to Dine," below. The hotel has a cozy bar.

Amenities: Jacuzzi, sauna, beauty salon, concierge, room service, dry cleaning/laundry, baby-sitting, solarium, indoor pool.

MODERATE

Haltmair am See. Seestrasse 33-35. D-83700 Rottach-Egern. ☎ **08022/2750.** Fax 08022/27564. 50 units. TV TEL. 180–200 DM ($102.60–$114) double; 250 DM ($142.50) suite. Rates include breakfast. No credit cards.

Unpretentious, and with a bit less experience in dealing with non-German clients than the other hotels recommended here, this hotel was expanded in the mid-1970s from a 100-year-old architectural core. The decoration is almost obsessively Bavarian, with lots of alpine accessories and dark wood paneling in the bedrooms. Suites are equipped with kitchenettes. It's near the center of the town, across the street from the edge of the lake. Other than a worthy buffet breakfast, no meals are served.

INEXPENSIVE

Gastehaus Maier-Kirschner. Seestrasse 23, D-83700 Rottach-Egern. ☎ **08022/67110.** Fax 08022/671137. 45 units. TV TEL. 165–180 DM ($94.05–$102.60) double; 240 DM ($136.80) suite. Rates include breakfast. No credit cards.

This is one of the best bets in town for comfortable, reasonably priced accommodations with a personal touch. The site has an ancient history, going back to 1350, when a farmhouse is recorded to have been here; however, such antique vestiges you may notice date from 1870 when the site was a local farmer's homestead. There's an amply proportioned central hallway and paneled public rooms that invite guests to linger over newspapers and coffee. Bedrooms contain simplified reproductions of antique baroque furniture and have comfortable armchairs. No meals, other than breakfast and midafternoon coffee and snacks, are served. Only the Seestrasse separates this hotel from the edge of the lake.

Gasthof zur Post. Nördliche Hauptstrasse 17–19, D-83700 Rottach-Egern. ☎ **08022/ 66780.** Fax 08022/667-8162. 17 units. TV TEL. 155–172 DM ($88.35–$98.05) double. MC, V.

The oldest hotel in town was built in the 1860s with an elaborately ornamented four-story facade accented with balconies. The interior is beautifully crafted, with wooden ceilings and furniture whose natural grain glows with a patina acquired over years of polishing. Guest rooms are equivalent to what you'd find in a woodsy chalet hotel in Switzerland—they are clean and comfortable and without unnecessary frills. On the premises are three dining rooms (Post Stübl, Postillion, and Nebenzimmer), all of which serve Bavarian and German food; main courses cost from 18 to 22 DM ($10.25 to $12.55). Dining hours are daily from 11:30am to 2pm and 5:30 to 9pm.

WHERE TO DINE

Dichterstube/Hubertus-Stüberl. In the Parkhotel Egerner Hof, Aribostrasse 19. ☎ **08022/ 6660.** Reservations recommended. In the Dichterstube, main courses 42–52 DM ($23.95–$29.65); fixed-price dinner 136 DM ($77.50). In the Hubertus-Stüberl, main courses 29–38 DM ($16.55–$21.65). AE, DC, MC, V. Daily noon–2pm (Hubertus-Stüberl only) and 6–10pm (both restaurants). CONTINENTAL (in Dichterstube)/BAVARIAN (in Hubertus-Stüberl).

Reaching these two restaurants requires a 20-minute pedestrian trek or a very brief drive south of the town center; however, it's worth the effort, considering the quality of the food. The less expensive of the two, Hubertus-Stüberl, is outfitted like the interior of a hunting lodge, with all the requisite references to "the Hunt." Here, menu items include cream of garlic soup with croutons, goulash soup, carpaccio of bonito with a paprika-flavored vinaigrette, smoked fillet of trout with horseradish sauce, and such main courses as ragout of venison with chive-flavored polenta, and veal schnitzel "in the style of the Tegernsee" with roasted potatoes.

Meals are more formal, more ambitious, and more expensive in the Dichterstube, site of the best cuisine in town. The seven-course, set-price menu is a veritable banquet that requires serious gastronomic attention. Ordering à la carte might be wise for persons with less hearty appetites. Depending on the season, menu items might include a galette of wild rice with tartare of salmon and caviar, braised zander with a ragout of crabs, glazed John Dory with chicory sauce, lobster salad with avocados and orange-pepper marmalade, and such desserts as a stuffed chocolate cake with champagne-flavored mousse and lemon-flavored sorbet.

3 Ammersee

24 miles W of Munich

Smaller and less popular than Starnberger See, Ammersee is a bit more rustic and wild than its cousin. In the past, Ammersee was thought too far from the city for excursions. For that reason, it was never overdeveloped and retains much of its natural splendor. Although it does have its share of summer homes and hotels, its shores are not quite so saturated or overcrowded.

ESSENTIALS

GETTING THERE

BY TRAIN   The suburban train (S-bahn 5) is a 40-minute ride from Marienplatz in the heart of Munich to Herrsching.

BY CAR   Take the A96 Autobahn west toward Lindau. Get off at the Herrsching/ Wessling exit (Highway 2068) and follow signs to Herrsching.

AROUND THE LAKE

The village of **Herrsching** with a population of 10,000 is home to an enormous villa with fabulous turrets, facades, and pagoda roofing, the **Kurpark Schlösschen** (☎ 08152/4250). It was constructed in the late 19th century as a summer getaway for the artist Ludwig Scheuermann. It is now home to the municipal cultural center and the venue for occasional summer evening concerts.

The small fishing village of **Diessen,** popular for its pottery and its church, the Marienmünster, is a short ferry ride from Herrsching. Ferries depart about nine times a day from the Seepromenade; the ride takes 20 minutes, and the fare to Diessen is 4.25 DM ($2.40) each way. Call ☎ 08143/94021 for information.

Also a short journey from Herrsching, and well worth the time, is the ancient monastery of **Andechs.** Set high on a mountain, the Heiliger Berg, this Benedictine monastery draws multitudes of pilgrims and beer aficionados. The pilgrims visit to venerate the religious relics from the Holy Land; the less devout make the journey for the stupendous beers and cheeses produced by the monks. The monastery is open daily from 7am to 7pm. Buses depart from the front of Herrshing's railway station every hour year-round. Contact Omnibusverhehr Rauner (☎ 08152/3457) for information. You can also hike the 3 uphill miles to the monastery—head east along the trails that are clearly marked from the center of town.

CRUISES & OUTDOOR PURSUITS   For a magnificent tour of the lake, take one of the steamship cruises. Boats depart hourly from 9am to 6pm. For information on various trips, contact Staatliche Schiffahrt (☎ 081/94021) at Landsberger Strasse 81 in Ammersee. You can also circumnavigate the lake by taking one of the ferryboats (see above) that departs seven times a day, making stops at seven lakefront towns. For 23 DM ($13.10) you can get on and off, boarding the next boat to continue the tour.

You can rent a Windsurfer, paddleboat, or rowboat at **Stummbaum** (☎ 08152/1375) at Summerstrasse 22, in Herrsching.

WHERE TO STAY

Ammersee-Hotel. Summerstrasse 32, D-82211 Herrsching. ☎ **08152/2011.** Fax 08152/53-74. 40 units. MINIBAR TV TEL. 195–235 DM ($111.15–$133.95) double. Rates include breakfast. Free parking.

This well-maintained and unpretentious three-star hotel sits behind a turn-of-the-century facade in the heart of town. Open all year long, it caters to business travelers in wintertime and to holidaymakers in summer. It has three floors of conservatively modern guest rooms, all renovated and upgraded in the late 1990s. Most have views over the lake. On the premises is a simple, Weinstube-style restaurant, plus a bar.

Hotel Promenade. Summerstrasse 6, D-82211 Herrsching. ☎ **08152/1088.** Fax 08152/5981. 11 units. MINIBAR TV TEL. 188–217 DM ($107.15–$123.70) double. Rates include breakfast. DC, MC, V. Closed Dec 20–Jan 20.

This is a small, businesslike hotel, with a staff that speaks almost no English, occupying a site directly in the center of the town. Built in 1988, and with fewer than a dozen guest rooms, it has a blandly modern decor, a bar, and a restaurant that serves Croatian and international food. Its position directly beside the lake permits sweeping views from the balconies of some rooms, and there's a lakeside terrace in case your room happens to face the wrong direction.

WHERE TO DINE

Andechser Hof. Zum Landungssteg 1. D-82211 Herrsching. ☎ **08152/8579.** Main courses 16–35 DM ($9.10–$19.95). AE, DC, MC, V. Daily 11am–10pm. BAVARIAN.

This popular dining spot is the kind of place that offers beer and snacks throughout the afternoon and substantial platters of Bavarian food at dinner. The setting is a solid 1905 building with a decor full of references to the Bavarian experience and style. A Biergarten adjacent to the hotel offers such specialties as ragout of beef or pork schnitzel with fresh vegetables of the day.

Don't overlook the possibility of an overnight stopover here. There's a total of 21 clean units, full of nostalgic charm, all with private baths, phones, and TVs, renting for 160 DM ($91.20) for a double.

4 Dachau

10 miles NW of Munich

In 1933 what had once been a quiet little artists' community outside Munich became a tragic symbol of the Nazi era. In March, shortly after Hitler became chancellor, Himmler and the SS set up the first German concentration camp on the grounds of a former ammunition factory. Countless prisoners arrived at Dachau between 1933 and 1945. Although the files show a registry of more than 206,000, the exact number of people imprisoned here is unknown.

ESSENTIALS

GETTING THERE

BY TRAIN The suburban train (S-2) is a 20-minute ride from Marienplatz in the heart of Munich. From the station, take bus no. 724 or 726 to the camp.

BY CAR The best road for motorists is a country road, B12. Motorists can also take the Stuttgart Autobahn, exiting at the signposted Dachau turnoff.

TOURING THE CAMP

Entering the camp, you are faced by three memorial chapels—Catholic, Protestant, and Jewish—built in the early 1960s. Immediately behind the Catholic chapel is the Lagerstrasse, the main camp road lined with poplar trees, once flanked by 32 barracks, each housing 208 prisoners. Two barracks have been rebuilt to give visitors insight into the horrible conditions endured by the prisoners.

The museum is housed in the large building that once contained the kitchen, laundry, and shower baths, where the SS often brought prisoners for torture. Photographs and documents show the rise of the Nazi regime and the superpower of the SS; there are also exhibits depicting the persecution of Jews and other prisoners. Every effort has been made to present the facts. The tour of Dachau is a truly moving experience. Admission is free, and the camp is open Tuesday to Sunday from 9am to 5pm. The English version of a documentary film, *KZ-Dachau,* is shown at 11:30am and 3:30pm. All documents are translated in the catalog, available at the museum entrance. Visitors are requested to wear appropriate attire (walking shorts and a T-shirt are acceptable).

5 Freising

20 miles N of Munich

Freising, one of Bavaria's oldest towns, grew up around a bishopric founded in the 8th century. By the 12th century, under Bishop Otto von Freising, the See had begun a spiritual and cultural boom. Freising was the scene of a bitter rivalry with Munich that had repercussions lasting from the 12th until the beginning of the 19th century. Bishop Otto owned a profitable toll bridge over the Isar until 1156 when Henry the Lion destroyed it and built his own bridge, wresting control of the lucrative salt route from the bishop and founding his settlement, München. As a result of the quarrel, up until 1803 Munich was forced to pay compensation to Freising for Henry's action.

ESSENTIALS
GETTING THERE
BY TRAIN   Take line 1 of the S-Bahn to Freising, a 25-minute ride.

BY CAR   Freising is northeast of Munich on the Bll.

VISITOR INFORMATION
The tourist information office is at Marienplatz 7 (☎ 08161/54122).

SEEING THE SIGHTS
All the main sights are within walking distance of the Bahnhof. The Altstadt contains a number of restored canons' houses with fine baroque facades along the Hauptstrasse and in the Marienplatz-Rindermarkt area. The Gothic **St. George's Parish Church** with its lovely baroque tower was built by the same architect who designed Munich's Frauenkirche. Opposite, in the former Lyzeum of the prince-bishops, is the **Asamsaal,** a room decorated by the father of the famous Asam brothers, with a fine stucco and fresco ceiling. Tours are offered occasionally; check the tourist office for information.

Southwest of the Altstadt on a gentle hill is the **Staatsbrauerei Weihenstephan,** the world's oldest brewery. The monks of the Benedictine monastery of Weihenstephan were granted the privilege of brewing and serving their own beer in 1040, a tradition that still continues. Guided tours, including beer tasting, are conducted on the hour from 9am to 2pm, except at noon, from Monday to Thursday, costing 3 DM ($1.70).

Located on the Domberg, a low hill above the Altstadt, **Mariendom** is a twin-towered Romanesque basilica, constructed between 1160 and 1205. The building is rather plain on the outside, but the interior was lavishly ornamented in the baroque style by the Asam brothers in 1723 to 1724. Egid Quirin Asam designed the interior, and Cosmas Damian Asam created the ceiling fresco of the *Second Coming,* with its floating figures and swirling clouds. A notable early medieval sculpture is the famous *Bestiensäule* (Beast Column), an entwined mass of men and monsters. The church's principal feature is the large Romanesque crypt, one of the oldest in Germany, which has survived in its original form.

The 15th-century **cloister** on the east side of the cathedral was decorated with frescoes and stuccowork by Johann Baptist Zimmerman. To the west of the church is the **Dombibliothek,** a library that dates from the 8th century. In the 18th century the library acquired a lively ceiling fresco designed by François Cuvilliés.

The **Diözesanmuseum** is the largest diocesan museum in Germany and contains a comprehensive collection of religious art, including the famous *Lukasbild,* an exceptional Byzantine icon. The museum's exhibits document the history of the Catholic Church over nine centuries. It's open Tuesday to Sunday from 10am to 5pm; there is an admission charge.

WHERE TO DINE
Gasthaus Landbrecht. Freisinger Strasse 1, Freising-Handlfinig. ☎ **08157/8926.** Reservations recommended. Main courses 18–32 DM ($10.15–$18.15). No credit cards. Sat–Sun

12:30–3pm, Wed–Sun 6–10:30pm. 3 miles NW of the town center; follow signs to Freising-Handlfinig. BAVARIAN.

Small scale and family run, this is an 1860s inn where food is prepared in the old-fashioned Bavarian style. In a country-rustic dining room you can begin with the "filet of beef" soup, one of the richest we've ever tasted, or a delicate cream of celery soup with fresh herbs. Main courses include roast suckling pig, roast rack of venison with red-wine sauce, a main dish of mushrooms, and fresh pike-perch in butter and parsley sauce.

6 Bad Tölz

31 miles S of Munich

The historic spa town of Bad Tölz offers something for all travelers. Situated where the rolling foothills become the mountains of the Alps, the town flanks both sides of the Isar River, which divides it into two distinct sectors. On the eastern side of the river stands the historic medieval town, complete with chapels, turrets, and walls. Older than Munich, this section offers fine examples of medieval and baroque art and architecture. The major attraction is **Stadtpfarrkirche,** a church built in 1466. It's an exquisite example of German late-Gothic architecture.

On the western bank of the Isar lies the *Kurverwaltung* or modern spa, whose waters are known for their soothing and healing powers. Treatments revolve around the iodine-rich springs and may also include climatic and terrain therapy, which are basically about exercise and constitutional walks in fresh air free from industrial pollutants.

ESSENTIALS
GETTING THERE
BY TRAIN   The train ride takes an hour from Munich's Hauptbahnhof.

BY CAR   From Munich, motorists can take the Autobahn A8 or A9 toward Salzburg. Exit at Holzkirchen and follow signs southward toward Bad Tölz.

VISITOR INFORMATION
For information, contact the **Kurverwaltung** (☎ 08041/70071), at Ludwigstrasse 11 in Bad Tölz, Monday to Friday from 9am to noon and 2 to 5:30pm and Saturday from 9am to noon and 4 to 6:30pm. Between June and August, it's also open every Sunday from 10am to noon.

SPORTS & OUTDOOR PURSUITS
Anyone interested in sports will never be bored in Bad Tölz. Golfers have access to two nine-hole courses. **Golf Club Isarwinkel** (☎ 08041/77878), on the town's northern tier was built for U.S. military officers when there was a local military base. On the western tier, **Golfplatz am Buchberg,** Strasse 124 (☎ 08041/9994) is a challenging but less prestigious course. Both charge greens fees of 60 DM ($34.20) and are open April through October, daily from 9am to 6pm. Advance reservations are a good idea.

Tennis players can play at **Tennisanlage am Isarstaussee,** Königsdorferstrasse (☎ 08041/74453) on the western bank of the Isar. Court time costs 14 DM ($8) per hour.

Alpamare, Ludwigstrasse 14 (☎ 08041/509331) is one of the most up-to-date swimming pools in the region, complete with water slides, waterfalls, kiddie pools, and saunas. Admission is 30 DM ($17.10), and it's open Monday to Friday from 9am to 9pm and Saturday and Sunday from 9am to 10pm. You can also swim in the Isar, but at your own risk. There are no official sites for swimming, and the river is both cold and swift moving.

For hiking or mountain biking, dozens of clearly marked trails converge at nearby points. For mountain bike rentals, contact **Fun-und-Trendsport Pirk,** Ludwigstrasse 30 (☎ **08041/730607**). Rentals cost 10 to 18 DM ($5.70 to $10.25) per day, depending on make and model.

The clear, swift waters of the Isar are perfect for white-water canoeing, kayaking, or rafting. Contact **Kajakschule Oberland,** Ganghoferstrasse 7, D-83661 Lenggries/ Fall (☎ **08045/275**), run by Gunther Carmelli, one of Bavaria's most experienced white-water guides, and his family. A 4-hour excursion in a rubber-sided raft costs 55 DM ($31.35). Lessons in kayaking and canoeing cost 250 DM ($142.50) per day per person, with discounts for the second and third participant in a party.

The nearest skiing slopes are on the Brauneck mountain. For information, contact **Ski-Centrum,** Berg Brauneck (☎ **08042/8910**), in the nearby hamlet of Lenggries, a 20-minute drive east of Bad Tölz. A day pass on any of the 30 lifts is 39 DM ($22.25).

WHERE TO STAY
MODERATE

Kurhotel Eberl. Buchenerstrasse 17. D-83646 Bad Tölz. ☎ **08041/78750.** Fax 08041/787278. 34 units. TV TEL. 245–265 DM ($139.65–$151.05) double; 285–305 DM ($162.45–$173.85) suite. Rates include half board. No credit cards. Closed Nov 20–Dec 15.

Set in a meadow about a quarter-mile west of the resort's center, this is a white-fronted, timber-studded replica of the kind of modern chalet you're likely to see a lot in Switzerland. Public rooms are lavishly finished with rough-textured beams and timbers for a look that—at least from the inside—might make you think that the hotel is older than it is. Guest rooms are conservatively and comfortably outfitted with pale colors and exposed wood, and many have balconies. This is the kind of hotel where guests (mostly German) expect to eat all their evening meals on-site. Only residents are allowed in the *Stübe*-like dining room and the lounges—the hotel is otherwise closed to the public. Although the town's public spa facilities are nearby, the hotel has its own indoor swimming pool, saunas, and array of spa facilities such as massages and mud packs—these can be bought as part of an all-inclusive health-and-rest regime package.

INEXPENSIVE

Alexandra. Kyreinstrasse 33, D-83646 Bad Tölz. ☎ **08041/78430.** Fax 08041/784399. 23 units. TV TEL. 138–180 DM ($78.65–$102.60) double. Rates include breakfast. MC.

This modern hotel has a facade of traditional dark-stained wood, lavishly accented with flower boxes. It was named after the then-infant daughter of the owner. It's near the town center, on the opposite side of the riverfront promenade from the banks of the Isar. Decor is all Bavarian, with fine interior woodwork. Rooms are unpretentious and outfitted—as you might guess—with reproductions of Bavarian furniture. Other than breakfast, no meals are served. Overall, it's a worthwhile and reasonably priced hotel choice.

Haus an der Sonne. Ludwigstrasse 12, D-83646 Bad Tölz. ☎ **08041/6121.** Fax 08041/2609. 23 units. TEL. 120–157 DM ($68.40–$89.50) double. Rates include breakfast. AE, DC, MC, V.

This is a cozy, unpretentious hotel whose country-baroque, ocher-colored facade is a 10-year-old copy of 18th-century models. In summer, cafe tables are set up on the pavement outside. The members of the Wosar family provide a well-managed retreat in a warmly paneled setting. Guest rooms contain modern pinewood furniture, some pieces accented with painted panels that evoke old Bavaria. A sauna is on the premises.

Jodquellenhof-Alpamare. Ludwigstrasse 13-15, D-83646 Bad Tölz. ☎ **08041/5090.** Fax 08041/509441. 81 units. TV TEL. 195–240 DM ($111.15–$136.80) double. Half board 50 DM ($28.50) extra per person per day. AE, DC, MC, V.

This is Bad Tölz's equivalent of a "grand hotel," with a longer history than any other hotel in town. Originally built in 1860, and modernized inside and out many times since then, it helped launch Bad Tölz into the full-fledged resort you see today. If you opt to stay here, however, don't expect 19th-century authenticity: From the outside the green-and-white premises still look vaguely Mediterranean, but the hotel has, both commercially and architecturally, kept up with the times. Unlike some spa hotels that appeal to older, more staid clients, Jodquellenhof attracts a family clientele on annual holiday. That's not surprising, for the hotel shares a verdant park with Alpamare, a water amusement area with a Disneyesque collection of water slides, Jacuzzis, and three indoor and two outdoor swimming pools. Parents and children can pad over to Alpamare in swimsuits and bathrobes in any weather, directly from their rooms. Entrance to Alpamare, open daily to residents of this hotel between 7am and 9pm, is free for guests but costs 50 DM ($28.50) per person for nonresidents. Also on the premises is an array of spa facilities, including soaking tubs filled with thermally heated water and all the mud packs, massage, and health or beauty treatments you'd expect. There's a pleasant hotel bar and a dining room where business mostly derives from feeding hotel guests on meal plans. Bedrooms at this place, incidentally, are outfitted in a neutral, rather bland style and all have balconies.

Kolbergarten. Fröhlichgasse 5. D-83646 Bad Tölz. ☎ **08041/9067.** Fax 08041/9069. 15 units. TV TEL. 150–160 DM ($85.50–$91.20) double. AE, DC, MC, V.

The finest and most lavish hotel in Bad Tölz, it's set in a historic zone on the east bank of the Isar that's sometimes used for outdoor concerts and parades. It was built in 1905 by the famous *Jugendstil* architect Gabriel von Seidel, who added many more folkloric touches, including lavishly ornate eaves, than are usual in his work. The interior has a turn-of-the-century dignity, always with a noteworthy emphasis on humanity, warmth, and charm. Guest rooms are as authentic and antique-laden as anything you'll find in the area.

The hotel's restaurant, Kolbergarten, is an upscale oasis of well-prepared cuisine dedicated to the traditions of South Tyrol, a German-speaking alpine region annexed by Italy from Austria after World War I. Lunch and dinner are served every day except Tuesday. Main courses cost from 16 to 34 DM ($9.10 to $19.40); set-price menus cost from 40 to 50 DM ($22.80 to $28.50).

Because of its limited number of bedrooms (although you'll probably appreciate the sense of intimacy this provides), management funnels the overflow to the larger and slightly less expensive sibling hotel, the Posthotel Kolberbräu, which is separately recommended below.

Posthotel Kolberbräu. Marktstrasse 29, D-83646 Bad Tölz. ☎ **08041/76880.** Fax 08041/768-8200. 45 units. TV TEL. 120–140 DM ($68.40–$79.80) double. Rates include breakfast. Half board 23 DM ($13.10) supplement per person per day. AE, DC, MC, V.

This hotel belongs to the same owner as the Kolbergarten (see above) but is in a less congested setting. Because it's in the center of town, it makes no attempt to surround itself with landscaping. What you'll find is a cozy, old-fashioned hotel with an identity firmly anchored in the commercial life of Bad Tölz. It has an imposing neoclassical facade whose foundations date from the 1600s. Its popular bistro is separately recommended below. Guest rooms are more prosaic than those at the more aristocratic Kolbergarten and have the kind of cozy, old-fashioned Teutonic decor that nobody dislikes, but nobody thrills to either. Ten of the rooms have private balconies.

Tölzer Hof. Rieschstrasse 21, D-83646 Bad Tölz. ☎ **08041/8060.** Fax 08041/806333. www.toelz.de-toelzer/hof. 82 units. MINIBAR TV TEL. 200–240 DM ($114–$136.80) double; 220–250 DM ($125.40–$142.50) suite. Half board 28 DM ($15.95) extra per person per day. AE, DC, MC, V.

This hotel is a worthy middle-bracket choice with almost no emphasis on old-timey nostalgia—a plain modern design of white stucco, blackened timber balconies, and terra-cotta roof tiles. Rooms are outfitted in a style that looks like a slightly more luxurious version of a bachelor's pad, complete with the kind of low-slung couches and coffee tables you don't feel guilty about putting your feet on. You'll be happiest here if you understand in advance that this is an honest, unassuming place, with an efficiency so pronounced that it almost verges on the spartan. The hotel's most unusual feature is a glass-sided greenhouse in the parking lot near the entrance, site of the reception desk and a cafe. There's a sauna on the premises and a swimming pool within walking distance.

WHERE TO DINE
MODERATE

✪ **Altes Fahrhaus.** An der Isarlust 1, D-83646 Bad Tölz. ☎ **08041/6030.** Reservations recommended. Main courses 38.50–47 DM ($21.95–$26.80); fixed-price dinner 88–138 DM ($50.15–$78.65). No credit cards. Wed–Sun 11:30am–2:30pm and 6pm–midnight. Closed 1 week in Nov and 1 week in Feb (dates vary). CONTINENTAL.

This is a *restaurant avec chambres* where the overnight accommodations, although comfortable, are less significant than the restaurant. Two miles south of the resort's center, adjacent to the right bank of the Isar River, it's in a 2-acre compound the centerpiece of which is a Bavarian-style, turn-of-the-century building adapted for use by the present owners around 1980.

The owner is Ely Reiser, who closely supervises (or prepares herself) everything coming out of her kitchens. The food is the best in the region, and Munich-based gastronomes often come here just to have a meal. Menu items change with the seasons but might include a salad of green asparagus with strips of braised goose liver, bouillon of venison with ravioli or a fillet of venison baked in herbs with a pepper-flavored cream sauce, fillet of turbot in champagne sauce, or fillet of veal with red wine sauce, noodles, and exotic mushrooms. Because the menu changes almost every day, even the owner is reluctant to name a particular house specialty, although one superb dish that's usually available is a well-seasoned rack of lamb served with eggplant, gratin of potatoes, and zucchini in a mustard sauce. Dessert might be a Grand Marnier soufflé with rhubarb.

On the premises are five bedrooms, each with its own terrace overlooking the river, TV, telephone, and minibar. With breakfast included, doubles cost 180 DM ($102.60).

INEXPENSIVE

Restaurant Posthotel Kolberbräu. Marktstrasse 29. ☎ **08041/76880.** Main courses 12–30 DM ($6.85–$17.10); fixed-price menus 29–52 DM ($16.55–$29.65). AE, DC, MC, V. Daily 11am–2pm and 5–9pm. GERMAN/BAVARIAN.

This is the kind of no-nonsense, high-volume restaurant that virtually everyone in town has visited at least once in his or her lifetime. A labyrinth of small dining areas, it's a civic rendezvous point where lots of deals have been made over steins of beer and hearty Germanic food. The place is always crowded during the lunch and dinner hours noted above, but throughout the afternoon it remains open for coffee, pastries, beer, wine, and an abbreviated roster of warm food and platters.

A SIDE TRIP TO BENEDIKTBEUREN

This 8th-century monastery is the oldest Benedictine site north of the Alps. It was a flourishing cultural center in the Middle Ages. The frescoes in the monastery's baroque church were painted by the father of the famous Asam brothers. It was here, in this ecclesiastical enclave, that the l2th-century secular musical work, the *Carmina Burana* (the Goliardic songs) first appeared, later to become a popular 20th-century work in a setting by Bavarian composer Carl Orff. Concerts of the work are regularly performed in the monastery courtyard.

Benediktbeuren is 9 miles southeast of Bad Tölz. Admission is 5 DM ($2.85). The church is open daily 8am to 6pm. Guided tours of the monastery are offered July through September, daily at 2:30pm; October through mid-May, Saturday and Sunday only at 2:30pm; mid-May through June, Saturday and Wednesday at 2:30pm and Sunday at 10:30am and 2:30pm. For information about the monastery and concerts, call ☎ **08857/248.**

The Bavarian Alps   11

If you walk into a rustic alpine inn along the German-Austrian frontier and ask the innkeeper if he or she is German, you'll most likely get the indignant response, "Of course not! I'm Bavarian." And the innkeeper is undoubtedly right, because even though Bavaria is a *Land* of Germany, some older inhabitants can still remember when Bavaria was a kingdom, although it was by then part of the German Reich (1871–1918).

The huge province of Bavaria includes not only the Alps but also Franconia, Lake Constance, and the capital city of Munich. However, we'll take this opportunity to explore separately the mountains along the Austrian frontier, a world unto itself. The Alps are a winter wonderland and a summer playground. Skiing is the best in Germany, centered around the chief resort, Garmisch-Partenkirchen. Within easy reach is the Zugspitze, Germany's tallest mountain peak at 9,720 feet above sea level. Many visitors come to the Alps in summer just to hike through the Berchtesgaden National Park, bordering the Austrian province of Salzburg. The area's hospitality is famous, and the picture of the plump, rosy-cheeked innkeeper who has a constant smile on his or her face is no myth.

Munich is the gateway to the region for those arriving by plane. From Munich, Autobahns lead directly to the Bavarian Alps. If you're beginning your tour in Garmisch-Partenkirchen in the west, you should fly to Munich. However, if you'd like to begin your tour in the east, at Berchtesgaden, then Salzburg in Austria has better plane connections.

OUTDOORS IN THE BAVARIAN ALPS

The Bavarian Alps are both a winter wonderland and a summer playground. Skiing, both alpine and cross-country, is the best in Germany. It's centered around the chief resort, Garmisch-Partenkirchen, famed as the site of the fourth Winter Olympics in 1936 and the World Alpine Ski Championships in 1978. A normal snowfall in January and February measures from 12 to 20 inches. This leaves about 6 feet of snow in the areas served by ski lifts. On the ski slopes of the Zugspitze, Germany's highest mountain peak, you can ski all summer.

The second great ski district is Berchtesgadener Land. Alpine skiing is centered on Jenner, Rossfeld, Götschen, and Hochschwarzeck, with consistently good snow conditions until March. There is a cross-country skiing center and many miles of tracks kept in first-class condition, natural toboggan runs, one artificial ice run for toboggan and skibob-runs, and ice-skating and ice-curling rinks.

In summer one of the best areas for climbing, hiking, and enjoying nature is 4,060-foot Eckbauer, on the southern fringe of Partenkirchen (see section 5, "Garmisch-Partenkirchen," below). Many visitors come to the Alps in summer just to hike through the Berchtesgaden National Park, which has well-mapped trails cut through protected areas, leading the hiker among spectacular flora and fauna (see section 2, "National Park Berchtesgaden," below). Hiking trails of all levels of difficulty exist, from gentle strolls around blue-green alpine lakes to overnight hikes through rugged terrain and across naked glaciers.

Mountain biking is available through the rental facilities of **Full Stall** in Berchtesgaden (☎ 08652/948450). Many rivers are suitable for **kayaking** or **white-water rafting** (water level permitting), such as the Ramsauer, Königisser, Bischofswiesener, and the Berchtesgadener Aches. Contact the **Outdoor-Club Berchtesgaden** (☎ 08652/5001). They also arrange other sports and activities. Both of these outfitters will provide directions and link-ups with their sports programs wherever you decide to stay in the area (see section 3, "Berchtesgaden," below).

Fishing, notably for salmon, pike-perch, and trout, is especially good on the Hintersee and the rivers Ramsauer Ache and Königsseer Ache. To acquire a fishing permit, contact the Kurdirektion at Berchtesgaden, which will direct you to any of four different authorities, based on where you want to fish. For fishing the Hintersee, contact officials at the Hotel Gamsboch in Ramsau (☎ 08657/98800).

Most of the resorts have ice-skating rinks (Berchtesgaden's Eisstadion is world-class), but for a real experience evocative of Bavaria's wild open spaces, try the Hintersee, once it's sufficiently frozen, or one of the other many smaller lakes. Once in a while, it's even possible to skate on the frozen Königssee.

Swimming in the frigid waters of Alpine lakes may not be to everyone's taste, but there are plenty of *lidos*, and lots of heated swimming pools in the resorts.

Maps of the alpine area are usually available free at the local tourist offices as are detailed topographical maps for a fee. Go to the **Kurdirektion** at Berchtesgaden (☎ 08652/9670) or the **Verkehrsamt** at Garmisch-Partenkirchen (☎ 08821/1806).

1 Exploring the Region by Car

One of Europe's most scenic drives is the **Deutsche Alpenstrasse (German Alpine Road),** which stretches for some 300 miles between Berchtesgaden in the east, all the way to Lindau on Lake Constance in the west. The road goes through mountains, lakes, "black" forests, and "castles in the sky." Where commercial reality hasn't intruded, it's a true fantasy. In winter, driving can be perilous, and mountain passes are often shut down. We always prefer to take the drive in early spring or early autumn.

DAY 1   From Munich, head south along Autobahn A8 (and drive in the right lane if you want to avoid the hysterical speeders on the left). Turn south on Route B20 for **Berchtesgaden,** 98 miles southeast of Munich. After settling in and having lunch, take an afternoon excursion to Obersalzberg and Kehlstein (you can go by bus). The Kehlstein road was blasted from bedrock, and a lift ascends to the summit, once Hitler's famed Eagle's Nest. The panorama is quite spectacular.

The Bavarian Alps

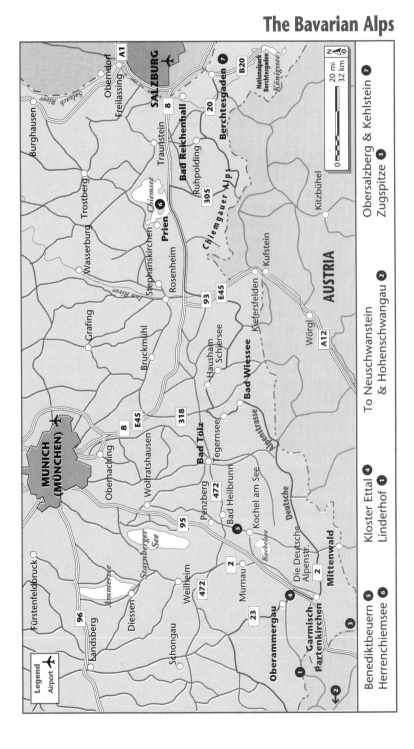

Benediktbeuern ❺
Herrenchiemsee ❻

Kloster Ettal ❹
Linderhof ❶

To Neuschwanstein
& Hohenschwangau ❷

Obersalzberg & Kehlstein ❼
Zugspitze ❸

Legend
✈ Airport

0   20 mi
0   32 km

DAY 2 While still based in Berchtesgaden, take the 2-hour boat ride on the **Königssee**, 3 miles to the south. This long, narrow lake, famed for its steep banks and dark waters, is one of Europe's most dramatic and romantic sights. In the afternoon, drive west along the alpine road and then north on Route B20 some 12 miles to **Bad Reichenhall.** This is one of Germany's most famous spas on the Saalach River. The town was built around its Kurpark (spa center), and it's filled with luxury and moderately priced hotels.

Right outside town in a tasteful baroque style, **Kirchberg-Schlössl** on Thumseestrasse (☎ **08651/2760**), is the best spot to dine in the area. Try its pike in beer sauce served with the inevitable sauerkraut, or filet of zander. A three-course lunch is 38 DM ($21.65), offered from 11am to 3pm. A four-course dinner is served from 6pm to midnight for 79 DM ($45.05). Main courses begin at 28 DM ($15.95). Return to Berchtesgaden for the night.

DAY 3 Get back on Autobahn A8 toward Munich but turn off at Prien am Chiemsee, 53 miles southeast of Munich. The premier attraction here is the **Neues Schloss,** a fantastic castle begun by Ludwig II in 1878 on the island of Herrenchiemsee. You can find food and lodging at Prien.

DAY 4 Get back on the Autobahn to Munich, but take a cross-country route (472) to **Bad Tölz,** one of Bavaria's leading spas. Its spa quarter (Kurverwaltung) makes a good place to take a break. **Hotel Am Wald,** Austrasse 39 in Bad Tölz (☎ **08041/ 78830**), is a reasonable place to dine, with meals beginning at 28 DM ($15.95). It serves good Bavarian fare—nothing fancy, but fit fortification for this breezy part of the country. Standing on its own grounds, the hotel lies about a 10-minute walk from the Altstadt (old town).

Leave Bad Tölz and go along Highway 472 for another 5 miles to Bad Heilbrunn, another typical Bavarian spa. There's not much to see, but in another 4 miles you reach **Benediktbeuern,** Upper Bavaria's oldest Benedictine monastery. Records trace it back to the year 739. After a look, continue along for 4 miles to Kochel am See, with its alpine vistas, and from here take B20 for 20 miles to **Mittenwald** on the Austrian frontier. Plan an overnight stay.

DAY 5 You'll want to spend as much time as possible in Mittenwald—Goethe called it a "living picture book." It is also a major center for violin making. At least give it a morning before driving northwest for 12 miles on Route 2 to **Garmisch-Partenkirchen,** two towns combined. After checking in, head for the major attraction, the **Zugspitze**, the highest peak in Germany (more about this later). Wear warm clothing.

DAY 6 Leaving Garmisch-Partenkirchen, head north for 12 miles to Oberammergau. Along the way you'll pass **Kloster Ettal,** founded by Ludwig the Bavarian in 1330. Its original 10-sided church is a stunning example of the Bavarian rococo style. Some 6 miles to the west is **Schloss Linderhof,** one of "Mad King" Ludwig's royal residences, built on the grounds of his hunting lodge between 1874 and 1878. These two attractions will take up most of your day, but you'll still arrive in the little old woodcarver's village of **Oberammergau,** 7 miles northeast of Linderhof, in time to wander and walk about. Later enjoy a hearty Bavarian dinner before turning in to your alpine bed.

2 National Park Berchtesgaden

This national park occupies the southeast corner of Germany, comprising a large portion of the state of Bavaria and bordering Austria's province of Salzburg. The park was established in 1978 by a decree from the Bavarian government. It is a lush expanse of 84 square miles, with altitudes ranging from 1,800 feet at lowland Königssee to the towering Watzmann Mountain.

The 8,900-foot Watzmann, the Königssee, and parts of the Jenner (the pride of Berchtesgaden's four ski areas), are within the boundaries of the national park, which has well-mapped trails cut through protected areas. Conservation goals and preservation of the natural ecosystems take precedence in the park. An effort is made to keep visitor impact low and to make visitors aware of the ecosystem's fragility.

Limestone dominates most of the rock bed, suggesting that this was once a highly aquatic region. Formed by sediment deposited on the ocean floor 200 million years ago, the rock folded and lifted. Although most of the accompanying sandstone has eroded away, the limestone remains. The steep mountain valleys and moraines suggest recent glacial recession was responsible for many of the grand landscapes found in the park. Of the several alpine lakes that dot the landscape, the most significant is the Königssee, Germany's cleanest, clearest lake (see "Day Trips from Berchtesgaden," below, for information about boat trips on the lake).

Atlantic and continental influences characterize the climate. A substantial annual rainfall fosters the heavy forestation of the region. The valleys receive approximately 60 inches of rainfall a year; the mountains are doused by approximately 110 inches annually.

Vegetation is affected by altitudinal gradient. Nearly half of the vegetation is remnants of deciduous forests, dominated by spruce, pines, and beeches. Nearly a third of the vegetation sprouts on rock debris and in crevices. The mixed mountain forest thrives below 4,500 feet; the coniferous forest above it reaches up to 5,500 feet, and above that, wind-dwarfed bushes and alpine meadows predominate. Once the forest was exploited for salt mines; it's now overpopulated and overgrazed by game.

In spring, summer, and autumn many different rare species of plants flower. They are protected, and don't live long once picked, so they should be left for the next person to enjoy. Alpine animals such as the chamois, ibex (reintroduced in 1930), the marmot, snow hare, alpine salamander, golden eagle, ptarmigan, black grouse, caipercaillie, alpine chough, black woodpecker, and the three-toed woodpecker still inhabit the area, but other animals—the wolf, lynx, bear, and golden vulture—once thriving inhabitants, have not survived. See "Hiking in the Bavarian Alps," below, for more specifics on vegetation and wildlife.

Information about hiking in the park is provided by the **Nationalparkhaus**, Franziskanerpl 7, D-83471 Berchtesgaden (☎ **08652/64343**).

3 Berchtesgaden

98 miles SE of Munich, 11 miles SE of Bad Reichenhall, 14 miles S of Salzburg

Ever since Ludwig I of Bavaria chose this resort as a favorite hideaway, the tourist business in Berchtesgaden has been booming. According to legend, the many summits of Watzmann Mountain that tower over the village were once a king and his family who were so evil that God punished them by turning them into rocks. The evil king has evidently not been completely silenced, however, because the Watzmann has been responsible for the deaths of a number of mountain climbers on the mile-high cliff on its eastern wall.

Berchtesgaden is an old alpine village with ancient winding streets and a medieval marketplace and castle square. Since the name of the village has often been linked with the Führer and the Nazi hierarchy, many visitors mistakenly believe they are seeing one of Hitler's favorite haunts. This impression is erroneous. Hitler's playground was actually at Obersalzberg, on a wooded plateau about half a mile up the mountain. Berchtesgaden is very much a quiet Bavarian town.

ESSENTIALS
GETTING THERE

BY TRAIN   The Berchtesgaden Bahnhof lies on the Munich-Freilassing rail line. Twelve trains a day arrive from Munich (trip time: 1½ hours). For rail information and schedules, call ☎ **08652/5074.** Berchtesgaden has three mountain rail lines—the Obersalzbergbahn, Jennerbahn, and Hirscheckbahn—that connect the mountain plateaus around the resorts. For more information, contact **Berchtesgadener Bergbahn AG** (☎ **08652/95810**) and **Obersalzbergbahn AG** (☎ **08652/2561**).

BY BUS   Long-distance bus service from Passau as well as from Bad Reichenhall is provided by **RBO Regionalbus Ostbayern GmbH in Passau** (☎ **0851/73435**). Regional bus service to alpine villages and towns around Berchtesgaden is offered by **Regionalverkehr Oberbayern RVO at Berchtesgaden** (☎ **08652/5473**).

BY CAR   Access by car is via the A8 Autobahn from Munich in the north or Route 20 from the south. The drive from Munich takes about 2 hours.

VISITOR INFORMATION

For tourist information, contact the **Kurdirektion,** Königssee Strasse 2 (☎ **08652/ 9670**), open Monday to Friday from 8am to 5pm and Saturday from 9am to noon.

SEEING THE SIGHTS

The **Schlossplatz,** partially enclosed by the castle and Stiftskirche, is the most attractive plaza in town. On the opposite side of the square from the church is a 16th-century arcade that leads to Marktplatz, with typical alpine houses and a wooden fountain from 1677 (restored by Ludwig I in 1860). Some of Berchtesgaden's oldest inns and houses border this square. Extending from Marktplatz is the Nonntal, lined with more old houses, some built into the rocks of the Lockstein Mountain that towers above.

A minor but interesting museum, **Heimatmuseum,** Schloss Aldelsheim, Schroffenbergallee 6 (☎ **08652/4410**), is devoted to alpine wood carving. Wood carving as a craft here predates the more fabled wood carving at Oberammergau. Some of the best examples in Germany are on display here. Entry is allowed only as part of a guided tour offered Monday to Friday at 10am and again at 3pm for a charge of 3 DM ($1.70).

Königliches Schloss Berchtesgaden. Schlossplatz 2. ☎ **08652/2085.** Admission 7 DM ($4) adults, 3 DM ($1.70) children 6–16, free for children 5 and under. Easter–Sept, Sun–Fri 10am–1pm and 2–5pm; Oct–Easter, Mon–Fri 10am–1pm and 2–5pm. Bus: 9539.

Berchtesgaden grew up around a powerful Augustinian monastery whose monks introduced the art of wood carving, for which the town is noted to this day. When the town became part of Bavaria in 1809, the abbey was secularized and eventually

---

Impressions

My memories of winter days in Berchtesgaden are ones of glorious sunshine, crisp air and a ring of sparkling mountains: a deep drink of blue fire from a chalice of ice.
                                                                    —Hugo von Hofmannsthal (1874–1929)

converted to a palace for the royal family of Wittelsbach. Now it is a museum, mostly devoted to the royal collection of sacred art, including wood sculptures by the famed artists Veit Stoss and Tilman Riemenschneider. You can also explore a gallery of 19th-century art. There's a collection of Italian Renaissance furniture from the 16th century and three armoires displaying many pistols and guns of the 17th and 18th centuries, plus swords and armor. Precious porcelain and hunting trophies are also shown.

Stiftskirche (Abbey Church). Schlossplatz.

Dating from 1122, the church is adjacent to the Königliches Schloss Berchtesgaden. The church is mainly Romanesque, with Gothic additions. One of its ancient twin steeples was destroyed by lightning and rebuilt in 1866. The church interior contains many fine works of art; the high altar has a painting by Zott dating from 1669. In the vestry is a small silver altar donated by Empress Maria Theresa of Austria.

Salzbergwerk Berchtesgaden. Bergwerkstrasse 83. ☎ **08652/60020.** Admission 19.50 DM ($11.10) adults, 9.50 DM ($5.40) children. May–Oct 15, daily 8:30am–5pm; Oct 16–Apr, Mon–Sat 12:30–3:30pm. Bus: 9539.

At the eastern edge of town are the salt mines once owned by the Augustinian monastery. Operations began here in 1517. The mines contain two types of salt, one suitable only for salt licks for cattle and other animals. The deposits are more than 990 feet thick and are still processed today from four galleries or "hills." Older children will especially enjoy the guided tours that begin with a ride into the mine on a small wagonlike train after donning protective miner's clothing. After nearly a half-mile ride, visitors leave the train and explore the rest of the mine on foot, sliding down a miner's slide and riding on the salt lake in a ferry. The highlight of the tour is the "chapel," a grotto containing unusually shaped salt formations illuminated for an eerie effect. The 1½-hour tour can be taken any time of the year, in any weather.

ORGANIZED TOURS

Guided tours in English are offered by the American-run **Berchtesgaden Mini Bus Tours,** Königsseerstrasse 2 (☎ **08652/64971**). Tours, including Obersalzberg, the Eagle's Nest, and the Bunker System as an afternoon history package, are conducted daily from mid-May through mid-October, starting at the Berchtesgaden tourist office. The service also takes visitors to sights such as the Salt Mines and the Königssee. A 3½-hour tour costs 47 DM ($26.80) adults, 13 DM ($7.40) for people under 25, and is free for children 6 and under. There's a tour information and ticket booth at the Berchtesgaden tourist office, across the street from the train station. One of the most popular tours offered is the "Sound of Music" tour to nearby Salzburg.

OUTDOORS IN THE AREA

Berchtesgaden has a world-class **ice-skating** rink, the **Eisstadion,** An der Schiessstätte (☎ **08652/61405**). A local variation of **curling (Eisstock)** that makes use of wooden, rather than stone instruments is also played there. It's open from October through February.

Mountain bike rentals are available through **Full Stall,** Maximilianstrasse 16 (☎ **08652/948-450**). They will also arrange **hang gliding** or **paragliding,** which can be thrilling, if dangerous, from the vertiginous slopes of Mount Jenner. You can also contact Full Stall's sibling organization, **Berchtesgadener Gleitschirmflieger** e.V., Königsseerstrasse 15 (☎ **08652/2363**).

Kayaking and **white-water rafting** as well as **ballooning** (weather permitting), can be arranged through **Outdoor Club Berchtesgaden,** Ludwig-Ganghofer-Strasse 20 (☎ 08652/5001).

WHERE TO STAY
EXPENSIVE

✪ **Hotel Geiger.** Berchtesgadenstrasse 111, D-83471 Berchtesgaden. ☎ **08652/9653.** Fax 08652/965400. 158 units. MINIBAR TV TEL. 220–350 DM ($125.40–$199.50) double; 400–700 DM ($228–$399) suite. Rates include continental breakfast. V. Free parking outdoors, 10 DM ($5.70) garage. Bus: 9539.

A traditional chalet inn on Berchtesgaden's upper fringes, the Geiger is a genuine antique—a gabled, extravagantly ornate hotel that looks like what every tourist imagines a German hotel to be. The hotel has more amenities and style than any other place in town. From its terraces, guest rooms, and breakfast rooms, you can enjoy panoramic views of the mountaintops. This remarkable retreat is owned by the Geiger family, who created the hotel more than a century ago.

Biedermeier enthusiasts will revel in the sitting rooms, completely furnished in that style. Any Geiger family member will give you the history of any furnishing, especially the painting in the paneled drawing room of *Silent Night* (it upset everyone by depicting Mary as awaiting the birth of Jesus on a Bavarian farm). The comfortable rooms are also furnished with antiques. Prices are based on whatever bath facilities you request and whether you have a balcony.

Dining/Diversions: Dining is a true event here (see "Where to Dine," below). Guests like to gather in the drawing room for after-dinner coffee and cognac in front of the fireplace.

Amenities: Room service, massage, laundry, open-air pool, indoor pool, sauna, solarium, fitness room.

MODERATE

✪ **Hotel Fischer.** Königsseer Strasse 51, D-83471 Berchtesgaden. ☎ **08652/9550.** Fax 08652/64873. 54 units. TV TEL. 198–246 DM ($112.85–$140.20) double. Half board available for stays of 3 days or more, 200–256 DM ($114–$145.90) double. Rates include buffet breakfast. MC, V. Closed Nov–mid-Dec and mid-Mar–Apr 10.

A short uphill walk from the Berchtesgaden railway station, in a spot overlooking the town, this hotel was built in the late 1970s in the Bavarian style. It is the second-ranking address in town, and, although comfortable in every way, it doesn't match the Geiger for charm. Fronted with dark-stained wooden balconies against a cream-colored facade, it rambles pleasantly along the hillside. The bedrooms are cozy and traditional, each with a regional theme. On the premises is an indoor swimming pool, a sauna, a solarium, and an alpine-style restaurant and bar.

Vier Jahreszeiten. Maximilianstrasse 20, D-83471 Berchtesgaden. ☎ **08652/9520.** Fax 08652/5029. 59 units. TEL. 160–260 DM ($91.20–$148.20) double. Rates include buffet breakfast. AE, MC, V. Free parking outside, 9 DM ($5.15) in the garage. Bus: 9539.

An old inn with modern extensions, Vier Jahreszeiten has been in the hands of the Miller family since 1876. It's in the heart of the village and has a colorful and distinguished restaurant. The inn has been remodeled and improved over the years and now offers a good level of comfort, making it a formidable rival of the Fischer. Some of the newer units, with tiny sitting rooms and balconies, resemble suites. Most of the accommodations have minibars and TVs. In addition to the main dining room, there's a terrace for summer dining and viewing. The hotel offers an indoor pool, a sauna, and a solarium.

Wittelsbach. Maximilianstrasse 16, D-83471 Berchtesgaden. ☎ **08652/96380.** Fax 08652/66304. 32 units. MINIBAR TV TEL. 100–160 DM ($57–$91.20) double; 200 DM ($114) suite. Rates include buffet breakfast. AE, DC, MC, V. Closed Nov–Dec 15. Free parking. Bus: 9539.

The Wittelsbach, a hotel that dates from the 1890s, has been stylishly modernized and now offers well-furnished rooms in the heart of Berchtesgaden. The rooms are quiet and sunny; most have balconies with fine views of the mountains. Breakfast is the only meal served. The hotel offers a solarium, as well as a bar with a lounge.

INEXPENSIVE

Watzmann. Franziskanerplatz 2, D-83471 Berchtesgaden. ☎ **08652/2055.** Fax 08652/5174. 38 units (16 with shower). 54–66 DM ($30.80–$37.60) double without shower; 98–138 DM ($55.85–$78.65) double with shower. AE, DC, MC, V. Closed Nov–Dec 25. Free parking. Bus: 9540 or 9541.

Built as part of a brewery 300 years ago, the Watzmann is your best budget bet in town, although it doesn't have the style or amenities of the properties previously described. Set opposite the church on the main square, it has a large outdoor terrace, a cozy Bavarian-inspired decor, and dozens of turn-of-the-century artifacts. Everyone in town seems to stop by sometime during the day or night for a beer, coffee, or lunch. Inside, you'll find huge carved wooden pillars, oak ceilings, wrought-iron chandeliers, and hunting trophies. The doors of the simply furnished guest rooms are painted with floral murals.

WHERE TO DINE

Demming-Restaurant Le Gourmet. Sunklergässchen 2, D-83471 Berchtesgaden. ☎ **08652/9610.** Reservations required. Main courses 23–35 DM ($13–$19.95). AE, DC, MC, V accepted for hotel guests only. Daily 11:30am–2pm and 5:30–8:30pm. Closed Oct 26–Dec 10. Bus: 9539. BAVARIAN/INTERNATIONAL.

The Demming Hotel contains one of the town's best restaurants. Formerly a wealthy private house, it looks over a panoramic view of mountains and forests. Many locals regard dining here as something of an event. Only fresh ingredients are used in the well-prepared dishes, including hearty mountain fare, such as roast beef with chive sauce and an array of veal and fish dishes. Sometimes we wish the chef could be less timid in his cookery, but what you get isn't bad unless you're seeking zesty flavors.

The hotel rents plainly furnished but comfortable bedrooms, costing 166 DM ($94.60) for a double.

✪ **Restaurant Geiger.** Berchtesgadenstrasse 111. ☎ **08652/9653.** Reservations required. Main courses 26–54 DM ($14.80–$30.80); fixed-price menus 45–72 DM ($25.65–$41.05). Tues–Sat 7–11:30am and 6:30–10pm, Sun 7am–1pm and 6:30–10pm. V. Bus: 9539. BAVARIAN/INTERNATIONAL.

Even if you don't stay here, you may want to visit for a meal, as the hotel has the finest cuisine in Berchtesgaden. Its owner makes guests feel well cared for in a cultivated atmosphere featuring hearty cuisine. Trout and game are specialties. Begin perhaps with a parfait of goose liver with a mango puree or lentil soup with sausages. At Christmas an old German favorite—a soup of baked apples with croutons—is served. For a main course, consider filet or saddle of veal on risotto with fresh truffles, salmon trout with vegetables, or "From Mother Nature's kitchen"— that is, spinach ravioli and small cakes made with red beets and served with Bavarian bleu cheese sauce. Desserts include old German favorites such as gingerbread mousse with a mulled claret pear.

DAY TRIPS FROM BERCHTESGADEN
✪ KÖNIGSSEE

This "jewel in the necklace" of Berchtesgaden is one of Europe's most scenic bodies of water. Its waters appear to be dark green because of the steep mountains that jut upward from its shores. On the low-lying land at the northern edge of the lake are a few charming inns and bathing facilities and also a parking lot, but the rest of the lake is enclosed by mountains, making it impossible to walk along the shoreline. The only way to explore the waters, unless you're like one of the mountain goats you may catch sight of above, is by boat.

Electric motorboats (no noisy power launches allowed) carry passengers on tours around the lake in summer, and occasionally even in winter. The favorite spot on Königssee is the tiny flat peninsula on the western bank. It was the site of a basilica as early as the 12th century. Today the Catholic Chapel of St. Bartholomew is still used for services (except in winter). The clergy must arrive by boat since there's no other way to approach the peninsula. The adjacent buildings include a fisher's house and a restaurant, which was once a favored hunting lodge of the Bavarian kings. Here you can sample trout and salmon caught in the crisp, clean waters. At the southern end of the lake you come to the Salet-Alm, where the tour boat makes a short stop near a thundering waterfall. If you follow the footpath up the hillside, you'll reach the summer pastures used by the cattle of Berchtesgaden Land.

Just over the hill is Lake Obersee, part of Königssee until an avalanche separated them 8 centuries ago. If you prefer a shorter trip, you can take the boat as far as St. Bartholomew and back. To reach the lake from Berchtesgaden by car, follow the signs south from the town (only 3 miles). It's also a pleasant hour's walk or a short ride by electric train or bus from the center of town.

For information about excursions, call **Schiffahrt Königssee** at ☎ **08652/ 963613.** An entire tour of Königssee requires about 2 hours. There are boats in summer every 15 minutes, so getting off one boat and climbing aboard another is easy if you want to break up the tour. During the summer, the first boat departs every morning at 7:15am and the last boat leaves at 5:30pm. In winter, boats leave about every 45 minutes. The important stops are at Salet and St. Batholomä. A round-trip fare for a lake tour is 21.50 DM ($12.25) for adults and half-fare for children.

✪ OBERSALZBERG

The drive from Berchtesgaden to Obersalzberg at 3,300 feet is along one of Bavaria's scenic routes. Here Hitler settled down in a rented cottage while he completed *Mein Kampf.* After he came to power in 1933, he bought Haus Wachenfeld and had it remodeled into his residence, the Berghof. Obersalzberg became the center of holiday living for Nazis such as Martin Bormann and Hermann Göring.

At Obersalzberg you can walk around the ruins of Hitler's **Berghof.** Here the 1938 meeting between Hitler and British Prime Minister Neville Chamberlain resulted in the Munich Agreement. Chamberlain came away hailing "peace in our time," but the Nazi dictator felt he had merely given the prime minister his "autograph" and continued preparations for World War II. The Berghof was destroyed in 1952 by Bavarian government authorities at the request of the U.S. Army—the Americans did not want a monument to Hitler. One of the only remaining structures from the Nazi compound is a guest house, the General Walker Hotel, used by U.S. troops stationed in Europe. Wear good walking shoes and be prepared to run into some VERBOTEN! signs.

Hitler built the **bunkers** and air-raid shelter in 1943. Three thousand laborers completed the work in 9 months, connecting all the major buildings of the Obersalzberg area to the underground rooms. Many readers have expressed their disappointment when reaching this site, apparently thinking they would tour Hitler's sumptuously decorated private apartments. A bunker, part of Hitler's air-raid-shelter system, is open for a visit. Newly opened are prison cells used by the Reichssicherheitsdienst (State Security Police). They were to be a last refuge for Hitler and other high officials of the Third Reich. Entrance to the bunker and prison cells is 5 DM ($2.85); they're open daily from 9am to 5pm. Guided tours in English are conducted daily from mid-May through mid-October, starting at the Berchtesgaden tourist office and offered by Berchtesgaden Mini Bus Tours (☎ **08652/64971;** see "Organized Tours," above).

A major point of interest to visitors is the **Kehlstein,** or Eagle's Nest, which can be reached only by a thrilling bus ride up a 4½-mile-long mountain road, blasted out of solid rock and considered an outstanding feat of construction and engineering when begun in 1937 under the leadership of Bormann, who intended it as a 50th birthday gift for Hitler. The Eagle's Nest was not, as the name may suggest, a military installation. It was a site for relaxation, a tea house, and was not popular with Hitler, who rarely visited it. To reach the spot, you must enter a tunnel and take a 400-foot elevator ride through a shaft in the Kehlstein Mountain. The building, with solid granite walls and huge picture windows, now houses a mountain restaurant. Called the **Kehlsteinhaus,** the restaurant is open from the end of May through the end of October.

You can also explore the rooms of the original tea house, which include Eva Braun's living room. Below you can see the Obersalzberg area where Hitler's Berghof once stood, and nearby, the site of Martin Bormann's house and the SS barracks. To the north you can see as far as Salzburg, Austria, and just below the mountain, to the west, is the village of Berchtesgaden, with its rivers dwindling off into threads in the distance.

For information about trips to Kehlstein, call ☎ **08652/5473.** RVO buses (local buses based in Berchtesgaden) run from the Berchtesgaden Post Office to Obersalzberg-Hintereck. Buses from the Hintereck parking lot run to the Kehlstein parking lot about every half hour. The ticket price includes the elevator ride to the Eagle's Nest at the top. By local bus the round-trip journey from Berchtesgaden to Obersalzberg costs 5.80 DM ($3.30). From Obersalzberg (Hintereck) the special mountain bus and elevator ride through the rock costs 20 DM ($11.40). If you're hearty, instead of taking the elevator, you can walk up the final stretch to the Eagle's Nest from the summit parking lot in about 30 minutes. The Kehlstein line operates daily from mid-May through mid-October, when there are full catering services offered at Kehlsteinhaus. The Kehlstein road is closed to private vehicles.

Obersalzberg is becoming an important health resort; the ruins of Bormann's Gusthof Farm are now the location of Skytop Lodge, a popular golfing center in summer and a ski site in winter.

WHERE TO STAY

Hotel Zum Türken. D-83471 Berchtesgaden-Obersalzberg. ☎ **08652/2428.** Fax 08652/4710. 17 units (13 with shower or bath). 115 DM ($65.55) double without shower or bath, 180 DM ($102.60) double with shower or bath. Rates include continental breakfast. AE, DC, MC, V. Closed Tues. Free parking. Obersalzberg bus from Berchtesgaden.

In Obersalzberg, the alpine-style Hotel zum Türken is legendary. On its facade is a large painted sign of "The Turk," and the foundation is stone, with the windows framed in shutters. A large handmade sign is written across the hillside, with a rather ominous pronouncement, pointing the way to the "Bunker." The story goes that the original building here was erected by a veteran from the Turkish war. At the turn of the century it was acquired by Karl Schuster, who turned it into a well-known restaurant that drew many celebrities of the day, including Brahms and Crown Prince Wilhelm of Prussia. However, anti-Nazi remarks he made in the 1930s led to trouble. Herr Schuster was arrested. Bormann took over the building as a Gestapo headquarters, and air raids and looting in April 1945 nearly destroyed the Türken. (Many tourists erroneously think that the Türken was Hitler's famed Berghof).

Herr Schuster's daughter, Therese Partner, was able to buy the ruin from the German government for a high price in 1949. She opened a cafe and rooms for overnight visitors. Today, the Türken is run by Frau Ingrid Scharfenberg, granddaughter of Karl Schuster. Pleasantly furnished units are rented, and a self-service bar is on the ground floor. The rooms have no private phones, but there is an international pay phone in the main hallway. Note that its terraces and views are for hotel guests only.

4 Chiemsee

Prien am Chiemsee: 53 miles SE of Munich, 14 miles E of Rosenheim, 40 miles W of Salzburg

Known as the "Bavarian Sea," Chiemsee is one of the Bavarian Alps' most beautiful lakes, set in a serene landscape. In the south the mountains reach almost to the water. Many resorts line the shores of the large lake, but the Chiemsee's main attractions are on its two islands, Frauenchiemsee, with its interesting local customs, and Herrenchiemsee, site of the palace built by Ludwig II, whose intent was to recreate Versailles.

ESSENTIALS
GETTING THERE

BY TRAIN The Prien Bahnhof is on the major Munich-Rosenheim-Freilassing-Salzburg rail line, with frequent connections in all directions. Ten daily trains arrive from Munich (trip time: 1 hour). For information, call ☎ 08051/19419.

BY BUS Regional bus service in the area is offered by **RVO Regionalverkehr Oberbayern, Betrieb Rosenheim** (☎ 08031/62006 for schedules and information).

BY CAR Access by car is via the A8 Autobahn from Munich.

VISITOR INFORMATION

For tourist information, contact the **Kur und Verkehrsamt,** Alte Rathausstrasse 11, in Prien am Chiemsee (☎ 0851/69050), open Monday to Friday from 8:30am to 6pm and Saturday from 9am to noon.

GETTING AROUND

BY STEAMER From the liveliest resort, Prien, on the west shore, you can reach either Frauenchiemsee or Herrenchiemsee via lake steamers that make regular trips throughout the year. The round-trip fare to Herrenchiemsee is 14 DM ($8), 16 DM ($9.10) to Fraueninsel. The steamers, operated by **Chiemsee-Schiffahrt Ludwig Fessler** (☎ 08051/6090), make round-trips covering the entire lake. Connections are made from Gstadt, Seebruck, Chieming, übersee/Feldwies, and Bernau/Felden. Large boats leave Prien/Stock for Herrenchiemsee at the island of

Herreninsel from May through September, daily about every 20 minutes between 9am and 5pm. The last return is at 7:25pm.

BY BUS   There is also bus service from the harbor to the DB station in Prien (Chiemsee-Schiffahrt) and around the lake by RVO.

EXPLORING THE ISLANDS
FRAUENCHIEMSEE

Frauenchiemsee, also called Fraueninsel, is the smaller of the lake's two major islands. Along its sandy shore stands a fishing village whose boats drag the lake for pike and salmon. At the festival of Corpus Christi, these boats are covered with flowers and streamers, the fishers are outfitted in Bavarian garb, and the young women of the village dress as brides. As the boats circle the island, they stop at each corner for the singing of the Gospels.

The island is also the home of a Benedictine nunnery, founded in 782. The convent is known for a liqueur called *Kloster Likör.* Sold by nuns in black cowls with white-winged head garb, it's supposed to be an "agreeable stomach elixir."

HERRENCHIEMSEE

Herrenchiemsee, also called Herreninsel, has the most popular visitor attraction on the lake, one of Ludwig's most fantastic castles.

✪ **Neues Schloss.** Herrenchiemsee 3 (☎ **08051/3069**). Admission (in addition to the round-trip boat fare) 7 DM ($4) adults, 4 DM ($2.30) students, free for children under 16. Apr–Sept 30, tours daily 9am–5pm; off-season, daily 10am–4pm.

Begun by Ludwig II in 1878, this castle was never completed. It was meant to be a replica of the grand palace of Versailles that Ludwig so admired. A German journalist once called it "a monument to uncreative megalomania." However, the creation of the castle gave impetus to a revival of arts and crafts. One of the architects of Herrenchiemsee was Julius Hofmann, whom the king had also employed for the construction of his fantastic alpine castle, Neuschwanstein. When money ran out and work was halted in 1886, only the center of the enormous palace had been completed. The palace and its formal gardens, surrounded by woodlands of beech and fir, remain one of the most fascinating of Ludwig's adventures, in spite of their unfinished state.

The palace entrance is lit by a huge skylight above the sumptuously decorated state staircase. Frescoes depicting the four states of existence alternate with Greek and Roman statues set in niches on the staircase and in the gallery above. The vestibule is adorned with a pair of enameled peacocks, Louis XIV's favorite bird.

The Great Hall of Mirrors is unquestionably the most splendid hall in the palace and the most authentic replica of Versailles. The 17 door panels contain enormous mirrors reflecting the 33 crystal chandeliers and the 44 gilded candelabra. The vaulted ceiling is covered with 25 paintings depicting the life of Louis XIV.

The dining room is a popular attraction for visitors because of the table nicknamed "the little table that lays itself." A mechanism in the floor permitted the table to go down to the room below to be cleared and relaid between courses. Over the table hangs an exquisite chandelier of Meissen porcelain, the largest in the world and the single most valuable item in the palace.

The state bedroom is brilliant to the point of gaudiness, as practically every inch of the room has been gilded. On the dais, instead of a throne stands the richly decorated state bed, its purple-velvet draperies weighing more than 300 pounds. Separating the dais from the rest of the room is a carved wooden balustrade

The Fairy-Tale King

Often called "Mad" King Ludwig (although Bavarians hate that label), Ludwig II, son of Maximilian II, was only 18 years old when he was crowned king of Bavaria. Handsome Ludwig initially took an interest in affairs of state, but he soon grew bored and turned to the pursuit of his romantic visions. He transformed his dreams into some of the region's most elaborate castles, nearly bankrupting Bavaria in the process.

Linderhof, the first and smallest of Ludwig's architectural fantasies, was his favorite castle, and the only one complete at the time of his death. His most elaborate effort was his attempt to construct his own Versailles on the island of Herrenchiemsee, but best known is the multiturreted Disneyland-like Neuschwanstein. From a distance the castle appears more illusory than real. It's the most photographed castle in Germany, and one of Germany's greatest tourist attractions.

The "dream" king was born in 1845 at Nymphenburg, the summer residence of the Bavarian rulers. A bisexual loner who never married, Ludwig's most intense relationship was his friendship with the composer Richard Wagner. An admirer of Wagner when that composer's music was considered crude, loud, and even demonic by almost everyone; it was Ludwig's enthusiastic and generous support that gave Wagner the opportunity to develop his art. It is probable that Ludwig, who was not musical, was captivated less by the music than by the operas' world of fantasy. The king sometimes had Wagner's operas mounted for his own pleasure and watched them in royal and solitary splendor. In the magical grotto at Linderhof, he recreated the Venus grotto from the Munich opera stage design for *Tannhäuser*. Although the money he lavished upon Wagner came from his own fortune, Ludwig's ministers became alarmed and Wagner was persuaded to leave Munich, although the friendship continued at a distance.

Ludwig had few close friends. He was devoted to his cousin Sissi—Elizabeth, the empress of Austria—but estranged from the rest of his family. He led a solitary life, slept most of the day, and spent his nights going for long, lonely rides through the countryside, often dressed in full kingly regalia. More and more he withdrew into his dream world; he ran up huge debts and refused all advice to curb his extravagant building projects. Finally the cabinet decided he had to go—his excesses were too much. He was declared insane in 1886 when he was 41 years old, and his uncle Luitpold was made regent.

Three days later he was found drowned in Lake Starnberg on the outskirts of Munich—he may have committed suicide, or he may have been murdered. His death remains a mystery. On the bank of the lake is a memorial chapel dedicated to him. He is buried with other royals in the crypt beneath the choir of St. Michael's Church.

Today Ludwig enjoys something of a cult status in Munich. Was he really insane? His theatricality, self-absorbed lifestyle, morbid shyness, and outbursts of temper certainly made him a very strange person, but there is not much evidence of real insanity. He seems mainly to have been an eccentric who had the means and power to try to turn his fancies and whims into reality.

covered with gold leaf. On the ceiling a huge fresco depicts the descent of Apollo, surrounded by the other gods of Olympus. The sun god's features bear a strong resemblance to Louis XIV.

WHERE TO STAY & DINE

Bayerischer Hof. Bernauerstrasse 3, D-83209 Prien am Chiemsee. ☎ **08051/6030.** Fax 08051/62917. 46 units. TV TEL. 165 DM ($94.05) double. Rates include buffet breakfast. V. Closed Nov and last week of Jan. Parking 10 DM ($5.70).

The Estermann family will welcome you to the Bayerischer Hof. The rustic aspects of the decor create the illusion that this relatively severe modern hotel is indeed older and more mellow than it is. Of particular note is the painted ceiling in the dining room, where regional meals are served. The rest of the hotel is more stream-lined—modern, efficient, but quite appealing.

Yachthotel Chiemsee. Harrasser Strasse 49, D-83209 Prien am Chiemsee. ☎ **08051/6960.** Fax 08051/5171. www.home.t-online.de/home/yachthotel_chiemsee. E-mail: yachthotel_chiemsee@t-online.de. 102 units. MINIBAR TV TEL. 245–315 DM ($139.65–$179.55) double; 335–465 DM ($190.95–$265) suite. Rates include buffet break-fast. AE, DC, MC, V. Free parking.

The best place to stay on the lake is the Yachthotel Chiemsee, on the western shore of the "Bavarian Sea." This modern hotel offers attractively furnished rooms, all with king-size beds and balconies or terraces opening onto the water. Lakeside rooms are equipped with two double beds and a pull-out sofa for groups of four or more.

Dining/Diversions: There's a choice of restaurants, complete with a lakeside ter-race and a marina, although you can order from the same menu in all three. The most elegant room, patronized for its view if not its food, is the Seepavillion. The See-restaurant is slightly more rustic but with an elegant flair, and the Zirbelstüberl goes alpine-Bavarian all the way.

Amenities: Room service (7am to midnight), laundry, baby-sitting. Sailing (a two-masted yacht with a skipper is available for sailing May through September), rowing, squash, tennis, riding, golf (nearby), horse-drawn carriage trips, spa depart-ment, beauty-care center, sauna, solarium, health and fitness center, outdoor whirlpool, indoor pool.

5 Garmisch-Partenkirchen

55 miles SW of Munich, 73 miles SE of Augsburg, 37 miles NW of Innsbruck

In spite of its urban flair, Garmisch-Partenkirchen, Germany's top alpine resort, has kept some of the charm of an ancient village. It's actually made up of two towns, the older Partenkirchen and the more modern Garmisch. Even today you occasionally see country folk in traditional costumes, and you may be held up in traffic while the cattle are led from their mountain-grazing grounds down through the streets of town.

ESSENTIALS

GETTING THERE

BY TRAIN The Garmisch-Partenkirchen Bahnhof is on the Munich-Weilheim-Garmisch-Mittenwald-Innsbruck rail line with frequent connections in all direc-tions. Twenty trains per day arrive from Munich (trip time: 1 hour and 22 minutes). For rail information and schedules, call ☎ **08821/19419.** Mountain rail service to several mountain plateaus and the Zugspitze is offered by the **Bayerische Zugspitzenbahn** at Garmisch (☎ **08821/7970**).

BY BUS   Both long-distance and regional buses through the Bavarian Alps are provided by **RVO Regionalverkehr Oberbayern** (☎ **08821/948274**).

BY CAR   Access is via the A95 Autobahn from Munich; exit at Eschenlohe.

VISITOR INFORMATION

For tourist information, contact the **Verkehrsamt der Kurverwaltung,** on Dr. Richard-Strauss-Platz (☎ **08821/1806**), open Monday to Saturday from 8am to 6pm and Sunday from 10am to noon.

GETTING AROUND

An unnumbered municipal bus services the town, depositing passengers at Marienplatz or the Bahnhof, from which it is possible to walk to all centrally located hotels. This free bus runs every 15 minutes.

EXPLORING THE AREA

The symbol of the city's growth and modernity is the **Olympic Ice Stadium,** built for the 1936 Winter Olympics and capable of holding nearly 12,000 people. On the slopes at the edge of town is the much larger **Ski Stadium,** with two ski jumps and a slalom course. In 1936 more than 100,000 people watched the events in this stadium. Today it's still an integral part of winter life in Garmisch—the World Cup Ski Jump is held here every New Year.

Garmisch-Partenkirchen is a center for winter sports, summer hiking, and mountain climbing. In addition, the town environs offer panoramic views and colorful buildings. The pilgrimage **Chapel of St. Anton,** on a pinewood path at the edge of Partenkirchen, is all pink and silver, inside and out. Its graceful lines are characteristic of 18th-century style. The **Philosopher's Walk** in the park surrounding the chapel is a delightful spot to wander, just to enjoy the views of the mountains around the low-lying town. Along Frülingstrasse are some beautiful examples of **Bavarian houses,** and the villa of composer Richard Strauss is at the end of Zöppritzstrasse. The **church of St. Martin,** off the Marienplatz, is worth a look for its stucco work.

This area of Germany has always attracted the German romantics, including the "Fairy Tale King," Ludwig II. Perhaps with Wagner's music sounding in his ears, the king ordered the construction of a hunting lodge in the style of a Swiss chalet, but commanded that the interior look like something out of *The Arabian Nights.* It's still here. The lodge, **Jagdschloss Schachen,** can only be reached after an arduous climb. The tourist office will supply details. Tours are offered at 11am and 2pm daily and often leave from the Olympic Ski Stadium heading for the lodge—but check that first.

SHOPPING   Your best bets are in the traffic-reduced Ludwigstrasse in Partenkirchen and in the almost traffic-free zone from Dr. Richard-Strauss-Platz to Marienplatz in Garmisch. There's a vast array of stores here selling everything from boots to boutique items, from clothing to jewelry, from art to antiques. An unusual store is **Kaufmann,** Am Kurkpark (☎ **08821/55248**), lithograph-meister to visitors to Garmisch. This shop not only sells a wide collection of artful lithographs depicting the glories of the Bavarian Alps but also offers tinsmith work, glass, ceramics, gold and silver jewelry, and various souvenirs of your visit. If you like traditional Bavarian folkloric dress but were scared off by the extremely high prices,

Garmisch-Partenkirchen

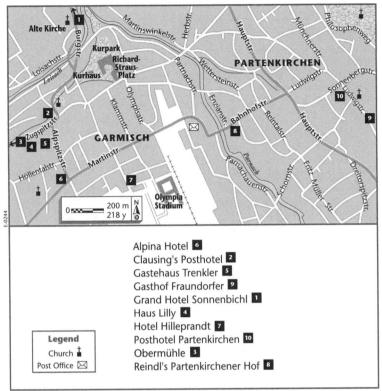

Alpina Hotel **6**
Clausing's Posthotel **2**
Gastehaus Trenkler **5**
Gasthof Fraundorfer **9**
Grand Hotel Sonnenbichl **1**
Haus Lilly **4**
Hotel Hilleprandt **7**
Posthotel Partenkirchen **10**
Obermühle **3**
Reindl's Partenkirchener Hof **8**

Legend
Church †
Post Office ✉

head for **Loisachtaler,** Burgstrasse 20 (☎ **08821/52390**). Here, Petra Ostler has assembled the area's finest collection of secondhand clothing, which for the most part is in such good shape it looks new. Take your pick: a jaegermeister loden coat, an alpine hat with pheasant feathers, or a cast-off dirndl.

WHERE TO STAY
EXPENSIVE
Alpina Hotel. Alpspitzstrasse 12, D-82467 Garmisch-Partenkirchen. ☎ **08821/7830.** Fax 08821/71374. 70 units. MINIBAR TV TEL. 240–330 DM ($136.80–$188.10) double. Rates include buffet breakfast. AE, DC, MC, V. Parking 15 DM ($8.55).

In this Bavarian hostelry only 3 minutes from the Hausberg ski lifts, guests have all sorts of luxury facilities, including a garden with wide lawns and trees and an open patio. But even so, this is not the town's leading hotel, an honor going to such classics as the Grand Hotel Sonnenbichl or the more traditional Posthotel Partenkirchen. Alpina has many winning features. Its facade is graced with a wide overhanging roof and Tyrolean-style entranceway and windows. Each of the guest rooms sports a personalized decor: Yours may have a snow-white sofa, chairs, walls, lamps, and carpet, with original paintings as accents; or it might feature sloped pine ceilings, a Spanish bedspread, and matching armchairs.

Dining/Diversions: The open tavern dining room has two levels, and there's an extensive brick wine cellar offering a wide choice. Bavarian and international dishes are served in a beamed rustic dining room and on the sun terrace.

Amenities: Room service, laundry, dry cleaning, covered pool with recreational terrace, open-air pool, sun terrace.

Grand Hotel Sonnenbichl. Burgstrasse 97, D-82467 Garmisch-Partenkirchen. ☎ **08821/ 7020.** Fax 08821/702131. 93 units. MINIBAR TV TEL. 350 DM ($199.50) double; 700–950 DM ($399–$541.50) suite. Rates include buffet breakfast. AE, DC, MC, V. Free parking. Take Route 23 toward Oberammergau.

The finest hotel in the area, but not the most atmospheric, is on the hillside overlooking Garmisch-Partenkirchen, 1 mile from the city center and 2 miles from the Bahnhof, with views of the Wetterstein mountain range and the Zugspitze from its front rooms (those in the rear open onto a rock wall). The hotel was built in 1898 by the family of Georg Bader. After World War II it was used as a military hospital. Some of the bedrooms are showing wear and tear, and, although usually spacious, some do not have a complete tub bath. The decor is more or less art nouveau.

Dining/Diversions: The hotel serves excellent food. You can have light, modern cuisine in the elegant gourmet restaurant, the Blauer Salon, or Bavarian specialties in the Zirbelstube. Afternoon coffee and fresh homemade cake are served in the lobby or on the sunny terrace. Drinks are available in the Peacock Bar.

Amenities: Room service, laundry, dry cleaning, pool, sauna, solarium, fitness and massage rooms, beauty farm.

Obermühle. Mühlstrasse 22, D-82467 Garmisch-Partenkirchen. ☎ **800/528-1234** in the U.S., or 08821/7040. Fax 08821/704112. 95 units. MINIBAR TV TEL. 250–325 DM ($142.50–$185.25) double; 330–450 DM ($188.10–$256.50) suite. Rates include buffet breakfast. AE, DC, MC, V. Free parking. Take Route 24 (Zugspitzstrasse) toward Griesen.

This hotel is a 5- to 10-minute walk from Garmisch's center, in a quiet, isolated spot much favored by repeat guests. The Wolf family, the owners, have operated a hotel on this spot since 1634, although the present building was constructed in 1969. They still maintain the traditional hospitality that has characterized their family for so long. Although a bit more sterile than either the Posthotel Partenkirchen or Alpina, the mountain panoramas from its beer garden and terrace are compensating factors. Most rooms have balconies with views of the Alps. Nearby are miles of woodland trails criss-crossing the nearby foothills. The rooms often have style and comfort, some with traditional Bavarian character.

Dining/Diversions: Bavarian and international dishes are featured in the excellent restaurant. The Weinstube is cozy and the garden a pleasant place to wander.

Amenities: Room service, laundry, baby-sitting, indoor pool set below a wooden roof shaped like a modified Gothic arch (at least it's pointed), sauna, solarium.

✪ **Posthotel Partenkirchen.** Ludwigstrasse 49, D-82467 Garmisch-Partenkirchen. ☎ **08821/51067.** Fax 08821/78568. 59 units. MINIBAR TV TEL. 200–280 DM ($114–159.60) double; 280–380 DM ($159.60–$216.60) suite. Rates include continental breakfast. AE, DC, MC, V. Free parking.

Once a posting inn, Posthotel Partenkirchen is now one of the town's most prestigious hotels and has the added asset of an unusually fine restaurant (see "Where to Dine," below). The traditional facade has decorative murals around the front entrance and window boxes planted with red geraniums. The U-shaped rooms are stylish, with hand-decorated or elaborately carved furnishings. The balconies are sun traps, overlooking a garden and parking for your car, and offer a view of the Alps. Here you'll experience old-world living, with personalized service offered by the owners.

Dining/Diversions: Of the two dining rooms, the larger is known for its decor: a wooden-beamed ceiling, wrought-iron chandeliers, and huge arches that divide the room, making it more intimate. In the rustic Weinlokal Barbarossa, there are nooks for quiet before- or after-dinner drinks. Musicians provide background music.

Amenities: Room service, laundry, and nearby golf, tennis, swimming, hiking, mountain climbing, skiing, cycling, hiking, horseback riding, paragliding.

MODERATE

Hotel Hilleprandt. Riffelstrasse 17, D-82467 Garmisch-Partenkirchen. ☎ **08821/2861.** Fax 08821/74548. 18 units. TV TEL. 142–178 DM ($80.95–$101.45) double; 190 DM ($108.30) suite. Rates include buffet breakfast. MC, V. Free parking. Town bus.

In a tranquil location, this cozy chalet is close to the Zugspitz Bahnhof and the Olympic Ice Stadium. Its cutout wooden balconies, attractive garden, and backdrop of forest-covered mountains give the impression of an old-time alpine building; however, a complete renovation in 1992 brought in streamlined modern comfort. Guests enjoy a fitness room, a sauna, a pleasant breakfast room, and the accommodating personality of owner Klaus Hilleprandt, who is also the chef, serving excellent Bavarian food. Each cozily furnished room opens to a private balcony.

✪ Reindl's Partenkirchner Hof. Bahnhofstrasse 15, D-82467 Garmisch-Partenkirchen. ☎ **08821/58025.** Fax 08821/73401. 88 units. MINIBAR TV TEL. 170–200 DM ($96.90–$114) double; 320–550 DM ($182.40–$313.50) suite. AE, DC, MC, V. Closed Nov 11–Dec 12. Parking 12 DM ($6.85).

Reindl's opened in 1911, and from the beginning it attracted a devoted following. Owners Bruni and Karl Reindl have kept this a special Bavarian retreat with high levels of luxury and hospitality. Balconies on the two annexes, the Wetterstein and the House Alpspitz, and wraparound verandas on the main four-story building give each guest room an unobstructed view of the mountains and town. The well-furnished rooms have all the amenities, including safes. The place is also known for Reindl's much honored restaurant (see "Where to Dine," below). Amenities include room service, laundry, a covered pool, sauna, sun room, health club, open terrace for snacks, and two attractive gardens.

✪ Romantik-Hotel Clausing's Posthotel. Marienplatz 12, D-82467 Garmisch-Partenkirchen. ☎ **08821/7090.** Fax 08821/709205. 43 units. TV TEL. 160–300 DM ($91.20–$171) double; from 450 DM ($256.50) suite. AE, DC, MC, V.

This historic hotel with its florid pink facade has seen a series of events that are a part of Garmisch's very identity. It was originally built in 1512 in the heart of town as a tavern. During the Thirty Years War, it became a haven for refugees when nearby Munich was ravaged and besieged. In 1891 it was sold to a prosperous beer baron from Berlin, whose claim to fame came from his invention of a new brand of beer, *Berliner Weissen,* with hints of yeast and raspberry flavoring, which quickly became one of the most popular brands in Garmisch.

In the early 1990s, the interior was radically upgraded without losing the establishment's historic ambience. Guest rooms successfully mingle antique charm with the modern, well-insulated comforts you'd expect. Unused space beneath the eaves has been transformed into what are now the inn's best accommodations.

The most glamorous restaurant here is the Stüberl, a paneled enclave of warmth and carefully presented cuisine. The Verandah offers simple platters, drinks, and glassed-in comfort in winter, and open-air access to the bustling Marienplatz in summer. Bavarian schmaltz is the venue at the Post-Hörnd'l, where live music is presented every evening between 7 and 11:30pm.

INEXPENSIVE

Gästehaus Trenkler. Kreuzstrasse 20, D-82467 Garmisch-Partenkirchen. ☎ **08821/3439.** Fax 08821/1562. 10 units (5 with shower). 85–90 DM ($48.45–$51.30) double without shower; 96–99 DM ($54.70–$56.45) double with shower. Rates include continental breakfast. No credit cards. Free parking.

For a number of years Frau Trenkler has made travelers feel well cared for in her guest house, which enjoys a quiet central location. She rents five doubles with showers and toilets and five doubles with hot and cold running water. The rooms are simple but comfortably furnished.

Gasthof Fraundorfer. Ludwigstrasse 24, D-82467 Garmisch-Partenkirchen. ☎ **08821/2176.** Fax 08821/92799. 30 units. TV TEL. 130–150 DM ($74.10–$85.50) double; 180–300 DM ($102.60–$171) family room for 2 to 5. Rates include buffet breakfast. AE, MC, V. Free parking.

The family-owned Gasthof Fraundorfer is directly on the main street of town, just a 5-minute walk from the old church. Its original style has not been updated, so it retains the character of another day. There are three floors under a sloping roof, with a facade brightly adorned with window boxes of geraniums and decorative murals depicting a family feast. You'll be in the midst of village-centered activities here, near interesting shops and restaurants. The guest rooms are furnished with traditional alpine styling, some with four-poster beds. Some larger units are virtual apartments, suitable for up to five guests. Owners Josef and Barbel Fraundorfer are proud of their country-style meals. There's Bavarian yodeling and dancing every night except Tuesday. Dinner reservations are advisable.

In addition, the owners operate the Gästehaus Barbara in back, with 20 more beds. A typical Bavarian decor includes a *Himmelbett* (a high four-poster bed with curtains). A double in their new house costs 150 DM ($85.50).

Haus Lilly. Zugspitzstrasse 20a, D-82467 Garmisch-Partenkirchen. ☎ **08821/52600.** 8 units. 103 DM ($58.70) double; 153 DM ($87.20) triple or quad. Rates include buffet breakfast. No credit cards. Free parking.

This spotlessly clean guest house, a 15-minute walk from the Bahnhof, wins prizes for its copious breakfasts and the personality of its smiling owner, Maria Lechner, whose English is limited but whose hospitality is universal. Each cozy room includes free access to a kitchen, so in-house meal preparation is an option for guests wanting to save money. Breakfast offers a combination of cold cuts, rolls, cheese, eggs, pastries, and coffee, tea, or chocolate.

WHERE TO DINE
EXPENSIVE

Posthotel Partenkirchen. Ludwigstrasse 49, Partenkirchen. ☎ **08821/51067.** Reservations required. Main courses 25–50 DM ($14.25–$28.50); fixed-price menus 32–76 DM ($18.25–$43.30). AE, DC, MC, V. Daily noon–2pm and 6–9:30pm. Eibsee bus no. 1. CONTINENTAL.

Posthotel Partenkirchen is renowned for its distinguished continental cuisine—in fact, its reputation is known throughout Bavaria. The interior dining rooms are rustic, with lots of mellow, old-fashioned atmosphere. Everything seems comfortably subdued, including the guests. Perhaps the best way to dine here is to order one of the fixed-price menus, which change daily depending on the availability of seasonal produce. The à la carte menu is extensive, featuring game in autumn. You can order fresh cauliflower soup followed by main dishes such as Schnitzel Cordon Bleu or mixed grill St. James. The Weiner schnitzel served with a large salad is the best we've had in the resort.

⊙ **Reindl's Restaurant.** In the Partenkirchner Hof, Bahnhofstrasse 15. ☎ **08821/58025.** Reservations required. Main courses 27–41 DM ($15.40–$23.35); fixed-price meals 50 DM ($28.50) at lunch, 120 DM ($68.40) at dinner. AE, DC, MC, V. Daily noon–2:30pm and 6:30–11pm. Closed Nov 11–Dec 12. CONTINENTAL.

One of the best places to dine in Partenkirchen is Reindl's, a first-class restaurant in every sense of the word. It is the only hotel in town that competes successfully with Posthotel Partenkirchen. The seasonal menu comprises *cuisine moderne* as well as regional Bavarian dishes. Some famous French wines and champagnes—Romanée Conti, Château Lafite Rothschild, and Château Petrus—are offered. The chef de cuisine is Marianne Holzinger, daughter of founding father Karl Reindl. She has worked in the kitchens of The Breakers in Palm Beach and Aubergine in Munich. The restaurant is known for honoring each "food season": For example, if you're here in asparagus season in spring, a special menu samples the dish in all the best-known varieties.

As a good opening to a fine repast, we suggest the scampi salad Walterspiel with fresh peaches, lemon, and tarragon or homemade goose-liver pâté with Riesling jelly. Among main dishes, we recommend coq au Riesling (chicken in wine) with noodles or veal roasted with Steinpilzen, a special mushroom from the Bavarian mountains. Among the fish dishes, try wild salmon with white and red wine and butter sauce. For dessert, you can select Grand Marnier sabayon with strawberry and vanilla ice cream or something more spectacular—a Salzburger Nockerl for two.

MODERATE

Alpenhof. Am Kurpark 10. ☎ **08821/59055.** Reservations recommended. Main courses 17.50–42 DM ($10–$23.95); fixed-price lunch 25–29 DM ($14.25–$16.50). DC, MC, V. Daily 11:30am–2pm and 5:30–9:30pm. Closed 3 weeks in Nov. BAVARIAN.

Alpenhof is probably the best restaurant in Garmisch outside the hotel dining rooms (see above). The cuisine here is neatly grounded in tradition, with a flavorful use of ingredients. In summer, try for an outside table; in winter, retreat to the cozy interior, which is flooded with sunlight from a greenhouse extension. Renate and Josef Huber offer a variety of Bavarian specialties, as well as trout "any way you want," salmon grilled with mousseline sauce, and ragout of venison. For dessert, try a soufflé with exotic fruits. An exceptional set meal for 28.50 DM ($16.25)—the best for value at the resort—is presented daily.

INEXPENSIVE

Flösserstuben. Schmiedstrasse 2. ☎ **08821/2888.** Reservations recommended. Main courses 12–32.50 DM ($6.85–$18.50). AE, MC. Daily 11am–2:30pm and 4:30–11pm (or as late as 1:30am, depending on business). Town bus. GREEK/BAVARIAN/INTERNATIONAL.

Regardless of season, a bit of the Bavarian Alps always seems to be in flower amid the wood-trimmed nostalgia of this intimate restaurant near the town center. The weathered beams are likely to reverberate with laughter and good times. You can select a seat at a colorful wooden table or on an ox yoke–inspired stool in front of the spliced saplings that decorate the bar. Moussaka and souvlaki, as well as sauer-braten and all kinds of Bavarian dishes, are abundantly available.

Riessersee. Reiss 6. ☎ **08821/95440.** Main courses 9.80–35 DM ($5.60–$19.95). Tues–Sun 8am–9pm. AE, MC, V. BAVARIAN.

On the shores of a small lake with emerald-green water, this restaurant is reached after a lovely 2-mile stroll from the center of town. A cafe-restaurant, it is the ideal place for a leisurely lunch, an afternoon tea or coffee and cake, ice cream, or chocolates. It makes a particularly good place to stop over after your exploration of the Zugspitze. The zither music played on Saturday and Sunday will soothe your nerves after such an adventure. You may like the place so much you'll stick around for one of the good-tasting dishes that feature Bavarian fish or game specialties. Caviar and lobster are available on occasion, and you can order some of the best-tasting veal dishes here at all times.

GARMISCH-PARTENKIRCHEN AFTER DARK

You can test your luck at the town's casino, **Spielbank Garmisch-Partenkirchen,** Am Kurpark 74 (☎ **08821/99590**). Admission costs 5 DM ($2.85) per person, and presentation of a passport is required. It's open daily from 3pm to 2am. Between 3 and 7pm, only roulette and the slot machines are available, and men must wear jackets. Beginning at 8pm, men must wear jackets and ties, and to the noise of the roulette tables and slot machines is added the sound of the blackjack tables. Baccarat, because of lack of interest, is no longer offered at the casino, but every Friday and Saturday, games of seven-card stud poker are arranged.

Many hotels have dance floors that keep the music pumping into the wee hours, but for earlier dancing of a different sort, check out the summer program of Bavarian folk music and dancing, held every Saturday night from mid-May through September in the **Bayernhalle,** Brauhausstrasse 19. During the same weeks from Saturday to Thursday, classical and pop concerts are sponsored at the **Garmisch Park bandstand.** On Friday these live shows move to the **Partenkirchen bandstand.** Check with the local tourist office (see above) for details about these programs as well as a 5-day **Wagner Festival** held in the dual resort during June.

If you'd like to join the locals at night, head for one of the taverns for a beer. All major hotels serve up a brew, but for a change-of-pace go to the **Irish Pub,** Rathausplatz 8 (☎ **08821/78798**), and order a Guinness. This pub, exactly in the center, attracts one of the most convivial crowds in town.

A particularly cozy way to spend about an hour on a winter's night involves being huddled with a companion in the back of a **horse-drawn sled.** For a fee of around 90 DM ($51.30) per hour, this can be arranged through Brandtner, GMbH, at the **Café Waldstein,** Königseer Fussweg 17 (☎ **08652/2427**).

6 Exploring the Alps

THE ZUGSPITZE

From Garmisch-Partenkirchen, you can see the tallest mountain peak in Germany, the ✪ **Zugspitze,** at the frontier between Austria and Germany. Its summit towers 9,720 feet above sea level, and you can ski all summer in the great Zugspitzplatt snowfield. Ski slopes begin at a height of 8,700 feet. For a panoramic view of both the Bavarian and the Tyrolean (Austrian) Alps, go all the way to the peak.

There are two ways to reach the Zugspitz peak from the center of Garmisch. We usually recommend that you ascend and descend via different trajectories, a plan that will allow maximum exposure to the panoramas that sweep outward en route. Both originate from the back side of Garmisch's main railway station. A cog railway, the **Zugspitzbahn,** departs daily every hour between 8:35am and 2:35pm. The train will meander uphill, past lichen-covered boulders and coursing streams, to a

The Alps Around Garmisch

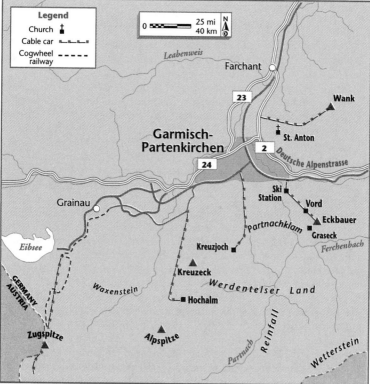

high-altitude alpine plateau, the **Zugspitzplatt,** where views sweep out over Bavaria. At the Zugspitzplatt, you'll transfer onto a cable car, the **Gletscher Sielbahn,** for a 4-minute uphill ride to the top of the Zugspitz. Here, far-reaching panoramas, a cafe and restaurant, a gift shop, and the terminus of many alpine trails provide options for diversions. Total travel time, including transfers at the Zugspitzplatt, is about 55 minutes.

An alternative means of reaching the summit of the Zugspitz involves taking the above-mentioned cog railway, the Zugspitzbahn, for a short distance, disembarking 9 miles southwest of Garmisch at the lower end of the **Eibsee Sielbahn (Eibsee Cable car).** The station for the Eibsee Cable car lies next to the edge of a clear alpine lake, the Eibsee. The cable car will carry you directly to the summit of the Zugspitz. Total transit time is about 38 minutes. The Sielbahn makes the summit run at least every half-hour from 8:30am to 4:30pm (until 5:30pm during July and August).

Regardless of which method you choose to ascend and descend the Zugspitz, the round-trip fare between April and October costs 75 DM ($42.75) for adults, 44 DM ($25.10) for travelers age 5 to 15, and 52 DM ($29.65) for persons aged 16 to 17. In winter, between November and March, round-trip fares are reduced to 61 DM ($34.75) for adults, 37 DM ($21.10) for children age 5 to 15, and 43 DM ($24.50) for persons age 16 to 17. For more information contact the **Bayerische Zugspitzbahn,** Olympiastrasse 27, in Garmisch-Partenkirchen (☎ 08821/79703).

The Natural World of the Alps

Many alpine animals such as the lynx, otter, and alpine ibex have all but disappeared from the Bavarian Alps during this century. Other endangered animals include wildcats, susliks, certain nesting birds, toads, and fish.

Efforts to reintroduce species eradicated from their habitats by hunters and farmers have been an unqualified success. Brown bears have been sighted in increased numbers over recent years, along with migrating elk. Wolves, however, have not reemerged since their final annihilation in the 1950s (attempts in the United States to reintroduce wolves in the American Rocky Mountains have been controversial). Without any check on their numbers by their natural enemies, the deer and stag population has enjoyed such exponential growth that hunting in some regions has become necessary to keep the population in check and preserve the natural balance.

Other species continue to thrive in the alpine environment. Unobtrusive hikers will find the Alps teeming with creatures—the chamois gracefully bounding up alpine heights, golden eagles in circling flight, the griffon vulture floating with its intimidating 9-foot wing spread. A hiker might even be befriended by a marmot or an alpine chough basking in a sunny meadow. Never threaten the gentle marmot or you might learn why it's nicknamed the whistle pig. The hill country and lower mountain ranges are often home to badgers, martens, and hares. Hedgehogs are rare, one of the endangered species of rodents.

Ornithologists literally have a field day in the Bavarian Alps. The range of birds is immense. Great white herons guide you on a teasing trail—they pause for respite along the Danube's banks long enough for you to catch up to them, only to depart in flight to another sanctuary 20 meters downstream. Storks, marsh warblers, gray geese, spoonbills, and terns can also be sighted. The streak of blue you see may be a blue kingfisher, diving for insects in the rippling of streams and rivers. The distinctive red and black wings of the gray alpine wall creeper distinguish it from the gray cliff faces it ascends. The spotted woodpecker, goldfinch,

From Garmisch-Partenkirchen, many other peaks of the Wetterstein range are accessible as well, via the 10 funiculars ascending from the borders of the town. From the top of the **Wank** (5,850 feet) to the east, you get the best view of the plateau on which the twin villages of Garmisch and Partenkirchen sit. This summit is also a favorite with patrons of Garmisch's spa facilities because the plentiful sunshine makes it ideal for the *Liegekur* (deck-chair cure).

HIKING IN THE BAVARIAN ALPS

Hiking is a national pastime in Bavaria. When winter snows melt, everybody seems to hit the trails, from preschoolers to seniors living on pensions. The tourist office in Garmisch-Partenkirchen will help you find trails of varying degrees of difficulty. After that, you just follow the signs.

One of the best places to begin is the 4,060-foot peak **Eckbauer** that lies on the southern fringe of Partenkirchen. The smallest of the Wetterstein mountain chain, its easy trails are recommended to first-time alpine hikers. A chairlift takes hikers to the top, where in real Bavarian style, they can refresh themselves with a glass of buttermilk at the Bergasthof. In less than an hour you can walk back down through a forest. If it's lunchtime, stop at the terraced restaurant of the Forsthaus Graseck (☎ 08821/54006), which opens onto a gorge.

redstart, thrush, and bluelit barter sing all winter, but the finch, lark, and song thrush save their voices for spring. Keen eyes only will spot falcons, buzzards, and other birds of prey. Don't forget to watch for nocturnal birds like the tawny owl if you're hiking at night.

Of course, if you spend the entire time with your head in the clouds, you'll miss what's underfoot. Edelweiss are the harbingers of spring. They blossom ahead of most wildflowers, often cropping up amid a blanket of snow, enjoying a short and fragile life. The season for mountain wildflowers varies depending on spring temperatures and snowpack. Most wildflowers blossom by the end of July or early August. Many are protected; it is against the law to pick them or take the plants. More than 40,000 plant species are threatened by extinction worldwide, and the Alps are no exception. In any case, the snowdrop, the pink meadow saffron, and the gorgeous colors of the mountain rose and gentian are finest in their natural setting in flowering alpine meadows. You can, however, pick the bluebills, pinks, cornflowers, buttercups, daisies, and primroses that blossom in such abundance.

You might even find a snack along your trail—wild raspberries, strawberries, bilberries, blackberries, cranberries, flap mushrooms, chanterelles, and parasol mushrooms are often found. However, edible varieties can be easily confused with inedible or poisonous varieties—know what you're picking and be careful. Autumn in the mountains brings an array of colors and splendor with the turning of the leaves. Those interested in finding out more about the flora of Bavaria can visit an alpine garden or an instructional guided path.

An ongoing effort is being made to conserve the area's valuable biotopes—high-altitude forests, water marshes, and the specialized plant life of steep cliffs and mountain banks. Nature reserves buffer the detrimental impact of agriculture and forestry, and outside their domains, farmland has been reallocated to include low-yield cultivation and extended pastures. But it's also important that hikers be sensitive to their ecological impact as they enjoy nature in the Alps.

An interesting hike is through the **Partnachklamm Gorge,** lying between the Graseck and Hausberg peaks. The gorge was created by the Partnach River. An open-sided tunnel has been drilled along it. After taking the cable car to the first station on the Graseck route, follow the paths along the sides of the slope to the right and trail the river as it cascades over the rocks. The path circles around by crossing the gorge and returns you to the point where you entered. Many readers have felt this to be one of their most memorable sightseeing adventures in Bavaria. The experience of walking along a rocky ledge just above a rushing river and often behind small waterfalls, while looking up at 1,200 feet of rocky cliffs, always fills one with awe. At the end of this sometimes wet tunnel walk, you can take a horse and buggy back to the chairlift.

The ✪ **Alpspitz** region is a paradise for hikers and nature lovers in general. From early spring until late fall, its meadows and flowers are a delight and its rocks evoke a prehistoric world. At altitudes of 4,600 to 6,300 feet, the Alps present themselves in a storybook fantasy. The highest trails are between Osterfelderkopf at 6,720 feet up and the final point of the Alpspitzbahn, which ends in Austria at 12,460 feet. Those who want to explore the northern foot of the Alpspitz can take the Alpspitz round-trip by going up on the Alpspitz cable car, over the Hochalm, and back down on the Kreuzeck or Hausberg cable car, allowing time in between for hikes lasting from half an hour to an hour and a half. Snacks are served at the Alpspitz cable car's top station or at the more rustic Hochalm Chalet.

The **Alpspitz cable car** to Osterfelderkopf, at a height of 6,300 feet, makes its 9-minute run at least every hour from 8am to 5pm. The round-trip cost is 42 DM ($23.95) for adults and 25 DM ($14.25) for children 4 to 14.

The **Hochalm cable car** from the Hochalm to Osterfelderkopf makes its 4-minute run at least every hour during the operating hours of the Alpspitz cable car. A single ride costs 6 DM ($3.40) for adults and 4 DM ($2.30) for children.

These fares and times of departure can fluctuate from season to season. Therefore, for the latest details, check with the tourist office, the **Verkehrsamt der Kurverwaltung,** on Dr. Richard-Strauss-Platz (☎ **08821/1806**), open Monday to Saturday from 8am to 6pm and on Sunday from 10am to noon only, or else call ☎ **08821/797991.**

The Zugspitzbahn, the rail line between Garmisch-Partenkirchen and Eibsee, at the base of the Zugspitze, offers a brochure outlining seven trails most favored by hikers. You don't have to be an Olympic athlete to try them. Some hikes will take 4 to 5 hours, and a few are suitable for the entire family.

Serious hikers can embark on overnight alpine treks from Garmisch-Partenkirchen, following clearly marked footpaths and staying in mountain huts maintained by the German Alpine Association. Some huts are staffed and serve meals. For the truly remote unsupervised huts, you'll be provided with information on how to gain access and your responsibility in leaving them tidy after your visit. For information, inquire at the local tourist office or write to the government-subsidized **German Alpine Association (Deutscher Alpenverein/DAV),** Am Perlacher Forst 186, D-80997 München (☎ **089/651-0720**). At the same address and phone number, you'll also be routed to staff members of a privately owned tour operator, the **Summit Club,** an outfit devoted to the organization of high-altitude expeditions throughout Europe and the world.

7 Oberammergau

59 miles SW of Munich, 12 miles N of Garmisch-Partenkirchen

In this alpine village the world-famous passion play is presented; performances are generally given every 10 years. The next one is scheduled for the year 2000, May through October. Surely the world's longest-running show (in more ways than one—it lasts about 8 hours), it began in 1634 when the town's citizens took a vow to present the play in gratitude for being spared from the devastating plague of 1633. The play is divided into episodes, each introduced by an Old Testament tableau connecting predictions of the great prophets to incidents of Jesus's suffering. The actors in the play are still the townspeople of Oberammergau.

Oberammergau stands in a wide valley surrounded by forests and mountains, sunny slopes, and green meadows. It has long been known for the skill of its wood-carvers. Here in this village right under the Kofel peak, farms are still intact, as well as first-class hotels, cozy inns, and family boarding houses.

Numerous hiking trails lead through the mountains around Oberammergau to hikers' inns such as the Kolbenalm and the Romanshohe. You can, however, simply go up to the mountaintops on the Laber cable railway or the Kolben chairlift. Oberammergau also offers opportunities for tennis buffs, minigolf players, cyclists, swimmers, hang-gliding enthusiasts, and canoeists. The recreation center, **Wellenberg,** with its large alpine swimming complex with open-air pools, hot water and fountains, sauna, solarium, and restaurant, is one of the most beautiful recreation centers in the Alps. The Ammer Valley, with Oberammergau in the (almost) center, is a treasure trove to explorers, who use it as a base for visiting Linderhof Castle, the Benedictine monastery at Ettal, or the fairy-tale Neuschwanstein and Hohenschwangau castles (see section 9, "Neuschwanstein & Hohenschwangau," below).

ESSENTIALS
GETTING THERE

BY TRAIN The Oberammergau Bahnhof is on the Murnau-Bad Kohlgrum-Oberammergau rail line, with frequent connections in all directions. Through Murnau all major German cities can be reached. Daily trains arrive from Munich (trip time: 2 hours) and from Frankfurt (trip time: 7 hours). For rail information and schedules, call ☎ 1-94-19.

BY BUS Regional bus service to nearby towns is offered by **RVO Regionalverkehr Oberbayern** in Garmisch-Partenkirchen (☎ 08821/948274). An unnumbered bus goes back and forth between Oberammergau and Garmisch-Partenkirchen.

BY CAR Oberammergau is 1½ hours from Munich and 5½ hours from Frankfurt. Take the A95 Munich–Garmisch-Partenkirchen Autobahn and exit at Eschenlohe.

VISITOR INFORMATION

For tourist information, contact the **Verkehrsbüro,** Eugen-Papst-Strasse 9A (☎ 08822/92310), open Monday to Friday from 8:30am to 6pm and Saturday from 8:30am to noon.

EXPLORING THE TOWN

If you visit Oberammergau in an "off" year, you can still see the **Passionspielhaus,** Passionwiese, the modern theater at the edge of town where the passion play is performed. The roofed auditorium holds 4,700 spectators, and the open-air stage is a wonder of engineering, with a curtained center stage flanked by gates opening onto the so-called streets of Jerusalem. The theater and production methods are contemporary, but the spirit of the play is marked by medieval tradition. The entire community is involved in the presentation—all those without speaking parts seem to be included in the crowd scenes. The impressive auditorium is open to the public daily from 9:30am to noon and 1 to 4pm May through October. Off-season hours are Tuesday to Sunday 10am to noon and 1:30 to 4pm. Admission is 4 DM ($2.30) for adults and 2 DM ($1.15) for children and students.

Aside from the actors, Oberammergau's most respected citizens include another unusual group, the woodcarvers, many of whom have been trained in the village woodcarver's school. In the **Pilatushaus,** Ludwigthomstrasse (☎ 08822/1682), you can watch local artists at work, including woodcarvers, painters, sculptors, and potters. Hours are Monday to Friday from 10:30am to 5:30pm. You'll see many examples of these art forms throughout the town, on the painted cottages and inns and in the churchyard. Also, when strolling through the village, watch for the houses with frescoes by Franz Zwink (18th century), named after fairy-tale characters, such as "Hansel and Gretel House" and the "Little Red Riding Hood House."

Heimatmuseum, Dorfstrasse (☎ 08822/94136), has a notable collection of Christmas crèches, all hand-carved and hand-painted, from the 18th through the 20th centuries. It's open May 15 through October 15, Tuesday to Saturday from 2 to 6pm; off-season, only on Saturday from 2 to 6pm. Admission is 3 DM ($1.70) for adults and 1.50 DM (85¢) for children and students.

The Passion Play & the Millennium

This famous play depicting the last days in the life of Christ, performed once per decade, will have its next presentation in the year 2000. Although its roots go back to 1634, its exposure to modern large-scale tourism began around 1910 when the present theater was constructed. Since then it has attracted millions of viewers, who approach the experience with a combination of cultural, historic, and religious interest.

If you plan to be in Oberammergau in the year 2000 between May 22 and October 8, you'll have a chance to attend a performance. Between those dates, performances are given every day except Tuesday and Thursday and last all day with a break for lunch. The morning session is from 9 to 11:30am and the afternoon session from 2:30 to 5:30pm.

You can take your chances and simply show up. About 20 tickets are held back every day for spontaneous arrivals. Don't count on this, however—you're much better off arranging in advance.

Phone, fax, write, or e-mail the **Geschaeftsstelle der Passionspiele 2000,** Eugen-Papst-Strasse 9A, DK 82487 Oberammergau (☎ **08822/92310;** fax 08822/923144; e-mail touristinfo@oberammergau.de). You can also access their web site www.oberammergau.de. Staff members prefer that you fill out an official order form before they mail you your tickets. Tickets cost 110 to 165 DM ($62.70 to $94.05). You can commute to Oberammergau from Munich or a nearby location, of course. But a convenient package deal is offered that includes tickets to the play and one or two nights in a local hotel with half board. Packages cost per person 300 to 800 DM ($171 to $456).

If you plan to drive, several enormous parking lots are on the town's perimeter. Parking is free, and shuttle buses haul you from the lots to the theater.

NEARBY ATTRACTIONS
✪ SCHLOSS LINDERHOF

Until the late 19th century, a modest hunting lodge stood on a large piece of land, 8 miles west of the village, owned by the Bavarian royal family. In 1869 "Mad Ludwig" struck again, this time creating a French rococo palace in the Ammergau Mountains. Unlike Ludwig's palace at Chiemsee, Schloss Linderhof was not meant to copy any other structure. And unlike his castle at Neuschwanstein, its concentration of fanciful projects and designs was not limited to the palace interior. In fact, the gardens and smaller buildings at Linderhof are, if anything, more elaborate than the two-story main structure. It is his most successful venture, and the only one that was completed.

The most interesting palace rooms are on the second floor, where ceilings are much higher because of the unusual roof plan. Ascending the winged staircase of Carrara marble, you'll find yourself at the West Gobelin Room (music room), with carved and gilded paneling and richly colored tapestries. This leads directly into the Hall of Mirrors. The mirrors are set in white and gold panels, decorated with gilded wood carvings. The ceiling of this room is festooned with frescoes depicting mythological scenes, including *The Birth of Venus* and *The Judgment of Paris*.

The king's bedchamber is the largest room in the palace and is placed in the back, overlooking the Fountain of Neptune and the cascades in the gardens. In the tradition of Louis XIV, who often received visitors in his bedchamber, the king's bed is closed off by a carved and gilded balustrade.

In the popular style of the previous century, Ludwig laid out the gardens in formal parterres with geometric shapes, baroque sculptures, and elegant fountains. The front of the palace opens onto a large pool with a piece of gilded statuary in its center, from which a jet of water sprays 105 feet into the air.

The park also contains several other small but exotic buildings, including the Moorish Kiosk, where Ludwig often spent hours smoking chibouk and dreaming of himself as an oriental prince. The magic grotto is unique, built of artificial rock, with stalagmites and stalactites dividing the cavelike room into three chambers. One wall of the grotto is painted with a scene of the Venus Mountain from *Tannhäuser*. The main chamber is occupied by an artificial lake illuminated from below; in Ludwig's time it had an artificial current produced by 24 dynamo engines. A shell-shaped boat, completely gilded, is tied to a platform called the Lorelei Rock.

The fantasy and grandeur of Schloss Linderhof, D-82488 Ettal-Linderhof (☎ **08822/3512**), is open to the public throughout the year and makes a day trip from Munich, as well as from Oberammergau. It's open April through September daily from 9am to 12:15pm and 12:45 to 5:30pm; from October through March, the grotto and Moorish Kiosk are closed, but the castle is open daily from 10am to 12:15pm and from 12:45 to 4pm. Admission is 9 DM ($5.15) for adults, 6 DM ($3.40) for students 16 to 24, and free for children 15 and under.

Buses run between Oberammergau and Schloss Linderhof seven times per day beginning at 9am; the last bus leaves Linderhof at 5:35pm. A round-trip passage costs 8.80 DM ($5).

✪ KLOSTER ETTAL

In a lovely valley sheltered by the steep hills of the Ammergau, Kloster Ettal, on Kaiser-Ludwig-Platz at Ettal (☎ **08822/740**), was founded by Ludwig the Bavarian in 1330. Monks, knights, and their ladies shared the honor of guarding the statue of the Virgin, attributed to Giovanni Pisano. In the 18th century, the golden age of the abbey, there were about 70,000 pilgrims every year. The Minster of Our Lady in Ettal is one of the finest examples of Bavarian rococo architecture in existence. Around the polygonal core of the church is a two-story gallery. An impressive baroque facade was built from a plan based on the designs of Enrico Zuccali. Inside, visitors stand under a vast dome to admire the fresco painted by John Jacob Zeiller in the summers of 1751 and 1752.

The abbey is 2 miles south of Oberammergau, along the road to Garmisch-Partenkirchen and Oberammergau. Admission is free, and it's open daily from 8am to 6:30pm (closes at 4:30pm in winter). Buses from Oberammergau leave from the Rathaus and the Bahnhof once an hour during the day, with round-trip passage costing 4.50 DM ($2.55). Call ☎ **8821/948274** for information.

SHOPPING

The region's wood carvings have always been sought after, and many an example has graced the mantel pieces, *étagères,* and what-not shelves of homes around the world. Know before you buy that even some of the most expensive pieces might have been roughed in by machine prior to being finished off (fine carved details) by hand. Most subjects are religious, deriving directly from 14th-century originals that usually, because of their exposure to the elements, war, or whatever, have not stood the test of time very well. To cater to the demands of modern tourism, there's been an increased emphasis lately on secular subjects, such as drinking or hunting scenes.

Competition for sales is fierce. Many objects are carved in the hamlets and farmhouses throughout the region.

In the town's wood carving school, conditions of study may remind you of the severity of the medieval guilds. Students who labor over a particular sculpture are required to turn it in to the school after its completion, where it's either placed on permanent exhibition or sold during the school's once-a-year sell-offs. These occur very briefly, usually over a two-day period in July and cannot be considered a steady or reliable source of supply for temporary visitors, who usually do better at any of the shops recommended below.

Josef Albl. Devrientweg 1. ☎ **08822/6433.**

Established sometime after World War II, this taciturn but prestigious woodcarver specializes in bas-reliefs. Although traditional art forms center on religious subjects, you'll find many carvings of secular scenes from Bavarian life, especially hunting scenes. Prices for some of the simple pieces sell for as little as 20 DM ($11.40), although more complicated or commissioned pieces can stretch into the tens of thousands of dollars. It's open from 9am to 1pm and 2 to 6pm daily, except Saturday afternoon and all day Sunday.

Peter Zwink. Schnitzlergasse 4. ☎ **08822/857.**

Long before the days of electricity, every self-respecting Bavarian home would have at least one, and often several, clocks designed in the rustic rococo tradition of the region. Don't ask for a cuckoo clock—although they do stock them, the staff will hurry to tell you that this tradition belongs to the Black Forest. Look instead for mantel clocks and floor clocks carved in baroque designs and crafted from pine, maple, or basswood. Some of the clocks need to be wound only once a year, a tradition that families carry out as part of their New Year's Day ritual. It's open from 9am to noon and from 2 to 6pm, but closed all day Wednesday and on Saturday afternoon.

Tony Baur. Dorfstrasse 27. ☎ **08822/821**.

This store contains the most sophisticated collection of wood carvings in Oberammergau. Established around 1980, it employs a small cadre of carvers who usually work from their homes. Carvings are often inspired by medieval originals and are fully rounded examples of religious subjects. Outgoing and personable, the sales staff is quick to admit that the rough forms of many of the pieces are done by machine, with most of the intricate work completed by hand. Most pieces are crafted from maple, pine, or linden (basswood), with special emphasis on religious and huntsman's motifs. Prices range from 40 DM ($22.80) to a high of 14,600 DM ($8,322) for pieces of museum quality. Although many carvings are left in their natural grain, sometimes using elaborately contrasting areas of light and dark wood, some of the most charming are polychromed, and in some instances, partially gilded. It's open Monday to Friday from 9am to 6pm and Saturday from 9am to 5pm. From Easter through October, it also opens every Sunday from 10am to 5pm.

WHERE TO STAY & DINE
MODERATE

Hotel Restaurant Böld. König-Ludwig-Strasse 10, D-82487 Oberammergau. ☎ **08822/ 9120.** Fax 08822/7102. 57 units. TV TEL. 180–238 DM ($102.60–$135.65) double. Rates include continental breakfast. AE, DC, MC, V. Free parking outside, 10–15 DM ($5.70–$8.55) in the garage. Bus: 30.

This inn has steadily improved in quality and now is among the town's premier choices. Only a stone's throw from the river, the well-designed chalet hotel offers comfortable public rooms in its central building and well-furnished guest rooms in its contemporary annex. All rooms have private baths and satellite TVs; most units open onto balconies. The restaurant features both international and regional cuisine. In the bar, you'll find a tranquil atmosphere, plus attentive service. There's a sauna, solarium, and whirlpool. Raimund Hans and family are the hosts.

Parkhotel Sonnenhof. König-Ludwig-Strasse 12, D-82487 Oberammergau. ☎ **08822/9130.** Fax 08822/3047. 77 units. TV TEL. 190–280 DM ($108.30–$159.60) double; 320–460 DM ($182.40–$262.20) suite. Rates include buffet breakfast. AE, DC, MC, V. Free parking.

Short on charm and alpine rusticity, this modern hotel still has a lot going for it. First, it's far enough away from the crowds that descend in summer—often in tour buses. It offers peace and tranquillity but is within walking distance of the center. The hotel overlooks the Ammer River and a beautiful Pfarrkirche (parish church). Every room has a balcony with an alpine vista, often of Oberammergau's mountain, the Kobel. Although devoid of old-fashioned charm, guest rooms are well maintained and filled with first-class comforts. The hotel has more amenities than most in the area—an indoor pool, sauna, and such extra features as a bowling alley. It's also a family favorite, with a children's playroom. Two restaurants serve many international dishes, although the Bavarian specialties are what's really good here.

INEXPENSIVE

Alte Post. Dorfstrasse 19, D-82487 Oberammergau. ☎ **08822/9100.** Fax 08822/910100. 32 units (28 with bath). TV TEL. 120 DM ($68.40) double without bath; 140 DM ($79.80) double with bath. Rates include continental breakfast. AE, MC, V. Closed Oct 25–Dec 19. Parking 6 DM ($3.40). Bus: 30.

A provincial inn in the village center, Alte Post is built in chalet style—wide overhanging roof, green-shuttered windows painted with decorative trim, a large crucifix on the facade, and tables along a sidewalk under a long awning. It's the village social hub. The interior has storybook charm, with a ceiling-high green ceramic stove, alpine chairs, and shelves of pewter plates. The rustic guest rooms have wood-beamed ceilings and wide beds with giant posts; most open onto views. The main dining room is equally rustic, with a collection of hunting memorabilia, and serves excellent Bavarian dishes. There's an intimate drinking bar.

Hotel Café-Restaurant Friedenshöhe. König-Ludwig-Strasse 31, D-82487 Oberammergau. ☎ **08822/3598.** Fax 08822/4345. 17 units. TEL. 100–170 DM ($57–$96.90) double. Rates include buffet breakfast. AE, DC, MC, V. Closed Nov–Dec 14. Free parking. Bus: 30.

The hotel name means "peaceful height." Built in 1906, the villa enjoys a beautiful location and is one of the better inns in town, although not in the same league as Böld or Parkhotel Sonnenhof. It was reconstructed into a pension and cafe in 1913; before that it hosted Thomas Mann, who stayed and wrote here. The guest rooms, furnished in tasteful modern style, are well maintained. TVs are available on request. The hotel offers a choice of four dining rooms, including an indoor terrace with a panoramic view and an outdoor terrace. The Bavarian and international cuisine is known for its taste and the quality of its ingredients.

Hotel Schilcherhof. Bahnhofstrasse 17, D-82487 Oberammergau. ☎ **08822/4740.** Fax 08822/3793. 26 units. 109–119 DM ($62.15–$67.85) double. Rates include buffet breakfast. AE, MC, V. Closed Nov 20–Christmas. Free parking. Bus: 30.

An enlarged chalet with surrounding gardens, the Schilcherhof has a modern wing with good-value rooms. In summer, the terrace overflows with beer and festivities. Five minutes away lies the passion-play theater; also nearby is the Ammer River. In summer you need to reserve well in advance to get a room. Although the house is built in the old style, with wooden front balconies and tiers of flower boxes, it has a fresh look.

Schlosshotel Linderhof. Linderhof 14, D-82488 Ettal. ☎ **08822/790.** Fax 08822/4347. 29 units. MINIBAR TV TEL. 120–180 DM ($68.40–$102.60) double. Rates include breakfast. AE, DC, MC, V. Free parking.

This hotel originally was constructed about a century ago as one of the outbuildings of the famous palace. Designed with gables, shutters, and half-timbering in the style of a Bavarian chalet, it has been tastefully enlarged and renovated by members of the Maier family. Bedrooms are dignified and high ceilinged, tasteful and comfortable, in a style that suggests 19th-century gentility.

Much of its business derives from its cozy restaurant, which extends onto a stone terrace accented with parasols and potted flowers. An array of fixed-price menus focuses on such hearty regional food as pork schnitzels with mixed salad and cream of tomato soup. Food orders are accepted daily from 8am to 8pm.

Turmwirt. Ettalerstrasse 2, D-82487 Oberammergau. ☎ **08822/92600.** Fax 08822/1437. 22 units. MINIBAR TV TEL. 140–190 DM ($79.80–$108.30) double. Rates include buffet breakfast. AE, DC, MC, V. Bus: 30.

A cozy Bavarian-style hotel, the Turmwirt offers many rooms with private balconies opening onto mountain views. It's an intricately painted, green-shuttered country house with a well-maintained homelike interior. A lodging house stood on this spot in 1742, and the present building was constructed in 1889. It has been altered and renovated many times over the past few decades. The owners are three generations of the Glas family, who often present Bavarian folk evenings. The town center is an invigorating 5-minute walk from the hotel.

Wolf Restaurant-Hotel. Dorfstrasse 1, D-82487 Oberammergau. ☎ **08822/3071.** Fax 08822/1096. 32 units. TV TEL. 110–180 DM ($62.70–$102.60) double. Rates include buffet breakfast. AE, DC, MC, V. Free parking. Bus: 30.

An overgrown Bavarian chalet, the Wolf Restaurant-Hotel is at the heart of village life. Its facade is much like others in the area: an encircling balcony, heavy timbering, and window boxes spilling cascades of red and pink geraniums. Inside it retains some local flavor, although certain concessions have been made: an elevator, conservative room furnishings, a dining hall with zigzag paneled ceiling, and spoke chairs. The hotel is also equipped with a lift, sauna, solarium, and outdoor pool. Only five singles are available.

The Hafner Stub'n is a rustic place for beer drinking as well as light meals. Dining here can be both economical and gracious. There's always a freshly made soup of the day, followed by a generous main course, such as Wiener schnitzel or roast pork with dumplings and cabbage.

8 Mittenwald

66 miles S of Munich, 11 miles SE of Garmisch-Partenkirchen, 23 miles NW of Innsbruck

The year-round resort of Mittenwald has often been called the most beautiful town in the Bavarian Alps. In 1996 it underwent a face-lift—a restoration that has made it more attractive than ever. The village is noteworthy for its photogenic painted houses with their intricate carved gables—even the baroque church tower is covered with frescoes. It's also noted as a center for the highly specialized craft of violin making. On the square stands a monument to Matthias Klotz, who introduced violin making to Mittenwald in 1684.

In the countryside around Mittenwald, the Wetterstein and Karwendel ranges offer constantly changing scenic vistas. In the winter, the town is a skiing center, and in the summer an even more popular range of outdoor activities invites the visitor.

ESSENTIALS
GETTING THERE

BY TRAIN Mittenwald is reached by almost hourly train service, since it lies on the express rail line between Munich and Innsbruck (Austria). From Munich, trip time is 1½ to 2 hours, depending on the train. It is about 5 or 6 hours by train from Frankfurt. Call ☎ **08821/19419** for information.

BY BUS Regional bus service from Garmisch-Partenkirchen and nearby towns is frequently provided by **RVO Regionalverkehr Oberbayern** at Garmisch. Call ☎ **08821/948274** for schedules and information.

BY CAR Access by car is via the A95 Autobahn from Munich.

VISITOR INFORMATION

For tourist information, contact the **Kurverwaltung und Verkehrsamt,** Dammkarstrasse 3 (☎ **08823/33981**), open Monday to Friday from 8am to noon and 1 to 5pm and Saturday from 10am to noon.

Horse and carriage trips or coach tours from Mittenwald to nearby villages are available; contact the tourist office for information.

EXPLORING THE AREA

Some 80 miles of hiking paths wind up and down the mountains around the village. Chairlifts make the mountain hiking trails readily accessible. Of course, where there are trails, there is mountain biking. A cycling map is available through Mittenwald's administration office. Besides hiking or biking through the hills on your own, you can take part in organized mountain-climbing expeditions. You can also take a cable car to the top of the Karwendel mountain for superb views.

Swimming in the brisk waters of the The Lautersee and Ferchensee is a good way to cool off on a hot summer's day. However, for those who find the waters too cold, Mittenwald has a heated adventure pool.

Mittenwald has good spa facilities, with large gardens landscaped with tree-lined streams and trout pools. Concerts during the summer are held in the music pavilion.

Geigenbau- und Heimatmuseum. Ballenhausgasse 3. ☎ **08823/2511.** Admission 3 DM ($1.70) adults, 1 DM (55¢) children. Mon–Fri 10–11:45am and 2–4:45pm; Sat–Sun 10–11:45am. Closed Nov 1–Dec 20.

This fascinating museum traces the history of violin making in Mittenwald and the development of the violin and other stringed instruments, from their invention through various stages of evolution. There is also a violin workshop.

SHOPPING

Mittenwald is internationally known for its classical stringed instruments, which have supplied professional musicians for centuries. Prices may be steep for the amateur violinist, but a visit to **Geigenbau Leonhardt,** Mühlenweg 53A (☎ **08823/8010**), is educational and interesting even if you're just browsing. If you're ambitious to traipse about in a dirndl, embroidered blouse, or lederhosen, head for **Trachtenstub'n,** Obermarkt 35 (☎ **08823/8555**), or **Trachten Werner-Leichtl,** Dekan-Karl-Platz 1 (☎ **08823/3785**); both stock a good selection of sizes and styles.

WHERE TO STAY
MODERATE

Hotel Post. Obermarkt 9, D-82481 Mittenwald. ☎ **08823/1094.** Fax 08823/1096. 95 units. TV TEL. 180–240 DM ($102.60–$136.80) double; 300–350 DM ($171–$199.50) suite. Rates include buffet breakfast. No credit cards. Closed Nov 22–Dec 17. Parking 8 DM ($4.55).

The Post is the most seasoned and established chalet hotel in the village—it's been here since 1632, when stagecoaches carrying mail and passengers across the Alps stopped here to refuel. Although it doesn't offer the tranquillity or the scenic views of Berghotel Latscheneck, it nevertheless is Mittenwald's finest address. Guest rooms are furnished in a comfortable although standard way. A delightful breakfast is served on the sun terrace, with a view of the Alps. On a cool day, take time out to enjoy a beer in the snug lounge-bar with an open fireplace. For a night of hearty Bavarian specialties, head for the wine tavern or the Poststüberl. The Poststüberl, with its deer antler collection, low beams, and wood paneling, is full of alpine charm. Available to guests are an indoor pool, massage facilities, and a sauna.

Rieger Hotel. Dekan-Karl-Platz 28, D-82481 Mittenwald. ☎ **08823/92500.** Fax 08823/925-0250. 45 units. TV TEL. 185–340 DM ($105.45–$193.80) double. Rates include buffet breakfast. AE, DC, MC, V. Closed Oct 21–Dec 19. Parking 8–10 DM ($4.55–$5.70).

The Rieger is attractive, whether snow is piled up outside or the window boxes are cascading with petunias. After the Post and Berghotel Latscheneck, the Rieger ranks number three in town. The living room has a beamed ceiling, wide arches, and a three-sided open fireplace. Guest rooms are pleasant and comfortable, with a certain amount of Bavarian charm. The indoor pool has a picture-window wall. Add to this a room for sauna and massages (segregated by sex except on Monday, family time, when both sexes join the crowd).

INEXPENSIVE

Alpenrose. Obermarkt 1, D-82481 Mittenwald. ☎ **08823/5055.** Fax 08823/3720. 18 units. MINIBAR TV TEL. 124–185 DM ($70.70–$105.45) double; 192 DM ($109.45) suite. Rates include buffet breakfast. AE, DC, MC, V. Free parking.

A particularly inviting place to stay is this inn in the village center at the foot of a rugged mountain. The facade is covered with decorative designs; window boxes hold flowering vines. The inn's basic structure is 14th century—it was once part of a monastery—although additions and improvements have been made over the years. The present inn is comfortable, with suitable plumbing facilities. The hotel's rooms are divided between the Alpenrose and its annex, the Bichlerhof; they're modernized but often with Bavarian traditional styling.

The tavern room, overlooking the street, has many ingratiating features, including coved ceilings (one decoratively painted), handmade chairs, flagstone floors, and a square tile stove in the center. In the Josefikeller, beer is served in giant steins, and musicians entertain guests in the evening. The dining room provides excellent meals, including Bavarian specialties.

✪ **Gästehaus Franziska.** Innsbruckerstrasse 24, D-82481 Mittenwald. ☎ **08823/92030.** Fax 08823/3893. www.werdenfelserland.de/e/franziska.html. E-mail: franziska@werdenfelserland.de. 18 units. MINIBAR TEL. 118–158 DM ($67.25–$90.05) double; 170–190 DM ($96.90–$108.30) suite. Rates include buffet breakfast. AE, V. Closed Nov 11–Dec 13. Free parking.

When Olaf Grothe built this guest house, he named it after the most important person in his life—his wife, Franziska. Both have labored to make it the most personalized guest house in town, with sympathetic attention given to their guests' needs. Rooms and suites are furnished tastefully in traditional Bavarian style. All have balconies opening onto mountain views; the suites also have safes and tea or coffee facilities. Breakfast is the only meal served, but there are plenty of restaurants nearby. Note that it's extremely difficult to obtain bookings between June 20 and October 2.

Gästehaus Sonnenbichl. Klausnerweg 32, D-82481 Mittenwald. ☎ **08823/92230.** Fax 08823/5814. www.werdenfelserland.de/e/sonenheim.html. E-mail: sonnenheim@werdenfelserland.de. 20 units. MINIBAR TV TEL. 114–154 DM ($65–$87.80) double. Rates include buffet breakfast. No credit cards. Closed Nov–Dec 15.

One of the more modest hostelries in town, this inn nevertheless offers good value and comfort. Lodged in a hillside, the chalet has a view of the village set against a backdrop of the Alps. The rooms have been freshly decorated in vivid natural colors. The guest house is often completely booked, so reserving well in advance is a good idea. Breakfast is the only meal served.

WHERE TO DINE

Restaurant Arnspitze. Innsbruckerstrasse 68. ☎ **08823/2425.** Main courses 29–42 DM ($16.50–$24); fixed-price meal 42.50 DM ($24.20) at lunch, 82.50 DM ($47.05) at dinner. AE. Wed 6–9pm, Thurs–Mon noon–2pm and 6–9pm. Closed Oct 25–Dec 19. Bus: RVO. BAVARIAN.

Housed in a modern chalet hotel on the outskirts of town, the Restaurant Arnspitze is the finest dining room in Mittenwald. Although you can also eat well at the inns previously recommended, over the years we've found the menus at this place more enticing. The restaurant is decorated in the old style; the cuisine is solid, satisfying, and wholesome. You might order sole with homemade noodles or veal steak in creamy smooth sauce, then finish with one of the freshly made desserts. There's an excellent fixed-price lunch.

9 Neuschwanstein & Hohenschwangau

The 19th century saw a great classical revival in Germany, especially in Bavaria, mainly because of the enthusiasm of Bavarian kings for ancient art forms. Beginning with Ludwig I (1786–1868), who was responsible for many Greek revival buildings in Munich, the royal house ran the gamut of ancient architecture in just three short decades. Its culmination was the remarkable flights of fancy of Ludwig II, often called "Mad King Ludwig." In spite of his rather lonely life and controversial alliances, both personal and political, he was a great patron of the arts.

In 1868, after a visit to the great castle of Wartburg, Ludwig wrote to his good friend, composer Richard Wagner: "I have the intention to rebuild the ancient castle ruins of Hohenschwangau in the true style of the ancient German knight's castle." The following year, construction began on the first of a series of fantastic edifices, a series that stopped only with Ludwig's untimely death in 1886 after he was deposed because of alleged insanity.

ESSENTIALS
GETTING THERE

BY CAR   From Munich, motorists can take the E533 toward Garmisch-Partenkirchen. At the end of the Autobahn, the road becomes Route 95 for its final run into Garmisch. From Garmisch, continue west on Route 187 to the junction

---

A Rococo Masterpiece

From Füssen you can take a fascinating side trip to the ✪ **Wieskirche,** (☎ **08862/501**) one of the most extravagant and flamboyant rococo buildings in the world, a masterpiece by Dominikus Zimmermann. Wieskirche is a noted pilgrimage church, drawing visitors from all over the globe. It's located on the slopes of the Ammergau Alps between Ammer and Lech, in an alpine meadow just off Route 17 near Steingaden. Inquire at the tourist office for a map and the exact location before setting out. Also, confirm that the church will be open at the time of your visit.

With the help of his brother, Johann Baptist, Zimmermann worked on the building from 1746 to 1754. It's amazing that such rich decoration could be crowded into so small a place. The great Zimmermann was so enchanted with his creation that he constructed a small home in the vicinity and spent the last decade of his life here. A bus heading for the church leaves Füssen Monday to Saturday at 11:05am and on Sunday at 1:05pm. You can return on the 3:50pm bus from the church. The trip takes 1 hour and costs 10 DM ($5.70) round-trip. For bus information, call ☎ **08362/37771.**

---

with Route 314, at which point you cut north to Füssen, where the castles are signposted.

BY TOUR BUS Panorama Tours offers an 8½-hour day tour from Munich to Neuschwanstein and Hohenschwangau that also includes Linderhof and a brief stopover in Oberammergau. For information see "Sightseeing Tours," in chapter 6.

VISITOR INFORMATION

Information about the castles and the region in general is available at the **Kurverwaltung,** Rathaus, Münchenerstrasse 2 in Schwangau (☎ **08362/81980**). It's open Monday to Friday from 8am to 5pm.

VISITING THE ROYAL CASTLES

The name "Royal Castles" is limited to the castles of Hohenschwangau (built by Ludwig's father, Maximilian II) and Ludwig's Neuschwanstein. Ludwig's other extravagant castles, Neues Schloss (Herrenchiemsee) and Linderhof (near Oberammergau), are described in sections 4 and 7, earlier in this chapter.

There are often very long lines in summer to these popular attractions, especially in August. With 25,000 people a day visiting, the wait in peak summer months can range from 4 to 5 hours for a 20-minute tour.

✪ NEUSCHWANSTEIN

This was the fairy-tale castle of Ludwig II. Construction went on for 17 years until the king's death, when all work stopped, leaving a part of the interior incomplete. Ludwig lived in the rooms on and off for a total of only about 6 months from 1884 to 1886.

The doorway off the left side of the vestibule leads to the king's apartments. The study, like most of the rooms, is decorated with wall paintings showing scenes from the Nordic legends (which also inspired Wagner's operas). The theme of the study is the *Tannhäuser* saga, painted by J. Aigner. The only fabric in the room is hand-embroidered silk, used in curtains and chair coverings, all designed with the gold and silver Bavarian coat-of-arms.

From the vestibule, you enter the throne room through the doorway at the opposite end. This hall, designed in Byzantine style by J. Hofmann, was never completed. The floor is a mosaic design depicting the animals of the world. The columns in the main hall are the deep copper red of porphyry. The circular apse where the king's throne was to have stood is reached by a stairway of white Carrera marble. The walls and ceiling are decorated with paintings of Christ in heaven looking down on the 12 apostles and six canonized kings of Europe.

The king's bedroom is the most richly carved in the entire castle—it took 4½ years to complete this room alone. Aside from the mural depicting the legend of Tristan and Isolde, the walls are decorated with panels carved to look like Gothic windows. In the center is a large wooden pillar completely encircled with gilded brass sconces. The ornate bed is on a raised platform with an elaborately carved canopy. Through the balcony window you can see the 150-foot waterfall in the Pollat Gorge, with the mountains in the distance.

The fourth floor of the castle is almost entirely given over to the Singer's Hall, the pride of Ludwig II and all of Bavaria. Modeled after the hall at Wartburg, where the legendary song contest of Tannhäuser supposedly took place, this hall is decorated with marble columns and elaborately painted designs interspersed with frescoes depicting the life of Parsifal.

The castle, at Neuschwansteinstrasse 20 (☎ **08362/81035**), can be visited year-round, and in September visitors have the additional treat of hearing concerts in the Singer's Hall. For information and reservations, contact the tourist office, **Verkehrsamt,** Schwangau, at the Rathaus (☎ **08362/81980**). The castle is open (guided tours only) April through September, daily from 9am to 5:30pm; off-season, daily from 10am to 4pm. Admission is 11 DM ($6.25) for adults, 7 DM ($4) for students and seniors over 65, and free for children 15 and under.

Reaching Neuschwanstein involves a steep half-mile climb from the parking lot for Hohenschwangau Castle (see below). This is about a 25-minute walk for the energetic, an eternity for anybody else. To cut down the climb, you can take a bus to Marienbrücke, a bridge that crosses over the Pollat Gorge at a height of 305 feet. From that vantage point you can, like Ludwig, stop and meditate on the glories of the castle and its panoramic surroundings. If you want to photograph the castle, don't wait until you reach the top where you'll be too close to the edifice to photograph it properly. It costs 3.50 DM ($2) for the bus ride up to the bridge or 2 DM ($1.15) if you'd like to take the bus back down the hill. Marienbrücke is still not at the castle. From the bridge it's a 10-minute walk to reach Neuschwanstein. This footpath is very steep and not easy to negotiate for anyone who has trouble walking up or down precipitous hills.

The most traditional way to reach Neuschwanstein is by horse-drawn carriage, costing 8 DM ($4.55) for the ascent, 4 DM ($2.30) for the descent. Some readers have objected to the rides, though, complaining that too many people are crowded in.

The Dream King

Plans are underway for Musical Theatre Neuschwanstein on the shores of nearby Forggen Lake, slated to open around the beginning of the millennium. A lavish musical based on the life of King Ludwig will be presented, along with other entertainment. For information, contact Ludwig Musical Project GambH, Maximilianstrasse 52, D-8538 München (☎ **89/2101480;** www.ludwigmusical.com).

✪ HOHENSCHWANGAU

Not as glamorous or as spectacular as Neuschwanstein, the neo-Gothic Hohenschwangau Castle nevertheless has a much richer history. The original structure dates back to the 12th-century Knights of Schwangau. When the knights faded away, the castle began to do so too, helped along by the Napoleonic Wars. When Ludwig II's father, Crown Prince Maximilian (later Maximilian II), saw the castle in 1832, he purchased it and in 4 years had it completely restored. Ludwig II spent the first 17 years of his life here and later received Richard Wagner in its chambers, although Wagner never visited Neuschwanstein on the hill above.

The rooms of Hohenschwangau are styled and furnished in a much heavier Gothic mode than those in the castle built by Ludwig. Many are typical of the halls of knights' castles of the Middle Ages in both England and Germany. There's no doubt that the castle's style greatly influenced young Ludwig and encouraged the fanciful boyhood dreams that formed his later tastes and character. Unlike Neuschwanstein, however, this castle has a comfortable look about it, as if it actually were a home at one time, not just a museum. The small chapel, once a reception hall, still hosts Sunday mass. The suits of armor and the Gothic arches here set the stage for the rest of the room.

Among the most attractive chambers is the Hall of the Swan Knight, named for the wall paintings depicting the saga of Lohengrin—before Wagner and Ludwig II. Note the Gothic grillwork on the ceiling with the open spaces studded with stars.

Hohenschwangau, Alpseestrasse 24 (☎ **08362/81127**), is open March 15 through October 15, daily from 8:30am to 5:30pm; October 16 through March 14, daily from 10am to 4pm. Admission is 10 DM ($5.70) for adults and 7 DM ($4) for children 6 to 15; children 5 and under enter free. There are several parking lots nearby where you can leave your car while visiting both castles.

WHERE TO STAY & DINE NEARBY

Hotel Lisl and Jägerhaus. Neuschwansteinstrasse 1-3, D-87643 Hohenschwangau. ☎ **08362/8870.** Fax 08362/81107. 47 units. MINIBAR TV TEL. 180–280 DM ($102.60–$159.60) double; 320–470 DM ($182.40–$267.90) suite. AE, DC, MC, V. Free parking.

This graciously styled villa with an annex across the street was seemingly made to provide views as well as comfort. Both houses sit in a narrow valley, surrounded by their own gardens. Most rooms have a view of at least one of the royal castles. In the main house, two well-styled dining rooms serve good-tasting meals. The restaurant features an international as well as a local cuisine.

Hotel Müller Hohenschwangau. Alpseestrasse 16, D-87645 Hohenschwangau. ☎ **08362/81990.** Fax 08362/819913. E-mail: hotel-mueller@T-online.de. 45 units. TV TEL. 200–260 DM ($114–$148.20) double; 300–400 DM ($171–$228) suite. Rates include buffet breakfast. AE, DC, MC, V. Closed Nov–Dec 20. Free parking.

The yellow walls, green shutters, and gabled alpine detailing of this hospitable inn make you want to stay here. However, its location near the foundation of Neuschwanstein is an additional advantage. The basic Bavarian lines were left intact when extra modern conveniences were added. On the premises are a well-maintained restaurant lined with burnished pinewood and a more formal evening restaurant with views over a verdant sun terrace. Nature lovers usually enjoy hiking the short distance to nearby Hohenschwangau castle.

Appendix

A Glossary

Altstadt old part of a city or town

Anlage park area

Apotheke pharmacy

Bad spa (also bath)

Bahn railroad, train

    Bahnhof railroad station

    Bergbahn funicular (cable railway)

    Hauptbahnhof main railroad station

— **Seilbahn** cable car

    Stadtbahn (S-Bahn) commuter railroad

    Strassenbahn streetcar, tram

    Untergrundbahn (U-Bahn) subway, underground transportation system in a city

Baroque ornate, decorated style of art and architecture in the 18th century; characterized by elaborate gilding and ornamentation

Bauhaus style of functional design for architecture and objects, originating in the early 20th century in Germany

Berg mountain

Biedermeier solid, bourgeois style of furniture design and interior decoration in the mid–19th century

Brücke bridge

Brunnen spring or well

Burg fortified castle

Damm dike, embankment

Der Blaue Reiter group of nonfigurative painters, founded in Munich in 1911 by Franz Marc and Wassily Kandinsky

Dom cathedral

Domplatz cathedral square

Drogerie shop selling cosmetics, sundries

"Evergreen" alpine traditional music

Fleet canal

Gasse lane

Gastarbeiter foreign worker

Gasthof   inn
Gemütlichkeit (adj. gemütlich)
comfort, coziness, friendliness
⚊ **Graben**   moat
Gutbürgerliche Küche   (German)
home cooking
Hof   court (of a prince), mansion
⚊ **Hotel garni**   hotel that serves no
meals or serves breakfast only
Insel   island
Jugendstil   art nouveau
Kai   quay
Kapelle   chapel
Kammer   room (in public
building)
Kaufhaus   department store
Kino   cinema
Kirche   church
Kloster   monastery
Konditorei   cafe for coffee and
pastries
Kunst   art
Land   state
Marktplatz   market square
Messegelände   exhibition center,
fairgrounds
Naturpark   protected natural area
Neue Küche   cuisine moderne
Neustadt   new part of city or town
Oper   opera
Platz   square

Rathaus   town or city hall
  Altes Rathaus   old town hall
  Neues Rathaus   new town hall
    (currently used as such)
Ratskeller   restaurant in Rathaus
cellar serving traditional German
food
Reisebüro   travel agency
Residenz   palace
Rococo   a highly decorative devel-
opment of baroque style
Saal   hall
Schauspielhaus   theater for plays
⚊ **Schicki-Micki**   yuppie
Schloss   palace, castle
⚊ **See**   lake (*der See*) or sea (*die See*)
⚊ **Spielbank**   casino
Stadt   town, city
Steg   footbridge
Strand   beach
Strasse   street
Tankstelle   filling station
Teich   pond
Tor   gateway
Turm   tower
Ufer   shore, riverbank
Verkehrsamt   tourist office
Weg   road
Weinstube   wine bar or tavern
serving meals
Zimmer   room

B Menu Terms

SOUPS (SUPPEN)

Erbsensuppe   pea soup
Gemüsesuppe   vegetable soup
Gulaschsuppe   goulash soup

Kartoffelsuppe   potato soup
Linsensuppe   lentil soup
Nudelsuppe   noodle soup

MEATS (WURST, FLEISCH & GEFLÜGEL)

Aufschnitt   cold cuts
Brathuhn   roast chicken
Bratwurst   grilled sausage
⚊ **Deutsches beefsteak**   hamburger
steak
⚊ **Eisbein**   pigs' knuckles
Ente   duck
Gans   goose
⚊ **Hammel**   mutton
Kalb   veal

Kaltes geflügel   cold poultry
⚊ **Kassler rippchen**   pork chops
Lamm   lamb
Leber   liver
⚊ **Nieren**   kidneys
⚊ **Ragout**   stew
⚊ **Rinderbraten**   roast beef
Rindfleisch   beef
Sauerbraten   marinated beef
Schinken   ham

Schweinebraten   roast pork
Truthahn   turkey

Wiener schnitzel   veal cutlet
Wurst   sausage

FISH (FISCH)

Aal   eel
Forelle   trout
- **Hecht**   pike
Karpfen   carp
Krebs   crawfish

Lachs   salmon
Makrele   mackerel
- **Rheinsalm**   Rhine salmon
- **Schellfisch**   haddock
- **Seezunge**   sole

EGGS (EIER)

Eier in der schale   boiled eggs
Mit speck   with bacon
Rühreier   scrambled eggs

Spiegeleier   fried eggs
- **Verlorene eier**   poached eggs

SALADS (SALAT)

Gemischter salat   mixed salad
Gurkensalat   cucumber salad

- **Rohkostplatte**   raw vegetable platter

SANDWICHES (BELEGTE BROTE)

Käsebrot   cheese sandwich
Schinkenbrot   ham sandwich

Schwarzbrot mit butter   pumpernickel with butter
Wurstbrot   sausage sandwich

VEGETABLES (GEMÜSE)

Artischocken   artichokes
Blumenkohl   cauliflower
Bohnen   beans
Bratkartoffeln   fried potatoes
Erbsen   peas
Grüne bohnen   string beans
Gurken   cucumbers
Karotten   carrots
- **Kartoffelbrei**   mashed potatoes
Kartoffelsalat   potato salad
Knödel   dumplings
Kohl   cabbage

Reis   rice
- **Rote Rüben**   beets
Rotkraut   red cabbage
Salat   lettuce
- **Salzkartoffeln**   boiled potatoes
Sauerkraut   sauerkraut
Spargel   asparagus
Spinat   spinach
Steinpilze   boletus mushrooms
Tomaten   tomatoes
Vorspeisen   hors d'oeuvres
- **Weisse Rüben**   turnips

DESSERTS (NACHTISCH)

- **Blatterteiggebäck**   puff pastry
Bratapfel   baked apple
Käse   cheese
Kompott   stewed fruit
Obstkuchen   fruit tart

Obstsalat   fruit salad
Pfannkuchen   sugared pancakes
Pflaumenkompott   stewed plums
Torten   pastries

FRUITS (OBST)

- **Ananas**   pineapple
Apfel   apple
- **Apfelsine**   orange
Banane   banana
Birne   pear

Erdbeeren   strawberries
Kirschen   cherries
- **Pfirsich**   peach
Weintrauben   grapes
Zitrone   lemon

BEVERAGES (GETRÄNKE)

Bier   beer
Ein dunkles   a dark beer
Ein helles   a light beer
Eine tasse kaffee   a cup of coffee
Eine tasse tee   a cup of tea

Milch   milk
Rotwein   red wine
Schokolade   hot chocolate
Tomatensaft   tomato juice
Wasser   water

CONDIMENTS & TABLE ITEMS

Brot   bread
Brötchen   rolls
Butter   butter
Eis   ice
Essig   vinegar
Gabel   fork
Glas   glass
Löffel   spoon

Messer   knife
Pfeffer   pepper
Platte   plate
Sahne   cream
Salz   salt
Senf   mustard
Tasse   cup
Zucker   sugar

COOKING TERMS

Gebacken   baked
Gebraten   fried
Gefüllt   stuffed
Gekocht   boiled

Geröstet   roasted
Gut durchgebraten   well done
Nicht durchgebraten   rare
Paniert   breaded

Index

ACCOMMODATIONS

RESTAURANTS

Frommer's® Complete Travel Guides

Alaska
Amsterdam
Arizona
Atlanta
Australia
Austria
Bahamas
Barcelona, Madrid & Seville
Belgium, Holland & Luxembourg
Bermuda
Boston
Budapest & the Best of Hungary
California
Canada
Cancún, Cozumel & the Yucatán
Cape Cod, Nantucket & Martha's Vineyard
Caribbean
Caribbean Cruises & Ports of Call
Caribbean Ports of Call
Carolinas & Georgia
Chicago
China
Colorado
Costa Rica
Denver, Boulder & Colorado Springs
England
Europe
Florida
France

Germany
Greece
Greek Islands
Hawaii
Hong Kong
Honolulu, Waikiki & Oahu
Ireland
Israel
Italy
Jamaica & Barbados
Japan
Las Vegas
London
Los Angeles
Maryland & Delaware
Maui
Mexico
Miami & the Keys
Montana & Wyoming
Montréal & Québec City
Munich & the Bavarian Alps
Nashville & Memphis
Nepal
New England
New Mexico
New Orleans
New York City
New Zealand
Nova Scotia, New Brunswick & Prince Edward Island
Oregon
Paris
Philadelphia & the Amish Country
Portugal

Prague & the Best of the Czech Republic
Provence & the Riviera
Puerto Rico
Rome
San Antonio & Austin
San Diego
San Francisco
Santa Fe, Taos & Albuquerque
Scandinavia
Scotland
Seattle & Portland
Singapore & Malaysia
South Pacific
Spain
Switzerland
Thailand
Tokyo
Toronto
Tuscany & Umbria
USA
Utah
Vancouver & Victoria
Vermont, New Hampshire & Maine
Vienna & the Danube Valley
Virgin Islands
Virginia
Walt Disney World & Orlando
Washington, D.C.
Washington State

Frommer's® Dollar-a-Day Guides

Australia from $50 a Day
California from $60 a Day
Caribbean from $60 a Day
England from $60 a Day
Europe from $50 a Day
Florida from $60 a Day

Greece from $50 a Day
Hawaii from $60 a Day
Ireland from $50 a Day
Israel from $45 a Day
Italy from $50 a Day
London from $75 a Day

New York from $75 a Day
New Zealand from $50 a Day
Paris from $70 a Day
San Francisco from $60 a Day
Washington, D.C., from $60 a Day

Frommer's® Portable Guides

Acapulco, Ixtapa & Zihuatanejo
Alaska Cruises & Ports of Call
Bahamas
California Wine Country
Charleston & Savannah
Chicago

Dublin
Las Vegas
London
Maine Coast
New Orleans
New York City
Paris

Puerto Vallarta, Manzanillo & Guadalajara
San Francisco
Sydney
Tampa & St. Petersburg
Venice
Washington, D.C.

FROMMER'S® NATIONAL PARK GUIDES

Family Vacations in the
    National Parks
Grand Canyon

National Parks of the
    American West
Yellowstone & Grand Teton

Yosemite & Sequoia/
    Kings Canyon
Zion & Bryce Canyon

FROMMER'S® MEMORABLE WALKS

Chicago
London

New York
Paris

San Francisco
Washington D.C.

FROMMER'S® IRREVERENT GUIDES

Amsterdam
Boston
Chicago

London
Manhattan

New Orleans
Paris

San Francisco
Walt Disney World
Washington, D.C.

FROMMER'S® DRIVING TOURS

America
Britain
California

Florida
France
Germany

Ireland
Italy
New England

Scotland
Spain
Western Europe

THE COMPLETE IDIOT'S TRAVEL GUIDES

Boston
Cruise Vacations
Planning Your Trip to Europe
Hawaii

Las Vegas
London
Mexico's Beach Resorts
New Orleans

New York City
San Francisco
Walt Disney World
Washington D.C.

THE UNOFFICIAL GUIDES®

Branson, Missouri
California with Kids
Chicago
Cruises
Disney Companion

Florida with Kids
The Great Smoky &
    Blue Ridge
    Mountains

Las Vegas
Miami & the Keys
Mini-Mickey
New Orleans

New York City
San Francisco
Skiing in the West
Walt Disney World
Washington, D.C.

SPECIAL-INTEREST TITLES

Frommer's Britain's Best Bike Rides
The Civil War Trust's Official Guide
    to the Civil War Discovery Trail
Frommer's Caribbean Hideaways
Frommer's Gay & Lesbian Europe
Israel Past & Present
Monks' Guide to California
Monks' Guide to New York City
New York City with Kids
New York Times Weekends
Outside Magazine's Adventure Guide
    to New England
Outside Magazine's Adventure Guide
    to Northern California

Outside Magazine's Adventure Guide
    to Southern California & Baja
Outside Magazine's Adventure Guide
    to the Pacific Northwest
Outside Magazine's Guide
    to Family Vacations
Places Rated Almanac
Retirement Places Rated
Washington, D.C., with Kids
Wonderful Weekends from Boston
Wonderful Weekends from New York City
Wonderful Weekends from San Francisco
Wonderful Weekends from Los Angeles